solutions@syngress.com

With over 1,500,000 copies of our MCSE, MCSD, CompTIA, and Cisco study guides in print, we have come to know many of you personally. By listening, we've learned what you like and dislike about typical computer books. The most requested item has been for a web-based service that keeps you current on the topic of the book and related technologies. In response, we have created solutions@syngress.com, a service that includes the following features:

- A one-year warranty against content obsolescence that occurs as the result of vendor product upgrades. We will provide regular web updates for affected chapters.

- Monthly mailings that respond to customer FAQs and provide detailed explanations of the most difficult topics, written by content experts exclusively for solutions@syngress.com.

- Regularly updated links to sites that our editors have determined offer valuable additional information on key topics.

- Access to "Ask the Author"™ customer query forms that allow readers to post questions to be addressed by our authors and editors.

Once you've purchased this book, browse to

www.syngress.com/solutions.

To register, you will need to have the book handy to verify your purchase.

Thank you for giving us the opportunity to serve you.

SYNGRESS®

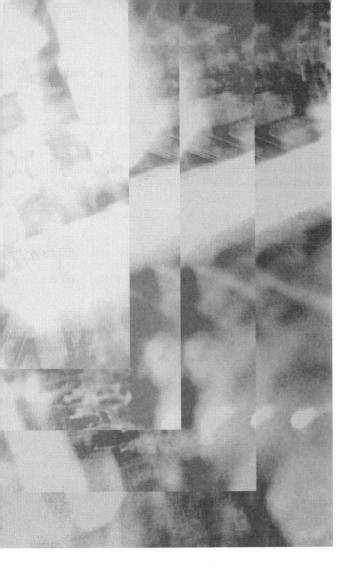

MANAGING **CISCO**
NETWORK SECURITY:
BUILDING ROCK-SOLID
NETWORKS

SYNGRESS®

KEY	SERIAL NUMBER
001	AWQ692ADSE
002	KT3LGY35C4
003	C3NXC478FV
004	235C87MN25
005	ZR378HT4DB
006	PF62865JK3
007	DTP435BNR9
008	QRDTKE342V
009	6ZDRW2E94D
010	U872G6S35N

PUBLISHED BY
Syngress Publishing, Inc.
800 Hingham Street
Rockland, MA 02370

Managing Cisco Network Security: Building Rock-Solid Networks

Printed in the United States of America

1 2 3 4 5 6 7 8 9 0

ISBN: 1-928994-17-2

Copy edit by: Adrienne Rebello
Technical review by: Stace Cunningham
Technical edit by: Florent Parent
Project Editor: Mark A. Listewnik

Proofreading by: Nancy Kruse Hannigan
Page Layout and Art by: Shannon Tozier
Index by: Robert Saigh
Co-Publisher: Richard Kristof

Distributed by Publishers Group West

Acknowledgments

We would like to acknowledge the following people for their kindness and support in making this book possible.

Richard Kristof, Duncan Anderson, Jennifer Gould, Robert Woodruff, Kevin Murray, Dale Leatherwood, Rhonda Harmon, and Robert Sanregret of Global Knowledge, for their generous access to the IT industry's best courses, instructors and training facilities.

Ralph Troupe and the team at Callisma for their invaluable insight into the challenges of designing, deploying and supporting world-class enterprise networks.

Karen Cross, Kim Wylie, Harry Kirchner, John Hays, Bill Richter, Kevin Votel, Brittin Clark, Sarah Schaffer, Ellen Lafferty and Sarah MacLachlan of Publishers Group West for sharing their incredible marketing experience and expertise.

Mary Ging, Caroline Hird, and Simon Beale of Harcourt International for making certain that our vision remains worldwide in scope.

Annabel Dent, Anneka Baeten, Clare MacKenzie, and Laurie Giles of Harcourt Australia for all their help.

David Buckland, Wendi Wong, David Loh, Marie Chieng, Lucy Chong, Leslie Lim, Audrey Gan, and Joseph Chan of Transquest Publishers for the enthusiasm with which they receive our books.

Kwon Sung June at Acorn Publishing for his support.

Ethan Atkin at Cranbury International for his help in expanding the Syngress program.

Special thanks to the professionals at Osborne with whom we are proud to publish the best-selling Global Knowledge Certification Press series.

From Global Knowledge

At Global Knowledge we strive to support the multiplicity of learning styles required by our students to achieve success as technical professionals. As the world's largest IT training company, Global Knowledge is uniquely positioned to offer these books. The expertise gained each year from providing instructor-led training to hundreds of thousands of students worldwide has been captured in book form to enhance your learning experience. We hope that the quality of these books demonstrates our commitment to your lifelong learning success. Whether you choose to learn through the written word, computer based training, Web delivery, or instructor-led training, Global Knowledge is committed to providing you with the very best in each of these categories. For those of you who know Global Knowledge, or those of you who have just found us for the first time, our goal is to be your lifelong competency partner.

Thank your for the opportunity to serve you. We look forward to serving your needs again in the future.

Warmest regards,

Duncan Anderson
President and Chief Executive Officer, Global Knowledge

Contributors

Russell Lusignan (CCNP, CCNA, MCSE, MCP+I, CNA) is a Senior Network Engineer for Bird on a Wire Networks, a high-end dedicated and fully managed Web server/ASP provider located in Toronto, Canada. He is also a technical trainer for the Computer Technology Institute.

Russell's main area of expertise is in LAN routing and switching technologies and network security implementations. *Chapters 3, 4, and 6.*

David G. Schaer (CCNA, CCDA, CCNP, CCSI, MCT, MCSE, MCP+I, MCNE, CCA) is President of Certified Tech Trainers, Inc., an organization specializing in the development and delivery of custom training for Cisco CCNA and CCNP certification. He has provided training sessions for major corporations throughout the United States, Europe, and Central America. David enjoys kayak fishing, horseback riding, and exploring the Everglades.

Oliver Steudler (CCNA, CCDA, CNE) is a Senior Systems Engineer at iFusion Networks in Cape Town, South Africa. He has over 10 years of experience in designing, implementing and troubleshooting complex networks. *Chapter 5.*

Jacques Allison (CCNP, ASE, MCSE+I) Jacques has been involved with Microsoft-related projects on customer networks ranging from single domain and exchange organization migrations to IP addressing and network infrastructure design and implementation. Recently he has worked on CA Unicenter TNG implementations for network management.

He received his engineering diploma in Computer Systems in 1996 from the Technicon Pretoria in South Africa. Jacques began his career with Electronic Data Systems performing desktop support, completing his MCSE in 1997.

Jacques would like to dedicate his contribution for this book to his fiancée, Anneline, who is always there for him. He would also like to thank his family and friends for their support.
Chapter 8.

John Barnes (CCNA, CCNP, CCSI) is a network consultant and instructor. John has over ten years experience in the implementation, design, and troubleshooting of local and wide area networks as well as four years of experience as an instructor.

John is a regular speaker at conferences and gives tutorials and courses on IPv6, IPSec, and intrusion detection. He is currently pursuing his CCIE. He would like to dedicate his efforts on this book to his daughter, Sydney.
Chapter 2.

Russell Gillis (CISSP, MCSE, CCNA) is Associate Director of Networking at Kalamazoo College in Kalamazoo, Michigan. Prior to joining "K" College, Russ worked for 11 years in the pharmaceutical industry. His experience includes workstation support, system administration, network design, and information security.
Chapter 1.

Pritpal Singh Sehmi lives in London, England. He has worked in various IT roles and in 1995 launched Spirit of Free Enterprise, Ltd. Pritpal is currently working on an enterprise architecture redesign project for a large company. Pritpal is also a freelance Cisco trainer and manages the Cisco study group www.ccguru.com. Pritpal owes his success to his family and life-long friend, Vaheguru Ji.
Chapter 7.

Technical Editor

Florent Parent is currently working at Viagénie, Inc. as a consultant in network architecture and security for a variety of organizations, corporations, and governments. For over 10 years, he has been involved in IP networking as a network architect, network manager, and educator.

He is involved in the architecture development and deployment of IPv6 in the CA*net network and the 6Tap IPv6 exchange. Florent participates regularly in the Internet Engineering Task Force (IETF), especially in the IPv6 and IPSec work groups.
In addition to acting as technical editor for the book, Florent authored the Preface and Chapter 9.

Technical Reviewer

Stace Cunningham (CMISS, CCNA, MCSE, CLSE, COS/2E, CLSI, COS/2I, CLSA, MCPS, A+) is a security consultant currently located in San Antonio, TX. He has assisted several clients, including a casino, in the development and implementation of network security plans for their organizations. He held the positions of Network Security Officer and Computer Systems Security Officer while serving in the United States Air Force.

While in the Air Force, Stace was involved for over 14 years in installing, troubleshooting, and protecting long-haul circuits ensuring the appropriate level of cryptography necessary to protect the level of information traversing the circuit as well the circuits from TEMPEST hazards. This included American equipment as well as equipment from Britain and Germany while he was assigned to Allied Forces Southern Europe (NATO).

Stace has been an active contributor to The SANS Institute booklet "Windows NT Security Step by Step." In addition, he has co-authored or served as the Technical Editor for over 30 books published by Osborne/McGraw-Hill, Syngress Media, and Microsoft Press. He is also a published author in "Internet Security Advisor" magazine.

His wife Martha and daughter Marissa have been very supportive of the time he spends with the computers, routers, and firewalls in the "lab" of their house. Without their love and support, he would not be able to accomplish the goals he has set for himself.

Contents

Preface

The Challenges of Security

Providing good internetwork security and remaining current on new hardware and software products is a never-ending task. Every network security manager aims to achieve the best possible security because the risks are real and the stakes are high. An enterprise must decide what level of security is required, taking into account which assets to protect as well as the impact of the measures on costs, personnel, and training. *Perfect* security is an impossibility, so one must aim for the best possible security by devising a plan to manage the *known* risks and safe-guard against the *potential* risks. Defining the enterprise security policy is the first step in implementing good security.

Many security tools are available to help reduce the vulnerability of your network. For example, a firewall can be deployed at the network perimeter to offer an effective protection against many attacks. But a firewall is only one piece in the network security infrastructure. Good host security, regular assessment of the overall vulnerability of the network (audits), good authentication, authorization, accounting practices, and intrusion detection are all valuable tools in combatting network attacks and ensure a network security manager's "peace of mind."

Cisco Systems is the worldwide leader in IP networking solutions. They offer a wide array of market-leading network security products: dedicated appliances, routers, and switches, most of which come with some form of security software. Currently, Cisco products comprise much of the Internet's backbone. An in-depth knowledge of how to configure Cisco IP network security technology is *a must* for anyone working in today's internetworked world. This book will provide you with the hands-on Cisco security knowledge you need to get ahead, and stay ahead.

About This Book

This book focuses on how to configure and secure IP networks utilizing the various security technologies offered by Cisco Systems. Inside are numerous configuration examples combined with extensive instruction from security veterans, that will provide you with the information you need to implement a network solution and manage any-sized IP network security infrastructure.

Although many books cover IP network security, we will concentrate specifically on security configurations using exclusively Cisco products. We supply you with exactly the information you need to know: what security solutions are available, how to apply those solutions in real-world cases, and what factors you should consider when choosing and implementing the technology.

Organization

Chapter 1 covers general system and network security concepts and introduces the different security mechanisms available through TCP/IP. Chapters 2, 3 and 4 deal with security through access control and advanced filtering mechanisms available in Cisco IOS routers and PIX firewall. Network Address Translation (NAT) is also covered in Chapter 3. Virtual Private Networks, AAA mechanisms, and intrusion detection follow in the next chapters. Network security management software available from Cisco is covered in Chapter 8. Chapter 9, the "Fast Track" chapter, provides an excellent review of the entire book and contains additional bonus coverage containing tips on general security processes. This will provide you with a quick jump on the key network security factors to weigh in choosing your security solutions.

Chapter 1: *Introduction to IP Network Security* provides an overview of the components that comprise system and network security. The chapter introduces some basic networking concepts (IP, TCP, UCP, ICMP) and discusses some of the security mechanisms available in TCP/IP. We also introduce some of the essential network security products available from Cisco

Chapter 2: *Traffic Filtering on the Cisco IOS* focuses on access control through traffic filtering. We cover some of the different traffic filtering mechanisms available on the Cisco IOS such as the standard, extended, and reflexive access lists, as well as Context-based Access Control (CBAC). Many configuration recommendations and examples are presented.

Chapter 3: *Network Address Translation (NAT)* provides detailed coverage of Network Address Translation (NAT) mechanisms with configuration examples on Cisco IOS and PIX firewall.

Chapter 4: *Cisco PIX Firewall* covers the main features of PIX firewall with recommendations on security policy configuration. Many configuration examples using advanced features such as AAA, NAT, and URL filtering are presented. Note that the PIX Firewall Manager graphical user interface is covered in Chapter 8.

Chapter 5: *Virtual Private Networks* provides an overview of Virtual Private Network (VPN) technologies available for the Cisco product line. A description of L2TP and IPSec protocols are presented and configuration examples using Cisco Secure VPN client and Windows 2000 are provided.

Chapter 6: *Cisco Authentication, Authorization, and Accounting Mechanisms* discusses the authentication, authorization, and accounting (AAA) security services available on Cisco products. The different security servers supported in Cisco, TACACS+, Radius and Kerberos are also explained. Note that the Cisco Secure Access Control Server is presented in Chapter 8.

Chapter 7: *Intrusion Detection* is the main focus of this chapter and includes an overview of several methods used to attack networks. We discuss host and network intrusion and focus on the intrusion detection and vulnerability scanner products available from Cisco.

Chapter 8: *Network Security Management* provides a look at the network security management tools available from Cisco: PIX Firewall Manager, CiscoWorks 2000 Access Control Lists Manager, Cisco Secure Security Manager (CSPM), and Cisco Secure Access Control Server.

Chapter 9: *Security Processes and the Managing Cisco Security Fast Track* provides a concise review of Cisco IP network security, detailing the essential concepts covered in the book. This chapter also includes a section on general security configuration recommendations for all networks. You can use these recommendations as a checklist to help you limit the exposure and vulnerability of your security infrastructure.

Audience

This book is intended primarily for network managers and network administrators who are responsible for implementing IP network security in a Cisco environment. However, it is also useful for people who are interested in knowing more about the security features available in Cisco products in general. The book is designed to be read from beginning to end, but each chapter can stand alone as a useful reference should you want detailed coverage of a particular topic. Readers who want a quick understanding of the information contained in the book can read Chapter 9 first.

This book will give the reader a good understanding of what security solutions are available from Cisco and how to apply those solutions in real-world cases. These solutions will give the security managers and administrators the necessary tools and knowledge to provide the best protection for their network and data.

Editor's Acknowledgement

I would like to thank Mark Listewnik from Syngress Publishing for his support; Marc Blanchet, colleague and friend, for his help, encouragement and guidance; all my colleagues and friends at Viagénie; and, especially, my wife Caroline for her exceptional support and patience.

—Florent Parent

Chapter 1

Introduction to IP Network Security

Solutions in this chapter:

- Protecting Your Site

- Network Communication in TCP/IP

- Security in TCP/IP

- Cisco IP Security Hardware and Software

Introduction

The "2000 CSI/FBI Computer Crime and Security Survey," conducted in early 2000 by the Computer Security Institute (CSI) with participation by the San Francisco office of the Federal Bureau of Investigation (FBI), showed that 90 percent of survey participants from large U.S. corporations, financial institutions, medical institutions, universities, and government agencies detected security breaches in 1999. About 70 percent of the participants experienced breaches more serious than viruses or employee Web abuse. Forty-two percent of survey participants (273 organizations) claimed financial losses totaling over 265 million dollars from cyber attacks. These security threats were composed of an assortment of attacks and abuses that originated both internally and externally to their network borders.

The CSI survey showed financial losses were larger than in any previous year in eight out of twelve categories. The largest loss was attributed to theft of proprietary information, followed by financial fraud, virus, insider net abuse, and unauthorized insider access.

Many organizations are increasing their use of electronic commerce for business-to-business and business-to-consumer transactions. New initiatives, such as Applications Service Providers (ASPs), expose vital corporate information and services to the Internet. People have altered the way that they work, now extending the workday or working full time from home. Telecommuters and mobile workers now require remote access to information resources normally protected within the organization's network.

Businesses and individuals now depend upon information systems and data communications to perform essential functions on a daily basis. In this environment of increasingly open and interconnected communication systems and networks, information security is crucial for protecting privacy, ensuring availability of information and services, and safeguarding integrity. These new technologies and increased connectivity via public access networks and extranets have allowed businesses to improve efficiency and lower costs, but at the price of increased exposure of valuable information assets to threats.

Protecting Your Site

Attack techniques are constantly evolving. Over the last twenty years, tools for attacking information systems have become more powerful, but more importantly, easier to use. Ease of use has lowered the technical knowledge required to conduct an attack, and has thus increased the pool of potential attackers exponentially. Script Kiddie is a term used to indicate a person that just needs to acquire a program to launch an attack and doesn't need to understand how it works.

Many network security failures have been widely publicized in the world press. An advantage to this unfortunate situation is the lowered resistance from upper management to support security initiatives. Getting upper management support is the first step in creating an effective network security program. Management must provide the authority to implement security processes and procedures. Management commits to security of information assets by documenting the authority and obligations of departments or employees in an information security policy, and supports it by providing the resources to build and maintain an effective security program.

An effective security program includes awareness, prevention, detection, measurement, management, and response to minimize risk. There is no such thing as perfect security. The determined and persistent attacker can find a way to defeat or bypass almost any security measure. Network security is a means of reducing vulnerabilities and managing risk.

Awareness should be tailored to the job requirements of employees. You must make employees understand why they need to take information security seriously. End-users choosing weak passwords or falling for social engineering attacks can easily neutralize the best technical security solutions. Upper management must provide for training, motivation, and codes of conduct to employees to comply with security measures.

NOTE

Don't ignore the human factors in designing or implementing a security plan. Security is a tradeoff between productivity and protection. If you want to realize acceptance and cooperation, avoid unreasonable constraints on end-users. If security measures are too cumbersome, people will circumvent them and take the path of least resistance to getting their work done. People will often fail before equipment fails.

Social engineering is when someone uses social skills to deceive an employee to gain unauthorized access. For example, an unauthorized person could pretend to help an authorized user in an attempt to trick them out of their passwords or access codes. Social engineering attacks bypass technical or logical security controls. Defeating social engineering attacks depends on having users that are aware of the need to protect information and can recognize attempts to deceive them. They follow procedures, like verifying the identity of anyone seeking sensitive information, that are designed to reduce the likelihood of inappropriate disclosure.

Awareness also applies to network and system administrators. Information security covers an enormous range of skills and knowledge. Pursue your education on a continuous basis. You need to be aware of trends in attack methods, the threats that could damage your systems, and the safeguards that you can deploy to counter them.

Security is a continuous process that includes the stages of protect, detect, analyze, manage, and recover. This book covers many of Cisco's security products that provide protection from threats, detection of network security incidents, measurement of vulnerability and policy compliance, and management of security policy across an extended organization. These are the tools that you have to mount defenses against threats.

Protection of assets must be cost effective. In analyzing your security needs, you first identify what assets you want to protect, and the value of those assets. Determine the threats that may damage these assets, and the likelihood of those threats occurring. Prioritize the relationships, so you concentrate on mitigating the risks with the highest potential damage, and greatest likelihood of occurring. To determine how to protect the asset, consider the cost of your protection measured against the value of the asset that you're trying to protect. You don't want to spend more for preventing a potential adversity than the asset is worth.

Monitor your network and systems to detect attacks and probes—and know what "normal" for your network and systems looks like. If you are not used to seeing normal behavior on your network, you may not recognize or be able to isolate an attack. Many systems on the network can provide clues and status information in their logs. Be sure to log enough information that you can recognize and record an attack, and examine these logs carefully. Use intrusion detection systems to watch the network traffic.

TIP

It is a good idea to synchronize the clocks of all your network devices and systems. Accurate time will help you compare logs that originate on different systems located in different parts of your network. You will be better able to reconstruct a complex sequence of events spanning multiple systems. Synchronized clocks will also assist forensic investigators coordinating events that may occur in various parts of the Internet. Distributed attacks or relayed attacks can involve many systems in different parts of the world.

Some services, such as Kerberos, are dependent on having a consistent time reference across systems. If the time on systems is outside of specification, Kerberos will deny access because the design assumes that it may be encountering a replay attack.

Recovery is as important as protection. A planned response to recover from incidents or attacks is a necessary part of network security. Have a plan in place, so you know what to do when a security crisis arises. It is a lot easier to think about what needs to be done and who needs to be notified while you're not in the middle of a crisis. A well thought-out plan can help you make the right decisions, save valuable time, and minimize damage in an emergency.

Management of security requires coordination and planning. The pervasive need for communications and the complexity of networks that support those needs has made security management a difficult task. Security will be only as good as the weakest link in the security chain. Security management tools that can create, distribute, and audit consistent security configurations and policies are critical for large and distributed organizations.

Typical Site Scenario

Business needs and technology are both evolving rapidly. A revolution in the ways that people work and companies interact is being brought about by the capabilities provided by telecommunications. Networks have to provide availability, integrity, and confidentiality under diverse conditions.

Networks must provide ubiquitous connectivity to all corners of your organization, including branch offices, mobile workers, and telecommuters. It may also include connections to business partners. Services made accessible to the public to improve availability and lower costs increase the exposure of some systems to millions of people. Figure 1.1 shows a typical site scenario.

The headquarters is a source of information vital to the operation of the organization. It also needs to collect data from all parts of the organization to conduct business, manage resources, and monitor the status of its business environment. This central site must accommodate many types of connections. It may use multiple wide area network (WAN) technologies to connect to branch offices or business partners. These connections may be permanent or on-demand. It should provide dial-up for mobile users or telecommuters. Most organizations also have an Internet connection to provide public information or business services.

The central site network is usually confined to a small geographic area. It may be a single building or a campus environment, but it will form the core of the network. Small or medium organizations may only have a presence at one geographic location, and large enterprises have several core sites on various continents, interconnected by a global WAN. This central site will have a mix of private servers, public servers, printers, workstations, and network equipment. The design of the network and the provision of services must be flexible to meet with changing needs and priorities of the organization.

Figure 1.1 A typical site scenario.

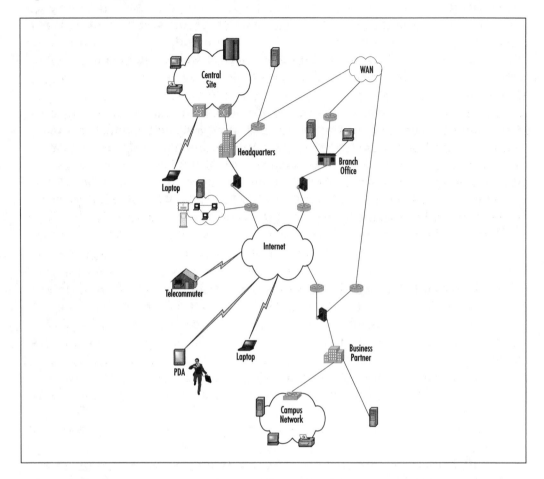

Before the advent of virtual private network (VPN) technology, remote connections were usually through expensive dedicated lines, or smaller organizations may have used on-demand connection technologies such as dial-up over Integrated Services Digital Network (ISDN) or Public Switched Telephone Network (PSTN). VPN has allowed companies to shift their connections to the Internet and save money, but still provide confidentiality and integrity to their communication traffic.

Branch offices can be located on the other side of the city or scattered across a continent. They may exist to provide business services, distribution, sales, or technical services closer to the location of customers. These offices can have one, two, or up to hundreds of employees. A branch office usually has business needs to access information securely at the headquarters site or other branch offices, but due to its smaller size, is constrained by cost for its connectivity options. When the cost or business needs are justified, the branch office would have a permanent connection to the central headquarters. Most branch offices will also have an Internet connection.

Business partners may be collaborative partners, manufacturers, or supply chain partners. Technologies such as Electronic Data Interchange (EDI) over proprietary networks have been used by large businesses to perform transactions, but are difficult and expensive to use. Many companies have implemented extranets by using dedicated network connections to share data and operate joint business applications. Extranets and business-to-business transactions are popular because they reduce business transaction cycle times and allow companies to reduce costs and inventories while increasing responsiveness and service. This trend will only continue to grow. Business-to-business interactions are now rapidly shifting to the Internet. Extranets can be built over the Internet using VPN technology.

Mobile users and telecommuters typically use dial-up services for connectivity to their headquarters or local office. Newer technologies such as Digital Subscriber Line (DSL) or cable modems offer permanent, high-speed Internet access to the home-based telecommuters.

TIP

It is well known that modems inside your campus network can create a backdoor to your network by dialing out to another network, or being left in answer mode to allow remote access directly to a workstation on your internal network. These backdoors bypass the firewall and other security measures that you may have in place.

The always-on Internet connections from home now offer the ability to create the backdoor remotely. It is possible to have an employee or contractor online with a modem to the corporate network remote access facility, while they still have an Internet connection through their DSL or cable modem. Attention to detail in the security policy, workstation configuration, and user awareness is critical to ensure that vulnerabilities don't creep into your system.

Host Security

Any vendor's software is susceptible to harboring security vulnerabilities. Almost every day, Web sites that track security vulnerabilities, such as CERT, are reporting new vulnerability discoveries in operating systems, application software, server software, and even in security software or devices. Patches are implemented for these known bugs, but new vulnerability discoveries continue. Sometimes patches fix one bug, only to introduce another. Even open source software that has been widely used for ten years is not immune to harbouring serious vulnerabilities. In June 2000, CERT reported that MIT Kerberos had multiple buffer overflow vulnerabilities that could be used to gain root access.

Many sites do not keep up with applying patches and thus, leave their systems with known vulnerabilities. It is important to keep all of your software up-to-date. Many of the most damaging attacks have been carried out through office productivity software and e-mail. Attacks can be directed at any software and can seriously affect your network.

The default configuration of hosts makes it easy to get them up and running, but many default services are unnecessary. These unnecessary services increase the vulnerabilities of the system. On each host, all unnecessary services should be shut down. Misconfigured hosts also increase the risk of an unauthorized access. All default passwords and community names must be changed.

TIP

SANS (System Administration, Networking, and Security) Institute has created a list of the top ten Internet security threats from the consensus of a group of security experts. The list is maintained at www.sans.org/topten.htm. Use this list as a guide for the most urgent and critical vulnerabilities to repair on your systems.

This effort was started because experience has shown that a small number of vulnerabilities are used repeatedly to gain unauthorized access to many systems.

SANS has also published a list of the most common mistakes made by end-users, executives, and information technology personnel. It is available at www.sans.org/mistakes.htm.

The increased complexity of systems, the shortage of well-trained administrators, and the lack of enough resources all contribute to reducing security of hosts and applications. We cannot depend on hosts to protect themselves from all threats.

To protect your infrastructure, you must apply security in layers. This layered approach is also called defense in depth. You should create appropriate barriers inside your system so that intruders who may gain access to one part of it do not automatically get access to the rest of the system. Use firewalls to minimize the exposure of private servers from public networks. Firewalls are the first line of defense while packet filtering on routers can supplement the protection of firewalls and provide internal access boundaries.

Access to hosts that contain confidential information needs to be carefully controlled. Inventory the hosts on your network, and use this list to categorize the protection that they will need. Some hosts will be used to provide public access, such as the corporate Web site or online storefront; others will contain confidential information that may be used only by a single department or workgroup. Plan the type of access needed and determine the boundaries of access control for these resources.

Network Security

The purpose of information and network security is to provide availability, integrity, and confidentiality (see Figure 1.2). These terms are described in the following sections. Different systems and businesses will place different importance on each of these three characteristics. For example, although Internet Service Providers (ISPs) may be concerned with confidentiality and integrity, they will be more concerned with protecting availability for their customers. The military places more emphasis on confidentiality with its system of classifications of information and clearances for people to access it. A financial institution must be concerned with all three elements, but they will be measured closely on the integrity of their data.

Figure 1.2 Balancing availability, integrity, and confidentiality.

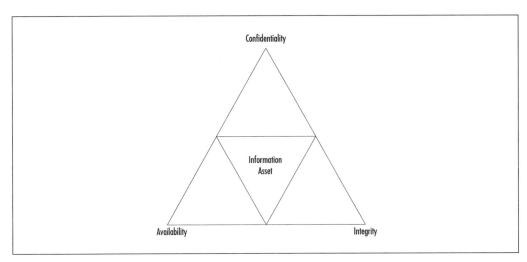

You should consider the security during the logical design of a network. Security considerations can have an effect on the physical design of the network. You need to know the specifications that will be used to purchase network equipment, software features or revision levels that need to be used, and any specialized devices used to provide encryption, quality of service, or access control.

Networks can be segmented to provide separation of responsibility. Departments such as finance, research, or engineering can be restricted so only the people that need access to particular resources can enter a network. You need to determine the resources to protect, the origin of threats against them, and where your network security perimeters should be located. Determine the level of availability, confidentiality, and integrity appropriate for controlling access to those segmented zones. Install perimeter devices and configurations that meet your security requirements. Controlling access to the network with firewalls, routers, switches, remote access servers, and authentication servers can reduce the traffic getting to critical hosts to just authorized users and services.

Keep your security configuration up-to-date and ensure that it meets the information security policy that you have set. In the course of operating a network, many changes can be made. These changes often open new vulnerabilities. You need to continuously reevaluate the status of network security and take action on any vulnerabilities that you find.

Availability

Availability ensures that information and services are accessible and functional when needed. Redundancy, fault tolerance, reliability, failover, backups, recovery, resilience, and load balancing are the network design concepts used to assure availability. If systems aren't available, then integrity and confidentiality won't matter.

Build networks that provide high availability. Your customers and end-users will perceive availability as being the entire system—application, servers, network, and workstation. If they can't run their applications, then it is not available. To provide high availability, ensure that security processes are reliable and responsive. Modular systems and software, including security systems, need to be interoperable.

Denial of Service (DoS) attacks are aimed at attacking the availability of networks and servers. DoS attacks can create severe losses for organizations. In February 2000, large Web sites such as Yahoo!, eBay, Amazon, CNN, ZDNet, E*Trade, Excite, and Buy.com were knocked off line or had availability reduced to about 10 percent for many hours by Distributed Denial of Service Attacks (DDoS). Actual losses were hard to estimate, but probably totalled millions of dollars for these companies.

TIP

Having a good inventory and documentation of your network is important for day-to-day operations, but in a disaster you can't depend on having it available. Store the configurations and software images of network devices off-site with your backups from servers, and keep them up-to-date. Include documentation about the architecture of your network. All of this documentation should be available in printed form because electronic versions may be unavailable or difficult to locate in an emergency. This information will save valuable time in a crisis.

Cisco makes many products designed for high availability. These devices are characterized by long mean time between failure (MTBF) with redundant power supplies, and hot-swappable cards or modules. For example, devices that provide 99.999 percent availability would have about five minutes of downtime per year.

Availability of individual devices can be enhanced by their configuration. Using features such as redundant uplinks with Hot Standby Router Protocol (HSRP), fast convergent Spanning Tree, or Fast Ether Channel provides a failover if one link should fail. Uninterruptible Power Supplies (UPSs) and back-up generators are used to protect mission-critical equipment against power outages.

Although not covered in this book, Cisco IOS includes reliability features such as:

- Hot Standby Router Protocol (HSRP)

- Simple Server Redundancy Protocol (SSRP)

- Deterministic Load Distribution (DLD)

Integrity

Integrity ensures that information or software is complete, accurate, and authentic. We want to keep unauthorized people or processes from making any changes to the system, and to keep authorized users from making unauthorized changes. These changes may be intentional or unintentional.

For network integrity, we need to ensure that the message received is the same message that was sent. The content of the message must be complete and unmodified, and the link is between valid source and destination nodes. Connection integrity can be provided by cryptography and routing control.

Integrity also extends to the software images for network devices that are transporting data. The images must be verified as authentic, and they have not been modified or corrupted. When copying an image into flash memory, verify that the checksum of the bundled image matches the checksum listed in the README file that comes with the upgrade.

Confidentiality

Confidentiality protects sensitive information from unauthorized disclosure or intelligible interception. Cryptography and access control are used to protect confidentiality. The effort applied to protecting confidentiality depends on the sensitivity of the information and the likelihood of it being observed or intercepted.

Network encryption can be applied at any level in the protocol stack. Applications can provide end-to-end encryption, but each application must be adapted to provide this service. Encryption at the transport layer is used frequently today, but this book focuses on encryption at the Open Systems Interconnection (OSI) network layer. Virtual private networks (covered in more detail in Chapter 5, "Virtual Private Networks") can be used to establish secure channels of communication between two sites or between an end-user and a site. Encryption can be used at the OSI data link layer, but at this level, encryption is a point-to-point solution and won't scale to the Internet or even to private internetworks. Every networking device in the communication pathway would have to participate in the encryption scheme. Physical security is used to prevent unauthorized access to network ports or equipment rooms. One of the risks at these low levels is the attachment of sniffers or packet analyzers to the network.

Access Control

Access control is the process of limiting the privilege to use system resources. There are three types of controls for limiting access:

Administrative Controls are based upon policies. Information security policies should state the organization's objectives regarding control over access to resources, hiring and management of personnel, and security awareness.

Physical Controls include limiting access to network nodes, protecting the network wiring, and securing rooms or buildings that contain restricted assets.

Logical Controls are the hardware and software means of limiting access and include access control lists, communication protocols, and cryptography.

Access control depends upon positively verifying an identity (authentication), and then granting privilege based upon identity (authorization). The access could be granted to a person, a machine, a service, or a program. For example, network management using SNMP has access control through the use of community names. One community name gives non-privileged access and another gives privileged access by the management program into the network device. A person can access the same device in user mode or privileged mode using different passwords. Network access control can be provided at the edge of a security perimeter by a firewall or a router using ACLs.

Authentication

Authentication is the verification of a user's, process's, or device's claimed identity. Other security measures depend upon verifying the identity of the sender and receiver of information. Authorization grants privileges based upon identity. Audit trails would not provide accountability without authentication. Confidentiality and integrity are broken if you can't reliably differentiate an authorized entity from an unauthorized entity.

The level of authentication required for a system is determined by the security needs that an organization has placed on it. Public Web servers may allow anonymous or guest access to information. Financial transactions could require strong authentication. An example of a weak form of authentication is using an IP address to determine identity. Changing or spoofing the IP address can easily defeat this mechanism. Strong authentication requires at least two factors of identity. Authentication factors are:

What a Person Knows Passwords and personal identification numbers (PIN) are examples of what a person knows. Passwords may be reusable or one-time use. S/Key is an example of a one-time password system.

What a Person Has Hardware or software tokens are examples of what a person has. Smart cards, SecureID, CRYPTOCard, and SafeWord are examples of tokens.

What a Person Is Biometric authentication is an example of what a person is, because identification is based upon some physical attributes of a person. Biometric systems include palm scan, hand geometry, iris scan, retina pattern, fingerprint, voiceprint, facial recognition, and signature dynamics systems.

A number of systems are available for network authentication. TACACS+ (Terminal Access Controller Access System), Kerberos, and RADIUS (Remote Access Dial In User Service) are authentication protocols supported by Cisco. These authentication systems can be configured to use many of the identification examples listed previously. The strength of the techniques used to verify an identity depends on the sensitivity of the information being accessed and the policy of the organization providing the access. It is an issue of providing cost-effective protection.

Reusable passwords, by themselves, are often a security threat because they are sent in cleartext in an insecure environment. They are easily given to another person, who can then impersonate the original user. Passwords can be accessible to unauthorized people because they are written down in an obvious location or are easy to guess. The password lifetime should be defined in the security policy of the organization, and they should be changed regularly. Choose passwords that are difficult to guess and that do not appear in a dictionary.

Although the details are beyond the scope of this book, Cisco routers can authenticate with each other. Router authentication assures that routing updates are from a known source and have not been modified or corrupted. Cisco can use the MD5 hash or a simple algorithm. Several Cisco routing protocols support authentication:

- Open Shortest Path First (OSPF)
- Routing Information Protocol version 2 (RIPv2)
- Enhanced Interior Gateway Routing Protocol (Enhanced IGRP)
- Border Gateway Protocol (BGP)
- Intermediate System-to-Intermediate System (IS-IS)

Authorization

Authorization is a privilege granted by a designated utility to enable access to services or information for a particular identity or group of identities. For highly secure systems, the default authorization should be no access, and any additional privileges are based on least privilege and need-to-know. For public systems, authorization may be granted to guest or anonymous users. You need to determine your security requirements to decide the appropriate authorization boundaries.

The granting of authorization is based on trust. The process granting access must trust the process that authenticated the identity. Attackers may attempt to get the password of an authorized user, hijack a Telnet session, or use social engineering to impersonate an authorized user and assume their access rights. Authentication is the key to ensuring that only authorized users are accessing controlled information.

Accounting

Accounting is the recording of network activity and resource access attempts. Though this information can be used for billing purposes, from a security perspective it is most important for detecting, analyzing, and responding to security incidents on the network. System logs, audit trails, and accounting software can all be used to hold users accountable for what happens under their logon ID.

For IT Professionals

A Duty to Prevent Your Systems from Being Used as Intermediaries for Parasitic Attacks

Parasitic attacks take advantage of unsuspecting accomplices by using their systems to launch attacks against third parties. One type of parasitic attack is the Distributed Denial of Service (DDoS) attack, like those used to bring down Yahoo! and eBay in February 2000. An attacker will install zombies on many hosts, and then at a time of their choosing, command the zombie hosts to attack a single victim, overwhelming the resources of the victim's site.

Your responsibility is not just to protect your organization's information assets, but to protect the Internet community as a whole. The following site www.cert.org/tech_tips/denial_of_service.html under Prevention and Response has recommendations that will help to make the Internet more secure for everyone.

In the future, we may see civil legal actions that will hold intermediaries used in an attack liable for damages if they have not exercised due care in providing security for their systems.

Network Communication in TCP/IP

The Transmission Control Protocol/Internet Protocol (TCP/IP) suite has become the de facto standard for open system data communication and interoperability. The suite is made up of several protocols and applications that operate at different layers. Each layer is responsible for a different aspect of communication.

The TCP/IP Internet model is organized into four layers as shown in Figure 1.3. The TCP/IP layers are compared to the equivalent layers in the seven-layer Open Systems Interconnection (OSI) reference model. The standards for TCP/IP are published as Requests for Comments (RFC) and are available at www.rfc-editor.org/. RFCs are categorized as standards, draft standards, proposed standards, experimental, informational, and historical. The list of current standards RFCs can be found at www.rfc-editor.org/categories/rfc-standard.html.

Figure 1.3 The layers of the TCP/IP protocol suite.

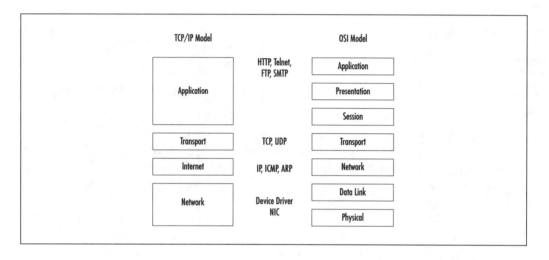

Layered protocols are designed so a specific layer at the destination receives the same object sent by the equivalent source layer. Each layer communicates with its corresponding layer on the other host. It does not worry about the parameters or formats used in the layers above or below it. Physically, a layer hands its data to the interface of the layer above or below on the same system. Figure 1.4 illustrates how the layers communicate. The vertical arrows show the physical communication within a host and the horizontal arrows show the logical communication between peer layers on different hosts.

As data is handed from the application, to transport, to Internet, and to the network, each protocol does its processing and prepends a header, encapsulating the protocol above it. On the system receiving this stream of information, the headers are removed as the data is processed and passed up the stack. This approach provides flexibility because, in general, upper layers don't need to be concerned with the technology used in the layers below. For example, if the IP layer is encrypted, the TCP and applications remain unchanged. Figure 1.5 shows an example of encapsulation on the source host.

Figure 1.4 Logical and physical communication between protocol layers.

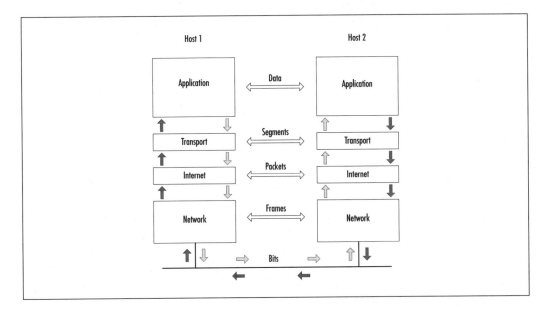

Figure 1.5 Encapsulation of protocol layers.

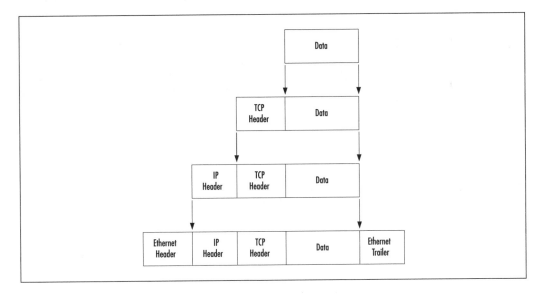

Application Layer

The application layer provides file transfer, print, message, terminal emulation, and database services. Some of the protocols that operate at this

layer include HyperText Transfer Protocol (HTTP), Telnet, File Transfer
Protocol (FTP), and Simple Mail Transfer Protocol (SMTP).

Transport Layer

The transport layer provides duplex, end-to-end data transport services
between applications. Data sent from the application layer is divided into
segments appropriate in size for the network technology being used.
Transmission Control Protocol (TCP) and User Datagram Protocol (UDP)
are the protocols used at this layer.

TCP

TCP provides reliable service by being connection-oriented and including
error detection and correction. The connected nature of TCP is used only
for two end points to communicate with each other. The connection must
be established before a data transfer can occur, and transfers are acknowledged throughout the process. Acknowledgments assure that data is being
received properly. The acknowledgment process provides robustness in the
face of network congestion or communication unreliability. TCP also determines when the transfer ends and closes the connection, thus freeing up
resources on the systems. Checksums assure that the data has not been
accidentally modified during transit. Figure 1.6 shows the format of the
TCP header.

Figure 1.6 The TCP header.

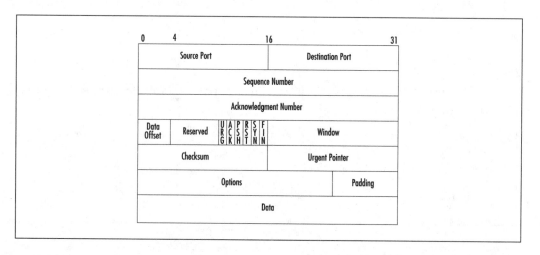

TCP ports are used to multiplex this protocol layer to the layer above
with multiple applications on the same host. A source port and a destination port are associated with the sending and receiving applications,

respectively. The ports from 0 to 1023 are Well Known Ports, and are assigned by Internet Assigned Numbers Authority (IANA). Ports from 1024 to 49151 are Registered Ports, and ports from 49152 through 65535 are Dynamic/Private Ports. The Well Known and Registered Port numbers are available at www.isi.edu/in-notes/iana/assignments/port-numbers.

The sequence numbers allow recovery by TCP from data that was lost, damaged, duplicated, or delivered out of order. Each host in the TCP connection selects an Initial Sequence Number (ISN), and these are synchronized during the establishment of the connection. The sequence number is incremented for each byte of data transmitted across the TCP connection, including the SYN and FIN flags. Sequence numbers are 32 bits and will wrap around to zero when it overflows. The ISN should be unpredictable for a given TCP connection. Some TCP implementations have exhibited vulnerabilities of predictable sequence numbers. Predicting the sequence number can allow an attacker to impersonate a host.

The acknowledgment number has a valid entry when the ACK flag is on. It contains the next sequence number that the receiver is expecting. Since every data segment sent over a TCP connection has a sequence number, it also has an acknowledgment number.

The following are flags used by TCP:

URG The urgent control bit indicates that Urgent Pointer is a valid offset to add to the Sequence Number. The sender of data can indicate to the receiver that there is urgent data pending.

ACK The acknowledgment control bit indicates that the Acknowledgment Number contains the value of the next sequence number the sender of the segment is expecting to receive. ACK is always set for an established connection.

PSH This indicates that all data received to this point has been pushed up to the receiving application. This function expedites the delivery of urgent data to the destination.

RST This TCP flag indicates that the connection is reset. This function flushes all queued segments waiting for transmission or retransmission, and puts the receiver in listen mode.

SYN This Synchronizes sequence numbers. The SYN control bit indicates that the Sequence Number contains the initial sequence number.

FIN This indicates that the sender has finished sending data. The FIN control bit is set by the application closing its connection.

The ACK and RST play a role in determining whether a connection is established or being established. Cisco uses the established keyword in

Access Control Lists (ACLs) to check whether the ACK or RST flags are set. If either flag is set, the packet meets the test as established. If neither flag is set, the device at the source TCP address is trying to establish a new connection to the device at the destination TCP address.

HTTP, SMTP, FTP, Telnet, and rlogin are examples of applications that use TCP for transport. Applications that need reliability support from the transport layer use Remote Procedure Calls (RPC) over TCP. Applications that do not depend on the transport layer for reliability use RPC over UDP.

TCP Connection

Figure 1.7 shows the establishment of a TCP/IP connection. Establishing a TCP connection requires three segments:

1. To initiate the connection, the source host sends a SYN segment (SYN flag is set) and an initial sequence number (ISN) in the sequence number field to the destination port and host address.

2. The destination host responds with a segment containing its initial sequence number, and both the SYN and ACK flags set. The acknowledgment number will be the source's sequence number, incremented by one.

3. The source host acknowledges the SYN from the destination host by replying with an ACK segment and an acknowledgment number that is the destination's sequence number incremented by one.

Figure 1.7 Establishing a TCP connection.

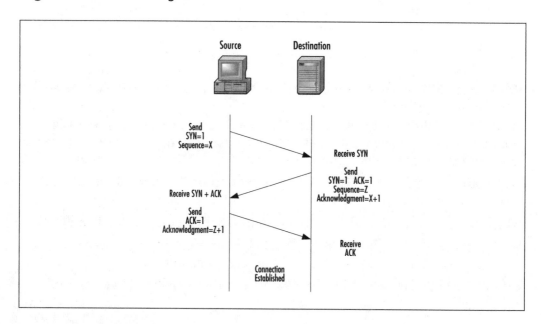

Once a TCP connection between the two systems exists, data can be transferred. As data is sent, the sequence number is incremented to track the number of bytes. Acknowledgment segments from the destination host increment the acknowledgment number as bytes of data are received.

The states that TCP goes through in establishing its connection allows firewalls to easily recognize new connections versus existing connections. Access lists on routers also use these flags in the TCP header to determine whether the connection is established.

A socket is the combination of IP address and TCP port. A local and remote socket pair (quadruplet) determines a connection between two hosts uniquely:

- The source IP address
- The source TCP port
- The destination IP address
- The destination TCP port

Firewalls can use this quadruplet to track the many connections on which they are making forwarding decisions at a very granular level. During the establishment of the connection, the firewall will learn the dynamic port assigned to the client for a particular connection. For the period of time that the connection exists, the dynamic port is allowed through the firewall. Once the connection is finished, the client port will be closed. By tracking the state of a particular connection in this way, security policy rules don't need to compensate for dynamic port assignments.

UDP

UDP is a simple, unreliable transport service. It is connectionless, so delivery is not assured. Look at the simple design of the UDP header in Figure 1.8, and you will understand the efficiency of this protocol. Since connections aren't set up and torn down, there is very little overhead. Lost, damaged, or out of order segments will not be retransmitted unless the application layer requests it. UDP is used for fast, simple messages sent from one host to another. Due to its simplicity, UDP packets are more easily spoofed than TCP packets. If reliable or ordered delivery of data is needed, applications should use TCP.

Simple Network Management Protocol (SNMP), Trivial File Transfer Protocol (TFTP), BOOTstrap Protocol (BOOTP), Network File System (NFS), and Dynamic Host Control Protocol (DHCP) are examples of applications that use UDP for transport. UDP is also used for multimedia applications. Unlike the connection-oriented TCP, which only can connect between two hosts, UDP can broadcast or multicast to many systems at once. The small overhead of UDP eases the network load when running time-sensitive data such as audio or video.

Secure Sockets Layer (SSL) was designed by Netscape in 1993 and provides end-to-end confidentiality, authentication, and integrity at the Transport layer (TCP). Transport Layer Security (TLS) is the IETF Internet standard version of SSL based on version 3. SSL and TLS are known mostly in the HTTP world, but the security features of SSL/TLS can be used for other protocols as well, such as Internet Mail Access Protocol (IMAP), Lightweight Mail Access Protocol (LDAP), and SMTP.

Figure 1.8 The UDP header.

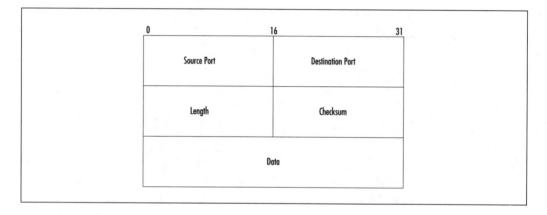

Internet Layer

The Internet layer is responsible for addressing, routing, error notification, and hop-by-hop fragmentation and reassembly. It manages the delivery of information from host to host. Fragmentation could occur at this layer because different network technologies have different Maximum Transmission Unit (MTU). Internet Protocol (IP), Internet Control Message Protocol (ICMP), and Address Resolution Protocol (ARP) are protocols used at this layer.

IP

IP is an unreliable, routable packet delivery protocol. All upper layer protocols use IP to send and receive packets. IP receives segments from the transport layer, fragments them into packets, and passes them to the network layer.

The IP address is a logical address assigned to each node on TCP/IP network. IP addressing is designed to allow routing of packets across internetworks. Since IP addresses are easy to change or spoof, they should not be relied upon to provide identification in untrusted environments. As shown in Figure 1.9, the source and destination addresses are included in the IP header.

The protocol parameter indicates the upper level protocol that is using IP. The decimal value for TCP is 6 and for UDP is 17. The list of assigned numbers for this field is available at www.isi.edu/in-notes/iana/assignments/protocol-numbers. The checksum is computed only on the header, so it does not check the integrity of the data payload.

Figure 1.9 The IP header.

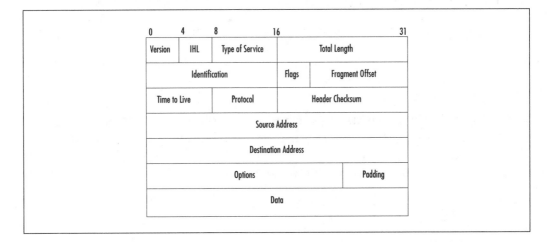

ICMP

ICMP provides diagnostic functions and error reporting for IP. For example, ICMP can provide feedback to a sending host when a destination is unreachable or time is exceeded (TTL=0). A ping is an ICMP echo request message, and the response is an ICMP echo reply.

ARP

ARP is responsible for resolving the logical IP address into the hardware address for the network layer. If the destination IP address is on the same subnet as the source host, then IP will use ARP to determine the hardware address of the destination host. If the destination IP address is on a remote subnet, then ARP will be used to determine the hardware address of the default gateway. The ARP cache, a table of translations between IP address and hardware, stores its entries dynamically and flushes them after a short period of time.

WARNING

Some attacks have been based upon forging the ARP reply and redirecting IP traffic to a system that sniffs for cleartext passwords or other information. This attack overcomes the benefit of a switched Ethernet environment because ARP requests are broadcast to all local network ports. The spoofing machine can respond with its hardware address and become a man-in-the-middle. Research is being conducted on a new ARP protocol that would be resistant to these types of attacks. In the meantime, avoid the use of cleartext passwords or community names.

Network Layer

The network layer includes the network interface card and device driver. These provide the physical interface to the media of the network. The network layer controls the network hardware, encapsulates and transmits outgoing packets, and accepts and demultiplexes incoming packets. It accepts IP packets from the Internet layer above.

Security in TCP/IP

The Internet provides no guarantee of privacy or integrity for data. Cryptography should be considered for private, valuable, or vulnerable data. Data is encrypted as it is transmitted, and decrypted as it is received. Most layers in the ISO model can be used to provide data integrity and confidentiality. The application of security to each layer has its own particular advantages and disadvantages. The characteristics of security applied at a particular layer provide features that can be used as a decision point in determining the applicability of each technique to solve a particular problem.

Cryptography

Cryptography is the science of writing and reading in code or cipher. Information security uses cryptosystems to keep information private, and to authenticate the identity of the sender or receiver of the information. Cryptography can also provide integrity for information, because it allows only authorized people or processes to access it, and can detect corruption or modification of the original message or file. Cryptography works by making the effort required to break the encryption much more expensive than the value of the data, or by taking much longer to break than the time the data will hold its value.

There are three categories of cryptographic functions: symmetric key, asymmetric key, and hash functions. Most of the standard algorithms are public knowledge, and have been thoroughly tested by many experts. Their security depends on the strength of the algorithm and the strength of the key. A key is a sequence that is used for the mathematical process of enciphering and deciphering information. The hash functions do not use a key. The hash is performed by a specialized mathematical function.

There are many algorithms for encrypting information. To exchange encrypted messages, the parties must agree on the algorithms that will be used, and the keys for each algorithm. The protocols will be configured to negotiate a particular algorithm, and a key management system will generate, distribute, and manage the keys.

Symmetric Cryptography

Symmetric key cryptography uses the same key to encrypt and decrypt the message. Each pair of users shares a key for exchanging messages. By being able to encrypt or decrypt a message, each partner assumes that the other entity is the same entity with which they exchanged keys. It provides some degree of authentication. For this scheme to work, the key must be kept secret between the two parties involved.

Examples of symmetric key algorithms are as follows:

- Data Encryption Standard (DES) (56 bits)
- Triple DES (3DES) (168 bits)
- International Data Encryption Algorithm (IDEA) (128 bits)
- Rivest Cipher 4 (RC4) (variable length key)
- Advanced Encryption Standard (AES) (will replace DES as a federal standard)

For stored files that are encrypted, the loss or destruction of the sole copy of a symmetric key could result in the loss of access to the files. Sometimes keys are archived or backed up to protect the organization from such potential loss. For network transfers, this vulnerability is not an issue. New keys can be generated, exchanged, and the information resent.

A symmetric key, including any backup copies, has to be protected to the same extent as the information that it protects. The distribution of the keys must be accomplished by a secure means. If someone intercepted a key during the exchange or acquired a key from a user's system, they could also participate in the exchange of encrypted information. Privacy and integrity would be lost.

Symmetric key algorithms are fast and can encrypt a lot of information in a short period of time. They are strong when large keys are used. Symmetric key algorithms are used for the bulk of communication link encryption.

Asymmetric Cryptography

Asymmetric key cryptography is also known as public key cryptography. It uses a pair of keys that are mathematically related, but given one key, the other is very unlikely to be calculated. One key is for encrypting or signing, and the other is used for decrypting or verifying. One of the keys is kept private or secret, and the other is distributed publicly.

Here are some examples of asymmetric key algorithms:

■ Diffie-Hellman

■ Rivest, Shamir, Adleman (RSA)

■ Digital Signature Algorithm (DSA) / El Gamal

■ Elliptic Curve Cryptosystem (ECC)

The asymmetric algorithms are trapdoor one-way functions. They are easy to compute in one direction, but extremely difficult to calculate in the reverse direction unless you have the other key to the trapdoor. Even with the keys, asymmetric key functions are very compute-intensive. They are about 100 times slower than symmetric key algorithms. They are not practical for encrypting and decrypting large amounts of data.

When used to provide confidentiality, the sender encrypts the message using the public key of the receiver. Only the intended receiver's private key can decrypt the message. Messages going to multiple receivers must be encrypted for each one of the receivers. When used for authentication in digital signatures, the message is encrypted with the sender's private key. Only the sender's public key can decrypt it, verifying that it came from the sender. Confidentiality is the most common use for public key cryptography. It is used to exchange the session keys for symmetric key algorithms.

Hash Function

A hash function is used to condense a variable-length message into a fixed-length code, known as a hash or message digest. Different algorithms will produce different length hashes. Some examples of hash functions are:

■ Message Digest 5 (MD5) (128 bits)

■ Secure Hash Algorithm (SHA) (160 bits)

■ Haval (variable length)

Hashes are a cryptographic checksum used to provide an integrity check on messages. A change of just one character in the original message can produce a change in a significant number of the hash bits. A hash function is a one-way function, and it is mathematically infeasible to compute the original message from the hash. The sender computes a hash of the original message and sends it with the encrypted message. The receiver decrypts the message, and also computes a hash. If the original hash and the computed hash are the same, then the receiver is confident that the message is complete and unmodified.

Computing a hash of the message, and encrypting the hash with the sender's private key can create a digital signature. The sender attaches this digital signature to the message. The receiver separates the digital signature and decrypts it with the sender's public key. A hash of the message received is computed. If the two hash values match, then it verifies that this is the authentic message from the sender.

Public Key Certificates

Public key certificates are data structures, signed by a trusted certificate authority (CA), that bind an identity to a public key and additional information. They provide a means of distributing public keys. The degree of trust that you put into the identity are dependent upon the procedures and trust that you place in the certificate authority. Public key certificates are used to support authentication, confidentiality, and integrity for such things as Web transactions, e-mail exchange, and IPSec. The certificate is signed with the private key of the certificate authority. The CA's public key is used to authenticate the certificate. Signed public key certificates, traceable via a hierarchical chain of trust, provide authentication and integrity of the public key and data included in the certificate.

The public key infrastructure provides a mechanism for generating keys, managing certificates, and ensuring integrity of the keys. Certificates are issued with expiration dates, after which they are no longer valid. Certificates may be revoked prior to the expiration date, for example due to personnel or organizational changes. Certificates are verified against recent certificate revocation lists (CRLs) or online query mechanisms to determine their validity. Certificate revocation lists can be downloaded from certificate authorities and used offline, but they need to be updated periodically.

Certificates are based on the formatting standards in X.509 v3. Version 3 improved the usefulness of certificates by adding standard and optional extension fields to the earlier formats. The standard extensions include such fields as Key Usage, Private Key Usage Period, Certificate Policies, and Policy Mappings.

Application Layer Security

Application layer security provides end-to-end security from an application running on one host through the network to the application on another host. It does not care about the underlying transport mechanism. Complete coverage of security requirements, integrity, confidentiality, and nonrepudiation can be provided at this layer. Applications have a fine granularity of control over the nature and content of the transactions. However, application layer security is not a general solution, because each application and client must be adapted to provide the security services. Several examples of application security extensions follow.

Pretty Good Privacy (PGP)

Phil Zimmerman created PGP in 1991. Individuals worldwide use it for privacy and digital signing of e-mail messages. PGP provides end-to-end security from the sender to the receiver. It can also be used to encrypt files. PGP has traditionally used RSA public key cryptography to exchange keys, and IDEA to encrypt messages.

PGP uses a *web of trust* or *network trust* model, where any users can vouch for the identity of other users. Getting the public keys of the intended person can be difficult to achieve in a secure manner. You can get a person's public key directly from that person, and then communicate the hash of the key in an out-of-band pathway. Keys are stored in files called key rings. There are some servers on the Internet with public key rings. These servers do not authenticate the keys, but merely store them. You should not trust keys that have an unknown heritage.

Secure HyperText Transport Protocol (S-HTTP)

S-HTTP is not widely used, but it was designed to provide security for Web-based applications. Secure HTTP is a secure message-oriented communications protocol, and can transmit individual messages securely. It provides transaction confidentiality, authentication, and message integrity. It extends HTTP to include tags for encrypted and secure transactions. S-HTTP is implemented in some commercial Web servers and most browsers. The S-HTTP server negotiates with the client for the type of encryption that will be used. Transactions can involve several types of encryption between a particular server and client.

S-HTTP does not require clients to have public key certificates because it can use symmetric keys to provide private transactions. The symmetric keys would be provided in advance using out-of-band communication.

Transport Layer Security

Transport layer security is directed at providing process-to-process security between hosts. Most schemes are designed for TCP to provide reliable, connection-oriented communication. Many transport layer security mechanisms require changes in applications to access the security benefits. The secure applications are replacements for standard unsecure applications and use different ports.

Secure Sockets Layer (SSL) and Transport Layer Security (TLS)

SSL was designed by Netscape and is used widely on the Internet for Web transactions such as sending credit card data. SSL can also be utilized for other protocols such as Telnet, FTP, LDAP, IMAP, and SMTP, but these are not commonly used. TLS is an open, IETF-proposed standard based on SSL 3.0. RFCs 2246, 2712, 2817, and 2818 define TLS. The two protocols are not interoperable, but TLS has the capability to drop down into SSL 3.0 mode for backwards compatibility. SSL and TLS provide security for a single TCP session.

SSL and TLS provide a connection between a client and a server, over which any amount of data can be sent securely. Server and browser must be SSL or TLS enabled to facilitate secure Web connections. Applications must be SSL- or TLS-enabled to allow their use of the secure connection. Figure 1.10 shows the relative location in the protocol stack of the SSL and TLS protocols.

Figure 1.10 The Secure Sockets Layer.

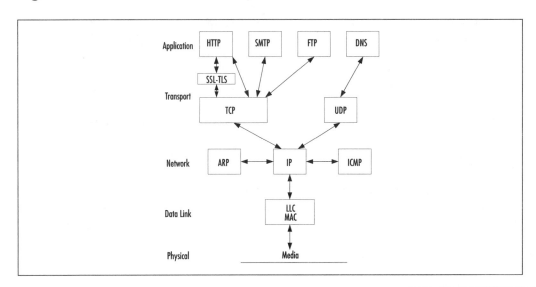

For the browser and server to communicate securely, each needs to have the shared session key. SSL/TLS use public key encryption to exchange session keys during communication initialization. When a browser is installed on a workstation, it generates a unique private/public key pair.

Secure Shell (SSH)

Secure shell protocol is specified in a set of Internet draft documents. SSH provides secure remote login and other secure network services over an insecure network. SSH is being promoted free to colleges and universities as a means for reducing cleartext passwords on networks. Middle and high-end Cisco routers support SSH, but only SSH version 1. SSH version 2 is completely rewritten to use different security protocols and has added public key cryptography.

The SSH protocol provides channels for establishing secure, interactive shell sessions and tunnelling other TCP applications. There are three major components to SSH:

Transport Layer Protocol provides authentication, confidentiality, and integrity for the server. It can also compress the data stream. The SSH transport runs on top of TCP. The transport protocol negotiates key exchange method, public key, symmetric encryption, authentication, and hash algorithms.

User Authentication Protocol authenticates the user-level client to the server and runs on top of SSH transport layer. It assumes that the transport layer provides integrity and confidentiality. The method of authentication is negotiated between the server and the client.

Connection Protocol multiplexes an encrypted tunnel into several channels. It is run on top of SSH transport and authentication protocols. The two ends negotiate the channel, window size, and type of data. The connection protocol can tunnel X11 or any arbitrary TCP port traffic.

Filtering

Packet filters can be implemented on routers and layer 3 devices to control the packets that will be blocked or forwarded at each interface. Routing decisions about whether to forward or drop the packet are made based on the rules in the access list. Standard access lists cannot filter on transport layer information. Only extended access lists can specify a protocol, and a parameter related to that protocol. TCP filtering options include established connections, port numbers or ranges of port numbers, and type of service values. UDP filter options only specify port numbers, since it is not a connection-oriented protocol.

Network Layer Security

Network layer security can be applied to secure traffic for all applications or transport protocols in the above layers. Applications do not need to be modified since they communicate with the transport layer above.

IP Security Protocols (IPSec)

IPSec protocols can supply access control, authentication, data integrity, and confidentiality for each IP packet between two participating network nodes. IPSec can be used between two hosts (including clients), a gateway and a host, or two gateways. No modification of network hardware or software is required to route IPSec. Applications and upper level protocols can be used unchanged.

IPSec adds two security protocols to IP, Authentication Header (AH) and Encapsulating Security Payload (ESP). AH provides connectionless integrity, data origin authentication, and anti-replay service for the IP packet. AH does not encrypt the data, but any modification of the data would be detected. ESP provides confidentiality through the encryption of the payload. Access control is provided through the use and management of keys to control participation in traffic flows.

IPSec was designed to be flexible, so different security needs could be accommodated. The security services can be tailored to the particular needs of each connection by using AH or ESP separately for their individual functions, or combining the protocols to provide the full range of protection offered by IPSec. Multiple cryptographic algorithms are supported. The algorithms that must be present in any implementation of IPSec follow. The null algorithms provide no protection, but are used for consistent negotiation by the protocols. AH and ESP cannot both be null at the same time.

- DES in CBC (Cipher Block Chaining) mode
- HMAC (Hash Message Authentication Code) with MD5
- HMAC with SHA
- Null Authentication Algorithm
- Null Encryption Algorithm

A Security Association (SA) forms an agreement between two systems participating in an IPSec connection. An SA represents a simplex connection to provide a security service using a selected policy and keys, between two nodes. A Security Parameter Index (SPI), an IP destination address, and a protocol identifier are used to identify a particular SA. The SPI is an arbitrary 32-bit value selected by the destination system that uniquely identifies a particular Security Association among several associations that may exist on a particular node. The protocol identifier can indicate either AH or ESP, but not both. Separate SAs are created for each protocol, and for each direction between systems. If two systems were using AH and ESP in both directions, then they would form four SAs.

Each protocol supports a transport mode and a tunnel mode of operation. The transport mode is between two hosts. These hosts are the endpoints for the cryptographic functions being used. Tunnel mode is an IP tunnel, and is used whenever either end of the SA is a security gateway. A security gateway is an intermediate system, such as a router or firewall, that implements IPSec protocols. A Security Association between a host and a security gateway must use tunnel mode. If the connection traffic is destined for the gateway itself, such as management traffic, then the gateway is treated as a host, because it is the endpoint of the communication.

In transport mode, the AH or ESP header are inserted after the IP header, but before any upper layer protocol headers. As shown in Figure 1.11, AH authenticates the original IP header. AH does not protect the fields that are modified in the course of routing IP packets. ESP protects only what comes after the ESP header. If the security policy between two nodes requires a combination of security services, the AH header appears first after the IP header, followed by the ESP header. This combination of Security Associations is called an SA bundle.

Figure 1.11 The IPSec transport mode in IPv4.

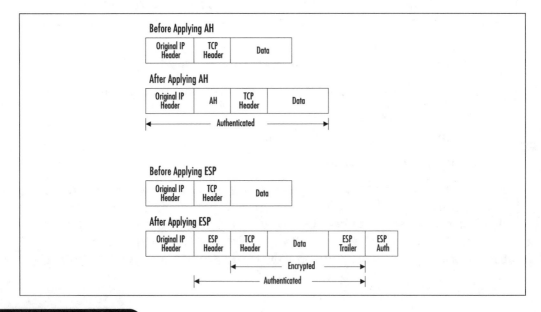

In tunnel mode, the original IP header and payload are encapsulated by the IPSec protocols. A new IP header that specifies the IPSec tunnel destination is prepended to the packet. The original IP header and its payload are protected by the AH or ESP headers. From Figure 1.12 you can see that, as in transport mode, AH offers some protection for the entire packet. AH does not protect the fields that are modified in the course of routing IP packets between the IPSec tunnel endpoints, but it does completely protect the original IP header.

Figure 1.12 The IPSec tunnel mode in IPv4.

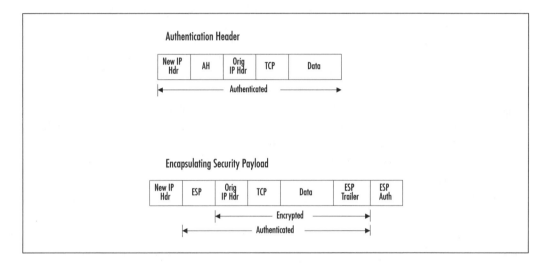

Key management is another major component of IPSec. Manual techniques are allowed in the IPSec standard, and might be acceptable for configuring one or two gateways, but typing in keys and data are not practical in most environments. The Internet Key Exchange (IKE) provides automated, bi-directional SA management, key generation, and key management. IKE negotiates in two phases. Phase 1 negotiates a secure, authenticated channel over which the two systems can communicate for further negotiations. They agree on the encryption algorithm, hash algorithm, authentication method, and Diffie-Hellman group to exchange keys and information. A single phase 1 association can be used for multiple phase 2 negotiations. Phase 2 negotiates the services that define the SAs used by IPSec. They agree on IPSec protocol, hash algorithm, and encryption algorithm. Multiple SAs will result from phase 2 negotiations. An SA is created for inbound and outbound of each protocol used.

Filtering (Access Control Lists)

Packet filters can be implemented on routers and layer 3 devices to control the source and destination IP addresses allowed to pass through the gateway. Standard access lists can filter on source address. Extended access lists can filter ICMP, IGMP, or IP protocols at the network layer. ICMP can be filtered based on the specific message. IP filtering can include port numbers at the transport layer to allow or disallow specific services between specific addresses. Access lists can also control other routed protocols such as AppleTalk or IPX.

Data Link Layer Security

Data Link security is done point-to-point, such as over a leased line or frame relay permanent virtual circuit. Dedicated hardware devices attached to each end of the link do encryption and decryption. Military, government, and banking organizations are the most common users of this approach. It is not scalable to large internetworks, because the packets are not routable in their encrypted state. This method does have the advantage that an eavesdropper cannot determine the source or destination addresses in the packets. It can also be used for any upper layer protocols.

Authentication

Authentication can be provided locally on each device on your network, but using an authentication server offers improved scalability, flexibility, and control. Firewalls, routers, and remote access servers enforce network access security. Configuring these devices to use one centralized database of accounts is easier on the administrator and the users who may access the network through multiple pathways.

A Cisco network access server (NAS), firewall, or router acts as the client and requests authentication from an authentication server. The access server or router will prompt the user for a username and password, and then verifies the password with the authentication server. TACACS+, RADIUS, and Kerberos are widely used authentication servers supported by Cisco. TACACS+ and RADIUS can also provide services for authorization and accounting.

Terminal Access Controller Access Control System Plus (TACACS+)

TACACS+ is an enhanced version of TACACS developed by Cisco. The enhancements include the separation of authentication, authorization, and accounting into three distinct functions. These services can be used independently or together. For example, Kerberos could be used for authentication, and TACACS+ used for authorization and accounting. Some of the characteristics of TACACS+ are:

- Whereas older versions of TACACS and RADIUS use UDP for transport, TACACS+ uses TCP (port 49) for reliable and acknowledged transport.

- TACACS+ can encrypt the entire payload of the packet, so it protects the password, username and other information sent between the Cisco access client and the server. The encryption can be turned off for troubleshooting. Communication from the workstation to the Cisco client providing access services is not encrypted.

- TACACS+ supports multiple protocols such as IP, AppleTalk Remote Access (ARA), Novell Asynchronous Services Interface (NASI), X.25 PAD connection, and NetBIOS.

- You can use TACACS+ to provide greater control over router management in either non-privileged or privileged mode, because you can authenticate individual users or groups rather than a shared password. Router commands can be specified explicitly on the TACACS+ server to allow specific commands.

Remote Access Dial-In User Service (RADIUS)

RADIUS is an open standard and available from many vendors. RADIUS can be a good choice in a heterogeneous network environment because of its widespread support, but some vendors have implemented proprietary attributes in RADIUS that hinder interoperability.

- RADIUS uses UDP, so it offers only best-effort delivery.

- For authentication, RADIUS encrypts only the password sent between the Cisco access client and RADIUS server. RADIUS does not provide encryption between the workstation and the Cisco access client.

- RADIUS does not support multiple protocols, and works only on IP networks.

- RADIUS does not provide the ability to control the commands that can be executed on a router.

Kerberos

Kerberos protocol can be used for network authentication and host authentication. Host-based applications must be adapted to use the Kerberos protocol. A Kerberos realm includes all users, hosts, and network services that are registered with a Kerberos server. Kerberos uses symmetric key cryptography and stores a shared key for each user and each network resource that is participating in its realm. Every user and network resource needs a Kerberos account. Knowing its shared key is proof of identity for each of those entities. Kerberos stores all passwords encrypted with a single system key. If that system key is compromised, all passwords need to be recreated.

The process of authenticating using Kerberos involves three systems: a client, a network resource, and the Kerberos server. The Kerberos server is called the Key Distribution Center (KDC). For remote network access, the client and network resource is the boundary network device, such as network access server or router. The remote user establishes a PPP connection to the boundary device, and the device prompts the user for username and password. The device, acting as the client, requests a ticket-granting ticket (TGT) from the Kerberos authentication server. If the user has an account, the authentication server generates a session key, and sends it to the ticket-granting server (TGS). The TGT is a credential that specifies the user's verified identity, the Kerberos server identity, and the expiration time of the ticket. By default, tickets expire after eight hours. The ticket-granting ticket is encrypted with a key known only to the ticket-granting server and the authentication server. The Kerberos server using a DES key generated from the users password encrypts the TGT, session key, and other information. Only the user and the Kerberos server should know the password. The Cisco access server will attempt to decrypt the TGT with the password that the user entered. If successful, the user is authenticated to the access server, and the user's workstation becomes part of the protected network.

Users who want to access services that are part of the Kerberos realm on the network must now authenticate against the Kerberos server and get authorization to access the services. The user first gets a ticket-granting ticket as described previously, which is used to request access to other services. The difference is that the client is now the user's workstation. The user then sends the TGT to the TGS to request access for a specific service on a specific server. The TGS generates a random session key and sends a server ticket containing the key to the client that requested the service. The client presents the new server ticket to the server in order to gain access. A server ticket must be created for each service that the client will access.

More details on AAA can be found in Chapter 6, "Cisco Authentication, Authorization, and Accounting Mechanisms."

Cisco IP Security Hardware and Software

Cisco provides a combination of dedicated security solutions, security options available for networking products, and consulting services. The following dedicated security products make up the Cisco Secure offerings:

- Cisco Secure PIX Firewall
- Cisco Secure Integrated Software
- Cisco Secure Integrated VPN Software
- Cisco Secure VPN Client
- Cisco Secure Access Control Server
- Cisco Secure Scanner
- Cisco Secure Intrusion Detection System
- Cisco Secure Policy Manager
- Cisco Secure Consulting Services

The breadth of these products provides a fairly complete set of security solutions for organizations to protect the availability, confidentiality, and integrity of their systems.

Cisco Secure PIX Firewall

Firewalls are typically placed at network borders to create a security perimeter. Most frequently, they are used to protect an internal network from external access. Firewalls may also be used internally to control network access to specific departments or resources. The Cisco Secure PIX Firewall series of products are dedicated firewall appliances. All models offer VPN, IPSec, and firewall capabilities. The three models—506, 515, and 520—provide performance levels ranging from small offices up to large enterprises and Internet Service Providers (ISPs). Choose the appropriate model based on the throughput and number of interfaces needed for your application.

Security policies can be enforced consistently across large enterprises and ISPs with the Cisco Secure Policy Manager. It can centrally manage up to 500 Cisco Secure PIX Firewalls. Organizations providing managed network security to many customers will also appreciate this centralized management feature.

www.syngress.com

Cisco Secure PIX Firewall 506 has two integrated10BaseT ports. The 515-R is limited to two 10/100 Ethernet interfaces. The 515-UR and the 520 provide up to six 10/100 Ethernet interfaces. The 520 also gives the option of up to four 4/16 Mbps Token Ring or two dual-attached, multi-mode FDDI interfaces.

Common features shared by all models are as follows:

Embedded, Real-Time Operating System The proprietary operating system was developed specifically for the PIX firewall. It provides high performance, is immune to UNIX security breaches, but is based upon security by obscurity. The code is a trade secret held by Cisco.

Stateful Inspection Cisco calls it Adaptive Security Algorithm (ASA). ASA tracks the state of connections based upon source address, destination address, sequence numbers, ports numbers, and TCP flags. Forwarding decisions are based on applying the configured security policy to these parameters.

VPN Tunnels Using DES or 3DES This feature provides confidentiality across untrusted networks. The addition of the PIX Private Link encryption card allows the PIX to create and/or terminate VPN tunnels between two PIX firewalls, between a PIX and any Cisco VPN enabled router, and between a PIX and the Cisco Secure VPN Client. The 506 supports up to 4 VPN peers. The 515 and 520 support up to 256 peers.

Java Applet Filter Java applets can be blocked when delivered in HTTP content. More sophisticated filtering requires a third-party product.

NOTE

Three basic types of firewalls are available today. Some firewall products combine more than one of these approaches to compensate for the strengths and weaknesses of each.

Packet Filters look at the protocol, address, or port information in each packet and make a forwarding decision for that packet based on rules. Access Control Lists (ACLs) on routers is an example of packet filters. Packet filters are useful for blocking source or destination addresses, and can restrict the services accessible.

Proxy Servers use a specific application for each service that will be forwarded through the firewall. The proxy application takes requests on one interface, examines the contents of the traffic, and makes a forwarding decision based on policy rules. Proxies offer excellent security, but you must have an application for each service that will be processed by the firewall. Proxy-based firewalls have the slowest performance of the three types.

Stateful Inspection analyzes all the communication layers, extracts the relevant communication and application state information, and dynamically maintains the state of communications in tables. Forwarding decisions are based upon the configured security policy. Stateful inspection offers flexibility and performance.

The 515 and 520 models offer additional features of interest to larger organizations:

Network Address Translation (NAT) NAT conserves the IP address space by translating up to 64,000 internal hosts to a single external IP address. The PIX firewall uses port address translation (PAT) to multiplex each internal host with a different port number. PAT does not work with H.323 applications, multimedia applications, or caching nameservers.

Failover/Hot Standby Option This feature improves availability of the network. It is not available on the 515-R. Cisco has created a Fail-Over Bundle (515-UR only) to add software and a second chassis to create a redundant firewall configuration.

Cut-through User Authentication A cut-through proxy is used to authenticate users with a TACACS+ or RADIUS server. This feature improves performance for authentication, authorization, and accounting. When the username and password are correct, PIX firewall lets further traffic between the specified authentication server and the connection interact directly.

URL Filtering A NetPartners WebSENSE server is needed to utilize this feature. The PIX firewall permits or denies connections based on the outbound URL requests and the policy on the WebSENSE server.

Table 1.1 compares the performance of the PIX firewalls offered by Cisco.

Table 1.1 Cisco Secure PIX Firewall Performance Comparison

Model	Throughput	Simultaneous Sessions
506	10Mbps	N/A
515-R	120Mbps	50,000
515-UR	120Mbps	125,000
520	370Mbps	250,000

You will find configuration details on Cisco Secure PIX Firewalls in Chapter 4, "Cisco PIX Firewall." Additional information on related topics is found in Chapter 3, "Network Address Translation," Chapter 5, "Virtual Private Networks" Chapter 6, and "Cisco Authentication, Authorization, and Accounting Mechanisms."

Cisco Secure Integrated Software

Cisco Secure Integrated Software (formerly called Cisco IOS Firewall Feature Set) is a bundle of security features that integrate with Cisco IOS software. It can add firewall, intrusion detection, Data Encryption Standard (DES) (56-bit) encryption, and secure administration capabilities to most of the following routers:

- 800
- UBR900 series
- 1600
- 1720
- 2500
- 2600
- 3600
- 7100
- 7200
- 7500
- RSM (Route Switch Module)

The 800, UBR904, 1600, and 2500 do not support authentication proxy or intrusion detection.

The authentication proxy can use TACACS+ or RADIUS protocols. These can be applied per-user on LAN or dial-up communication links.

The Cisco Secure Intrusion Detection System described next is a separate appliance and merely watches the network traffic. The Cisco Secure Integrated Software is an integral part of Cisco IOS. This difference can affect performance, because the Cisco Secure Integrated Software lies in the critical packet path.

Cisco Secure Integrated VPN Software

Cisco Secure Integrated VPN Software adds 3DES (168-bit) encryption, and authentication through digital certificates, one-time password tokens, and preshared keys to the Cisco Secure Integrated Software features described previously. The package is available for the following routers:

- 1720
- 2600
- 3600
- 7100

VPNs can be established over remote access, intranet, or extranets.

Cisco Secure VPN Client

The Cisco Secure VPN Client enables secure connectivity for remote access VPNs. It can be used for applications such as e-commerce, mobile user, and telecommuting. It provides Microsoft Windows 95/98 and NT 4.0 users with a complete implementation of IPSec, including support for DES (56-bit) and 3DES (168-bit) encryption, and authentication through digital certificates, one-time password tokens, and preshared keys.

The security policy for end-users can be managed centrally, and protected as read-only for the client. This feature prevents users from by-passing the policy that has been put in place and ensures that policy is applied consistently among users.

More details about VPNs can be found in Chapter 5, "Virtual Private Networks."

Cisco Secure Access Control Server

The Cisco Secure Access Control Server (ACS) provides authentication, authorization, and accounting (AAA) for users accessing network services. Cisco Secure ACS supports TACACS+ and RADIUS protocols. The Windows NT version can also do pass-through authentication to the NT user accounts. The ACS can be used as a centralized server or a distributed system composed of multiple ACS systems. It can also interface to other third-party RADIUS or TACACS+ systems in a distributed configuration. In a distributed environment, the ACS can act as a proxy and automatically forward an authentication request to another AAA server.

The accounting function can record each user session that was authenticated by the server. The accounting information can be used by ISPs to provide billing or usage reports for customers. It can also serve as data for security or forensic analysis.

More details about AAA can be found in Chapter 6, "Cisco Authentication, Authorization, and Accounting Mechanisms."

Cisco Secure Scanner

Cisco Secure Scanner (formerly called NetSonar) is a vulnerability assessment tool for network hosts. This scanner software package is available to run on Windows NT, Solaris, and Solaris x86. It will map all devices connected to the scanned network. Vulnerability assessment can be performed on:

- UNIX hosts
- Windows NT hosts
- Network TCP/IP hosts
- Mail servers
- Web servers
- FTP servers
- Routers
- Firewalls
- Switches

The scanner comes with a database of known security vulnerabilities. The database contains information about repairing any of the vulnerabilities that it finds, and is updated periodically as new vulnerabilities are discovered. You can also create customized scanning rules tailored to your environment or security policies.

More details about Cisco Secure Scanner can be found in Chapter 7, "Intrusion Detection."

Cisco Secure Intrusion Detection System

An intrusion detection system (IDS) can help to make you aware of the nature and frequency of attacks against your network and systems. From the information provided by the IDS, you can design an appropriate response to reduce the risks to your systems from these attacks.

Cisco Secure Intrusion Detection System (formerly called NetRanger) is a real-time network intrusion detection system. The system consists of sensors and a director. A system can be implemented with a single sensor at a strategic location, or multiple sensors placed at many well-chosen locations in the network. Sensors operate in promiscuous mode and passively analyze the network traffic that appears on its interface for unauthorized activity. The IDS sensor will report traffic matching attack signatures to the director. The sensor can also be configured to actively change ACLs on Cisco routers in response to attack signatures. The sensor is a hardware and software appliance that is available for five network technologies:

- Ethernet
- Fast Ethernet
- Token Ring
- Single attached FDDI
- Dual attached FDDI

The director is the management station. It receives the alerts from sensors locally or remotely located. You can have one central director, or you can have multiple directors receiving alerts from any of your network sensors. The director can be configured to send alarms to a pager or e-mail address.

More details about intrusion detection can be found in Chapter 7, "Intrusion Detection."

Cisco Secure Policy Manager

The Cisco Secure Policy Manager (formerly called Cisco Security Manager) is a comprehensive security management system for Cisco Secure products. You can define, distribute, enforce, and audit security policies for multiple PIX Firewalls and VPN routers from a central location. Cisco Secure Policy Manager supports IPSec VPN, user authentication, and in a future version will support intrusion detection and vulnerability scanning technologies. Its use on routers requires that Cisco Secure Integrated Software be installed.

Policy Manager centralizes the management of security policies, monitoring of status, and reporting of policy events. It can help to ensure a consistent application of policies across hundreds of devices, and will save your time by automating portions of the policy creation and distribution.

More details about Cisco Secure Policy Manager can be found in Chapter 8, "Network Security Management."

Cisco Secure Consulting Services

Cisco Secure Consulting Services are targeted to large corporate and government customers. Consulting services is beyond the scope of this book, but it does round out the Cisco Secure product line for those of you who need expert assistance. It offers two types of professional services:

Security Posture Assessments This service provides comprehensive security analysis of large, complex networks. Cisco will test your network security from the perspective of external attackers, disgruntled employees, or contractors. They will make recommendations on security measures needed to improve network security.

Incident Control and Recovery This service is an emergency response to a hostile network incident. Cisco can provide short-notice assistance to restore control and availability of your network.

Summary

The growth of the Internet and its reach into the fabric of business and personal life has outdistanced most organizations' ability to protect the confidentiality and integrity of information. Many organizations are increasing their use of electronic commerce for business-to-business and business-to-consumer transactions. This increased exposure and the constant escalation of threats to network security have increased the need for effective controls that can restore availability, confidentiality, and integrity to information systems. Although no one product or system can provide complete protection, security can be layered to provide reasonable risk management reduction of vulnerabilities.

The TCP/IP stack consists of four layers and provides data communications under a diversity of conditions. The application layer provides file transfer, print, message, terminal emulation, and database services. The transport layer provides duplex, end-to-end data transport services between applications. The TCP port determines which application on the end system is sending and receiving data. The Internet layer provides routing and delivery of datagrams to end nodes. The IP address determines the end system to send or receive communications. The network layer communicates directly with the network media. The hardware address is translated to an IP address to allow IP to traverse each network segment. Any of the protocol layers are vulnerable to attack.

Network security continues to be a very dynamic area as new protocols and technologies are evolving. Security can be provided in TCP/IP at any layer, but each approach has advantages and disadvantages. Application layer security protocols require modifications to each application that will use them, but they can provide fine granularity of control. Transport layer security protocols can also require modifications at the application layer and have been limited in practice to a few specific applications. Network layer security protocols promise to become widely used and will likely replace many of the more limited solutions in use today. Cisco offers a number of products that together can provide a fairly complete security solution. Firewalls provide network access control at security zone perimeters. The PIX firewall can also be the endpoint of a VPN tunnel from site to site or site to end-user. Cisco Secure Scanner tests system security with vulnerability assessment. Cisco Secure Intrusion Detection System monitors network traffic for unauthorized activity. Management tools allow you to improve the consistency and effectiveness of security policies with improved efficiency.

FAQs

Q: Why are local area networks more vulnerable to data abuse than mainframe computers?

A: The mainframe environment is referred to as the "glass house" and is a static, centrally controlled environment. LANs provide multiple points of access in a dynamic, distributed environment. Anyone can connect a self-contained, locally controlled computer to a LAN port. Implementing security services in a complex, networked environment requires controls to be coordinated at many points.

Q: What is the difference between IPSec and IP Security?

A: IP Security is a broad term that describes securing communications at the IP protocol layer. For example, packet filtering could provide some level of IP Security. IPSec is IP Security Protocols, a standard architecture defined by the Internet Engineering Task Force in RFCs 2401–2411 and 2451. IPSec is the dominant security solution at the IP layer because it is a global standard supported by many vendors.

Q: What authentication mechanisms can be used with IKE?

A: Preshared keys (HASH), public key cryptography (NONCE), and digital signatures (SIG) are commonly implemented generic authentication mechanisms.

Q: Why should Telnet or other unencrypted protocols not be used to manage routers, firewalls, switches, servers, or other infrastructure devices?

A: If someone can acquire the passwords or community names to your network infrastructure devices, they have the keys to the kingdom. The dangers of packet sniffing on shared network media have been known for a long time, but many people mistakenly believe that switched networks protect from sniffing by reducing the collision domain to each port on the switch. Although limited to the same subnet as one of the communicating devices, ARP spoofing is an easy and effective technique that negates the protection of a switched network. It fools devices into communicating with a different hardware address than that of the intended IP destination. ARP spoofing allows the capture of cleartext passwords, and other interesting information.

Q: While traveling and using a VPN tunnel from my laptop to the corporate headquarters, is my e-mail protected from disclosure?

A: The encryption of the VPN would protect your e-mail and any other data in transit between the endpoints of the tunnel. Copies of the message stored on the mail server, your laptop, or the recipient's computer would not be protected unless some other measures are taken. PGP, S/MIME, or some other means of encrypting the message would protect it from end-to-end.

Chapter 2

Traffic Filtering on the Cisco IOS

Solutions in this chapter:

- Access Lists
- Lock-and-Key Access Lists
- Reflexive Access Lists
- Context-based Access Control
- Examples

Introduction

Traffic filtering controls the type of traffic that can be forwarded to and from a network. This function enforces security policies in a specific point on a network, often between networks with different level of security.

This chapter covers the different traffic filtering mechanisms available in Cisco IOS and Cisco Secure Integrated Software. In the simplest case, IP filtering consists of an access list that permits or denies traffic based on the source or destination IP address.

Often, however, basic traffic filtering is not sufficient to provide adequate security in a network. Today, modern security products provide more control over the network traffic entering and exiting the network. To achieve that, the traffic must be inspected and the state of the connection must be kept. These advanced features require the router or firewall to understand the internal workings of the protocol it is trying to secure.

Access Lists

A very important step to security is the capability to control the flow of data within a network. A way to accomplish this is to utilize one of the many features of the Cisco Internetwork Operating System (IOS), known as an access list. The function of an access list will depend of the context in which it is used. For instance, access lists can:

- Control access to networks attached to a router or define a particular type of traffic that is allowed to pass to and from a network.

- Limit the contents of routing updates that are advertised by various routing protocols.

- Secure the router itself by limiting access to services such as SNMP and Telnet.

- Define "interesting traffic" for Dial-on-Demand routing. Interesting traffic defines which packets allow the dial connection to occur.

- Define queuing features by determining what packets are given priority over others.

An access list is composed of a sequential series of filters defined globally on the router. Think of each filter as a statement that you enter into the router. Each of these filters performs a comparison or match, and it permits or denies a packet across an interface. The decision to permit or deny is determined by the information contained inside the packets. This process is commonly referred to as *packet filtering*. The criteria that must be met for action to be taken can be based on only a source address or a source and destination address, a protocol type, a specific port or service type, or other type of information. This information typically is contained within the layer 3 and layer 4 headers. Once an access list is defined, it will need to be applied on the interface where access control is required.

We previously stated that we define access lists globally on the router. The key here is to remember that after defining the access list it must be applied on the interface or your access list will have no effect. Also remember, traffic moves both in and out of the interface of the router. Access lists can be applied either in the inbound or in the outbound direction on a specific interface. One method commonly used to avoid confusion is to assume you are inside the router; simply ask yourself if you want to apply the access list statements as traffic comes in (inbound) or as traffic moves out (outbound). You can have one access list per protocol, per interface, per direction. So, for example, it is possible to have one access list for outbound IP traffic and one access list for inbound IP traffic applied to the same interface. See Figure 2.1 for an illustration of this concept.

Figure 2.1 Managing traffic entering and exiting the router interface.

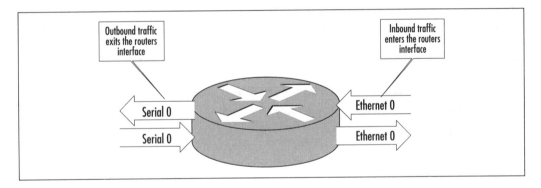

Access List Operation

When a packet enters a router, a route is looked up for the packet's destination, and an interface is determined for the packet to exit the router. When using access lists, before the packet can enter or exit the router, there is a "stack" of filters that are applied to the interface through which the packet must pass. The stack we are referring to here would be the commands you entered on your router with the **access-list global configuration** command. An access list consists of a list of rules or statements that are sequentially tested against incoming or outgoing packets. Those rules can test for specific information inside an IP packet, such as the IP addresses or port numbers. The packet entering or exiting the router will be tested against each condition until a match occurs.

    If no match occurs on the first rule, the packet moves to the second line, and the matching process happens again. When a match is established, a permit or deny action, which is specified on each filter statement, will be executed. What happens if the packet ends up at the end of the stack or at the last rule of our access list, and a match has never occurred? There is an implicit **deny all** at the end of every access list. Any packet that passes through an access list with no match is automatically dropped. You will not see this line on any access list that you build—just think of it as a default line that exists at the end of your access rule. In some cases, you may want to enter the last rule of the access list as permit any. With this line in place, all packets that pass through the access list with no match will be permitted and will never reach the implicit **deny all**. In Figure 2.2 we can see the direction of a packet as it flows through the access list.

Figure 2.2 A packet flows through the access list.

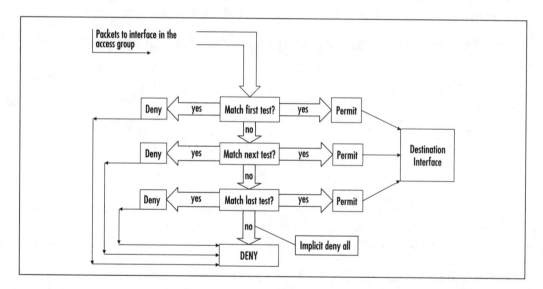

Types of Access Lists

There are several types of access lists available on Cisco routers; the two basic types are known as standard and extended. Lock-and-key, and reflexive are also access lists available on the router and will be discussed later in the chapter. A list name or number identifies each access list. Table 2.1 shows the various access list types and the range of numbers that correlates with each.

Table 2.1 Access List Numbers

Access List Type	Range of Numbers
Standard IP access list	1–99
Standard IP access list (IOS 12.1 number ranges were extended)	1300–1399
Extended IP access list	100–199
Extended IP access list (IOS 12.1 number ranges were extended)	2000–2699
Ethernet type code	200–299
Transparent bridging (protocol type)	200–299
Source-route bridging (protocol type)	200–299
DECnet and extended DECnet	300–399
XNS	400–499
Extended XNS	500–599
AppleTalk	600–699
Transparent bridging (vendor code)	700–799
Source-route bridging (vendor code)	700–799
Standard IPX	800–899
Extended IPX	900–900
IPX SAP	1000–1099
Extended transparent bridging	1100–1199
NLSP route summary	1200–1299

Notice that some of the number ranges are the same for different protocols. For example, Ethernet Type Code and Source Route Bridging have the same number but are different protocols. In this case, the router will distinguish between the access list types by the format of the access list instead of the number. You can choose any number in the range of the access you are creating and do not have to follow any order. For example, when using a standard IP access list, you can choose any number in the range of 1 through 99. The first standard IP access list on the router does not have to be access list 1; however, each list must be uniquely numbered on the router.

Access lists may also be identified by name instead of by number. Named access lists are beneficial to the administrator when dealing with a large number of access lists for ease of identification and also if there are more than 99 standard or if extended access lists are needed. Another advantage of named access lists over numbered access lists is in modifying the access list. With numbered access lists, the entire access list and all its statements are considered one entity. To delete or change a statement, you will have to delete the entire numbered access list and re-enter the statements you want to keep. Named access lists allow you to delete one statement in the access list.

Standard IP Access Lists

Standard access lists can be used to filter packets based on the source IP address in the packet. For example, one could define a standard access list that would deny all incoming traffic on the router except if the traffic is from a specific IP address (source). The source address specified in the standard access list can be configured to represent a host or a network.

In the following example, any field represented by {} is mandatory for the access list. Any field represented by [] is optional. The syntax of a standard IP access list is:

```
access-list list-number {permit | deny} source-address
 [wildcard-mask][log]
```

Table 2.2 lists the configuration for a standard IP access list.

Table 2.2 Standard IP Access List Configuration

Command	Description
access-list list number	Defines the number of the access list. The standard access list numbers range from 1–99.
permit	If conditions are met, traffic will be allowed.
deny	If conditions are met, traffic will be denied.
source-address	Identifies the host or network from which the packet is being sent. The source can be specified by an IP address or by using the keyword **any**.
wildcard-mask	By default, this field will be 0.0.0.0. This defines the number of wildcard bits assigned to the source address. The wildcard-mask can be specified by using the keyword **any**.
log	This keyword results in the logging of packets that match the **permit** or **deny** statement.

Note first that a hyphen is required between the words **access** and **list**. Next is the list number. Since we are referencing a standard IP access list, the numbers would range from 1–99. The access list number actually serves a dual purpose here. Typically, you will find several access lists on one router; therefore, the router must have a way to distinguish one access list from another. The number performs this purpose along with tying the lines of an access list together. The number also tells the router the type of the access list.

The keyword **permit** or **deny** indicates the action to be performed if a match occurs. For example, the keyword **permit** would allow the packet to be forwarded by the interface. The keyword **deny** will drop the packet if a match is found. If a packet is dropped an ICMP error message of destination unreachable will be sent back to the source. Table 2.3 describes the following access list commands:

```
access-list 3 permit 192.168.10.15 0.0.0.0

access-list 3 permit 192.168.10.16 0.0.0.0

access-list 3 permit 192.168.10.17 0.0.0.0

access-list 3 deny 192.168.10.0 0.0.0.0.255

access-list 3 permit 0.0.0.0 255.255.255.255
```

Table 2.3 Description of Access List Commands

Command	Description
access-list 3 permit 192.168.10.15 0.0.0.0 access-list 3 permit 192.168.10.16 0.0.0.0 access-list 3 permit 192.168.10.17 0.0.0.0	Allow hosts 192.168.10.15, 192.168.10.16, and 192.168.10.17
access-list 3 deny 192.168.10.0 0.0.0.0.255	Deny any host from network 192.168.10.0
access-list 3 permit 0.0.0.0 255.255.255.255	Allow any host

Source Address and Wildcard Mask

When using a standard IP access list, the source address must always be specified. The source address can refer to the address of a host, a group of hosts, or possibly an entire subnet. The scope of the source address is specified by the wildcard mask field.

The wildcard mask is typically one of the most misunderstood topics when dealing with access lists. The wildcard mask will be discussed more in depth in the extended IP access list section. When using the wildcard mask, think of the reverse manner in which a subnet mask works. The job of a subnet mask is to specify how many bits of an IP address refer to the subnet portion. Remember, a binary 1 in the subnet mask indicates the corresponding bit is part of the subnet range, and a binary 0 in the subnet mask indicates the corresponding bit is part of the host portion. For example, take the following IP address and subnet mask:

```
Source address   =172.16.130.77    -10101100.00010000.10000010.01000110
Subnet Mask      =255.255.255.0    -11111111.11111111.11111111.00000000
Subnet           =172.16.130.0     -10101100.00010000.10000010.00000000
```

In the first three octets of the subnet mask, we have set all the bits to one (decimal 255 = 11111111 in binary). This tells us that all of the bits in the first three octets are now part of the subnet field. This is accomplished by using what is known as a Boolean AND operation. A Boolean AND is performed on the host address and the subnet mask, giving us a subnet or network number. When comparing two bits in the previous example, the result will be one only if both of the bits are set to one.

Now let's move from the subnet mask to the wildcard mask. When using a wildcard mask, a zero is used for each bit that should be matched, and a one is used when the bit position doesn't need to be matched. Take the following IP address and wildcard mask (our wildcard mask here is 0.0.0.255):

```
Source address  =172.16.130.77-    10101100.00010000.10000010. 01000110
Wildcard Mask    =0.0.0.255    -    00000000.00000000.00000000.11111111
Subnet           =172.16.130.255-10101100.00010000.10000010.11111111
```

Here a Boolean OR is performed. When comparing two bits here, the result will be zero only if both of the bits are set to zero. The meaning of both bits here are the 32 bits in the source address and the 32 bits in the wildcard mask. So, in the previous example, the router will perform the Boolean OR starting with the leading bit in the first octet of the source address and the leading bit in the first octet of the wildcard mask. Then continue with the Boolean or through all 32 bits of the source address and wildcard mask. Therefore, in the previous example, all of the host addresses on subnet 172.16.130.0 will be permitted or denied depending on what is specified in the access list. The first three octets (172.16.130) must match, and the last octet (.255) is not concerned with matching any bits. The default wildcard mask for a standard IP access list is 0.0.0.0. The 0.0.0.0 indicates that all bits in the source address must match. In the following access list, the IP address in each line must be matched exactly (all 32 bits). Table 2.4 describes the following access list commands:

```
access-list 17 deny 172.16.130.88 0.0.0.0
access-list 17 deny 172.16.130.89 0.0.0.0
```

```
access-list 17 deny 172.16.130.90 0.0.0.0
access-list 17 permit 0.0.0.0 255.255.255.255
```

Table 2.4 Description of Access List Commands

Command	Description
access-list 17 deny 172.16.130.88 0.0.0.0	Deny host 172.16.130.88
access-list 17 deny 172.16.130.89 0.0.0.0	Deny host 172.16.130.89
access-list 17 deny 172.16.130.90 0.0.0.0	Deny host 172.16.130.90
access-list 17 permit 0.0.0.0 255.255.255.255	Allow any host

Now let's look at the last line in the access list in Table 2.4. Remember that we are performing an OR on the bits here, so using the wildcard mask of 0.0.0.0 255.255.255.255 tells us that all bits will be permitted. (The 255.255.255.255 means any source address will be permitted.) There is an implicit deny all at the end of every access list. To change that behavior to a permit by default, you must enter a permit statement at the end of your access list as shown in the example. Since the default wildcard mask for a standard IP address is 0.0.0.0, we could write the access list as follows with the same effect:

```
access-list 17 deny 172.16.130.88

access-list 17 deny 172.16.130.89

access-list 17 deny 172.16.130.90

access-list 17 permit any
```

Table 2.5 describes these access list commands.

Table 2.5 Description of Access List Commands

Command	Description
access-list 17 deny 172.16.130.88	Deny host 172.16.130.88
access-list 17 deny 172.16.130.89	Deny host 172.16.130.89
access-list 17 deny 172.16.130.90	Deny host 172.16.130.90
access-list 17 permit any	Allow any host

Notice that we have removed the wildcard mask for the access list because the value of 0.0.0.0 is the default. Remember, this mask will try any match on all 32 bits of the IP address so if you choose not to enter a wildcard mask an exact match is assumed. We also changed the last line of our access list by using permit any. This has the same effect as using a source address of 0.0.0.0 with a wildcard mask of 255.255.255.255.

What would happen in the lines if the access list were reversed? Let's rewrite our access list as follows:

```
access-list 17 permit any
access-list 17 deny 172.16.130.88
access-list 17 deny 172.16.130.89
access-list 17 deny 172.16.130.90
```

Table 2.6 describes these access list commands.

Table 2.6 Description of Access List Commands

Command	Description
access-list 17 permit any	Allow any host
access-list 17 deny 172.16.130.88	Deny host 172.16.130.88
access-list 17 deny 172.16.130.89	Deny host 172.16.130.89
access-list 17 deny 172.16.130.90	Deny host 172.16.130.90

Access lists operate in sequential order. They test packets one statement at a time from top to bottom. In the preceding example, all traffic would be permitted when it is tested on the first statement. No packet would ever have the chance to be denied.

WARNING

Access lists operate in sequential order, from top to bottom. It is easy to inadvertently make a mistake that can interrupt services or cause other serious effects. Access lists should be double-checked to make sure that the logic is correct. (Having someone else check them is a good idea.)

Keywords any and host

Keywords typically are used in an extended access list statement; however, some are applicable in standard access lists. In the previous example, we used the keyword **any** to specify that we will permit any IP address as a source. The keyword **host** can be used in our access to indicate a wildcard mask of 0.0.0.0, or more specifically, an exact match. This would be written as follows:

```
access-list 17 deny host 172.16.130.88
access-list 17 deny host 172.16.130.89
```

```
access-list 17 deny host 172.16.130.90
access-list 17 permit any
```

Keyword log

When including the keyword **log** in an access list statement, a match of that statement will be logged. That is, any packet that matches the access list will cause a message to be sent to the console, memory, or a syslog server. Using the global **logging console** command controls this. This feature is available with standard access lists since IOS 11.3. Previously, this capability was available only in extended IP access lists. When using the log keyword, the first packet that matches the access list causes a logging message immediately. Following matching packets are gathered over a five-minute interval before they are displayed or logged. Let's look at how this would work in the following example:

```
access-list 17 deny 172.16.130.88 log
access-list 17 deny 172.16.130.89 log
access-list 17 deny 172.16.130.90 log
access-list 17 permit any
```

Suppose the interface receives 10 packets from host 172.16.130.88, 15 packets from host 172.16.130.89, and 20 packets from host 172.16.130.90 over a five-minute period. The first log will look as follows:

```
list 17 deny 172.16.130.88 1 packet
list 17 deny 172.16.130.89 1 packet
list 17 deny 172.16.130.90 1 packet
```

After five minutes, the log would display the following:

```
list 17 deny 172.16.130.88 9 packets
list 17 deny 172.16.130.89 14 packets
list 17 deny 172.16.130.90 19 packets
```

When using the keyword **log**, we are provided with an observant capability. Here you are able to analyze not only who has tried to access your network, but you are also able to determine the number of attempts. The log message will indicate the number of packets, whether the packet was permitted or denied, the source address, and the access list number. There will be a message generated for the first packet that matches the test, and then at five-minute intervals, you will receive a message stating the number of packets matched during the previous five minutes. Table 2.7 lists the keywords available for use with standard access lists.

Table 2.7 Keywords Available with Standard Access Lists

Keyword	Description
any	Available as an abbreviation for an address or the wildcard-mask value of 0.0.0.0 255.255.255.255. Can be used in source and destination address fields.
host	Available as an abbreviation for a wildcard mask of 0.0.0.0. Can be used in source and destination address fields.
log	Used for logging of packets that match **permit** and **deny** statements.

Applying an Access List

When applying an access list to an interface, there are three steps to follow. The first step is to create the access list. You can create your access list on the router when attached through the console or with a word processor or text editor. If using a word processor, the file is stored in ASCII text. To load this file from the PC to the router, you will need to install a TFTP program on the PC. When using TFTP software, the file is stored on the TFTP server in ASCII text and the router will act as a client to retrieve the file that you created. Next, you must specify the interface where you plan to apply the access list. For example, to apply the access list to the Ethernet interface 0, you must first define the interface. This is accomplished with the following command in configuration mode (configure terminal):

```
interface ethernet 0
```

You have the option to abbreviate keywords in a command. The preceding command could be used as follows:

```
interface e0
```

If you plan to apply the access list to a serial port on your router the command would look as follows:

```
interface serial 0
```

The next step is to actually apply the access list to the interface and define the direction of the access list. This is accomplished by using the **ip access-group** command. Table 2.8 describes the ip access-group command. The format of the command is as follows:

```
ip access-group {list number}[in|out]
```

Table 2.8 IP Access-Group Command

Command	Description
ip	Defines the protocol used
access-group	Applies the access list to the interface
list number	Identifies the access list
in|out	Keyword in or out defines the direction in which the access list will be applied. This indicates whether packets are examined as they leave or as they enter the router.

For example, if we want to apply the access list 17 defined in a previous example to incoming traffic on the ethernet interface 0, the commands shown in Table 2.9 would be used.

Table 2.9 Applying an Access List

Command	Description
configure terminal	Enters the configuration mode on the router.
interface ethernet 0	Identifies the interface where the access list will be applied.
ip access-group 17 in	Applies access list 17 to the interface in the inbound direction. (in)

Extended IP Access Lists

An option for more precise traffic-filtering control would be an extended IP access list. Here, both the source and destination addresses are checked. In addition, you also have the ability to specify the protocol and optional TCP or UDP port number to filter more precisely. In the following example, any field represented by {} is mandatory for the access list. Any field represented by [] is optional. The format of an extended IP access list is:

```
access-list access-list-number {permit | deny} protocol source
  source-wildcard [operator port] destination destination-wildcard
  [precedence precedence number] [operator port] [tos tos]
  [established] [log]
```

Bold items represent keywords that are part of the access list syntax. Table 2.10 lists the configuration for a standard IP access list.

Table 2.10 Standard IP Access List Configuration

Command	Description
access-list list number	Defines the number of the access list. The standard access list numbers range from 100–199.
permit	If conditions are met, traffic will be allowed.
deny	If conditions are met, traffic will be denied.
protocol	Defines the protocol for filtering. Available options here are keywords such as TCP or UDP.
source-address	Identifies the host or network from which the packet is being sent. The source can be specified by an IP address or by using the keyword **any**.
source wildcard-mask	This defines the number of wildcard bits assigned to the source address. The source wildcard-mask can be specified by an IP address or by using the keyword **any**.
operator port	Defines the name or decimal number of a TCP or UDP port. operator ? complete.
destination-address	Identifies the host or network to which the packet is being sent. The destination can be specified by an IP address or by using the keyword **any**.
destination wildcard-mask	This defines the number of wildcard bits assigned to the destination address. The destination wildcard-mask can be specified by an IP address or by using the keyword **any**.
precedence / precedence number	Used for filtering by the precedence level name or number.
TOS	Defines filtering by service level specified by a name or number (01–5).
Established	RST or ACK bits are set.
Log	Log the event when a packet matches the access list statement.

In the following access list, we get very specific about what host we want to access a particular network or host on a network. In the first three lines we are permitting or allowing packets from individual hosts on subnet 172.16.130.0 to any host on network 10.0.0.0. In line 4, we are denying packets with the source address that belongs to subnet 172.16.130.0 to the destination of host 192.168.10.118. Line 5 tells us that we are permitting all IP packets with no concern of a source or destination address. The implicit **deny all** will deny all other traffic that passes through the interface to which we have applied the access list. In Figure 2.3, we would apply this access list on the serial 0 interface in the outbound direction as follows:

```
Router(config)# interface serial 0
Router(config-if)# ip access-group 141 out
```

An example of an extended access list is as follows:

```
access-list 141 permit ip 172.16.130.88 0.0.0.0 10.0.0.0 0.255.255.255
access-list 141 permit ip 172.16.130.89 0.0.0.0 10.0.0.0 0.255.255.255
access-list 141 permit ip 172.16.130.90 0.0.0.0 10.0.0.0 0.255.255.255
access-list 141 deny ip 172.16.130.0 0.0.0.255 192.168.10.118 0.0.0.0
access-list 141 permit ip 0.0.0.0 255.255.255.255 0.0.0.0
 255.255.255.255
```

Table 2.11 describes the extended access list commands.

Table 2.11 Description of Extended Access List Commands

Command	Description
access-list 141 permit ip 172.16.130.88 0.0.0.0 10.0.0.0 0.255.255.255	Allows host 172.16.130.88 to any host on network 10.0.0.0.
access-list 141 permit ip 172.16.130.89 0.0.0.0 10.0.0.0 0.255.255.255	Allows host 172.16.130.89 to any host on network 10.0.0.0.
access-list 141 permit ip 172.16.130.89 0.0.0.0 10.0.0.0 0.255.255.255	Allows host 172.16.130.90 to any host on network 10.0.0.0.
access-list 141 deny ip 172.16.130.0 0.0.0.255 192.168.10.118 0.0.0.0	Denies any host on network 172.16.130.0 to host 192.168.10.118.
access-list 141 permit ip 0.0.0.0 255.255.255.255 0.0.0.0 255.255.255.255	Allows all hosts from any network to any network.

Just as in our standard access list, the extended access list will require a hyphen between the words **access** and **list**. Next is the list number. Since we are referencing an extended IP access list, the numbers would range from 100–199. The access list number serves the same dual purpose here as we looked at earlier with the standard access list. The router must have a way to distinguish between access lists. The number performs this purpose along with tying the lines of an access list together and designates in which access-list the filter is a part. The number also tells the router the type of the access list.

Keywords permit or deny

The keywords **permit** and **deny** have the same meaning as for a standard access lists.

Protocol

You have the option of filtering several different protocols using the extended access list. The protocol field defines what protocol to filter such as TCP, UDP, ICMP, and IP, to name a few. It is important to remember here that an IP header is used to transport TCP and UDP; therefore, if you choose to filter the IP protocol, you will permit or deny all the protocols transported over IP such as an ICMP message, TCP, or UDP. If you plan to filter a specific protocol you must specify that protocol. You must use a systematic approach here when designing your access list.

For example, if your first line in the access list permits IP for a specific address, and the second line denies UDP for the same address, the second statement would have no effect. The first line would permit IP, including all the above layers. An option here may be to reverse the order of the statements. With the statements reversed, UDP would be denied from that address and all other protocols would be permitted.

Source Address and Wildcard-Mask

The source address and wildcard-mask perform the same function here as in a standard IP access list. So in our preceding example, we could have used the keyword host followed by the IP address. The access list would look as follows:

```
access-list 141 permit ip host 172.16.130.88 10.0.0.0 0.255.255.255
access-list 141 permit ip host 172.16.130.89 10.0.0.0 0.255.255.255
access-list 141 permit ip host 172.16.130.90 10.0.0.0 0.255.255.255
access-list 141 permit ip 172.16.130.0 0.0.0.255 192.168.10.118 0.0.0.0
access-list 141 permit ip 172.17.0.0 0.0.31.255 192.168.10.0 0.0.0.255
```

In the first three lines, we are permitting or allowing packets from individual hosts on subnet 172.16.130.0 to any host on network 10.0.0.0. In line 4, we are permitting packets with the source address that belongs to subnet 172.16.130.0 to the destination of host 192.168.10.118. Line 5 tells us that we are permitting packets with a source address between 172.17.0.0 and 172.17.31.255 with a destination of network 192.168.10.0. The implicit deny all will deny all other traffic that passes through the interface to which we have applied the access list. Remember that standard IP access lists have a default mask of 0.0.0.0. This does not apply to extended access lists, so we must specify one. There are some short cuts available such as the keyword **host**, as we used earlier and the keyword **any**.

Destination Address and Wildcard Mask

The destination address and wildcard mask have the same effect and structure as the source address and wildcard mask. So here the keywords **host**, and **any** are also available. You can utilize these keywords to specify any destination address as well as a specific destination without using the wildcard mask. Remember that extended access lists try a match on both source and destination. A common mistake here is trying to build an extended access list with the idea of filtering only the source address and forget to specify the destination address. Figure 2.3 shows an example of our network with the access list applied to interface serial 0 outbound.

Figure 2.3 The access list applied to interface serial 0 outbound.

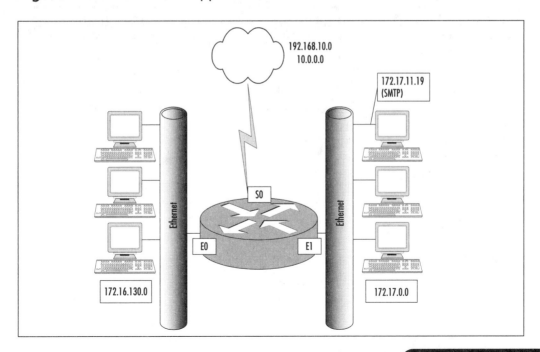

Source and Destination Port Number

The destination port can be specified the same as for a source port. We must apply the access list to the interface. The access list will be applied to the serial interface, inbound. Let's look at the following example:

```
Router(config)# interface Serial 0
Router(config-if)# ip access-group 111 in


access-list 111 permit tcp any host 172.17.11.19 eq 25
access-list 111 permit tcp any host 172.17.11.19 eq 23
```

Table 2.12 describes these access list commands.

Table 2.12 Router Commands and Descriptions

Router Command	Description
access-list 111 permit tcp any host 172.17.11.19 eq 25	Permits SMTP to host 172.17.11.19.
access-list 111 permit tcp any host 172.17.11.19 eq 23	Permits Telnet to host 172.17.11.19.
interface Serial 1	Enters interface submode.
ip access-group 111 in	Applies access list inbound on interface.

In line 1, we are permitting TCP packets from any source to the destination of host 172.22.11.19 if the destination port is 25 (SMTP). In line 2, we are permitting TCP packets from, and source to, the destination of host 172.22.11.19 if the destination port is 23 (Telnet).

Let's take a look at filtering with TCP and UDP. When using TCP, for example, the access list will examine the source and destination port numbers inside the TCP segment header. When using an extended access list, you have the capability to filter to and from a network address and also to and from a particular port number. You have several options when using the operator port such as:

- **eq** equal to
- **neq** not equal to
- **gt** greater than
- **lt** less than
- **range** an inclusive range or ports (here two port numbers are specified)

The port specifies the application layer port to be permitted or denied.

Established

One of the options available for use with an extended access list is the established option. This option is available only with the TCP protocol. The idea here is to restrict traffic in one direction as a response to sessions initiated in the opposite direction.

Look at the following access-list:

```
Router(config)# interface Serial 0

Router(config-if)# ip access-group 111 in

access-list 111 permit tcp any host 172.17.0.0 0.0.255.255 established

access-list 111 permit tcp any host 172.17.11.19 eq 25

access-list 111 permit tcp 12.0.0.0 0.255.255.255 172.22.114.0
 0.0.0.255 eq 23
```

Figure 2.4 shows an example of our network with the access list applied inbound on interface serial 0 (S0). The first line of the access list permits TCP packets from any source to the network 172.17.0.0 with the TCP flag ACK or RST bit set. This is beneficial if you need to prevent TCP sessions from being established into your network. It also ensures that incoming traffic from the TCP session initiated from network 172.17.0.0 would be allowed. The second line tells the router to permit TCP packets from any source if the destination is 172.17.11.19 and the destination port is 25 (SMTP). Line 3 is allowing a TCP segment with a source address from network 12.0.0.0 to port 23 (Telnet), to any address on subnet 172.22.114.0. What will happen to all other packets? Once again, the implicit deny all will drop any other packets.

In the TCP segment, there are six flag bits, two of which are the ACK and RST. If one of these bits is set, then a match will occur. The SYN bit indicates that a connection is being established. A packet with a SYN bit without an ACK bit is the very first packet sent to establish a TCP connection. Figure 2.5 shows the TCP setup handshake.

Another issue to consider here is that as the administrator, you may not be certain what protocols the host may be using. However, we do know ports are chosen by workstations randomly between the port ranges of 1024 through 65535. Keeping this in mind, we could modify the first line of the access list as follows:

```
access-list 111 permit tcp any host 172.17.0.0 0.0.255.255 gt 1023
 established
```

Figure 2.4 The access list applied to serial 0 inbound.

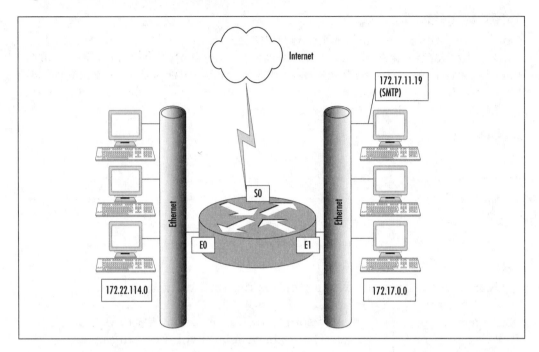

Figure 2.5 A TCP session being established.

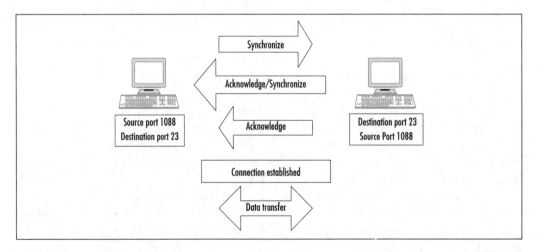

This would ensure that no packets would be accepted inbound to our network unless the destination port is higher that 1023. The hacker could spoof the ACK or RST bit in the packet, but the destination port would still have to be higher than 1023. Typically, our servers running services such as DNS run below port 1024. However, it is not a good idea to let through all ports over 1023. You become vulnerable to network scans and Denial-of-Service attacks.

Now let's look at what happens when we decide to allow a restricted TFTP access to host 172.17.11.19, DNS access to host 172.17.11.20, and unrestricted SNMP access. TFTP, DNS, and SNMP are UDP-based protocols. We have added to our extended access list again in the following example:

```
access-list 111 permit tcp any host 172.17.0.0 0.0.255.255 established

access-list 111 permit tcp any host 172.17.11.19 eq 25

access-list 111 permit tcp 12.0.0.0 0.255.255.255 172.22.114.0

 0.0.0.255 eq 23

access-list 111 permit udp 192.168.10.0 0.0.0.255 host 172.17.11.19

 eq 69

access-list 111 permit udp any host 172.17.11.20 eq 53

access-list 111 permit udp any any eq 161
```

You will notice there is no keyword established here. Remember that UDP is a connectionless protocol; therefore, no connections will be established between hosts and there is no SYN-ACK negotiation. Since we have not changed the first three lines of our access list, we will begin by discussing line 4. Line 4 is allowing UDP datagrams from subnet 192.168.10.0 to port 69 (TFTP) on host 172.17.11.19. Line 5 is allowing UDP datagrams from any source to host 172.17.11.20 with a destination port of 53 (DNS). Line 6 allows all SNMP (port 161) to and from any destination. Remember, any packets not matching the list will be dropped by the implicit deny all. Figure 2.6 shows the addition of a DNS server in our network. Here we would apply the access list inbound on interface serial 0.

Named Access Lists

Each access list type has a range of acceptable numbers that can be used. For example there are 99 standard (1–99) and 100 extended (100–199) access lists available in the Cisco IOS. This seems to be more than enough, but you may need to create more than 100 extended IP access lists on your enterprise router. Named access lists provide an alternative to allow this. Also, named access lists provide a description that is typically more manageable than a large group of numbers.

Named access lists are just as the title implies, access lists that are referenced by name instead of a number. They also allow you to delete a specific entry in your access list. When using numbered access lists this is not an option. When using a numbered access list you, must recreate the

Figure 2.6 The access list applied to serial 0 inbound.

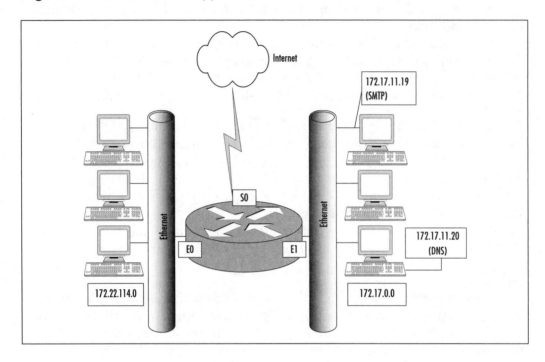

entire access list to remove an unwanted entry. When adding to an access list, both the named and numbered will place the new line at the bottom of the access list.

When creating a named access list it must begin with a standard alphabetic ASCII character. Names are case sensitive so the access list SYDNEY and Sydney will be looked at as two unique names or as two different access lists. With the exception of the number, the named access list will look identical to a numbered access list. The following is an example of a named access list:

```
ip access-list extended filter_tx
```

```
permit tcp any 172.17.0.0 0.0.255.255 established
permit tcp any host 172.17.11.19 eq smtp
permit tcp 12.0.0.0 0.255.255.255 172.22.114.0 0.0.0.255 eq 23
permit udp 192.168.10.0 0.0.0.255 host 172.17.11.19 eq 69
permit udp any host 172.17.11.20 eq 53
permit udp any any eq 161
```

Editing Access Lists

When applying access lists there are several factors to consider. One of the most important things to remember is that access lists are evaluated from the top down, so packets will always be tested starting with the top line of the access list. Be sure you carefully consider the order of your access list statements. The most frequent match should always be at the beginning of the access list.

Another thing to consider is the placement of the access list. When looking at your network, a standard access list should be placed closest to the destination of where you are trying to block the packets. Remember that a standard IP access list filters on the source IP address. If the IP address is blocked then the entire protocol suite (IP) typically would be denied. So if you denied an IP address close to the source, the user would be denied access anywhere on the network. When applying an extended access list, the access list should be placed closest to the source. When using an extended access list, both the source and destination address are checked along with a protocol; therefore, the access list will be most effective if applied to the source. For example, if denying Telnet from one network to another, the access list would have very little effect if applied near the destination. The user could Telnet to another router on the network, then establish a new Telnet session with a different IP address.

TIP

Packets generated by the router are not affected by an outbound access list, so to filter routing table updates or any traffic generated by the router, you should consider inbound access lists.

When using a named access list, we can delete a specific entry; however, with a numbered access list we do not have this option. We have learned that when you need to add an entry into the access list in a specific position (such as the fifth line) the entire access list must be deleted and then recreated with new entries. This applies to both numbered and named access lists. This tells me I have just created a 35-line access list and need to make a change. Is the only option here to start over? Not really. There are several ways to avoid recreating your entire access list.

One option to explore here may be the use of the TFTP protocol. When utilizing TFTP, we have the ability to copy our configuration to a server as a text file. Remember, when you copy from anywhere to the running configuration a merge will occur. If your intention is to change line 14, make your changes to the configuration file while on the TFTP server; then, when you copy the file to the running configuration, the merge will replace line 14 with your new changes. Once on the server, we can use a text editor to modify and then reload the configuration to our router. Another option may be to have a template of an access list on your TFTP server. Having the template will help ensure that you enter the command correctly.

Remember that the commands you use here will be the exact commands you would enter at the command line of the router. When copying this file to your running configuration, it will merge the new access list with your current configuration; if the syntax is incorrect, the operation will fail.

In the following example, a configuration file is uploaded on the Cisco router from a TFTP server. The command **copy tftp running-config** instructs the router to copy from a remote TFTP server a file that will be merged into the running configuration. The router then prompts the user for additional information such as the address of the TFTP server and the name of the remote file that should be loaded.

The text in bold shows the user input.

```
copy tftp running-config
Address or name of remote host []? 172.16.1.1
Source filename []? accesslist.txt
Destination filename [running-config]?
Accessing TFTP://172.16.1.1/accesslist.txt... OK - 1684/3072 bytes]
Loading accesslist.txt from 172.16.1.1 (via Ethernet 0): !! [OK -
1388/3072 bytes]
1388 bytes copied in 3 secs (462 bytes/sec)
```

After a successful copy, the running configuration must be saved into non-volatile memory (write memory); otherwise, the modification will be lost after a reload or if the router is powered off.

Problems with Access Lists

Some issues you may encounter with access lists are their limited capability to test information above the IP layer. Extended access lists have the capability to check on layer 4 but not in the detailed sense.

Another issue to consider is that the access list will examine each packet individually and does not have the capability of detecting if a packet is part of an upper layer conversation. The keyword **established** can be used to match TCP packets that are part of an established TCP session. You need to be cautious when relying on the keyword established. Remember that "established" is applicable only when using TCP for the presence of an RST, and an ACK flag in the packet automatically makes this packet part of an established TCP session. Although this filtering technique is suitable in many cases, it does not protect against forged TCP packets (commonly used to probe networks), nor does it offer any facility to filter UDP sessions. Reflexive access list and CBAC, introduced later in this chapter, offer better control and more facilities to do session filtering.

Last but not least, we must take into consideration human error. You must remember the basics here; for example, after you create the access list, be sure to apply it to an interface. The access list must be created in the correct order, and when changes are made the new entries must be placed in the correct order.

Lock-and-Key Access Lists

Lock-and-key is a traffic filtering security feature that can automatically create access lists on the router to allow incoming traffic from an authenticated source. These access lists are also referred to as dynamic access lists. Lock-and-key can be used in conjunction with other standard and extended access lists. Traditional standard and extended access lists cannot create lock-and-key access list entries. Once an entry is added to a traditional access list, it remains there until it is removed manually. With lock-and-key you can create a temporary opening in an access list by utilizing a response to a user authentication procedure. The idea here is to give temporary access, after proper authentication, to designated users who normally have their IP traffic blocked at the router. Lock-and-key reconfigures the interface's existing IP access list to permit designated users to reach their destination.

When the connection is terminated, the interface is configured back to its original state.

Let's say, for example, that a user in Figure 2.7 is working at a branch office and needs to log into the corporate office. The user will attempt to log in from a PC that is connected to a router (typically via LAN). A Telnet session will be opened to the router to provide authentication. The router at the corporate site (which is configured for lock-and-key) receives the Telnet packet and opens a Telnet session. Next, the router will prompt for a password and then perform authentication by using a test that is configured by the administrator, such as a name and password. The authentication process can be done locally by the router using local username/ password configuration, or through an external AAA server such as

TACACS+ or RADIUS. When the user successfully authenticates, the Telnet session closes and a temporary entry is created in the dynamic access list. This dynamic access list typically will permit traffic from the user's source IP address to some predetermined destination. This dynamic access list will be deleted when a timeout is reached or when it can be cleared by the administrator. A timeout can be configured as an idle-timeout or when the maximum-timeout period expires.

Figure 2.7 Using lock-and-key.

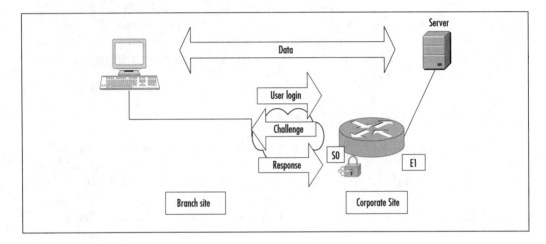

A user may not have a static IP address in a situation where a DHCP is in use in a LAN environment or when a user is connected through a dial up to an Internet Service Provider. In both cases, users may typically get a different IP address. Lock-and-key access lists can be used to implement a higher level of security without creating large holes in your network. The format of a lock-and-key access list is as follows:

```
access-list access-list-number [dynamic dynamic-name[timeout minutes]]
   {deny | permit} protocol source source-wildcard destination
   destination-wildcard[precedence precedence] [tos tos] [established]
   [log]
```

Table 2.13 describes lock-and-key access lists.

Table 2.13 Lock-and-Key Access List Configuration

Command	Description
access-list list number	Defines the number of the access list. The standard access list numbers range from 100–199.
dynamic dynamic-name	Designates the name of the dynamic access list.
timeout minutes	The timeout is optional and designates an absolute timeout for dynamic entries.
permit	If conditions are met, traffic will be allowed.
deny	If conditions are met, traffic will be denied.
protocol	Defines the protocol for filtering. Available options here are keywords such as TCP or UDP.
source-address	Identifies the host or network from which the packet is being sent. The source can be specified by an IP address or by using the keyword **any**.
source wildcard-mask	This defines the number of wildcard bits assigned to the source address. The source wildcard-mask can be specified by an IP address or by using the keyword **any**.
destination-address	Identifies the host or network to which the packet is being sent. The destination can be specified by an IP address or by using the keyword **any**.
destination wildcard-mask	This defines the number of wildcard bits assigned to the destination address. The destination wildcard-mask can be specified by an IP address or by using the keyword **any**.
precedence / precedence number	Used for filtering by the precedence level name or number.
TOS	Defines filtering by service level specified by a name or number (01–5).
Established	When using TCP, filtering will occur if RST or ACK bits are set.
Log	This keyword results in the logging of packets that match the permit or deny statement.

- The access-list number has the same format as an extended access list using the number 100–199.

- The dynamic-name parameter is used to name your access list.

- The timeout parameter here is optional. This is where a maximum timeout for your dynamic access list is configured. If no timeout is specified, the temporary access list entry will remain configured indefinitely on the interface. The entry would have to be removed manually.

- The permit or deny field tells the router the action to perform.

- The protocol field can be any TCP/IP protocol field; TCP will be used in most cases. When using UDP, remember that it is a connectionless protocol and contains no SYN-ACK bits for negotiation. UDP also contains no bits in the header for us to determine if it is part of an existing conversation.

- The source IP address is always replaced with the IP address of the authenticating host so the keyword **any** is typically used here.

- The destination address and destination wildcard mask will specify the destination that will be allowed by the dynamic access list.

Previously when defining standard and extended access lists, we had two steps: build the access list and then apply it to an interface. When using lock-and-key access lists, there are a few more steps we must follow. After creating the access list and applying the access list to an interface, we must configure our virtual terminal (VTY) ports.

By default, the router has 5 VTY ports available for Telnet sessions. They are numbered 0 through 5. When a user connects to a router, the connection will reserve a VTY port for the duration of that session, so five different Telnet sessions can be established on the router simultaneously. If you specify multiple VTY ports, they must all be configured identically because the software hunts for available VTY ports on a round-robin basis. If you do not want to configure all your VTY ports for lock-and-key access, you can specify a group of VTY ports for lock-and-key support only.

We have chosen to use three VTY ports in the following configuration:

```
Line vty 0 2
login local
autocommand access-enable host timeout 10
```

You must use the autocommand here. When using the autocommand the host parameter is an important player also. Without the host parameter the dynamic entries would not replace the source IP address of the authenticating host; therefore, any host would be allowed. The timeout parameter is optional here and specifies the idle-timeout. If no maximum-timeout or idle-timeout is specified, the entry will not be removed until the router is rebooted. If you use both timers, the idle-timeout should be set to a lower number than the maximum-timeout.

For IT Professionals

Prevention of IP Spoofing Attacks

One thing to consider is an attacker using IP spoofing. IP spoofing is where a hacker changes the source IP address of the packets that are sent to an IP address believed trusted by the network.

When packets arrive at your router, it is nearly impossible to determine if the packets are from a real host. Lock-and-key access lists play a big role in assisting here due to the fact the openings are only temporary. This lowers the chance of the hacker determining the trusted source IP address.

It doesn't lower the chance of determining the source IP, but it does reduce the window of opportunity to exploit the temporary opening.

One drawback to consider is when a client is behind NAPT (PAT in Cisco nomenclature). If that client uses lock-and-key to a remote site to get access to some private resource, the dynamic access list on the remote router will use the external or public address of the NAPT device. That address is potentially used by a number of users; therefore, they will automatically be allowed access without any authentication. This is a serious security consideration.

Another issue to consider when using a lock-and-key access list is that if no additional steps are taken, every Telnet session incoming to the router will be treated as an attempt to open a dynamic entry. Remember here that after authentication the Telnet session is closed, so we would never be able to Telnet to our router for management purposes. We have to specify another command in our router to alleviate this problem. Beneath our remaining VTY ports, the rotary 1 command is needed. The rotary 1 command will enable normal Telnet access to our router on port 3001. You will need to specify the use of port 3001 when attempting to access the router via a Telnet session by specifying the port number immediately after the destination IP address. The following is an example:

```
telnet 172.16.1.1 3001
Line vty 3 4
login local
rotary 1
```

We must ensure that our configuration looks like this before we save it. There is no autocommand associated with lines 3 and 4. If our VTY ports are not configured properly, we could disable all Telnet capability to the router. When establishing a Telnet session to the router you must specify the port number after the destination IP address. The command would look as follows:

```
telnet 192.168.200.1 3001
```

Let's look at how this would be configured on our router. In the following example, only relevant portions of the configuration are shown:

```
Username cisco password san-jose
!
interface serial 1
ip address 192.168.200.1 255.255.255.0
ip access-group 114 in
!
access-list 114 permit tcp any host 172.16.4.1 eq telnet
access-list 114 dynamic cisco timeout 10 permit ip any any
!
line vty 0 2
login local
autocommand access-enable host timeout 10
line vty 3 4
login local
rotary 1
```

In this example, our username is *cisco* and is referenced in the second line of our access list. You have the option to specify only the password here, but it is not recommended. In specifying one generic password for all users, it is far easier for a hacker to create an opening to the router. Also, if only using a password, it is impossible to track the individual user's actions. When using both the ID and password, the hacker must guess both before access is gained. Remember, when using Telnet with a conventional username and password, everything is sent in cleartext, allowing anyone to capture your authentication data.

It should be reiterated that using cleartext passwords over an untrusted network such as the Internet could be detrimental to the security of your network. The preceding configuration would not be recommended due to the fact that the passwords are in cleartext.

The first line of the access list enables users to establish a Telnet session for authentication. In the next line, we see the words dynamic and timeout. Dynamic signals the use of a dynamic access list and timeout is the maximum timeout period. We are allowing all IP packets in this statement also. The dynamic entry created will allow all IP packets from authenticated hosts to any IP address. This could be changed to permit only certain protocols or destinations. Remember, only the source IP address is replaced so all users will have the same access.

NOTE

Lock-and-key will install only one dynamic access list in any given access list. Although the router will allow you to specify more than one entry in a dynamic access list, these will not have any effect. After entering multiple entries in your access list, enter the **show access-list** command and you will see only the results of the original entry, so it is meaningless to specify multiple entries.

Reflexive Access Lists

The reflexive access list alleviates some of the limitations of basic and extended access lists. Reflexive access lists allow IP packets to be filtered based on upper-layer session information as in extended access lists, but the reflexive access list can do session filtering by creating dynamic openings for IP traffic that is part of the allowed session. In so doing, reflexive access lists provide a way to maintain information about existing connections. You have the option to permit IP traffic for sessions originating from within your network, but to deny IP traffic for sessions originating from outside your network. This sounds the same as an extended access list. Although reflexive access lists are referred to as a separate type of access list, it is important to note that a reflexive access list is a feature added to an extended access list. Reflexive access lists can be defined only using extended named IP access lists.

One instance where a reflexive access list could be used is when an IP upper-layer session (such as TCP or UDP) is initiated from inside the network, with an outgoing packet traveling to the external network. In this case a new, temporary entry will be created. Here, the ingoing traffic would be permitted only if it were part of the session; all other traffic will be denied. For example, a temporary access list will be created inside the reflexive access list when an outbound TCP packet is forwarded outside of your network. This temporary access list will permit ingoing traffic corresponding to the outbound connection.

Reflexive access lists are similar to other access lists in several ways. As with other access lists, reflexive access lists contain entries that define criteria for permitting IP packets. These entries are evaluated in a top-down process in form until a match occurs. Reflexive access lists have significant differences; for example, they contain only temporary entries. The idea here is that we create a reflexive access list that will contain temporary entries.

As stated earlier, these temporary entries are created automatically when a new IP session begins and matches a reflexive permit entry (for example, with an outbound packet), and the entries will be removed when the session ends. Reflexive access lists are not applied directly to an interface. They are placed within an extended named IP access list that is applied to the interface. Reflexive access lists do not have the implicit deny all at the end of the list. Remember, they are nested in another access list.

The idea with a reflexive access list is to create a mirror image of the reflected entry. For example, in Figure 2.8, host0 on network 172.22.114.0 initiates a Telnet session to host1 on network 172.17.0.0. Telnet uses the TCP protocol; therefore, host0 will pick a random source port number—let's use port 1028. Also, here we will have a source IP address, destination IP address, and destination TCP port number. Since we are using Telnet, the destination port number will be 23. So far we have the following information:

```
Source TCP port-1028
Destination TCP port-23
Source IP address-172.22.114.1
Destination IP address-172.17.0.1
```

In our configuration, we will have a reflexive access list statement that will trigger the creation of a reflected access list entry. This will allow inbound return traffic and would look as follows:

```
#permit tcp host 172.17.0.1 eq 23 host 172.22.114.1 eq 1028
```

The following shows our information as a reflected access list entry:

```
Source TCP port-23

Destination TCP port-1028

Source IP address-172.17.0.1

Destination IP address-172.22.114.1
```

In this example of a reflected entry, the source and destination address have been swapped, along with the source and destination port numbers giving the mirror image.

Figure 2.8 Reflexive access list example.

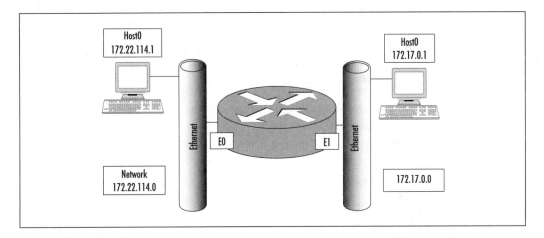

Building Reflexive Access Lists

When building a reflexive access list, we must first design an extended named access list. Remember that you must use an extended named access list when defining your reflexive access list, and there is no implicit **deny all** at the end. Here we enter a **permit** statement to allow all protocols in which you want a reflected entry created. So what must we do to indicate a reflexive opening? You need to use the keyword **reflect** in each of your permit statements. This tells us that a reflexive opening will occur. The following example shows the format of a reflexive access list.

permit protocol source destination **reflect** name [**timeout** seconds]

Table 2.14 describes reflexive access lists.

Table 2.14 Reflexive Access Lists

Command	Description
Permit	This entry will always use the keyword **permit**.
Protocol	Any TCP/IP protocol that is supported by an extended named IP access list.
Source	Identifies the host or network from which the packet is being sent. The source can be specified by an IP address or by using the keywords **any** or **host**.
Destination	Identifies the host or network to which the packet is being sent. The destination can be specified by an IP address or by using the keywords **any** or **host**.
Reflect	Allows the permit statement to create a temporary opening.
Name	The name must be included so a reflexive entry can be used.
Timeout	Timeout is optional and has a default value of 300 seconds.

Let us outline the format further here:

- This entry will always use the keyword **permit**. The keywords **permit** and **reflect** work hand-in-hand. To allow the permit statement to create a temporary opening, you must have the reflect statement.

- The protocol field can depict any UDP, TCP, IP, and ICMP protocol that is supported by an extended named IP access list.

- The source field represents the source IP address. Keywords such as **any** and **host** are applicable here.

- The destination field represents the destination IP address. Keywords such as **any** and **host** are applicable here.

- You must include the name of the access list. Remember that a reflexive entry can be used only with an extended IP named access list.

- The timeout field is optional. If no value is specified, a default of 300 seconds will be used. The timeout is necessary when using connectionless protocols such as UDP. UDP offers nothing in the header to determine when the entry should be deleted. When using TCP, the timeout is not used. Instead, the reflexive access list is deleted after receiving a packet with the RST flag set or when the TCP session closes (both ends have sent FIN packets); the reflexive access list is deleted within five seconds of detecting the bits.

To nest our reflexive access list within an access list, we use the evaluate command. This is done with the keyword **evaluate.** By default, the reflexive access list does not evaluate. This command is used as an entry in the access list and points to the reflexive access list to be evaluated; therefore, traffic entering your network will be evaluated against the reflexive access list.

The following example shows that we are using a named IP access list, named Sydney. The entry would be as follows:

```
evaluate Sydney
```

Refer back to Figure 2.8. In our network, we need to allow from network 172.17.0.0, dynamic openings in response to any host that Telnets to network 172.22.114.0. Our named extended IP access list is represented by the name Sydney. The entry would be as follows:

```
permit tcp any any eq 23 reflect Sydney
```

Even though reflexive access lists give more control in our networks, they do have a major shortcoming. As a rule of thumb, reflexive access lists are only capable of handling single channel applications such as Telnet. An application such as Telnet uses a single static port that stays the same throughout the conversation. Reflexive access lists do not offer the ability to support applications that change port numbers in a session. So how do we handle FTP? Normal mode FTP is a multi-channel operation that uses one channel for control and the second channel for data transmission, and is not supported by reflexive access lists because the data port is chosen by the server not the client. Using the passive mode FTP generally gives us a more favorable result. With passive mode, the server does not perform an active open to the client. The client uses the command channel to exchange port information and then performs an open to the server on an agreed port. So, both of the sessions we just discussed are outbound from the client. Therefore, the reflexive access list would create an additional entry. Here we would have success! FTP is not the only protocol that might be a potential problem here. Many other protocols with similar behavior such as RPC, SQL*Net, Stream works, and multimedia such as H.232 (Netmeeting, Proshare) will have problems.

When applying a reflexive access list, there are a few things to consider. Do you need to apply this on an internal interface or external interface? Just as it sounds, an internal interface refers to the internal network: for example, your Ethernet port on the router and the external interface refers to the external network, your serial port on the router, and, typically, your connection to the Internet. In most cases, the reflect statements will be defined in an outbound extended named access list. Here, a temporary opening in the inbound direction will be created. This opening would be created only if it were part of a session already established from within the internal network. This prevents unwanted IP traffic from entering the router, thereby protecting the internal network.

Applying Reflexive Access Lists

The first step in applying a reflexive access list is to define the access list in an inbound or outbound extended named access list. Determine if your access list needs to be applied inbound or outbound. Next, we have to nest the access list in an inbound or outbound extended named access list. Then we have the option of setting a global timeout value. When using an entry in an extended named IP access list, the entry must contain the **reflect** keyword in each permit statement.

You can use the keyword **timeout** to specify a timeout period for individual entries. If the timeout field is not used, a default value of 300 seconds is used. Remember, this will not apply when using TCP. When using TCP, the access list will close immediately after receiving the RST bit or within five seconds after both ends have closed the TCP session. To set the timeout, the following format is used:

```
ip reflexive-list timeout seconds
```

The following command is used to define a named extended access list (see the section "Named Access Lists" for more details on named access list):

```
ip access-list extended name
```

Normally, when a packet is tested against entries in an access list, the entries are tested in sequential order, and when a match occurs, no more entries are tested. When using a reflexive access list nested in an extended access list, the extended access list entries are tested sequentially up to the nested (reflexive) entry. From there, the reflexive access list entries are tested sequentially, and the remaining entries in the extended access list are tested sequentially. After a packet matches *any* of these entries, no more entries will be tested. As stated earlier, you must use the **evaluate** command to nest a reflexive access list.

Reflexive Access List Example

Refer to Figure 2.9 for this example. Our serial port provides Internet access, and our internal network is connected to the Ethernet 0 port. We want to allow users on network 172.22.114.0 to access the Internet and DNS information along with providing Telnet capability. First, let's create our extended named access lists. Here we will use a permit statement for all the protocols for which we want a reflexive entry created. Remember, we must use a named IP extended access list. Our access list could look as follows:

```
ip access-list extended protection-out
permit tcp 172.22.114.0 0.0.0.255 any eq 23 reflect Sydney
permit tcp 172.22.114.0 0.0.0.255 any eq 80 reflect Sydney
permit udp 172.22.114.0.0.0.0.255 any eq 53 reflect Sydney


ip access-list extended protection-in
evaluate Sydney
```

Now, we need to apply our access list to the appropriate interface. Here we will apply the extended IP named access list of protection-out, in the outbound direction on the serial port. This will allow for dynamic openings in the inbound direction. These openings will only be created in response to network 172.22.114.0 initiating the three sessions that we defined. It is important to remember the default deny all at the end of both access lists. In Figure 2.9, we would apply the access lists to the interface as follows:

```
Interface serial 0
Ip access-group protection-in in
Ip access-group protection-out out
```

Figure 2.9 Applying the access list to the interface.

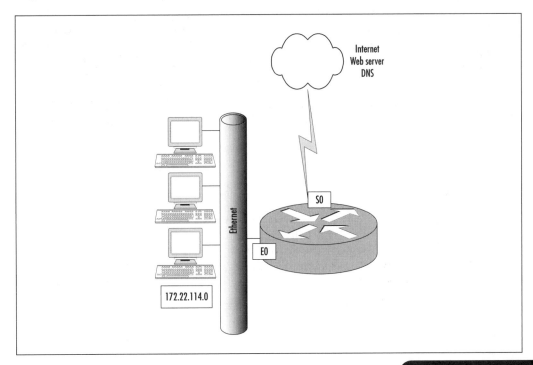

Context-based Access Control

As discussed earlier, the reflexive access list can handle only single-channel applications. This could prove to be detrimental in your enterprise network. Now we will discus how CBAC overcomes some of these issues. Provided in Cisco Secure Integrated Software, Context-based Access Control (CBAC) includes an extensive set of security features. The purpose of Context-based Access Control is to inspect outgoing sessions and create temporary openings to enable the return traffic. Sound familiar? We just described a reflexive access list—the difference here is that CBAC can examine and securely handle various application-based upper-layer information.

For example, when the traffic that you specify leaves the internal network through an interface, an opening is created. This allows returning traffic based on the traffic that was part of the data session initiated from an internal network. These openings are created when specified traffic exits your internal network through the router and allows returning traffic that would normally be blocked in a similar manner to a reflexive access list. The openings also allow additional data channels to enter your internal network back through the router if it is part of the same session as the originating traffic.

With other types of access lists such as reflexive or extended access list, traffic filtering is limited to filtering packets at the network layer or transport layer. CBAC examines the network layer and transport layer along with application-layer protocol information to learn about the state of the TCP or UDP session. Some protocols create multiple channels as a result of negotiations used in the control channel, and it is not possible to filter those protocols using only the information available in the IP and transport layers. By examining the information at the application layer, CBAC provides support for some of these protocols. As previously stated, CBAC inspects outgoing sessions and creates temporary openings to enable the return traffic just as a reflexive access list does. However, unlike reflexive access lists, CBAC has the ability to make decisions based on the behavior of the application. With a reflexive access list, the information inside the packet can be examined up to the transport layer, or layer 4, only.

When using CBAC, the packets are examined when leaving or entering an interface on the router; the information will be placed in a packet state information table. The information may be an IP address and port numbers from layer 4. This state table is used by CBAC to create a temporary opening in the access list for return traffic. CBAC also inspects application-layer information to ensure that the traffic being allowed back through the router is applicable. Recall the issue we had earlier with FTP. Reflexive access lists could support only passive mode where a single channel is used. Now we can use normal mode where multiple channels are used. CBAC observes the outgoing session, then permit the data connection that will be established from the server to the client by creating an opening in the inbound access list. Another difference with CBAC is that a CBAC access list can be created separately from extended or standard access lists and are applied to the interface. The list of protocols and applications where CBAC performs the equivalent function in IOS 12.1 is as follows:

- Single-channel TCP
- Single-channel UDP
- CU-SeeME
- FTP
- H.323
- Java (applets embedded in HTTP)
- Microsoft Netshow
- Unix r commands
- RealAudio
- RPC
- SMTP
- SQL*Net
- StreamWorks
- TFTP
- VDOLive

Just as with everything, there are a few limitations when using CBAC:

- Any packets in which the router is the source address or destination address will not be inspected. Only TCP and UDP packets are inspected, so traffic originating from or destined to the router itself cannot be controlled with CBAC.
- CBAC cannot inspect IPsec traffic. If the traffic needs to be inspected, the router must be configured as the IPsec tunnel endpoint.
- IP traffic such as ICMP must be filtered with an extended or named access list.

The Control-based Access Control Process

The following is a sample process of the events that occur when we configure CBAC on an external interface.

1. The outgoing packet reaches the router and is evaluated against the outgoing access list (inspected by CBAC) and is permitted.

2. Information is recorded including the source and destination IP address and port numbers. The information is recorded in a state table entry created for the new connection.

3. A temporary access list entry is created based on the preceding state information. This access list entry is placed at the beginning of the extended access list on the router's external interface.

4. This temporary opening is designed to permit inbound packets that are part of the same connection as the outbound packet that was inspected previously. The outbound packet now leaves the interface.

5. The return packet is tested against the inbound access list and permitted because of the temporary access list previously created. Here CBAC will modify the state table and inbound access list if necessary.

6. All inbound and outbound traffic in the future will be tested; therefore, the state table access list will be modified as required.

7. When the connection is closed, the state table entry is deleted along with the temporary access list.

Configuring Control-based Access Control

Before configuring CBAC, we must specify which protocols you want to be inspected. We must also specify an interface and direction where the inspection originates. Context-based Access Control will inspect only the protocols we specify here. For the specified protocols, packets entering or exiting the router are inspected. They must flow through the interface where inspection is configured. The packets must pass the inbound access list applied on the interface to be inspected by CBAC. If a packet is denied by the access list, the packet is dropped and CBAC will have no effect. Figure 2.10 diagrams a CBAC configuration.

Figure 2.10 Configuring Context-based Access Control.

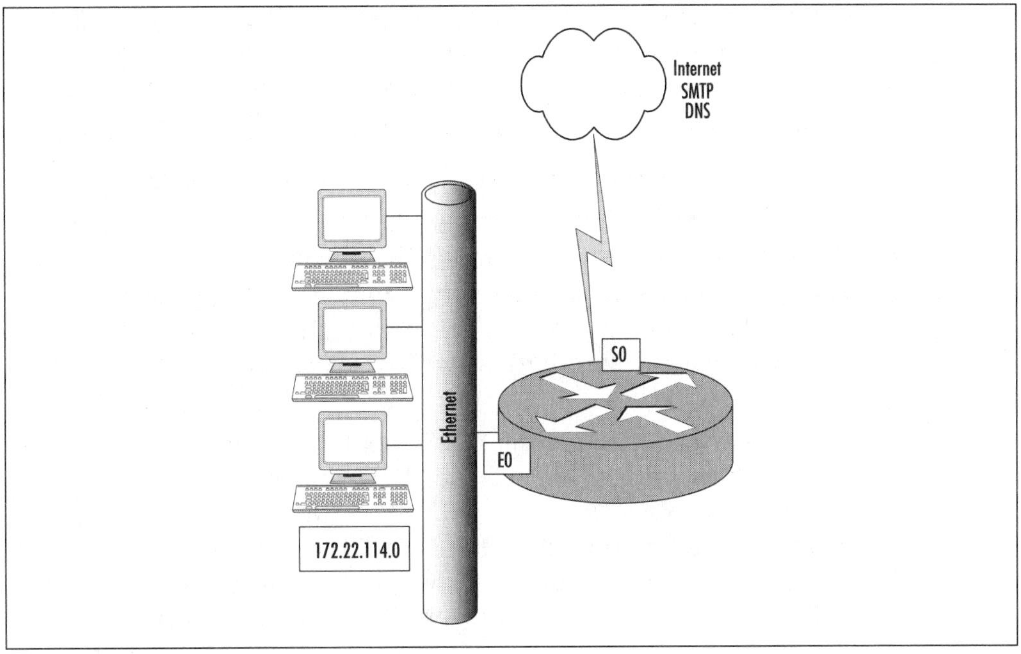

Configuring CBAC involves the following steps.

1. **Choose the interface** Here the decision is made to configure CBAC on an internal or external interface such as Ethernet 0 or Serial 0. The internal interface is where the client sessions originate. The external interface is where the client sessions exit the router. In most cases, CBAC will be configured on the external interface inspecting any traffic entering the network.

2. **Configure access lists** When using CBAC, the access list must be configured for both inbound and outbound traffic to operate properly. The traffic to be inspected by CBAC is specified in the outbound or inbound access list. The outbound access list may be a standard or extended IP access list. The temporary openings are created and managed by CBAC with the inbound access list. This must be an extended IP access list. It is important to note that an access list filtering inbound traffic could be applied either inbound (on the untrusted interface) or outbound (on the trusted interface).

3. **Configuring global timeouts and thresholds** CBAC uses timeouts and thresholds to determine the duration of an inactive session before it is deleted. CBAC helps prevent Denial-of-Service

(DoS) attacks. This is accomplished by monitoring the number and frequency of half-open connections. For example, when using TCP, an example of a half-open session is one that has not completed the three-way handshake, or, if using UDP, a session in which the router has not detected return traffic. CBAC counts both TCP and UDP when determining the number of half-open sessions. Half-open sessions are monitored only for connections configured for inspection by CBAC. These timeouts and thresholds apply globally to all sessions. You can use the default timeout and threshold values, or you can change to values more suitable to your security requirements. You should make any changes to the timeout and threshold values before you continue configuring CBAC. Table 2.15 lists available CBAC commands used to configure timeouts and thresholds.

4. **Inspection rules** After configuring global timeouts and thresholds, you must define an inspection rule. This specifies which application-layer protocols will be tested by CBAC at an interface. Typically, you define only one inspection rule. One exception might be if you want to enable CBAC in two directions. In this case, you should define two rules, one in each direction. The inspection rule should specify each desired application-layer protocol as well as TCP or UDP if desired. The inspection rule consists of a series of statements, each listing a protocol and specifying the same inspection rule name. Included here are rules for controlling alert and audit trail messages and for checking IP packet fragmentation.

Table 2.15 Available Timeout Commands and Thresholds

Command	Description	Default values
IP inspect tcp synwait-time *seconds*	Length of time of wait for TCP session to establish	30 seconds
IP inspect tcp finwait time *seconds*	Length of time TCP is managed after FIN exchange	5 seconds
IP inspect tcp idle-time *seconds*	TCP idle timeout	3,600 seconds
IP inspect udp idle-time *seconds*	UDP idle timeout	30 seconds
IP inspect dns-timeout *seconds*	DNS lookup idle timer	5 seconds
IP inspect max-incomplete high *number*	Max number of half-open connections before CBAC begins closing connections	500 sessions

Continued

Table 2.15 Continued

Command	Description	Default values
IP inspect max-incomplete low *number*	Max number of half-open connections causing CBAC to stop closing connections	400 sessions
IP inspect one-minute high *number*	Rate of half-open sessions per minute before CBAC begins closing connections	500 sessions
IP inspect one-minute low *number*	Rate of half-open sessions per minute causing CBAC to stop deleting connections	400 sessions
IP inspect tcp max-incomplete host *number* block-time *seconds*	Number of existing half-open sessions with the same destination address before CBAC begins closing sessions	50 sessions

Inspection Rules

The following format defines inspection rules:

```
ip inspect name inspection-name protocol [alert {on|off}
 [audit-trail{on|off}] [timeout seconds]
```

The keyword **alert** allows CBAC to send messages to a syslog server when a violation occurs in a monitored application. Each application will have an individual alert the router will send to the server for illegal conditions. The keyword **audit trail** permits the tracking of connections used for a protected application. Here the router logs information about each connection including ports used, number of bytes transferred, and source and destination IP address. A key issue here is if a large amount of traffic is being monitored, the logging produced will be significant!

Applying the Inspection Rule

Now that we have defined the inspection rule, the final step is to apply it to an interface. You will apply the inspection rule the same way we apply access lists on the interface. You must also specify inbound, for traffic entering the interface, or outbound for traffic exiting the interface. The command is as follows:

```
ip inspect inspection-name {in | out}
```

To perform Java blocking, a list of permitted IP addresses must be created using a standard IP access list, as shown in the following example:

```
access-list list-number {permit | deny} source-address
  [wildcard-mask][log]
ip inspect name inspection-name http [java-list access-list]
  [alert {on | off}] [audit-trail {on | off}] [timeout seconds}
```

By default, an undefined access list in the java-list definition will deny
all Java applets. CBAC can block only Java applets, not Active X.

There are several commands that are useful in gathering information
about CBAC. The **sh ip inspect config** will be discussed first. This command allows all specific portions of a configuration, as shown in the following example:

```
Router# sh ip inspect config
Session alert is enabled
One-minute (sampling period) thresholds are [400:500] connections
max-incomplete sessions thresholds are [400:500]
max- incomplete tcp connections per host is 50.
Block-time 0 minute.
tcp synwait-time is 30 sec - tcp finwait - time is 5 sec
tcp idle - time is 3600 sec - udp idle - time is 30 sec
dns - timeout is 5 seconds
```

The **show ip inspect interfaces** command shows the interfaces that
CBAC inspection is configured. For example:

```
Router# sh ip inspect interfaces
Interface FastEthernet 3/0
Inbound inspection rule is Protector
tcp alert is on audit-trail is off timeout 3600
udp alert is on audit-trail is CBAC off timeout 30
fragment Maximum 50 In Use 0 alert is on audit-trail is off timeout 1
Inbound access list is 114
Outbound access list is not set
```

Refer to the section "Connecting Public Servers Connected to the
Internet" for the required configuration for CBAC.

Configuring Port to Application Mapping

A limitation of CBAC is the fact that only services running on standard ports can be controlled. For example, traffic going to a Web server running on a port other than the standard HTTP port (80) cannot be inspected and protected using CBAC. Port to Application Mapping (PAM) can be used to override this limitation. Port to Application Mapping gives you the capability to customize TCP or UDP port numbers for network services or applications. Upon startup, PAM will build a table containing ports associated with their default application known as a PAM table or database. All of the services supported by CBAC are kept in this table. This is where the link with CBAC comes into play. The information built in the PAM table will give CBAC the ability to function on a nonstandard port. If you are running applications on nonstandard ports, PAM and CBAC have the ability to work together to identify the ports associated with their applications. Without the use of PAM, CBAC is limited to well-known ports and their applications.

PAM comes standard with the Cisco Secure Integrated Software Feature Set. Network services or applications that use non-standard ports will require you to place entries in the PAM table manually. You can also specify a range of ports used by an application by establishing a separate entry in the PAM table for each port number in the range. All manual entries are saved with the default mapping information when you save the router configuration, so upon startup the mapping will be in the PAM table. If you use an application that requires a non-standard port you will need to enter this manually in the PAM table (for example, if you use the Telnet application with port 8000 instead of port 23).

Configuring PAM

When configuring PAM the following format is used:

```
ip port-map application_name port port number m
```

Mapping the well-known port 23 (Telnet) to port 8000 may look like this:

```
ip port-map telnet port 8000
```

Let's take this example a step farther and define a range of non-standard ports for well-known port 23. Here's an example:

```
Ip port-map telnet port 8001
```

```
Ip port-map telnet port 8002

Ip port-map telnet port 8003

Ip port-map telnet port 8004
```

We also have the option of mapping application to a port for a specific host or subnet. Mapping an application to a host would look as follows:

```
Access-list 1 permit 172.16.144.1

Ip port-map Telnet port 8000 list 1
```

When mapping to a specific subnet, the list may look as follows:

```
Access-list 1 permit 172.16.144.0

Ip port-map Telnet port 8000 list 1
```

Protecting a Private Network

When only protecting a private network, the security factors concerning the Internet have already been addressed or are not an issue. However, with the networks of today and the future, it is almost a given that this will be an issue. Previously, the concern to protect a network was generally from the outside, which is no longer true. Security concerns are an issue internally as well as externally.

The concern in this example is only internal; let's say you want to protect your accounting department from internal unauthorized access. For this scenario, a standard or extended access list is all that is necessary. You can create an access list that allows traffic from only two subnets, for example. The access list may look as follows:

```
access-list 7 permit 172.17.0.0

access-list 7 permit 10.0.0.0
```

This is a very simple standard access list that meets our requirements in Figure 2.11. We are allowing only traffic from network 172.16.0.0 and network 10.0.0.0; traffic from 192.168.0.0 will be blocked due to the implicit deny all at the end of the access list. For the access list to be effective, it could be applied as follows:

```
Router1# config t

Router(config)# interface ethernet 1

Router(config-if)#ip access-group 7 in
```

Figure 2.11 Protecting a private network.

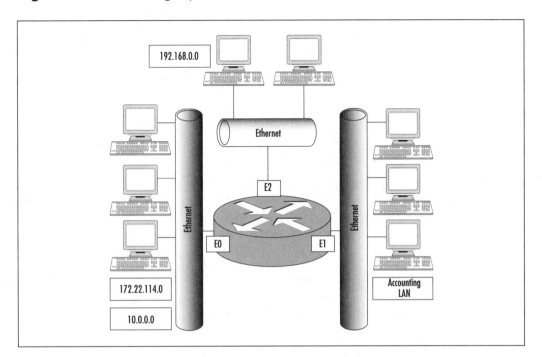

Protecting a Network Connected to the Internet

Now our concern has moved to protecting a network that is connected to the Internet. The connection from the network to the Internet has the potential to be an open door if no restrictions are applied. If there are no restrictions on your network to and from the Internet, then anyone with the proper IP address can access your network.

Here we are not concerned with restricting packets going out to the Internet; we are interested only in restricting what comes in. For example, let's say we want to allow external users to establish TCP connections to a server for HTTP access to our Web page, Telnet, and SMTP sessions for mail. We also need to allow UDP packets to pass for DNS traffic. Remember that the TCP ports we are concerned with here are 80 (HTTP), 23 (Telnet), and 25 (SMTP). UDP ports are 53 (DNS). Our access list needs to permit connections using ports 80, 23, 53, and 25 to the IP address of the server only and apply that access list to packets inbound. Our access list may look as follows:

```
access-list 111 permit tcp any host 201.12.12.1 eq 80
access-list 111 permit tcp any host 201.12.12.1 eq 23
```

```
access-list 111 permit tcp any host 210.12.12.1 eq 25
access-list 111 permit ucp any host 210.12.12.2 eq 25
```

We would apply the access list to the serial 0 interface of the router. The command would be as follows:

```
interface s0
ip access-group 111 in
```

Figure 2.12 shows our configuration in action.

Figure 2.12 Protecting a private network.

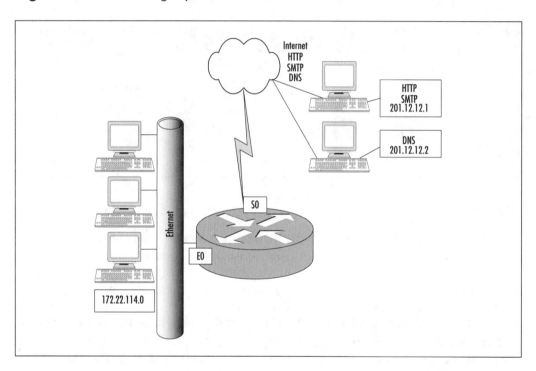

Protecting Server Access Using Lock-and-Key

The concern here is protecting a server on our trusted network from unwanted users from the Internet. Not only do we have to consider the server we are protecting, but we must also keep the rest of our network the server resides on in mind. There is also another factor here which is an additional internal network that we must take into account when designing our access list. We need to allow the users on the network access to the Internet.

Our organization has a router with two Ethernet segments, one attached to interface E0 (172.16.4.0) and the other attached to E1 (192.168.200.0). We also have an Internet connection on our serial port (10.1.1.1). We need to restrict when we allow external users to connect to the server using the IP address 172.16.4.1. Also, we want our internal users on the 192.168.200.0 network to have access to the Internet for browsing and DNS. Lastly, we need to block access from E0 to E1. Our access list may look as follows:

```
access-list 118 permit udp any eq 53 192.168.200.0 0.0.0.255 gt 1023

access-list 118 permit tcp any eq 80 192.168.200.0 0.0.0.255 gt 1023
established

access-list 118 dynamic test timeout 90 permit ip any host 172.16.4.1
time-range my-time log

access-list 118 deny ip any 192.168.200.0 0.0.0.255

access-list 118 permit tcp any any established

time-range my-time

periodic weekdays 8:00 to 18:00

line vty 0 2

 login local

 autocommand  access-enable host timeout 10

line vty 3 4

 login local

 rotary 1
```

Here we have permitted incoming packets from any source IP address if the source port is 53(DNS) or 80(HTTP). All DNS requests should be originated from a source port above 1024. The idea here is that a hacker could send UDP packets from source 53 and try a Denial-of-Service attack on the internal servers. Notice, on the next line we have added the established keyword. We are saying here that the ACK or RST bit must be set in the TCP header. This will allow return traffic from a converstion initiated by an internal host.

The access list would be applied to the serial 0 interface inbound as follows:

```
Router1# config t

Router(config)# interface serial 0

Router(config-if)#ip access-group118 in
```

Figure 2.13 illustrates the configuration.

Figure 2.13 Protecting a server using access using lock-and-key.

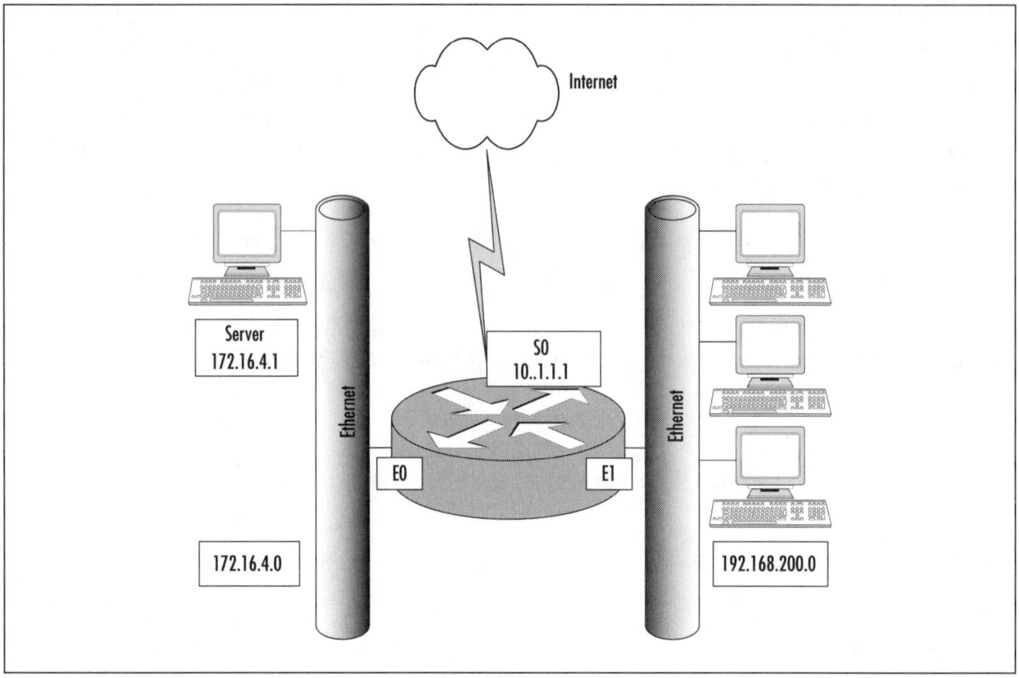

Protecting Public Servers Connected to the Internet

Our focus now turns to protecting a public server on the Internet. Even though the term is "public server," that doesn't imply that it has public access. You want to allow access only to particular applications on the server and ensure that nothing else is susceptible to a hacker.

Here we have serial interface 0 on our router connected to the Internet, and Ethernet interface 0 connected to our internal network. We need to permit our internal users to access the Internet for Web browsing, e-mail, and FTP. We also want to know how much FTP traffic is in use. The internal users need to be able to ping and trace route to hosts on the Internet for troubleshooting purposes. We have no internal servers, so all services are provided by the ISP. (Please refer back to Figure 2.10 for an illustration this situation.) Our access list may look as follows:

```
ip inspect alert-off
ip inspect name protector ftp audit-trail on
ip inspect name protector smtp
```

```
ip inspect name protector udp

ip inspect name protector tcp

interface Ethernet 0

ip address 172..22.14.1 255.255.255.0

ip access-group 111 in

interface serial 0

ip address 12.1.1.1 255.255.255.252

ip inspect protector out

ip access-group 112 in

ip access-list 1 permit 209.12.12.0 0.0.0.255

ip access-list 111 permit ip any any

ip access-list 112 permit icmp any any echo-reply

ip access-list 112 permit icmp any any time-exceeded

ip access-list 112 permit icmp any any unreachable
```

Here we have used a context-based access control access list. We would like to know how much FTP traffic is in use so the audit trail was enabled. We also defined the protocols we want to inspect with CBAC. Users will have the ability to ping and trace routes for troubleshooting purposes.

Summary

A standard IP access list filters on source IP addresses only. With extended access lists, we have the capability of filtering on source and destination addresses along with specific protocols, source, and destination ports. When using named access lists, we create access lists by name instead of number.

Lock-and-key access lists offer our first look at enhanced access-list capability. Lock-and-key are also known as dynamic access lists that create dynamic entries. Traditional access lists do not offer this capability. Remember that with a traditional access list, the entry remains until you delete it manually. Dynamic access lists create a temporary, specific opening in an access list after a user is authenticated.

Reflexive access lists automatically create and delete temporary access list entries that will allow traffic associated with an IP session. This offers a stronger control over what traffic is allowed into a network.

CBAC can be used with multiple applications and provides a higher level of security than a traditional access list. Here we create dynamic openings in an inbound access list in response to an outbound data connection. Traffic is permitted from untrusted networks to our internal network only when traffic is part of a session that was initiated from the internal network.

FAQs

Q: You have created your access list, and there seems to be no effect on traffic entering or exiting the router. What could be the problem?

A: After creating the access list globally on the router, you must remember to apply the access list to an interface and give a direction, inbound or outbound. The default direction for access lists is outbound.

Q: After applying an access list on your enterprise router, there has been a drastic decrease in throughput. What could be a potential problem here?

A: First, recall how an access list works. An access list utilizes "top-down" processing when testing traffic. Typically on an enterprise router, an access list can get quite lengthy. A problem here could be that the majority of your traffic is permitted or denied near the end of the access list. When creating an access list, it is important to test the majority of your traffic first.

Q: A customer wants you to configure an access list that has an opening only when a user establishes an outbound Telnet session. What type of access list could apply here?

A: A reflexive access list would be a good choice. When using reflexive access lists, an entry is created enabling inbound return traffic.

Chapter 3

Network Address Translation (NAT)

Solutions in this chapter:

- NAT and NAPT
- Deploying NAT and NAPT in a Network
- Configuring NAT on Cisco IOS
- Examples
- Considerations on NAT and NAPT

Introduction

In today's world of Enterprise networks, one of the major problems facing IT professionals is the rapidly depleting supply of legal network addresses. Measures have been taken to slow the rate at which IP addresses are being allocated; such measures include Classless Inter-Domain Routing (CIDR), Network Address Translation (NAT), and Network Address Port Translation (NAPT or PAT). This chapter will discuss NAT and NAPT and how they can contribute to a security policy, implications of NAT, and considerations when implementing NAT.

NAT is a mechanism that can be used to translate the IP addresses inside IP packets. The mechanism is commonly used today to allow a site using private IP addresses to acheive connectivity the Internet. NAT operates on a device, usually connecting two networks together, allowing them to communicate. Typically one network uses RFC1918 IP addresses, which will be translated into globally unique IP addresses. Other scenarios in which NAT can be utilized will be discussed later in this chapter.

NAT by itself is not a security measure, and should not be implemented in such a fashion. A common misconception is that NAT will allow a company to "hide" your internal network. That can be an added security benefit, but you should not rely on it as the only security measure. A network using private IP address space is not reachable from the Internet because the Internet routing tables cannot contain such private IP addresses. If routing between the company and the ISP is not done properly, a route to the company may be leaked throughout the ISP, possibly exposing the company's network to the public.

NAT Overview

In today's world of technology, different vendors have implemented Network Address Translation in their devices. Because there are so many vendors, dealing with devices from multiple vendors can be confusing. Terms used in one vendor's documentation may be used differently in another vendor's documentation. This section will introduce and clarify terms used in Network Address Translation using the document RFC2663 "IP Network Address Translator (NAT) Terminology and Considerations" as a reference.

Overview of NAT Devices

Generally, NAT is used when a company's internal addresses are not globally unique and thus cannot be routed on the Internet (for example, using RFC1918 private addresses), or because two separate networks that need to communicate are using an overlapping IP address space.

NAT allows (in most cases) hosts in a private network (inside network) to transparently communicate with destination hosts (outside network) in a global or public network. This is achieved by modifying the *source address* portion of an IP packet as it traverses the NAT device. The NAT device will keep track of each translation (conversation) between the source host (inside network) and destination host (outside network), and vice versa. This means that NAT is a stateful device.

Throughout this chapter and in Cisco documentation, the networks will be described and referred to as being either an *inside* network or *outside* network. An inside network is the set of networks that are subject to translation; all other networks are considered outside networks.

One of the variations of NAT is Network Address Port Translation (NAPT). Cisco documentation refers to NAPT as Port Address Translation (PAT). Both of these terms mean the same thing, which will be discussed later in this chapter.

This solution works only if the application does not rely on an IP address in the data portion of the packet for functionality. In these cases, Application Layer Gateways included inside the NAT (discussed later) may be needed to assist a NAT device.

The following is a series of terms and their descriptions used when referring to NAT. Keep in mind that different vendors may refer to these terms in varying contexts.

Address Realm

An address realm is a network in which the network addresses (IP addresses) are uniquely assigned to hosts such that traffic can be routed to them. Routing protocols used within the network are responsible for routing traffic to the destination network. Often referred to as inside and outside networks, address realms help define zones that are separated and need to communicate with each other. For example, a company's internal networks can be considered as one address realm. This realm is under a single administrative authority, which needs to communicate with networks outside of its authority. These outside networks, which could be the Internet or another company's network, are also considered an address realm. The definition of realm will vary depending on the context in which it is used.

NAT

The basic configuration of NAT operates on a device that connects two networks together; one of these networks (designated as inside) is addressed with either private RFC1918 or other addresses that need to be converted into legal addresses before packets are forwarded to their destination network (designated as outside).

NAT is a method by which IP addresses are mapped from one address realm to another. This type of translation provides transparent routing from host to host. There are many variations of address translation that assist in translating different applications; however, all NAT implementations on various devices should share the following characteristics:

- Transparent address assignment
- Transparent routing through address translation (routing refers to forwarding packets and not exchanging routing information)
- ICMP error packet data translation

Transparent Address Assignment

NAT translates addresses from an inside network to addresses in an outside network and vice versa. This provides transparent routing for the traffic traversing between both networks. The translation in some cases may extend to transport-level identifiers such as TCP/UDP ports. Address translation is done at the start of a session; the following describes two types of address assignment:

Static Address Assignment Static address assignment is a one-to-one address mapping for hosts between an inside network and an outside network for the duration of the NAT session. Static address assignment ensures that the translation table is static and not dynamic. Using static address assignment, your internal host is visible from the outside network since it is always assigned the same global IP address. This can be useful for some applications, but care must also be taken to secure that machine.

TIP

Think of static address assignment as a static IP address that has been assigned by an administrator to a host. This IP address will never change unless administrators do so themselves. Dynamic address assignment can be compared to a DHCP server, which dynamically assigns IP address (as well as other information) to hosts. DHCP IP address assignment is based on a lease time, which can also be compared to the duration of a NAT translation. Once the lease expires, that IP address may be assigned to another host. Once a dynamic NAT translation to a global IP address is no longer needed, it can be used to translate another inside host to that global IP address.

Dynamic Address Assignment Dynamic address assignment is the process in which hosts are translated by the NAT device dynamically based on usage requirements. Once a NAT is no longer being used, it is terminated. NAT would then free that translation so the global address could be used in another translation.

Transparent Routing

Transparent routing refers to routing traffic between separate address realms (inside network to outside network) by modifying address contents in the IP header so that they will be valid in the address realm into which the traffic is routed. A NAT device is placed at the border between two address realms and translates addresses in IP headers so that when the packet leaves one realm and enters another, it can be routed properly.

Typically there are three phases to address translation:

Address Binding Address binding is the phase in which an inside IP address is associated with an outside address, or vice versa. This assumes that dynamic NAT is being used and not static NAT. Address binding is fixed with a pool of static addresses to be assigned. These addresses are dynamically assigned on a per-session basis. For example, whenever a host on the inside network must reach another host on the outside network, it will begin a session with that host. A translation will occur on the NAT device associating a global IP address on the outside network with the IP address of the host on the inside network. Once a session is created, all traffic originating from the same inside host will use the same translation. The start of each new session will result in the creation of a new translation. A NAT device will support many simultaneous sessions; consult the vendor's documentation for specific information.

Address Lookup and Translation Once a translation is established for a session, all packets belonging to the session will be subject to address lookup and translation.

Address Unbinding Address unbinding is the phase in which an inside host IP address is no longer associated with a global address. NAT will perform address unbinding when it believes the last session using an address binding has terminated.

An example of transparent routing is when a company's inside network uses the subnet 192.168.1.0/24, and the outside network uses the subnet 207.139.221.0/24—transparent routing would occur on the device that separates the two subnets. Instead of using a router to route packets based on destination address, NAT alters the source address of an IP packet originating from the inside network and changes it to a valid IP address in the outside network. The NAT device then builds a table to keep track of the translations that have occurred to maintain communications between a host on the inside network and a host on the outside network. Figure 3.1 illustrates this example.

Figure 3.1 The NAT device maintaining communications between inside network and outside network hosts.

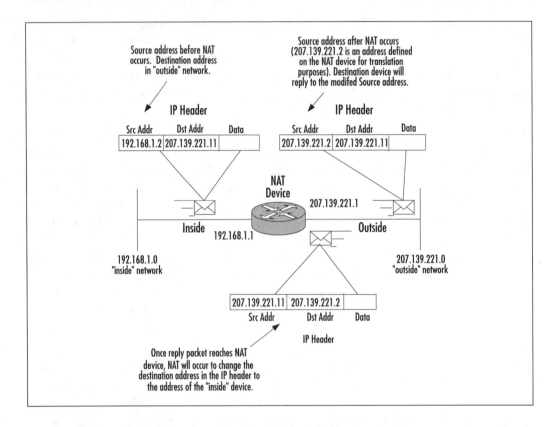

Public, Global, and External Networks

A public, global, or external network is an address realm with a unique network address assigned by the Internet Assigned Numbers Authority or an equivalent address registry.

NOTE

Do not confuse public, global, and external networks with the term outside network. Outside is more of a generic term to describe a destination network in which NAT must occur in order to communicate with that network. Outside networks may refer to networks using global IP addresses, but they also may refer to the destination network in a situation where both networks use private IP addresses.

Private and Local Networks

A private or local network is an address realm independent of external network addresses. A private or local network uses IP addresses specified in RFC1918. These addresses are private—they should never be used globally. Transparent routing between hosts in a private realm and external realm is made possible by a NAT device.

NOTE

Do not confuse private and local networks with the term inside network. As with the term outside network, inside network is more of a generic term to describe the source network in which NAT must occur in order for two hosts to communicate. An inside network may refer to a network that uses the private IP addresses (RFC1918), but it may also refer to the source network in which both networks use global IP addresses but must communicate through a NAT device.

Application Level Gateway

Not all protocols are easily translated by NAT devices, especially those that include IP addresses and TCP/UDP ports in the data portion of the packet. Simple NAT may not always work with certain protocols; this is why most modern implementations of NAT include built-in Application Layer Gateway functionality. Application Level Gateways (ALGs) are application-specific translation agents that allow an application on a host in one address realm to connect to another host running a translation agent in a different realm transparently. An ALG may interact with NAT to set up state, use NAT state information, alter application specific data, and perform whatever else is necessary to get the application to run across different realms.

For example, recall that NAT and NAPT can alter the IP header source and destination addresses, as well as the source and destination port in the TCP/UDP header. RealAudio clients on the inside network access TCP port 7070 to initiate a conversation with a real-audio server located on an outside network, and to exchange control messages during playback such as pausing or stopping of the audio stream. Audio session parameters are embedded in the TCP control session as a byte stream. The actual audio traffic is carried in the opposite direction (originating from the real-audio server, destined for the real-audio client on the inside network) on ports ranging from 6970–7170.

As a result, RealAudio will not work with a traditional NAT device. One work-around is for an ALG that will examine the TCP traffic to determine the audio session parameters and selectively enable inbound UDP sessions for the ports agreed upon in the TCP control session. Another work-around could have the ALG simply redirecting all inbound UDP sessions directed to ports 6970–7170 to the client address on the inside network.

ALGs are similar to proxies in that both ALGs and proxies aid application-specific communication between clients and servers. Proxies use a special protocol to communicate with proxy clients and relay client data to servers, and vice versa. Unlike proxies, ALGs do not use a special protocol to communicate with application clients and do not require changes to application clients.

NAT Architectures

Many variations of NAT aid different applications. The following headings outline some of the variations of NAT.

Traditional or Outbound NAT

Traditional NAT is a dynamic translation that allows hosts within the inside network to transparently access hosts in the outside network. In a traditional NAT, the initial outbound session is unidirectional (one-way), outbound from the private network. Once a session has been established with a device on the outside network, bidirectional communication will occur for the duration of that session.

IP addresses of hosts in the outside network are unique. IP addresses of hosts in the inside network use RFC1918 private IP addresses. Since the IP addresses of the inside network are private and cannot be used globally, they must be translated into global addresses.

The traditional NAT router in Figure 3.2 would allow Host A to initiate a session to Host Z, but not the other way around. Also, the address space from the global address pool used on the outside is routable, whereas the inside address space cannot be routed globally.

Figure 3.3 shows the reply packets sent by Host Z to Host A. Since Host A originated a session from inside, any packets originating from Host Z in response to Host A will be permitted provided that the security rules on the NAT device permit it. If Host Z attempted to initiate a session with Host A, traditional NAT will not permit this because Host A has a private IP address. This IP address is reserved for private networks and will therefore never be routed globally. From the perspective of Host Z, Host A's IP address is 207.139.221.2 (the translated address). If Host Z attempts to initiate a session with this IP address, the NAT device will not be able to associate 207.139.221.2 with an inside IP address with traditional NAT. In order to allow Host Z to initiate a session with Host A, static NAT (explained later) will need to be configured.

Figure 3.2 A diagram of traditional NAT.

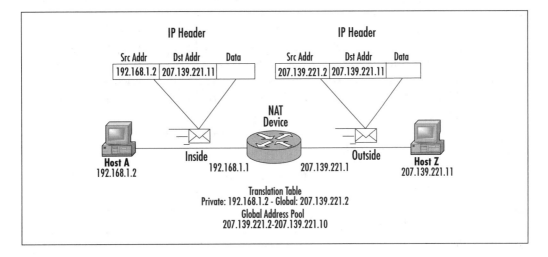

Figure 3.3 Traditional NAT reply.

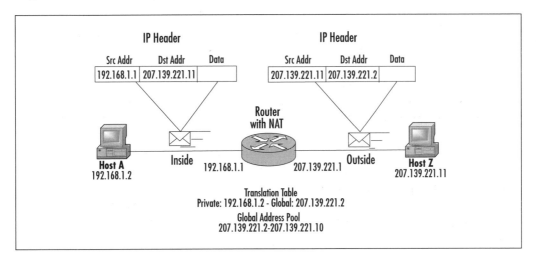

Network Address Port Translation (NAPT)

NAPT extends the concept of translation one step further by also translating transport identifiers—TCP and UDP port numbers—and ICMP query identifiers. This allows the transport identifiers of a number of private hosts to be multiplexed into the transport identifiers of a single global IP address. NAPT allows numerous hosts from the inside network to share a single outside network IP address. The advantage of this type of translation is that only one global IP address is needed for every 6,400 simultanious sessions, whereas with NAT, each inside host must translate to a unique outside IP address.

TIP

Both NAT and NAPT can be combined; the advantage is that when NAT exhausts the pool of global IP addresses, NAPT can then be used until one of the NAT translations is timed out. This method ensures that all inside hosts can be translated successfully into outside global IP addresses.

Figure 3.4 illustrates NAPT. Host A on the inside network needs to communicate with Host Z on the outside network. Because these two hosts are on different networks and the inside network uses IP addresses from a private address space, NAT/NAPT is needed to allow the two hosts to communicate. Unfortunately the administrator has only a limited number of global IP addresses, many of which have already been assigned to various devices. Therefore NAT cannot be used for translations.

As an alternative, NAPT can be used instead. To perform NAPT:

1. Host A attempts to initiate a session with Host Z. Since Host Z is not on the same network as Host A, Host A must send the packet to the router (default gateway) in order for it to be routed correctly.

2. Once the packet reaches the inside interface of the router in which NAPT is enabled, the router examines the translation table for an existing translation. Since this is a new session, the router creates a new translation record in the table. Since only one IP address is assigned to the pool of IP addresses to translate to, a unique port number is added to the *source address*. This will allow the router to keep track of the translation for the duration of the session:

```
PAT Global 207.139.221.2(1576) Local 192.168.1.2
```

The router then alters the IP header and changes the *source address* to the IP address of the outside interface of the router.

Figure 3.4 How NAPT functions.

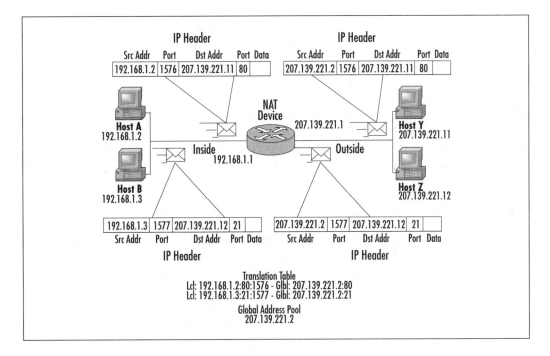

3. The packet is transparently routed to Host Z.

4. Host Z replies to Host A by sending the packet to the outside interface of the router (*destination address*).

5. Once the packet reaches the outside interface, the router examines the IP header and checks the translation table for an existing translation. Since a translation already exists in the table, the router changes the *destination address* to the IP address of Host A.

6. The process is repeated until the session between Host A and Host Z is terminated.

Static NAT

With a static NAT, sessions can be initiated from hosts in the inside or outside network. Inside addresses are bound to globally unique addresses using static translations as the connections are established in either direction. A translation that occurs from the inside network to the outside network will be translated with the statically configured address on the NAT device. When a session must be established from an outside network to an inside network, the static translation must already be set up manually on the router. By creating a static translation, you are translating an inside IP address to a fixed outside global IP address. This translation will never change and will always remain in the translation table.

For example, if there is a resource on the inside network that must be made accessible to the outside network, the global IP address of the resource can be advertised worldwide through the DNS. Since this resource has been statically translated into a global IP, this IP can be advertised in a DNS record. If the resource is a mail server, an MX record may be created in the company's zone associating the MX record with the global IP that was statically assigned to the resource in the inside network. By doing this, even though the mail server is not physically located in the outside network, it can still be accessed as if it were.

TIP

A configuration allowing global access to resources has security related advantages. If the NAT device is a Cisco PIX firewall or Cisco router running FW IOS, Access Control Lists can be used to limit the type of traffic permitted to reach the resource. Compare this with having a server that is physically placed in the outside network allowing global access, limiting the type of traffic would be very difficult if not impossible, therefore becoming a security risk.

Figure 3.5 illustrates a static NAT translation. A session is initiated from Host Z on the outside network. Since the NAT device has a static translation for Host A's IP address to a global IP address, the NAT device can forward the packet from Host Z to Host A's static NAT public IP address. Recall that with traditional or outbound NAT, a session can be initiated only from the inside host, which causes a dynamic translation to occur on the NAT device. Once this translation has been created, only then can the outside host reply back to the inside host. Once the session times out, the inside host will need to start a new session with the outside host, causing the NAT device to create a new translation and possibly allocating a new global IP address to the inside host for the duration of the session (if NAT is used). With a static NAT, the translation is always active; the global IP address will never be allocated dynamically to another host on the inside network for translation purposes.

Figure 3.5 A Static NAT translation.

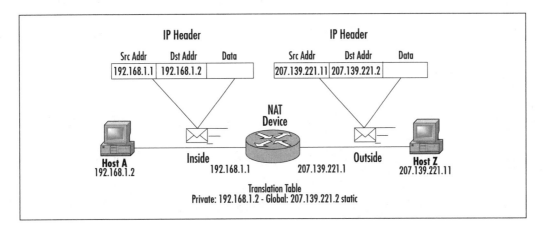

Twice NAT

Twice NAT is a variation of NAT—both the source and destination addresses are modified by the NAT device as the packet crosses address realms. Compare this to traditional NAT, where only one of the addresses (either source or destination) is translated when traversing the NAT device.

Twice NAT is necessary when both inside and outside networks have overlapping address space. Although this type of problem does not occur often, a need for Twice NAT would arise when two companies merge their networks together and they use overlapping address space, or when a company chooses an IP subnet that is already in use on the Internet. Figure 3.6 illustrates Twice NAT.

The router performs the following process when translating overlapping addresses:

1. The device Host 1.1.1.1 opens a connection to Host C by DNS name. A name-to-address lookup request is sent to DNS server x.x.x.x.

2. The router intercepts the DNS reply and translates the returned address (Data portion of packet) if there is an overlap (that is, the resulting legal address resides illegally in the inside network). To translate the return address, the router creates a simple translation entry mapping the overlapping address 1.1.1.3 to an address from a separately configured, outside local address pool. The router examines every DNS reply from everywhere, ensuring that the IP address is not in the inside network. If it is, the router translates the address.

Figure 3.6 Twice NAT.

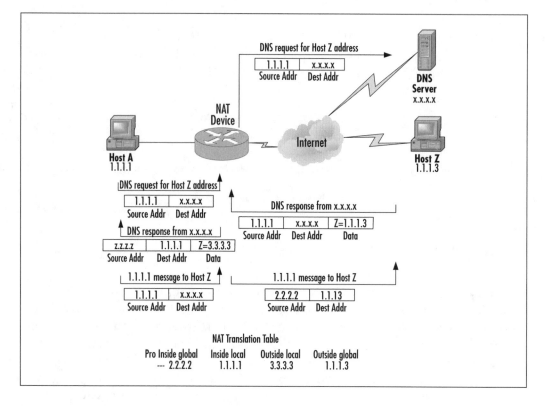

3. Host 1.1.1.1 opens a connection to 3.3.3.3.

4. The router sets up translations mapping inside local and global addresses to each other, and outside global and local addresses to each other.

5. The router replaces the source address with the inside global address and replaces the destination address with the outside global address.

6. Host C receives the packet and continues the conversation.

7. The router does a lookup, replaces the destination address with the inside local address, and replaces the source address with the outside local address.

8. Host 1.1.1.1 receives the packet and the conversation continues, using this translation process.

Guidelines for Deploying NAT and NAPT

When deploying NAT and NAPT in a network, there are many things to take into consideration. Various factors will contribute to which type of NAT is used, such as the number of available global IP addresses for translations, if the inside network uses global or RFC1918 IP addresses. The following are general guidelines for deploying NAT:

- How many public IP addresses are available for inside IP addresses to be translated to? If only a limited number of global IP addresses exist for many inside hosts (for example, 8 global addresses for 250 inside hosts), NAPT or a combination of dynamic NAT and NAPT may be necessary.

- Router performance needs to be considered for all types of NAT. NAT increases the time it takes for a packet to arrive at a destination address. When a packet traverses a NAT device, the IP header must be modified. This is currently done using process switching. Table 3.1 shows performance statistics on various router platforms.

Table 3.1 Statistics on Router Platforms

Routing Platform	Packet Size (bytes)	Data Throughput (Mbps)
Cisco 7500 Series	64	24
	200	50
	1000	89
	1500	96
Cisco 4700 Series	64	10
	200	10
	1000	10
	1500	10.5
Cisco 4500 Series	64	7.5
	200	7.5
	1000	7.5
	1500	8

- What type of addressing scheme is being used on the inside network? Are private RFC1918 addresses being used? If so, then NAT will need to occur for the inside network(s) to be able to reach the outside networks.

- Not all applications will work with NAT. Be aware of what type of traffic will be translated and if the functionality of those applications will be affected by NAT. If this is the case, an ALG may need to be implemented to assist in the translation process. Application types that do not need an ALG or that have an ALG built into Cisco's NAT implementation are listed later in this chapter.

- A disadvantage of NAT is the loss of end-to-end IP connectivity. It becomes much harder to trace packets that undergo numerous IP address changes over multiple NAT hops. On the other hand, an advantage to this is that it becomes difficult if not impossible for hackers to determine a packet's source to trace or obtain the original source or destination addresses.

TIP

Process switching occurs when a device must examine every packet to decide whether it has to translate it, and then alter the IP header and possibly the TCP header.

Some guidelines to follow for implementing static NAT are as follows:

- How many inside devices need to be statically translated? Remember that each global IP used for static translations cannot be used for dynamic translations.

- A security policy should be in place to limit the type of traffic permitted to reach that statically translated device. When an inside device is statically translated into a global IP address, any devices on the outside networks can initiate a session with the inside device.

Some guidelines to follow for implementing NAPT are as follows:

- Should NAPT be the only type of translation used or can NAPT be used once the addresses in the NAT pool are all used? For example, if 128 global IP addresses are available for NAT translations, 127 can be used for NAT and the last IP address can be used for NAPT. Once NAT has used up all 127 address with active translations, the NAT device can then use NAPT until a NAT translation times out and the global address can then be reallocated to the global IP address pool.

For IT Professionals

What Applications Need an ALG?

Application Layer Gateways (ALG) have been mentioned several times throughout this chapter, but the questions of what applications may or may not need an ALG have not been answered. Here are some examples of traffic types that the Cisco IOS NAT supports:

- Any TCP/UDP traffic that does not carry source and/or destination IP addresses in the data portion of an IP packet
- HTTP
- TFTP
- Telnet
- Archie
- Finger
- NTP
- NFS
- rlogin, rsh

Although the following traffic types carry IP addresses in the data portion of an IP packet, Cisco IOS NAT provides ALG functions.

- ICMP
- FTP (including PORT and PASV commands)
- NetBIOS over TCP/IP
- RealAudio
- CuSeeMe
- Streamworks
- DNS name-lookup queries and reverse name-lookup queries

Continued

- H.323/NetMeeting (IOS 12.0(1)/12.0(1)T or later)
- VDOLive (IOS 11.3(4), 11.3(4)T or later)
- Vxtreme (IOS 11.3(4), 11.3(4)T or later)
- IP Multicast (IOS 12.0(1)T source address translation only)

The following traffic types are not currently support by Cisco IOS NAT.

- Routing table updates
- DNS zone transfers
- BOOTP
- Talk, ntalk
- SNMP
- NetShow

Configuring NAT on Cisco IOS

Cisco's implementation of NAT functionality on a router is fundamentally the same as the implementation of NAT on a PIX Firewall. Performance-wise, the NAT session limit on a router depends on the amount of DRAM available on the router. Each NAT translation consumes approximately 160 bytes of DRAM. As a result, 10,000 translations would consume about 1.6MB; this should not impose a burden on a typical router. NAPT (Network Address Port Translation) as described previously is handled differently. The translations occur with one global IP address. The translation table maintains each translation by assigning a unique port number to each translation. Since the port numbers are encoded in 16 bits, there are theoretically 65,536 possible values.

The following section will outline the commands necessary to implement and verify NAT operation on a Cisco router. The commands necessary to configure NAT on the Cisco PIX Firewall differ from the ones used in the IOS. These commands will be covered in detail in Chapter 4, "Cisco PIX Firewall."

Configuration Commands

Let us now cover the commands necessary to implement NAT on a Cisco router. You will find the configuration commands necessary to implement NAT on a Cisco Secure PIX Firewall will be covered in the next chapter.

Before NAT can be implemented, the inside and outside networks must be defined. To define the inside and outside networks, use the **ip nat** command:

```
ip nat inside | outside
```

inside indicates that the interface is connected to the inside network (the network subject to NAT translation), and **outside** indicates that the interface is connected to the outside network.

Mark the interface as being on the inside or outside realms with the following:

```
interface ethernet0
ip nat inside
```

Enter interface configuration mode and designate **ethernet0** as the inside network interface.

```
interface serial1
ip nat outside
```

Enter interface configuration mode and designate **serial0** as the outside network interface.

Once the inside and outside network interfaces have been defined, an access list must be created to define the traffic that will be translated. This will define only the traffic to be translated and will not control any NAT functions by itself. To create an access list, use the **access-list** command:

access-list access-list-number **permit** | **deny** source [source-wildcard]

To further explain:

Access-list-number is the number of an access list. This is a decimal number from 1 to 99.

Deny denies access if the conditions are matched.

Permit permits access if the conditions are matched.

Source is the number of the network or host from which the packet is being sent. Use the keyword *any* as an abbreviation for *source* 0.0.0.0 and *source-wildcard* 255.255.255.255.

Source-wildcard (optional) are wildcard bits to be applied to the *source*. Use the keyword **any** as an abbreviation for *source* 0.0.0.0 and *source-wildcard* 255.255.255.255.

```
access-list 10 permit ip 192.168.1.0 0.0.0.255 any
```

This specifies that traffic originating from the 192.168.1.0 subnet destined to any other network should be translated. By itself, the access list will not translate the specified traffic.

A pool of IP addresses must be defined for dynamic NAT translations. To do this, use the **ip nat** command:

```
ip nat pool name start-ip end-ip {netmask netmask | prefix-length
 prefix-length}
    [type rotary]
```

To further explain:

Name is the name of the pool.

Start-ip is the starting IP address for range of addresses in the address pool.

End-ip is the ending IP address for range of addresses in the address pool.

Netmask *netmask* specifies the netmask of the network to which the pool addresses belong.

Prefix-length *prefix-length* is the number that indicates how many bits of the netmask are ones.

Type-rotary (optional) indicates that the range of addresses in the address pool identify real, inside hosts among which TCP load distribution will occur.

Define a pool of global addresses to be allocated as needed.

```
ip nat pool net-208 207.139.221.10 207.139.221.128 netmask >255.255.255.0
```

This specifies a pool of global IP addresses with the name **net-208**, which will contain the range of IP addresses 207.139.221.10–207.139.221.128.

To enable NAT of the inside destination address, the ip nat inside destination command will be used:

```
ip nat inside destination list {access-list-number | name} pool name
```

To further explain:

List *access-list-number* is the standard IP access list number. Packets with destination addresses that pass the access list are translated using global addresses from the named pool.

List *name* is the name of a standard IP access list.

pool *name* is the name of the pool from which global IP addresses are allocated during dynamic translation.

```
ip nat pool net-208 207.139.221.10 207.139.221.128 netmask >255.255.255.0
```

This defines a pool of global IP addresses called **net-208** with the IP addresses *207.139.221.10–207.139.221.128*.

```
access-list 10 permit any 204.71.201.0 0.0.0.255
```

This specifies that traffic destined for the network 204.71.201.0 will be translated to global addresses defined in the pool **net-207**.

```
ip nat inside destinationn list 10 pool net-207
```

This enables NAT for traffic defined in access list 10 to be translated to addresses from the **net-207** pool. This will translate the destination address and not the source.

To enable NAT of the inside source address, use the **ip nat inside source** command:

```
ip nat inside source {list {access-list-number | name} pool name
 [overload] | static local-ip global-ip
```

To further explain:

List *access-list number* is the standard IP access list number. Packets with source addresses that pass the access list are dynamically translated using global addresses from the named pool.

List *name* is the name of the standard IP access list.

Pool *name* is the name of the pool from which global IP addresses are allocated dynamically.

Overload (optional) enables the router to use one global address for many local addresses (NAPT).

Static *local-ip* sets up a single static translation.

Global-ip sets up a single static translation. This argument establishes the globally unique IP address to which an inside host will be translated.

Establish dynamic source translation, using an access list to define the traffic to be translated based on source address.

```
ip nat pool net-207 207.139.221.10 207.139.221.128 netmask >255.255.255.0
```

Define a pool of IP addresses with the name **net-207** and a range of IP addresses from *207.139.221.10-207.139.221.128*.

```
access-list 10 permit ip 192.168.1.0 0.0.0.255 any
```

Specify that traffic originating from the *192.168.1.0* network destined anywhere will be translated.

```
ip nat inside source list 10 pool net-207
```

Enable dynamic NAT for traffic defined in access list 10 to be translated to addresses from *net-207* pool. This will translate the source address and not the destination address. To enable static NAT translation for the inside host 192.168.1.10 to the global IP address 207.139.221.10 use the following command:

```
ip nat inside source static 192.168.1.10 207.139.221.10
```

To enable NAPT in conjunction with or instead of NAT, use the following:

```
ip nat pool net-207 207.139.221.10 netmask 255.255.255.0
```

Define a single global IP addresses with the name *net-207* and an IP addresses of *207.139.221.10*.

```
access-list 10 permit ip 192.168.1.0 0.0.0.255
```

Specify that traffic originating from the *192.168.1.0* network destined anywhere will be translated.

```
ip nat inside source list 10 pool net-207 overload
```

Enable NAPT for traffic defined in access list 10 to be translated to the address defined in **net-207** pool. This will translate the source address.

To enable NAT of the outside source address, use the **ip nat outside source** command:

```
ip nat outside source {list {access-list-number | name} pool name |
 static global-ip local-ip}
```

In this case:

List *access-list-number* is the standard IP access list number. Packets with source addresses that pass the access list are translated using the global addresses from the named pool.

List *name* is the name of a standard IP access list.

Pool *name* is the name of the pool from which global IP addresses are allocated.

Static *global-ip* sets up a single static translation. This argument establishes the globally unique IP address assigned to an outside host.

Local-ip sets up a single static translation. This argument establishes the local IP address of an outside host as it appears to the inside world.

```
ip nat translation {timeout | udp-timeout | dns-timeout | tcp-timeout |
  finrst-timeout} seconds
```

To further clarify:

Timeout specifies that the timeout value applies to dynamic translations except for overload translations. Default is 86400 seconds (24 hours).

Udp-timeout specifies that the timeout value applies to the UDP port. Default is 300 seconds (5 minutes).

Dns-timeout specifies that the timeout value applies to connections to the Domain Name System. Default is 60 seconds.

Tcp-timeout specifies that the timeout value applies to the TCP port. Default is 86400 seconds (24 hours).

Finrst-timeout specifies that the timeout value applies to Finish and Reset TCP packets, which terminate a connection. Default is 60 seconds.

Seconds is the number of seconds the specified port translation times out.

```
ip translation timeout 300
```

This example specifies that translations will timeout after 300 seconds (5 minutes) of inactivity.

```
ip nat translation timeout 600
```

This specifies that NAT translations will timeout after 600 seconds (10 minutes) of inactivity.

Verification Commands

The following are commands used to verify the operation of NAT on a Cisco router:

show ip nat statistics, which displays NAT statistics.

show ip nat translations [verbose], which displays NAT translations, where **verbose** optionally displays additional information for each translation table entry, including how long ago the entry was created and used.

The following is a sample output from the **show ip nat statistics**. Table 3.2 outlines the significant fields in the sample output.

```
Router#show ip nat statistics
Total translations: 2 (0 static, 2 dynamic; 0 extended)
Outside interfaces: Serial0
Inside interfaces: Ethernet1
```

```
Hits: 135   Misses: 5

Expired translations: 2

Dynamic mappings:

- Inside Source

access-list 1 pool net-208 refcount 2

  pool net-208: netmask 255.255.255.240

          start 171.69.233.208 end 171.69.233.221

          type generic, total addresses 14, allocated 2 (14%), misses 0
```

Table 3.2 Explanation of the Significant Fields from the *show ip nat statistics* sample output

Field	Description
Total translations	Number of translations active in the system. This number is incremented each time a translation is created and is decremented each time a translation is cleared or timed out.
Outside interfaces	List of interfaces marked as outside with the **ip nat outside** command.
Inside interfaces	List of interfaces marked as inside with the **ip nat inside** command.
Hits	Number of times the software does a translations table lookup and finds an entry.
Misses	Number of times the software does a translation table lookup, files to find an entry, and must try to create one.
Expired translations	Cumulative count of translations that have expired since the router was booted.

Configuring NAT between a Private Network and Internet

Let us now take an example. Company XYZ management has decided to allow employees access to the Internet. A leased line to their ISP has been purchased and installed, a Cisco router has been purchased to route the company's internal traffic to their ISP. The ISP has assigned a range of 128 global IP addresses (207.139.221.0/25) to the company to use as they see fit. Administrators have used a private 192.168.1.0/24 subnet for their internal hosts. Figure 3.7 illustrates the design.

Figure 3.7 NAT and Internet Design for Company XYZ.

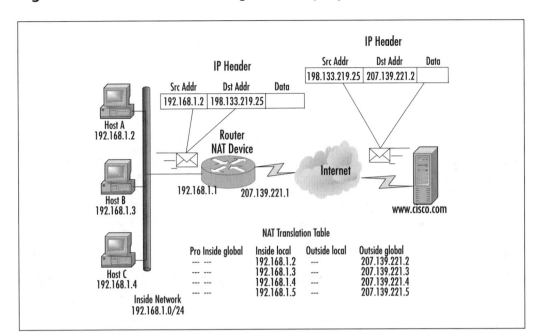

Here are the steps to follow for the configuration example, with explanations for clarification as you go through the commands:

```
configure terminal
interface ethernet0
ip address 192.168.1.1 255.255.255.0
```

This assigns an IP address to ethernet0 interface.

```
ip nat inside
```

This designates **ethernet0 interface** as an inside network.

```
no shutdown
```

This serves to remove the **interface** from shutdown status:

```
interface serial0
ip address 207.139.221.1 255.255.255.128
Assign IP address to serial0 interface.ip nat outside
```

This designates **serial0 interface** as an outside network.

```
no shutdown
```

This removes the **interface** from shutdown status.

```
exit
access-list 10 permit ip 192.168.1.0 0.0.0.255
```

This specifies that traffic originating from 192.168.1.0 network will be translated.

```
ip nat pool net-207 207.139.221.2 207.139.221.126 netmask 255.255.255.128
```

This defines a pool of global IP addresses named **net-207** with an address range of 207.139.221.2-207.139.221.126 to be used for NAT.

```
ip nat pool net-207-napt 207.139.221.127 netmask 255.255.255.128
```

This defines a single global IP address named **net-207-napt** with the address 207.139.221.127 to be used for NAPT.

```
ip nat inside source list 10 pool net-207
```

This specifies that the source IP address of traffic defined in access list 10 will be NAT'd with the IP addresses defined in **net-207** pool.

```
ip nat inside source list 10 pool net-207-napt overload
```

Lastly, this specifies that the source IP address of traffic defined in access list 10 will be NAPTed with the IP address defined in **net-207-napt** pool. NAPT will occur once NAT has used all available addresses in **net-207** pool. Once a translation has timed out due to inactivity, that global IP address will be reused for future NAT translations.

Configuring NAT in a Network with DMZ

Company XYZ has decided to host a Web server and e-mail server on their LAN. They would like to make these servers publicly available yet provide full security for them. It has been decided that a demilitarized zone (DMZ) will be created to keep the servers separated from the company's local LAN. The Cisco router currently used has an additional Ethernet port that will be designated as the DMZ. The DMZ subnet will use the private IP address space of 192.168.2.0/24. The Web server and e-mail server will be statically translated into two global IP addresses currently used in the NAT global pool. Figure 3.8 illustrates the new scenario.

Figure 3.8 NAT with DMZ.

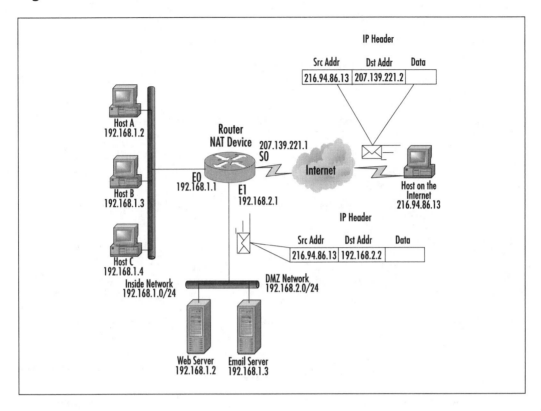

Here are the steps to follow in walking through the configuration example, with explanations for clarification after each step as you go through the commands:

```
configure terminal
interface ethernet0
ip address 192.168.1.1 255.255.255.0
```

This assigns the IP address to ethernet0 interface.

```
ip nat inside
```

This designates ethernet0 interface as an inside network.

```
no shutdown
```

This removes the **interface** from shutdown status.

```
interface serial0
ip address 207.139.221.1 255.255.255.128
```

This assigns the IP address to **serial0 interface**.

```
ip nat outside
```

This designates the **serial0 interface** as an outside network.

```
no shutdown
```

As in the previous example, this removes the interface from shutdown status.

```
interface ethernet1
ip address 192.168.2.1 255.255.255.0
```

This assigns the IP address to **ethernet1 interface**.

```
ip nat inside
```

This designates **ethernet1 interface** as an inside network.

```
no shutdown
```

This removes the interface from shutdown status.

```
access-list 10 permit ip 192.168.1.0 0.0.0.255
```

This specifies that traffic originating from 192.168.1.0 network will be translated.

```
ip nat pool net-207 207.139.221.4 207.139.221.126 netmask 255.255.255.128
```

This defines a pool of global IP addresses named **net-207** with an address range of 207.139.221.4-207.139.221.126 to be used for NAT.

```
ip nat pool net-207-napt 207.139.221.127 netmask 255.255.255.128
```

This defines a single global IP address named **net-207-napt** with address 207.139.221.127 to be used for NAPT.

```
ip nat inside source list 10 pool net-207
```

This specifies that the source IP address of traffic defined in access list 10 will be NAT'd with the IP addresses defined in **net-207** pool.

```
ip nat inside source list 10 pool net-207-napt overload
```

This specifies that the source IP address of traffic defined in access list 10 will be NAPTed with the IP address defined in **net-207-napt** pool. NAPT will occur once NAT has used all available addresses in **net-207** pool. Once a translation has timed out due to inactivity, that global IP address will be reused for future NAT translations.

```
ip nat inside source static 192.168.2.2 207.139.221.2 netmask
 >255.255.255.128
```

Create a static translation for inside IP address 192.168.2.2 to global IP address 207.139.221.2. Any traffic destined for 207.139.221.2 will be statically translated to 192.168.2.2.

```
ip nat inside source static 192.168.2.3 207.139.221.3 netmask
 >255.255.255.128
```

Considerations on NAT and NAPT

Even though NAT helps to avoid the problem of scarce availability of globally routable IP addresses, NAT has an impact on the functionality of certain protocols, therefore complicating their deployment. This section will outline some of the problems that are associated with NAT.

IP Address Information in Data

Numerous applications fail when packets traverse a NAT device. These packets carry IP address or port information in the data portion of the packet. Since NAT only alters the IP header to perform the translation, the data portion is left untouched. With the aid of an ALG, a work-around may be provided in some cases. But if the packet data is IPSec secured (or secured by another transport or application level mechanism), the application is going to fail.

Bundled Session Applications

Bundled session applications such as FTP, H.323, SIP, and RTSP, which use a control connection to establish data flow are also usually broken by NAT devices. This occurs because the applications exchange address and port information within control session to establish data sessions and session orientations. NAT cannot know the interdependency of the bundled sessions and would treat each session as if they were unrelated to each other. Applications like these can fail for a variety of reasons. Two of the most common reasons for failures are as follows:

- Addressing information in the data portion of the packet is realm specific and is not valid once the packet crosses the originating realm

- Control sessions create new data sessions about which NAT has no information. These will fail in many cases.

Peer-to-Peer Applications

Peer-to-peer applications are more prone to failure than client/server-based applications. Peer-to-peer applications can be originated by any of the peers; if the peers are located in different realms, NAT translations may not be established because the host on the inside network is not visible to the host on the outside network. This is more problematic with traditional NAT (dynamic NAT and NAPT) where connections are client to server.

IP Fragmentation with NAPT En Route

IP fragmentation with NAPT can occur when two hosts originate fragmented TCP/UDP packets to the same destination host, and they happen to use the same fragmentation identifier. When the target host receives the two unrelated packets, carrying the same fragmentation id, and from the same assigned host address, the target host is unable to distinguish which of the two sessions the packets belong to (due to the translation of the local source address, to that used in the global NAPT address); therefore, both sessions will be corrupted.

Applications Requiring Retention of Address Mapping

When a session is established across realms through the use of NAT, the translation for that session will eventually time out and then be utilized by another session's traversing realms. This can be a problem for applications that require numerous sessions to the same external address. NAT cannot know this requirement ahead of time and may reassign the global address between sessions. For example, if Host A on the inside network has established a session with Host Z on the outside network, the application will function properly. Once the session stops sending traffic and the NAT timer expires, the translation will be terminated and the global IP allocated for that specific translation will be used for another translation. What happens if Host Z requires more data and tries to initiate a session with the IP address that Host A had while it was translated? At this point, the application will no longer function properly.

To remedy this problem, keepalive messages need to be sent between hosts to keep the translation active. This can be especially annoying and may not be possible in some situations. An alternative is to use an ALG to keep the address mapping from being discarded by NAT.

IPSec and IKE

NAT operates by modifying source addresses within the IP header while it passes through the NAT device. Due to the nature of IPSec, the AH protocol is designed to detect alterations to an IP packet header. So when NAT alters the source address information, the destination host receiving the altered packet will discard the packet since the IP headers have been altered. The IPSec AH secure packet traversing NAT will simply not reach the target application.

IPSec ESP encrypted packets may be altered by NAT devices only in a limited number of cases. In the cases of TCP/UDP packets, NAT would need to update the checksum in the TCP/UDP headers whenever the IP header is changed. However, because the TCP/UDP header is encrypted by the ESP, NAT would not be able to make this checksum update because it is now encrypted. TCP/UDP packets that are encrypted and traverse a NAT device will fail because the TCP/UDP checksum validation is on the receiving end and will not reach the target application.

Internet Key Exchange (IKE) protocol can potentially pass IP addresses as node identifiers during the Main, Aggressive, and Quick Modes. In order for an IKE negotiation to correctly pass through NAT, these data portions would need to be modified. However, these payloads are often protected by encryption. For all practical purposes, end-to-end IPSec is almost impossible to accomplish with NAT translation en route.

Summary

NAT solves the problem of the limited available supply of global IP addresses. By implementing a private IP address scheme in a private network, those addresses can then be translated into global IP addresses via a NAT device. This chapter covered various generic terms used by NAT, variations of NAT, deploying NAT on a network, and considerations for using NAT. As I stated at the beginning of the chapter, NAT is not a security feature and should not be used for security. It simply allows private IP addresses to be translated into global IP addresses. The myth that NAT "hides" a network is exactly that, a myth. A company's ISP may have knowledge of that private network and can therefore inject a route to that network in their routing tables, therefore exposing the private network.

FAQs

Q: Should I use NAT or NAPT?

A: It is a good idea to implement both, depending on how many global addresses are available and how many local hosts need to be translated. If a NAT pool is implemented, NAPT can then be used once all of the NAT translations are used up. Once a translation times out, it will be reallocated to another local host trying to open a session with a host on the outside.

Q: How do I know if NAT should be used on my network?

A: Typically, NAT must be used if your network is using a private IP address space and traffic must be routed globally (Internet). Another instance when NAT would be used is when two companies merge two LANs that use an overlapping IP subnet.

Q: I have implemented NAT on my network; at different points in time, hosts are no longer being translated. Why is this happening?

A: Check the number of global addresses in your global pool. The number of hosts requiring translation may be outnumbering the available addresses. If this is the case, remove one of the addresses from the NAT pool and assign that address for NAPT.

Q: RFC1918? RFC2663? What are these?

A: RFC is short for Request for Comments. RFCs are standards that are published on various topics. For a listing of RFCs, visit www.rfc.net or www.normos.org (official mirror site for internet drafts and RFCs).

Chapter 4

Cisco PIX Firewall

Solutions in this chapter:

- Overview of the Security Features

- Initial Configuration

- Configuring NAT and NAPT

- Security Policy Configuration

- PIX Configuration Examples

- Securing and Maintaining the PIX

Introduction

A firewall is a security mechanism located on a network that protects resources from other networks and individuals. A firewall controls access to a network and enforces a security policy that can be tailored to suit the needs of a company.

There is some confusion on the difference between a Cisco PIX firewall and a router. Both devices are capable of filtering traffic with access control lists, and both devices are capable of providing Network Address Translation (NAT). PIX, however, goes above and beyond simply filtering packets, based on source/destination IP addresses, as well as source/destination TCP/UDP port numbers. PIX is a dedicated hardware device built to provide security. Although a router can also provide some of the functions of a PIX by implementing access control lists, it also has to deal with routing packets from one network to another. Depending on what model of router is being used, access lists tend to burden the CPU, especially if there are numerous access lists that must be referenced for every packet that travels through the router. This can impact the performance of the router, causing other problems such as network convergence time.

Cisco Systems offers a number of security solutions for networks, including Cisco Secure PIX Firewall series. The PIX firewall is a dedicated hardware-based firewall that utilizes a version of the Cisco IOS for configuration and operation. This chapter will introduce and discuss security features, Network Address Translation (NAT), Network Address Port Translation (NAPT, or referred to as PAT in the PIX firewall IOS), developing a security policy for your network, applying the security policy on the PIX, and finally, maintaining your PIX and securing it from unauthorized individuals.

The PIX Firewall series offers several models to meet today's networks' needs, from the Enterprise-class Secure PIX 520 Firewall to the newly introduced Small Office/Home Office (SOHO) class Secure PIX 506 Firewall model.

520 and 520 DC The largest of the PIX Firewall series, it is meant for Enterprise and Internet Service Provider (ISP) use. It has a throughput of 385 Mbps and will handle up to 250,000 simultaneous sessions. The hardware specifications include two Fast Ethernet ports, 128MB of RAM, a floppy disk drive for upgrading the IOS image, and support for up to six additional network interface cards in the chassis. Additionally, other available interfaces are 10/100 Ethernet cards, Token Ring cards, and dual-attached multimode FDDI cards.

515R and 515UR This particular model is intended for small- to medium-sized businesses and remote offices. The 515R and 515UR have a throughput of 120 Mbps with the capacity to handle up to 125,000 simultaneous connections. The hardware specifications include two Fast Ethernet 10/100 ports, 32MB of RAM for the 515R and 64MB of RAM for the 515UR model, and will support up to two additional network interface cards in the chassis. Additionally, 10/100 Ethernet cards are available, but Token Ring cards are not supported on the 515 model.

506 The most recent addition to the Secure PIX Firewall series is the 506, intended for high-end small office/home office use, with a throughput measured at 10 Mbps. The 506 offers two Fast Ethernet 10/100 ports, and does not support any additional network interface cards in the chassis. The 506 comes with 32MB of RAM and does not support additional RAM upgrades.

Overview of the Security Features

With the enormous growth of the Internet, companies are beginning to depend on having an online presence on the Internet. With that presence come security risks that allow outside individuals to gain access to critical information and resources.

Companies are now faced with the task of implementing security measures to protect their data and resources. These resources can be very diversified, such as Web servers, mail servers, FTP servers, databases, or any type of networked devices. Figure 4.1 displays a typical company network with access to the Internet via a leased line without a firewall in place.

As you can see in Figure 4.1, company XYZ has a direct connection to the Internet. They are also using a class C public IP address space for their network, therefore making it publicly available to anyone who wishes to access it. Without any security measures, individuals are able to access each of the devices on the network with a public IP. Private information can be compromised, and other malicious attacks such as Denial of Service (DoS) can occur. If a firewall was placed between company XYZ's network and the Internet, security measures can then be taken to filter and block unwanted traffic. Without any access control at the network perimeter, a company's security relies on proper configuration and security on each individual host and server. This can be an administrative nightmare if hundreds of devices need to be configured for this purpose.

Figure 4.1 Typical LAN with no firewall.

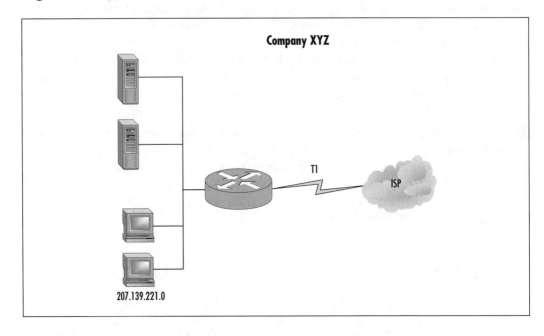

Routers have the ability to filter traffic based on source address, destination address, and TCP/UDP ports. Using that ability as well as a firewall can provide a more complete security solution for a network.

Another example of how a PIX firewall can secure a network is in a company's intranet. Figure 4.2 illustrates a network in which departments are separated by two different subnets. What is stopping an individual from the Human Resources network from accessing resources on the Finance network? A firewall can be put in place between the two subnets to secure the Finance network from any unauthorized access or to restrict access to certain hosts.

Since the PIX is designed as a security appliance, it provides a wealth of features to secure a network. These features include:

- **Packet Filtering** A method for limiting inbound information from the Internet. Packet filters use access control lists (ACL) similar to those used in routers to accept or deny access based on packet source address, destination address, and TCP/UDP source and destination port.

- **Proxy Server** A device that examines higher layers of the Open Systems Interconnection (OSI) model. This will act as an intermediary between the source and destination by creating a separate connection to each. Optionally, authentication can be achieved by requiring users to authenticate with a secure system by means of a proxy such as a Cisco IOS Firewall Authentication Proxy Server. Some of the drawbacks for this method of security are that it provides authentication at the cost of performance, and that a proxy supports only a limited number of protocols.

Figure 4.2 LAN segmented by a department with no firewall.

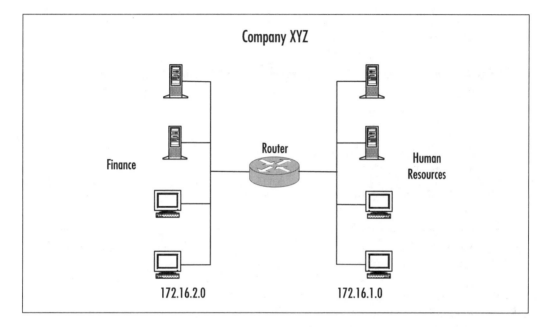

- **Stateful Filtering** A secure method of analyzing packets and placing extensive information about that packet in a table. Each time a TCP connection is established from an inside host accessing an outside host through the PIX firewall, the information about the connection automatically is logged in a stateful session flow table. The table contains the source and destination addresses, port numbers, TCP sequencing information, and additional flags for each TCP connection associated with that particular host. Inbound packets are compared against the session flows in the table and are permitted through the PIX only if an appropriate connection exists to validate their passage. Without stateful filtering, access lists would have to be configured to allow traffic originating from the inside network to return from the outside network.

- **Network Address Translation and Network Address Port Translation** Using NAT is often mistaken as a security measure. Translating private IP addresses into global IP addresses was implemented to assist in the problem of rapidly depleting public IP addresses. Even though private IP addresses are used for an inside network, an ISP is still directly connected. It is not unheard of that a sloppy routing configuration on behalf of the ISP will leak a route to your network, to other clients. NAT will hide your network, but it should not be relied upon as a security measure.

- **IPSec** IPSec provides VPN (Virtual Private Network) access via digital certificates or preshared keys.

- **Flood Defender Flood Guard, and IP Frag Guard** These protect a network from TCP SYN flood attacks, controlling the AAA service's tolerance for unanswered login attempts and IP fragmentation attacks.

- **DNS Guard** This identifies an outbound DNS resolve request, and allows only a single DNS response.

- **FTP and URL Logging** These allow you to view inbound and outbound FTP commands entered by users, as well as the URLs they use to access other sites.

- **Mail Guard** This provides safe access for SMTP (Simple Mail Transfer Protocol) connections from the outside to an inside e-mail server.

- **ActiveX Blocking** This blocks HTML object commands and comments them out of the HTML Web page.

- **Java Filtering** This allows an administrator to prevent Java applets from being downloaded by a host on the inside network.

- **URL Filtering** When used with NetPartners WebSENSE product, PIX checks outgoing URL requests with policy defined on the WebSENSE server, which runs on either Windows NT/2000 or UNIX.

- **AAA** AAA provides authentication, authorization, and accounting with the aid of an AAA server such as a RADIUS or TACACS+ server.

Differences Between IOS 4.x and 5.x

The following new features are available in the recent release of the PIX IOS:

- Cisco IOS access lists
- IPSec
- Stateful failover
- Voice-over IP support

Cisco IOS access lists can now be specified in support of the IPSec feature. In addition, access lists can now be used to specify the type of traffic permitted through the PIX in conjunction with the **access-group** command. IOS 4.x used **conduit** and **outbound** statements to limit the type of traffic permitted through the interface. For example, the following command set can be rewritten using **access-list** and **access-group** statements.

```
pixfirewall(config)#write terminal
static (inside,outside) 207.139.221.10 192.168.0.10 netmask
>255.255.255.255
```

This creates a static translation for private 192.168.0.10 to globally unique IP 207.139.221.10.

```
conduit permit tcp any host 207.139.221.10 eq www
```

This specifies that only HTTP traffic will be permitted to reach host 207.139.221.10.

```
outbound 10 permit any any 80 tcp
outbound 10 permit any any 23 tcp
outbound 10 deny any any any tcp
outbound 10 deny any any any udp
```

This specifies that HTTP and Telnet traffic will be permitted from a higher level security interface to a lower level security interface (inside, outside), followed by an explicit deny all statement.

```
apply (inside) 10 outgoing_src
```

This command applies outbound list 10 to inside interface. This configuration can be rewritten using **access-list** and **access-group** commands available in 5.x IOS.

```
pixfirewall(config)#write terminal
static (inside,outside) 207.139.221.10 192.168.0.10 netmask
>255.255.255.255
```

This creates a static translation for private 192.168.0.10 to globally unique IP 207.139.221.10.

```
access-list acl_out permit tcp any any eq www
access-list acl_out permit tcp any any eq telnet
access-list acl_out deny tcp any any
access-list acl_out deny udp any any
```

This specifies that HTTP and Telnet traffic will be permitted, followed by an explicit deny all statement.

```
access-list acl_in permit tcp any host 207.139.221.10 eq www
access-list acl_in permit tcp any host 207.139.221.10 eq ftp
```

This specifies that HTTP and FTP traffic will be permitted from any source to host 207.139.221.10.

```
access-group acl_out in interface inside
```

This applies access list acl_out to the inside interface.

```
access-group acl_in in interface outside
```

This applies access list acl_in to the outside interface.

Using the **access-list** and **access-group** commands instead of the **outbound** and **conduit** statements provides a common operating environment across various platforms. If an individual is able to implement access lists on a router, then implementing access lists on a PIX should be no different.

The IPSec feature is based on the Cisco IOS IPSec implementation and provides functionality with those IPSec-compliant devices. IPSec provides a mechanism for secure data transmission by providing confidentiality, integrity, and authenticity of data across a public IP network. Refer to the chapter on VPN for more information on IPSec.

The stateful failover feature provides a mechanism for hardware and software redundancy by allowing two identical PIX units to serve the same functionality in case one fails in an unattended environment. One PIX is considered an active unit, and the other is in standby mode. In the event that the active unit fails, the standby unit becomes active, therefore providing redundancy.

PIX provides support for Voice-over IP in its H.323 RAS feature; however, Cisco CallManager is not supported. For more information on Voice-over IP, please refer to Cisco's Web site (www.cisco.com).

Other new commands that were introduced in the 5.x IOS are as follows:

- **ca** provides access to the IPSec certification authority feature.

- **Clear flashfs** clears Flash memory. Use before downgrading to any version 4.x release.

- **Crypto-map** provides IPSec cryptography mapping.

- **Debug crypto ca** debugs certification authority (CA) processing.

- **Debug crypto ipsec** debugs IPSec processing.

- **Debug crypto isakmp** debugs ISAKMP processing.

- **Domain-name** changes the domain name.

- **Failover link** enables stateful failover support.

- **Ipsec** is shortened for the **cyrpto ipsec** command.

- **Isakmp** lets you create an IKE security association.

- **Sysopt connection permit-ipsec** specifies that the PIX implicitly permit IPSec traffic and bypass the checking of the conduit or access-group commands that are associated with IPSec connections.

Initial Configuration

The initial configuration of the Secure PIX Firewall greatly resembles that of a router. A console cable kit consisting of a rollover cable and DB9/DB25 serial adapter is needed to configure the device out of the box. It is recommended that the initial configuration not take place on a live network until the initial set up has been completed and tested. Initial configuration should take place in a test bed environment, which is isolated from any production network. If initial configuration takes place on a production network and an incorrect IP address is assigned to an interface on the PIX, and is already in use on the network, IP address conflicts will occur. It is generally a bad idea to set up a firewall or other security device on a non-isolated network. The default configuration is often not secure and can be compromised between the set-up stage and the security-policy stage. Installing the PIX consists of removing the unit from the packaging, installing any optional hardware such as an additional NIC, mounting the PIX in a rack (optional), and connecting all the necessary cables such as power and network cables. Once the hardware portion of the PIX setup has been completed the software portion of the setup can begin.

Before configuring the software, be sure to have a design plan already in place. Items such as IP addresses, security policies, and placement of the PIX should already be mapped out. With a proper design strategy the basic configuration will have to be done only once to make the PIX functional.

Installing the PIX Software

In this section we will discuss the initial software configuration of the PIX to allow traffic to pass through it. Other features such as configuring NAT, NAPT, and Security Policies will be covered later in this chapter.

When the PIX is first powered on, the software configuration stored in Flash memory permits the PIX to start up, but will not allow any traffic to pass through it until configured to do so. Newer versions of the IOS may be available from Cisco depending on what version shipped with the PIX, so it may be a good idea to complete the basic configuration to establish connectivity and then upgrade the version of the IOS.

Basic Configuration

We will now detail the basic configuration of the PIX, how to connect to it, as well as how to identify each interface.

Connect to the PIX

To upgrade the IOS or to begin allowing traffic to pass through the PIX, some basic configuration is needed to make the PIX operational.

1. Connect the serial port of your PC to the console port on the PIX firewall with the serial cable supplied with the PIX.

2. Using a Terminal Emulation program such as HyperTerminal, connect to the COM port on the PC.

NOTE

Make sure the COM port properties in the terminal emulation program match the following values:
- 9600 baud
- 8 data bits
- No parity
- 1 stop bit
- Hardware flow control

3. Turn on the PIX.

4. Once the PIX has finished booting up, you will be prompted as follows:

```
pixfirewall>
```

5. Type **enable** and press the Enter key. The follow prompt appears:

```
Password:
```

6. Press the Enter key again and you will now be in privileged mode, which is represented by the following prompt:

```
pixfirewall#
```

7. Set an enable password by going into configuration mode. A good, non-guessable password should be chosen. The example uses <password> to designate where your password should be typed.

```
pixfirewall#configure terminal
pixfirewall(config)#enable password <password>
```

8. Permit Telnet access to the console from the inside network:

```
pixfirewall(config)#telnet 0.0.0.0 0.0.0.0 inside
```

9. Set the Telnet console password. This password should be different from the enable password chosen in step 7.

```
pixfirewall(config)#passwd  <password>
```

10. Save your changes to NVRAM with the **write** command:

```
pixfirewall(config)#write memory
```

Note that the configuration used in the following examples are based on IOS version 5.1(1).

Identify Each Interface

On new installations with only two interfaces, PIX will provide names for each interface by default. These can be viewed with the **show nameif** command. The **show nameif** command output will resemble the following:

```
pixfirewall# show nameif
nameif ethernet0 outside security0
nameif ethernet1 inside security100
```

If additional NICs are going to be used, you must assign a unique name and security value to each additional interface.

The default behavior of the PIX includes blocking traffic originating from the *outside* interface destined for the *inside* interface. Traffic originating from the *inside* interface destined to the *outside* interface will be permitted until access lists are implemented to restrict traffic. The inside interface will be assigned a security value of 100 and the outside interface will be assigned a value of 0. These values are important when creating security policies in which traffic will flow from a lower security interface to higher security level interface. If additional interfaces are added to the PIX, it is important to properly plan which interfaces will be used for what purposes. For example, in a situation where three interfaces are used to separate an inside network, outside network, and DMZ (discussed later in this chapter), assign the DMZ interface a security value between the inside and outside interfaces, such as 50. This configuration will reflect the purpose of the DMZ, which is a network separated from the inside and outside networks, yet security can still be controlled with the PIX.

To assign a name to an interface use:

Nameif *hardware_id name security_level*

To further explain:

- *Hardware_id* is either **ethernet***n* for Ethernet or **token***x* for Token Ring interfaces, where *n* and *x* are the interface numbers.

- *Name* is the name to be assigned to the interface

- *Security_level* is a value such as **security40** or **security60**. You can use any security value between 1 and 99.

```
pixfirewall#configure terminal
pixfirewall(config)#nameif ethernet2 dmz1 security40
pixfurewall(config)#show nameif
pixfirewall(config)#nameif ethernet0 outside security0
pixfirewall(config)#nameif ethernet1 inside security100
pixfirewall(config)#nameif ethernet2 dmz1 security40
```

> **TIP**
>
> Be sure to use a naming convention that will easily describe the function of each interface. The dmz1 interface represents a "demilitarized zone," which is intended to be an area between the inside and outside networks. This is a common implementation for companies that host Web servers, mail servers, and other resources.

By default each interface is in a shutdown state and must be made active. Use the **interface** command to activate the interfaces:

```
Interface hardware_id hardware_speed [shutdown]
```

In this case:

- *Hardware_id* –is either **ethernet***n* for Ethernet or **token***x* for Token Ring interfaces.

- *Hardware_speed* is either **4mpbs** or **16mpbs** for Token Ring, depending on the line speed of the Token Ring card, or, if the interface is Ethernet, use **auto**.

- **Auto** activates auto-negotiation for the Ethernet 10/100 interface.

- **Shutdown** disables the interface. When the PIX is configured for the first time, all interfaces will be shutdown by default.

The following examples will enable the **ethernet0** interface into auto negotiation mode, and the Token Ring interface token into 16 Mbps mode.

```
pixfirewall(config)#interface ethernet0 auto
pixfirewall(config)#interface token0 16mpbs
```

Installing the IOS over TFTP

The following steps will guide you through upgrading the PIX IOS.

1. Download the latest version of the IOS from Cisco's Web site (www.cisco.com).

2. Download and install the TFTP server application, which can also be found on Cisco's Web site. The TFTP server is an application that is installed on a host computer to provide a TFTP service. This service is used by the PIX firewall to download or upload software images and configuration parameters.

3. Make sure the TFTP software is running on a server. Also confirm that the server is on the same subnet as one of the interfaces.

4. Once the connection to the PIX console port has been established, power on the PIX.

5. Immediately send a BREAK character by pressing the Escape (ESC) key. The monitor prompt will appear.

6. Use the **address** command to specify an IP address on the interface in the same network where the TFTP resides.

7. Use the **server** command to specify the IP address of the TFTP server.

8. Use the **file** command to specify the name of the file to download from the TFTP server.

9. If the TFTP server resides on a different subnet than that of the PIX interface, use the **gateway** command to specify the IP address of the default gateway in order to reach the TFTP server.

10. To test connectivity, use the **ping** command to ping the TFTP server.

11. Finally, use the **TFTP** command to start the TFTP download of the IOS.

Note that you need to download the TFTP server software if you are using a Windows NT/2000 machine as a server. A UNIX server has a TFTP server by default.

For example, assume that the TFTP server has been configured with the IP address 172.16.0.39, and that a new software image file *pix512.bin* is stored on that server. We can download this new image on the PIX as follows:

```
monitor>
monitor>address 172.16.0.1
monitor>server 172.16.0.39
monitor>file pix512.bin
monitor>ping 172.16.0.39
Sending 5, 100-byte 0x5b8d ICMP Echoes to 172.16.0.39, timeout is 4
seconds:
!!!!!
Success rate is 100 percent (5/5)
monitor>tftp
```

```
tftp pix512.bin@172.16.0.39..............................
Received 626688 bytes


PIX admin loader (3.0) #0: Mon July 10 10:43:02 PDT 2000
Flash=AT29C040A @ 0x300
Flash version 4.9.9.1, Install version 5.1.2


Installing to flash
```

The following commands are available in monitor mode:

- **Address** Set IP address.

- **File** Specify boot file name.

- **Gateway** Set gateway IP address.

- **Help** List available help commands and syntax.

- **Interface** Specify type of interface (Ethernet, Token Ring).

- **Ping** Test connectivity by issuing echo-requests to a specified IP address.

- **Reload** Halt and reload system.

- **Server** Specify server by the IP address in which the TFTP application is running.

- **Tftp** Initiate the TFTP download.

- **Trace** Toggle packet tracing.

Command Line Interface

The Command Line Interface (CLI) used on the PIX is very similar to the one used on routers. Three modes exist in order to perform configuration and troubleshooting steps: unprivileged, privileged, and configuration. When you first initiate a console or Telnet session to the PIX, you will be in unprivileged mode. Virtually no commands will be available in unprivileged mode; only the **enable, pager,** and **quit** commands are permitted. Once in privileged mode, commands such as **show, debug,** and **reload** are available. From privileged mode, configuration tasks may take place by entering the **configure** command followed by the location from which the PIX will accept configuration commands. For example, when you first connect to the PIX either through a Telnet or console session, you will be in unprivileged mode (unprivileged mode password must be entered when accessing the PIX by Telnet). Unprivileged mode is represented by the following prompt:

```
Pixfirewall>
```

To access privileged mode, you must type **enable** at the prompt. After providing the required authentication you will be in privileged mode. Privileged mode is represented by the following prompt:

```
Pixfurewall>enable
Password: ********
Pixfirewall#
```

If the system did not request a password after typing **enable**, it means that no enable password has been configured as described earlier in the section "Basic Configuration." It is very important that an enable password be configured.

Finally, to perform configuration tasks, you must be in configuration mode. This mode is represented by the following prompt:

```
Pixfurewall#configure terminal
Pixfirewall(config)#
```

Table 4.1 lists some of the shortcut key combinations that are available on the PIX CLI.

Table 4.1 Key Combination Shortcuts

Command	Result
TAB	Completes a command entry
Ctrl-A	Takes cursor to beginning of the line
Ctrl-E	Takes cursor to end of the line
Ctrl-R	Redisplays a line (useful if command gets interrupted by console output)
Arrow up or Ctrl-P	Displays previous line
Arrow up or Ctrl-N	Displays next line
Help or ?	Displays help

IP Configuration

Once the interfaces on the PIX have been named and assigned a security value (additional interfaces only), IP must be configured on the interfaces in order to allow traffic to pass through the PIX.

IP Address

Once the interfaces have been named and are activated, an IP address needs to be assigned to them. To assign an IP address to an interface, use the command:

ip address interface-name netmask

To further explain:

- *Interface-name* is the name assigned to the interface using the **nameif** command.
- *Netmask* is the network mask that will be assigned to the interface.

```
pixfirewall(config)#interface ethernet0 auto
pixfirewall(config)#interface ethernet1 auto
pixfirewall(config)#ip address inside 172.16.0.1 255.255.255.0
pixfirewall(config)#ip address outside 207.139.221.1 255.255.255.0
pixfirewall(config)#show interface ethernet1
interface ethernet1 "inside" is up, line protocol is up
   Hardware is i82559 ethernet, address is 0050.54ff.2aa9
   IP address 172.16.0.1, subnet mask 255.255.255.0
   MTU 1500 bytes, BW 100000 Kbit full duplex
         147022319 packets input, 3391299957 bytes, 0 no buffer
         Received 12580140 broadcasts, 0 runts, 0 giants
         0 input errors, 0 CRC, 0 frame, 0 overrun, 0 ignored, 0 abort
         166995559 packets output, 1686643683 bytes, 0 underruns
         0 output errors, 0 collisions, 0 interface resets
         0 babbles, 0 late collisions, 0 deferred
         0 lost carrier, 0 no carrier
```

Once the interfaces have been configured, test them to make sure they have been configured properly. A simple connectivity test is to ping another interface on your network or test lab environment. To do this, use the following:

Ping interface ip_address

In this case:

- *Interface* is the interface from which you want the ping to originate (similar to an extended ping on a router).

- *Ip_address* is the target IP address to ping.

```
pixfirewall#ping inside 172.16.0.2
        172.16.0.2 response received — 0ms
        172.16.0.2 response received — 0ms
        172.16.0.2 response received — 0ms
```

If no response is received, confirm that the network cables are connected to the interfaces and that the interfaces have been configured correctly.

```
pixfirewall#ping inside 172.16.0.4
        172.16.0.4 NO response received — 940ms
        172.16.0.4 NO response received — 900ms
        172.16.0.4 NO response received — 920ms
```

Default Route

Now that all the interfaces have been configured, a default gateway must be assigned. A typical implementation will have a PIX firewall positioned between the ISP and the company's network (see Figure 4.3).

A default gateway must be assigned to the outside interface to allow traffic to reach the ISP. To do this use the command:

route interface_name ip_address netmask gateway_ip [metric]

To further explain:

- *Interface_name* is the internal or external network interface name.

- *Ip_address* is the internal or external IP address. Use **0.0.0.0** to specify a default route. The **0.0.0.0** can be abbreviated as **0**.

- *Netmask* specifies a network mask to apply to *ip_address*. Use **0.0.0.0** to specify a default route. The **0.0.0.0** can be abbreviated as **0**.

- *Gateway_ip* is the IP address of the gateway router (next hop address for this route).

- *Metric* specifies the number of hops to *gateway_ip*.

```
pixfirewall>enable
pixfirewall#configure terminal
pixfirewall(config)#route outside 0 0 207.139.221.1
```

Figure 4.3 Default route.

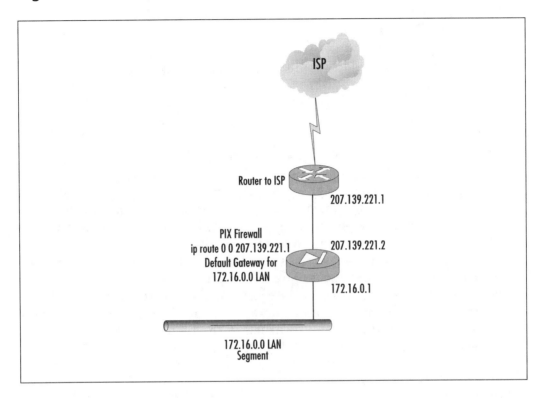

If different networks are present on the inside or outside interface, the PIX will need information about how to reach those networks. Since the PIX is not a router, it does not support the different routing protocols that a router does. Currently the PIX only supports RIP as its routing protocol. Since PIX is not a router, it is not recommended to use RIP; instead, add static routes to the PIX to make other networks reachable.

To add a static route:

```
pixfirewall>enable
pixfirewall#configure terminal
pixfirewall(config)#route inside 192.168.1.0 255.255.255.0 172.16.0.2 1
```

Configuring NAT and NAPT

Now that the interfaces have been named and security values have been assigned, and network connectivity has been established by configuring and testing the IP settings, NAT and PAT can be configured to allow traffic to pass through.

Permit Traffic Through

When an outbound packet arrives at a higher security level interface (inside), the PIX checks the validity of the packet based on the adaptive security algorithm, and then checks whether or not a previous packet has come from that host. If no packet has originated from that host, then the packet is for a new connection, and PIX will create a translation in its table for the connection.

The information that PIX stores in the translation table includes the inside IP address and a globally unique IP address assigned by the Network Address Translation or Network Address Port Translation. The PIX then changes the packet's source IP address to the global address, modifies the checksum and other fields as required, and then forwards the packet to the lower security interface (outside, or DMZ).

When an inbound packet arrives at a lower security level interface (outside, or DMZ), it must first pass the PIX Adaptive Security criteria. If the packet passes the security tests (static and Access Control Lists), the PIX removes the destination IP address, and the internal IP address is inserted in its place. The packet is then forwarded to the higher security level interface (inside). Figure 4.4 illustrates the NAT process on the PIX.

Figure 4.4 NAT example.

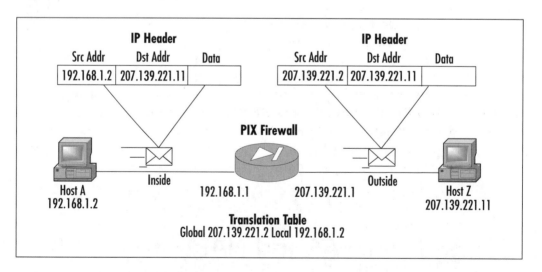

In the example, Host A initiates a session with Host Z. Since Host A is not on the same subnet as host Z, the packet must be routed. When the packet arrives at the inside interface of the PIX, it examines the source address. NAT has been enabled on the PIX, and a global pool of IP addresses has been allocated for translations. The PIX then modifies the IP header and alters the source address of the IP header to an IP address from the global pool of IP addresses. Once the translation occurs, the packet is then routed to Host Z. When Host Z replies to Host A, the PIX examines the packet that arrives on the outside interface. Since there is an active translation for Host A, the PIX knows that packets destined for IP address 207.139.221.2 must be translated back to 192.168.1.2. Once the PIX alters the IP header, it then routes the packet back to Host A. This process occurs until no more traffic needs to be translated between the two devices and the translation times out.

To allow traffic to flow from a higher level security interface to a lower level security interface (inside, outside), you must use the **nat** and **global** commands. To permit traffic from a lower level security interface to flow through a higher level security interface, you must use the **access-list** and **access-group** command.

Network Address Translation (NAT) is a feature that dynamically maps IP addresses originating from the higher security level interface into IP addresses on the same subnet as the lower level security interface (for more information on NAT and NAPT, refer to Chapter 3, "NAT and NAPT").

To enable NAT on an interface use the command:

```
nat [(interface_name)] nat_id local_ip [netmask [max_conns [em_limit]]]
  [norandomseq]
```

To further explain:

- *Interface_name* is the internal network interface name.

- *Nat_id* is used in the **global** command statement. All **nat** commands with the same *nat_id* are in the same **nat** group.

- *Local_ip* is the internal network IP address to be translated. You can use **0.0.0.0** to allow all hosts to start an outbound connection originating from the inside interface. The **0.0.0.0** IP can be abbreviated as **0**.

- *Netmask* is the network mask for *local_ip*. You can also use the **0.0.0.0** to allow all outbound connections originating from the inside interface.

- *Max_cons* is the maximum TCP connections limit. The default is 0, which will allow unlimited connections.

- *Em_limit* is the embryonic connection limit. The default is also 0, which will allow unlimited connections.

- **Norandomseq** Specifies not to randomize TCP packet sequence numbers. Because this is one of the security features of PIX, it is not recommended that this option be used.

```
pixfirewall(config)#nat (inside) 1 0.0.0.0 0.0.0.0
pixfirewall(config)#nat (inside) 2 172.16.0.0 255.255.0.0
```

The first *nat_id* will translate all traffic from the inside interface, whereas the second *nat_id* will translate only traffic originating from the 172.16.0.0 subnet.

NOTE

When PAT is used, the PIX will keep track of each translation by adding a unique source port number to the source IP address for each translation. This feature is valuable when only limited IP address space is available from the Service Provider. To display the active translations, use the command **show xlate** from the enable prompt.

Once the traffic to be translated has been specified on the inside interface, it is time to specify the IP address pool to which the inside traffic will be translated. To do this the **global** command will be used:

```
global [(interface_name)] nat_id global_ip[-global_ip] [netmask
global_mask]
```

In this case:

- *Interface_name* is the external network interface that these global addresses will use.

- *Nat_id* is the number shared with the **nat** command that will group the **nat** and **global** statements together.

- *Global_ip* is one or more global IP address to which the PIX will translate the inside interface traffic. If the external network interface is connected to the Internet, each global IP must be registered with the Network Information Center (NIC). You can either specify a single IP address or a range of IP addresses by separating the addresses with a dash (-).You can create a Port Address Translation (PAT) by specifying a single IP address in the **global** statement.

- *Global_mask* is the network mask for the *global_ip* statement.

```
pixfirewall(config)#global (outside) 1 207.139.221.1-207.139.221.254
netmask >255.255.255.0
Global 207.139.221.1-207.139.221.254 will be Network Address Translated
pixfirewall(config)#global (outside) 1 207.139.221.1 255.255.255.255
Global 207.139.221.128 will be Port Address Translated
```

WARNING

If PAT is used, the IP address must be different from the IP address assigned to any of the interfaces on the PIX.

In the first statement, inside IP addresses will be translated to an IP address in the range of 207.139.221.1 to 207.139.221.254. In the second statement, inside IP addresses will be Port Address Translated in a single IP address, 207.139.221.128.

TIP

When NAT is used, the PIX has a specified range of global IP addresses with which to perform translations. Once the last available global IP is used, no other traffic from the inside interface will be permitted through until one of the translations times out. It is a good idea to use a NAT statement followed by a PAT statement. This way when all IP addresses are used in NAT, the PAT will then be used until a NAT address has timed out.

Security Policy Configuration

Security Policy configuration is probably one of the most important factors in establishing a secure network. The following sections present security strategies and "best practice" policies that you can implement to ensure the best possible security.

Security Strategies

In order for the PIX to protect a network, managers and administrators must figure out what type of security strategy to employ. Do we deny everything that is not explicitly permitted, or do we allow everything and deny only certain things? The security policy is the most important element when designing a secure network. Without a policy, the necessary devices and configurations cannot be implemented properly. The security policy should aim for a balance between security and cost/productivity. It is impossible for a network to be totally secure; the security policy should reflect the risks of a potential security incident that the company is willing to take. For example, by allowing users the ability to browse Web sites to perform research on the Internet, a company opens itself up to numerous security risks that can be exploited. Weigh this against restricting access to browsing Web sites in a company that relies heavily on that information to function. If the security policy is designed and implemented properly, these risks will be minimal. Once a security policy has been established, a firewall can then be used as a tool to implement that security policy. It will not function properly at protecting your network if the security policy is not carefully defined beforehand.

Deny Everything That Is Not Explicitly Permitted

One of the most common strategies used for security policies is to permit only certain IP traffic and to deny the rest. For example, Company XYZ wishes to permit HTTP, FTP, and Telnet traffic for users. Managers and administrators agreed that as a company policy, only these three types of traffic are to be permitted. All other traffic, such as Real Audio, ICQ, MSN Messenger, etc., will be blocked. Using Access Control Lists (ACLs) similar to those used on routers, the PIX will allow an administrator to specify which type of IP traffic to permit or deny based on destination address/ network, source address/network, TCP port number, and UDP port number. This implementation makes configuring the security policy for the administrator very simple. The administrator has to worry only about entering statements to permit HTTP, FTP, and Telnet traffic, and then at the end of the ACL he/she will add an explicit Deny All statement.

Allow Everything That Is Not Explicitly Denied

On a network where many different types of IP traffic will be permitted, it may be easier for an administrator to use a different approach for a security policy. This strategy is to allow all types of traffic and deny specific IP traffic. For example, suppose Company XYZ is not concerned about the types of traffic users are going to access, but managers and administrators agreed that since they only have a T1 connection to their Internet Service Provider that services 1000 users, they do not wish their users to use Real Player because it is bandwidth intensive. To implement this strategy, only one Access Control List needs to be implemented on the PIX. This ACL will deny the TCP/UDP port that Real Audio uses, but will allow everything else.

For Managers

The Importance of Security Policies

A security policy is the most important aspect in network security. As a manager, you must take many things into careful consideration when planning your policy. Tasks such as identifying the resources to protect, balancing security risks with cost/productivity, and the ability to log items are very important. Creating regular reports on usage will assist in identifying possible weaknesses in your security policy. If weaknesses have been overlooked they can then be remedied quickly. PIX allows you to utilize a feature called a syslog. With the addition of third-party software such as Open Systems Privatel, detailed analysis on the contents of a syslog can be achieved. The ability to generate reports on the types of traffic that are being permitted or denied by the PIX is crucial to a security policy. If you suspect that your network is being attacked, the ability to look at logs over certain time periods is invaluable in proving your suspicion.

As a manager, proactive measures are always better then reactive measures. Instead of generating reports and looking for weaknesses after the fact, it may be beneficial to create a strict policy and then remove elements of that policy as necessary. For example, if a company has set up a Web server on the inside network and has used PIX to translate that inside address to a globally unique address on the outside, the server has now become fully exposed. To reduce the risk of the server being compromised, access lists can be used to limit the type of TCP/UDP traffic that will be permitted to reach the server through the PIX. By allowing only HTTP traffic to reach the Web server from the outside network and explicitly denying all other traffic, the risk of it being comprised has been greatly reduced. If the server becomes an FTP server as well as a Web server, the security policy can be modified to permit FTP as well as HTTP traffic to the server from the outside interface by adding another access list that permits FTP traffic. A security policy can take many forms, depending on the needs of an organization. Careful planning is a necessity prior to implementing the PIX firewall.

Note that this is not a recommended strategy. Be sure to plan in advance what types of traffic will be permitted through the firewall. This example was shown as an alternative to the "Deny Everything That Is Not Explicitly Permitted" strategy, and in some network scenarios may be useful. By using this type of implementation in a situation where the ISP charges by the byte may cause quite a shock when the first bill from the ISP arrives.

Identify the Resources to Protect

In the context of a security policy, a resource can be defined as any network device that is susceptible to attack, which will then cost a company either financially or otherwise. Examples of resources can be Web servers, mail servers, database servers, servers that contain sensitive information such as employee records, or even just a stand-alone server that does not provide any services to clients. If any of these servers are attacked, functionality can be affected, which then costs a company money.

It is important to evaluate carefully the assets a company wishes to protect. Are some resources more important than others, therefore requiring a higher security? Is a mail server more important to the operation of the company than a print server?

Areas of weaknesses must also be identified prior to implementing the security policy. If a company uses an ISP for Internet access, a pool of modems for dial-in access, and remote users tunneling into the LAN via the Internet through VPN, each of these points of entry must be looked at as a weakness. Once weaknesses have been identified, a security policy can be shaped to protect a company's LAN from those various weaknesses. For example, using the previous scenario of an ISP, dial-in access, and remote VPN access, placement of the PIX will be critical to the overall security of the LAN. If the PIX is placed between the LAN and the ISP, how does this protect the LAN from unauthorized dial-in users? By adding an additional NIC to the PIX, a DMZ (covered later) can be used to isolate the dial-in and VPN users from the rest of the LAN.

An example of protecting resources is in a situation where a public Web site is hosted internally by the company. The Web server is definitely considered an asset and must be protected. Some decisions will need to be made as to how the PIX will secure the Web server. Since only one Web site, which uses a private IP address space, is hosted by the company, a static translation in which the Web server is assigned an internal IP address is then translated by the PIX firewall with a Global IP address allowing outside users to gain access to it.

Depending on the security policy, having servers on an internal network—which are then translated to global IP addresses—may be too risky. An alternative is to implement a demilitarized zone in which the public resources will reside.

Demilitarized Zone (DMZ)

A DMZ is a zone that is logically and physically separated from both the inside network and outside networks. A DMZ can be created by installing additional NICs to the PIX. By creating a DMZ, administrators can remove devices that need to be accessed publicly from the inside and outside zones, and can place them into their own zone. By implementing this type of configuration, it helps an administrator establish boundaries on the various zones of his/her network.

NOTE

Remember that only the PIX 515 and 520 models will allow additional interfaces to be added. The PIX 506 is a SOHO class firewall and currently does not support additional interfaces.

Figure 4.5 illustrates how a DMZ zone is used to secure public resources.

In this scenario, a DMZ has been used to separate the public servers from the inside and outside zones. This will allow administrators to control the flow of traffic destined for the DMZ zone. Since all traffic must pass through the outside interface in order to reach the DMZ zone, Access Control Lists can be applied to the outside interface specifying the type of traffic permitted to reach the DMZ zone. For example, since the public servers are Web, e-mail, and DNS servers, HTTP, DNS, and SMTP traffic will be permitted to reach the DMZ zone—everything else will be denied.

It is very difficult to secure a server. The operating system and software applications can contain bugs and security flaws and need to be updated continuously. As soon as you install a server that offers a public service, there is always a risk that the server can be compromised. Creating a new perimeter (DMZ) where the public servers are located allows more control over the traffic that will be permitted towards the internal network. For example, once a DMZ has been set up and the public servers have been removed from the inside network, a rule can be created that denies all traffic destined for the inside network, therefore increasing the security.

Figure 4.5 Securing Public Resources with a DMZ zone.

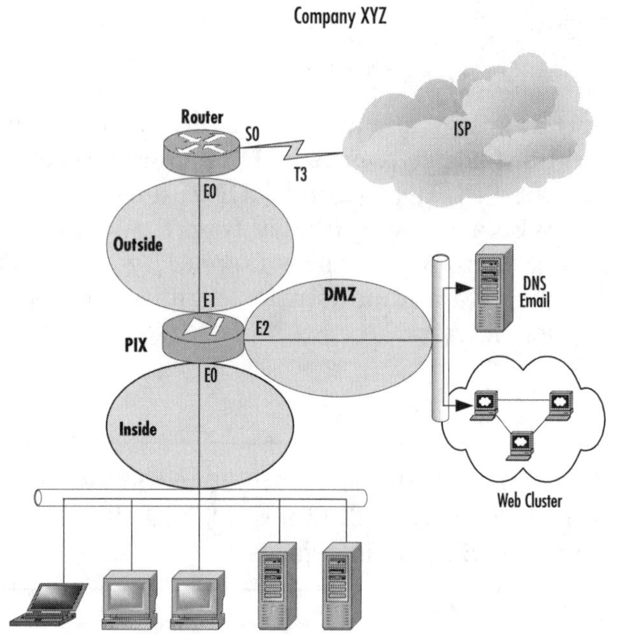

No matter what type of network a company has, careful planning will be needed well in advance to implement a successful security policy. Planning in advance will help to avoid making unnecessary changes in the way the PIX operates while in production. If a company continuously alters how resources are to be protected, availability of those resources will fluctuate. In a situation where a company relies heavily on that availability, careless planning may cost the company money.

Identify the Security Services to Implement

Depending on how your security policy is designed will reflect on how you design and implement your network. Various factors such as resources to protect, user authentication, traffic filtering, and confidentiality all come into play when designing the security policy.

Authentication and Authorization

Authentication is a mechanism that verifies that users are who they say they are. Authorization is a mechanism that will determine what services a user can use to access a host. An administrator must design a security policy that will specify the resources that need to be protected, what type of user will be able to access those resources, and which services a user will be able to use to access those resources. Once a security policy that requires authentication has been outlined, an authentication server such as a RADIUS or TACACS+ server must be put in place in order to implement the security policy.

Once authentication and authorization have been enabled on the PIX, it will provide credential prompts on inbound and outbound connections for FTP, Telnet, and HTTP access. The authentication and authorization server will make the actual decision about which users are permitted or denied, and which services are used. For more information on AAA, please refer to Chapter 6, "Cisco Authentication, Authorization, and Accounting Mechanisms."

Access Control

In a network of any size, various administrators have control over different areas of the network. How does one administrator know where his or her responsibility stops and another administrator's responsibility begins? It is important to lay out the perimeters either inside a network or surrounding a network. For example, if a network is connected to the Internet via a T1 leased line, does the administrator maintain the network on the other side of the T1? Probably not—that is where the ISP will take over responsibility. Perimeters must be established in order to help with designing a security policy. By defining perimeters, an administrator can secure resources under their control, and this will also aid in the decision of where traffic should be filtered. Access control lists (ACLs) are used to permit or deny traffic based on various criteria. These ACLs are used to assist in securing various resources by filtering the traffic that will get to them.

Confidentiality

Confidentiality is achieved by encrypting the information that travels along the network. If an individual used a network monitoring tool, there is a good chance they would be able to look at the data in the packets. An example of this is Password Authentication Protocol (PAP). When using point-to-point (PPP) with PAP, information is sent in clear text during the authentication phase. If a network monitor is used to capture these packets, the password used to authenticate the two parties would be readily available. To remedy this problem Challenge Handshake Authentication Protocol (CHAP) encrypts the negotiation phase. IPSec was developed to provide confidentiality, access control, authentication, and integrity for data traversing a network. IPSec is a suite of protocols to assist in the encryption of data across a network. Commonly found in VPN tunnels, IPSec uses various encryption algorithms, keys, and certificates to validate information passed throughout a network. For more information on IPSEC, refer to Chapter 5, "Virtual Private Networks."

URL, ActiveX, and Java Filtering

Access control lists are limited to certain criteria; destination address, source address, and ports are all taken into consideration for ACLs. ActiveX blocking occurs by the PIX commenting out HTML <object> commands on Web pages. As a technology, ActiveX creates many potential problems for clients including causing workstations to fail, introducing network security problems, or causing servers to fail.

Java filtering is accomplished by denying applets that are downloaded to a client once they access a URL.

URLs themselves can also be filtered. Typically a company will introduce an AUP (Acceptable Usage Policy) that dictates the usage of the Internet for the employees. This can be enforced somewhat by the PIX as well as third-party applications. The PIX can redirect URL requests to a server running a third-party application. This application will decide whether to permit or deny access to that URL and then pass response back to the PIX.

NOTE

URL filtering can be accomplished with the addition of a server running WebSENSE (www.websense.com). The configuration on the PIX will allow URLs to be forwarded to the WebSENSE server, which will then permit or deny the destination URL.

Implementing the Network Security Policy

Once a security policy has been created, it is time to implement that security policy on the PIX. To completely implement a policy, other devices (such as AAA server or IPSec) must be used. This section will cover the commands to enable these features on the PIX, but the actual configuration on the other devices will be discussed in later chapters.

Authentication Configuration in PIX

To configure authentication on the PIX, it must first be enabled. To enable AAA authentication, use **aaa-server** and **aaa** commands:

```
aaa-server group_tag if_name host server_ip key timeout seconds
```

In this case:

- *Group_tag* is an alphanumeric string that is the name of the server group. Use the *group_tag* in the **aaa** command to associate **aaa authentication** and **aaa accounting** command statements to an AAA server.

- *If_name* is the interface name on which the server resides.

- **Host** *server_ip* is the IP address of the TACACS_ or RADIUS server.

- *Key* is a case-sensitive, alphanumeric keyword of up to 127 characters. The key must be the same one that is used on the TACACS+ server.

- **Timeout** *seconds* is a retransmit timer that specifies the duration that the PIX retries access four times to the AAA server before choosing the next AAA server.

- **Protocol** *auth_protocol* is the type of AAA server, either **tacacs+** or **radius**.

```
aaa authentication include | exclude authen_service inbound |
  outbound | if_name local_ip local_mask foreign_ip foreign_mask group_tag
```

In this case:

- **Accounting** enables or disables accounting services with the authentication server.

- **Include** creates a new rule with the specified service to include.

- **Exclude** creates an exception to a previously stated rule by excluding the specified service from authentication, authorization, or accounting to the specified host.

- *Acctg_service* is the account service. Accounting is provided for all services, or you can limit it to one or more services. Possible values are **any, ftp, http, telnet**, or *protocolport*.

- **Authentication** enables or disables user authentication, prompts user for username and password, and verifies information with the authentication server.

- *Authen_service* is the application with which a user is accessing a network. Use **an, ftp, http,** or **telnet**.

- **Authorization** enables or disables TACACS+ user authorization for services (PIX does not support RADIUS authorization).

- *Author_service* are the services that require authorization. Use **any, ftp, http, telnet,** or *protocolport*.

- **Inbound** authenticates or authorizes inbound connections.

- **Outbound** authenticates or authorizes outbound connections

- *If_name* is the interface name from which users require authentication. Use *if_name* in combination with the *local_ip* address and the *foreign_ip* address to determine where and from whom access is sought.

- *Local_ip* is the IP address of the host or network of hosts that you want to be authenticated or authorized. Set this to **0** for all hosts.

- *Local_mask* is the network mask of *local_ip*. If IP is 0, use **0**. Use **255.255.255.255** for a host.

- *Foreign_ip* is the IP address of the hosts you want to access the *local_ip* address. Use **0** for all hosts and **255.255.255.255** for a single host.

- *Foreign_mask* is the network mask of *foreign_ip*. Always specify a specific mask value. Use **0** if the IP address is 0, use **255.255.255.255** for a single host

- *Group_tag* is the group tag set with the **aaa-server** command.

```
pixfirewall>enable
pixfirewall#configure terminal
pixfirewall(config)#aaa-server AuthOutbound protocol tacacs+
pixfirewall(config)#aaa-server tacacs+ (inside) host 172.16.0.10 cisco
 >timeout 20
pixfirewall(config)#aaa authentication include any outbound 0 0 0 0
 >AuthOutbound
pixfirewall(config)#aaa authorization include any outbound 0 0 0 0
```

The first **aaa-server** statement specifies TACACS+ as the authentication protocol to use, and the second **aaa-server** statement specifies the server that is performing the authentication. The last two statements indicate that all traffic outbound will need to be authenticated and authorized.

Access Control Configuration in PIX

Access control can be achieved through the use of access control lists (ACLs). Similar to those used on routers, ACLs can limit the traffic able to traverse the PIX based on several criteria including source address, destination address, source TCP/UDP ports, and destination TCP/UDP ports.

To implement access control lists on a PIX, the **access-list** and **access-group** commands are used:

```
access-list acl_name deny | permit protocol src_addr src_mask operator
 port dest_addr dest_mask operator port
```

To further explain:

- *Acl_name* is the name of an access list.

- **Deny** does not allow a packet to traverse the PIX. By default PIX denies all inbound packets unless explicitly permitted.

- **Permit** allows a packet to traverse the PIX.

- *Protocol* is the name or number of an IP protocol. It can be one of the keywords **icmp, ip, tcp**, or **udp**.

- *Src_addr* is the address of the network or host from which the packet originated. To specify all networks or hosts, use the keyword **any**, which is equivalent to a source network and mask of 0.0.0.0 0.0.0.0. Use the **host** keyword to specify a single host.

- *Src_mask* are netmask bits to be applied to the *src_addr*, if the source address is for a network mask. Do not apply if the source address is a host.

- *Dst_addr* is the IP address of the network or host to which the packet is being sent. Like the *src_addr*, the keyword **any** can be applied for a destination and netmask of 0.0.0.0 0.0.0.0, as well as the **host** abbreviation for a single host.

- *Dst_mask* are netmask bits to be applied to the *dst_addr*, if the destination address is for a network mask. Do not apply if the destination address is a host.

- *Operator* is a comparison that lets you specify a port or port range. Use without the operator and port to indicate all ports. Use **eq** and a port to permit or deny access to just that single port. Use **lt** to permit or deny access to all ports less than the port specified. Use **gt** and a port to permit or deny access to all ports greater than the port you specify. Use **neq** and a port to permit or deny access to every port except the ports you specify. Finally, use **range** and a port range to permit or deny access to only those ports named in the range.

- *Port* is a service or services you permit to be used while accessing *src_addr* or *dest_addr*. Specify services by port number or use the literal name.

- *Icmp_type* permits or denies access to ICMP message types.

access-group *acl_name* **in interface** *interface-name*

Here we see:

- *Acl_name* is the name associated with an access list.

- **In interface** filters on inbound packets at the given interface.

- *Interface_name* is the name of the network interface.

```
pixfirewall>enable
pixfirewall#configure terminal
pixfirewall(config)#access-list acl_out permit tcp any any eq http
pixfirewall(config)#access-list acl_out permit tcp any any eq ftp
pixfirewall(config)#access-list acl_out permit tcp any any eq ftp-data
pixfirewall(config)#access-list acl_out permit tcp any any eq telnet
pixfirewall(config)#access-list acl_out permit tcp any any eq smtp
pixfirewall(config)#access-list acl_out deny tcp any any
pixfirewall(config)#access-list acl_out deny udp any any
pixfirewall(config)#access-group acl_out in interface inside
```

The **access-list** statements for ACL *acl_out* will permit http, ftp, ftp-data, telnet, and smtp traffic. The last two statements of the **access-list** will explicitly deny all traffic.

The **access-group** statement will apply ACL *acl_out* to the inside interface.

Securing Resources

An example of securing resources would arise if Company XYZ has numerous consultants that need access to a resource on the internal LAN. Previously the consultants have been using a RAS connection to dial in but have complained several times that the link to their work is too slow. To remedy this, administrators have decided to permit terminal access to the server via the Internet. The internal server is a Windows NT 4.0 Terminal Server and the consultants have been provided with the Terminal Server client. For security reasons, administrators have also requested the IP and subnet from which the consultants are going to be connecting.

This configuration example will explain the commands necessary to protect a server with a private IP address that is translated to a global IP address.

To create a translation for an internal IP address to a public IP address, use the **static** command:

```
static (internal_if_name, external_if_name) global_ip local_ip netmask
  network_mask max_conns em_limit norandomseq
```

To further explain:

- *Internal_if_name* is the internal network interface name (the higher security level interface you are accessing).

- *External_if_name* is the external network interface name (the lower security level interface you are accessing).

- *Global_ip* is a global IP address. This address cannot be a Port Address Translation IP address.

- *Local_ip* is the local IP address from the inside network.

- **Netmask** specifies the network mask.

- *Network_mask* pertains to both *global_ip* and *local_ip*. For host addresses, always use the 255.255.255.255. For networks, use the appropriate class mask or subnet mask.

- *Max_cons* is the maximum number of connections permitted through the static at the same time.

- *Em_limit* is the embryonic connection limit. An embryonic connection is one that has started but not yet completed. Set this limit to prevent attack by a flood of embryonic connections.

- **Norandomseq** specifies not to randomize the TCP/IP packet's sequence number. Use this option only if another inline firewall is also randomizing sequence numbers. Using this feature opens a security hole in the PIX.

Once a translation for an internal IP to an external IP has been made, you must specify the type of traffic that will be permitted to access it. To do this, use the **access-list** command:

```
access-list acl_name deny | permit protocol src_addr src_mask operator
  port dest_addr dest_mask operator port
```

To further clarify:

- *Acl_name* is the name of an access list.

- **Deny** does not allow a packet to traverse the PIX. By default PIX denies all inbound packets unless explicitly permitted.

- **Permit** allows a packet to traverse the PIX.

- *Protocol* is the name or number of an IP protocol. It can be one of the keywords **icmp, ip, tcp**, or **udp**.

- *Src_addr* is the address of the network or host from which the packet originated. To specify all networks or hosts, use the keyword **any**, which is equivalent to a source network and mask of 0.0.0.0 0.0.0.0. Use the **host** keyword to specify a single host.

- *Src_mask* are netmask bits to be applied to the *src_addr*, if the source address is for a network mask. Do not apply if the source address is a host.

- *Dst_addr* is the IP address of the network or host to which the packet is being sent. Like the *src_addr*, the keyword **any** can be applied for a destination and netmask of 0.0.0.0 0.0.0.0, as well as the **host** abbreviation for a single host.

- *Dst_mask* are netmask bits to be applied to the dst_*addr*, if the destination address is for a network mask. Do not apply if the destination address is a host.

- *Operator* is a comparison that lets you specify a port or port range. Use without the operator and port to indicate all ports. Use **eq** and a port to permit or deny access to just that single port. Use **lt** to permit or deny access to all ports less that the port specified. Use **gt** and a port to permit or deny access to all ports greater than the port you specify. Use **neq** and a port to permit or deny access to every port except the ports you specify. Finally, use **range** and a port range to permit or deny access to only those ports named in the range.

- *Port* is a service or services you permit to be used while accessing *src_addr* or *dest_addr*. Specify services by port number or use the literal name.

- *Icmp_type* permits or denies access to ICMP message types.

```
pixfirewall>enable

pixfirewall#configure terminal

pixfirewall(config)#static (inside,outside) 207.139.221.10 172.16.0.32
 >netmask 255.255.255.255

pixfirewall(config)#access-list acl_consult permit tcp 198.142.65.0
 >255.255.255.0 host 207.139.221.10 eq 3389

pixfirewall(config)#access-list acl_consult permit tcp 64.182.95.0
 >255.255.255.0 host 307.139.221.10 eq 3389

pixfirewall(config)#access-group acl_consult in interface outside
```

TIP

TCP port 3389 is the corresponding port for Microsoft Terminal Server client. For a listing of valid TCP and UDP port numbers, refer to www.isi.edu/in-notes/iana/assignments/port-numbers.

The first **static** statement will provide a translation for the inside server with an IP address of 172.16.0.32 to a global IP address of 207.139.221.10.

The **access-list** statements specify that ACL *acl_consult* will permit only Microsoft Terminal Server client traffic originating from 198.142.65.0 and 64.182.95.0.

Finally, the **access-group** statement will apply the *acl_consult* access control list to the outside interface.

It is also important to note that implementing a security policy does not revolve around configuration of the PIX. In the previous example, a PIX will not assist as a security measure if the information passed from terminal server to terminal server client is not encrypted. If information is passed as clear text, a network monitoring tool could be used to capture packets, which can then be analyzed by other individuals. Once a consultant has connected to the terminal server, how is the authentication handled? What permissions does that account have? Have various Windows NT security flaws been addressed with the latest service packs?

URL, ActiveX, and Java Filtering

To implement URL, ActiveX, and Java filtering, use the **filter** command:

```
filter activex port local_ip mask foreign_ip mask
```

In this case:

- **Activex** blocks outbound ActiveX tags from outbound packets.

- *Port* (**filter activex** only) is the port at which Web traffic is received on the PIX firewall.

- *Local_ip* is the IP address of the highest security level interface from which access is sought. You can set this address to **0** to specify all hosts.

- *Mask* is the network mask of *local_ip*. You can use **0** to specify all hosts.

- *Foreign_ip* is the IP address of the lowest security level interface to which access is sought. You can use **0** to specify all hosts.

- *Foreign_mask* is the network mask of *foreign_ip*. Always specify a mask value. You can use **0** to specify all hosts.

```
filter java port[-port] local_ip mask foreign_ip mask
```

To further explain:

- **Java** blocks Java applets returning to the PIX firewall as a result of an outbound connection.

- *Port[-port]* (**filter java** only) is one or more ports on which Java applets may be received.

- *Local_ip* is the IP address of the highest security level interface from which access is sought. You can set this address to **0** to specify all hosts.

- *Mask* is the network mask of *local_ip*. You can use **0** to specify all hosts.

- *Foreign_ip* is the IP address of the lowest security level interface to which access is sought. You can use **0** to specify all hosts.

- *Foreign_mask* is the network mask of *foreign_ip*. Always specify a mask value. You can use **0** to specify all hosts.

```
filter url http|except local_ip local_mask foreign_ip foreign_mask
[allow]
```

Here we see:

- **url** filters URLs from data moving through the PIX firewall.

- **http (filter url** only) filters HTTP URLs.

- **except (filter url** only) creates an exception to a previous **filter** condition.

- *Local_ip* is the IP address of the highest security level interface from which access is sought. You can set this address to **0** to specify all hosts.

- *Mask* is the network mask of *local_ip*. You can use **0** to specify all hosts.

- *Foreign_ip* is the IP address of the lowest security level interface to which access is sought. You can use **0** to specify all hosts.

- *Foreign_mask* is the network mask of *foreign_ip*. Always specify a mask value. You can use **0** to specify all hosts.

- **Allow (filter url** only) lets outbound connections pass through PIX firewall without filtering when the server is unavailable. If you omit this option and if the WebSENSE server goes offline, the PIX firewall stops outbound port 80 traffic until the WebSENSE server is back online.

Once filtering has been enabled on the PIX, to successfully filter URLs, you must designate a WebSENSE server with the **url-server** command.

```
url-server (if_name) host ip_address timeout seconds
```

To further explain:

- *If_name* is the network interface where the authentication server resides. Default is inside.

- **Host** *ip_address* is the server that runs the WebSENSE URL filtering application.

- **Timeout** *seconds* is the maximum idle time permitted before PIX switches to the next server you specify. The default is 5 seconds.

```
pixfirewall>enable

pixfirewall#configure terminal

pixfirewall(config)#filter url http 0 0 0 0

pixfirewall(config)#filter activex 80 0 0 0 0

pixfirewall(config)#filter java 80 0 0 0 0

pixfirewall(config)#url-server (inside) host 172.16.0.38 timeout 5
```

The **filter url** statement specifies that all http traffic passing through the PIX will be filtered. In addition, the **url-server** statement will specify which server is running WebSENSE to provide the actual filtering.

The **filter activex** and **filter java** statements specify that all http traffic will be filtered for ActiveX controls and Java applets.

PIX Configuration Examples

The following examples will illustrate how a PIX firewall can be used in various real world scenarios, as well as the configuration needed on the PIX.

Protecting a Private Network

For security reasons, Company XYZ management has decided to restrict access to the Finance servers. Management has assigned the task of securing the Finance network from unauthorized access. Only individuals who are in the Finance departments network will have access to any of the Finance resources, any traffic originating from the Finance LAN will be permitted to any destination, and all other departments will not be permitted to access the Finance LAN. Figure 4.6 illustrates how the LAN will be set up.

To begin, execute the following:

```
pixfirewall(config)#write terminal

nameif ethernet0 public security0

nameif ethernet1 finance security100
```

This assigns names and security values to each of the interfaces.

```
interface ethernet0 inside auto

interface ethernet1 outside auto
```

This sets each Ethernet interface to 10/100 auto negotiation.

```
ip address public 172.16.2.1 255.255.255.0

ip address finance 172.16.1.1 255.255.255.0
```

Figure 4.6 Secure department to department.

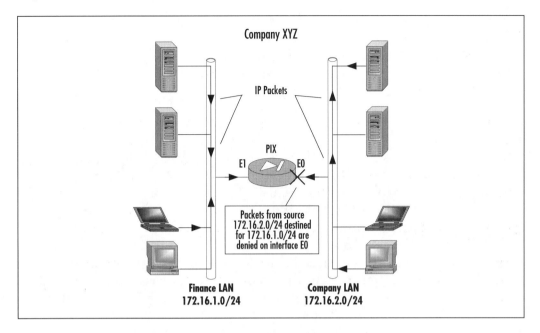

This assigns unique RFC1918 IP addresses to each of the interfaces.

```
access-list deny tcp any 172.16.1.0 255.255.255.0
    >eq any
access-list deny udp any 172.16.1.0 255.255.255.0
    >eq any
```

This specifies that traffic originating from the 172.16.1.0/24 subnet will be denied.

```
access-group acl_out in interface public
```

This applies access-list acl_out to public interface.

```
telnet 172.16.1.0 255.255.255.0 public
telnet 172.16.2.0 255.255.255.0 finance
```

This specifies that only clients from the 172.16.1.0/24 and 172.16.2.0/24 subnets will be able to Telnet to the PIX.

NOTE

A configuration where two departments are separated for security reasons can easily be achieved by using a router with access control lists. The PIX is a very versatile device and can also be used to protect internal networks as shown in this example.

Protecting a Network Connected to the Internet

Company XYZ management has decided that in order to keep up with the rapidly evolving world of technology, Internet access is a necessity. Managers and administrators have decided that a T1 leased line will be sufficient for their users to access the Internet, and an ISP has already been chosen. Since the LAN uses an IP address scheme using the private 172.16.0.0 network, Network Address Translation or Network Address Port Translation will be needed in order to translate internal IP addresses to Global IP addresses. The ISP has also provided the company with eight public addresses, which consist of 207.139.221.1 to 207.139.221.8. A Cisco Secure PIX 515 Firewall has been chosen to provide security for Company XYZ.

Management and administrators have established a security policy in which users will be permitted to access only HTTP, FTP, Telnet, e-mail, DNS, and News. Web site filtering will be performed by a third-party application called WebSENSE web filtering software (www.websense.com). ActiveX controls will be also filtered due to the security problems associated with them. The ability to Telnet to the inside interface will be restricted to the administrator's workstation. Figure 4.7 shows how the network will be set up.

To begin, execute the following:

```
pixfirewall(config)#write terminal
interface ethernet0 inside auto
interface ethernet1 outside auto
```

This sets each Ethernet interface to 10/100 auto negotiation.

```
ip address inside 172.16.0.1 255.255.0.0
ip address outside 207.139.221.2 255.255.255.248
```

Figure 4.7 Securing a Network from the Internet.

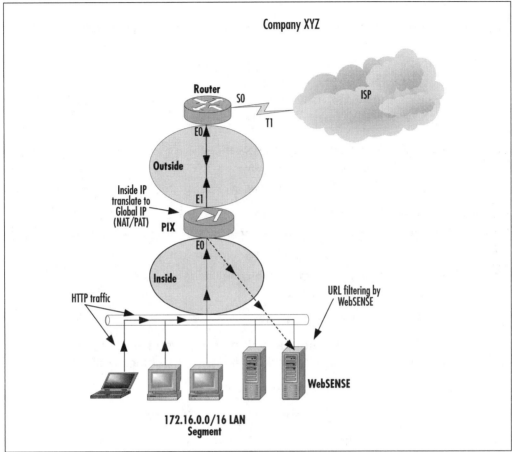

This assigns unique IP addresses to each of the interfaces.

```
route outside 0.0.0.0 0.0.0.0 207.139.221.1
```

This adds a static route for outside interface.

```
nat (inside) 1 0.0.0.0 0.0.0.0
```

This allows any address on the inside interface to be NAT'd.

```
global (inside) 1 207.139.221.3
```

This sets up a global pool using the unique IP address 207.139.221.3 for NAPT.

```
filter url http 0 0 0 0
```

This filters any HTTP URL requests to any destination address.

```
filter activex 0 0 0 0
```

This filters any ActiveX controls in HTML pages to any destination address.

```
url-server (inside) host 172.16.0.10 timeout 5
```

This specifies the server in which WebSENSE is running for URL filtering.

```
access-list acl_out permit tcp any any eq http
access-list acl_out permit tcp any any eq ftp
access-list acl_out permit tcp any any eq ftp-data
access-list acl_out permit tcp any any eq smtp
access-list acl_out permit tcp any any eq telnet
access-list acl_out permit tcp any any eq nntp
access-list acl_out permit tcp any any eq domain
access-list acl_out permit udp any any eq domain
access-list acl_out deny tcp any any
access-list acl_out deny udp any any
```

This specifies types of traffic that will be permitted through the PIX (inside, outside) with an explicit deny all statement to block any other traffic.

```
access-group acl_out in interface inside
```

This applies access-list acl_out to the inside interface.

```
telnet 172.16.0.50 255.255.255.255. inside
```

This permits only host 172.16.0.50 for Telnet sessions on the inside interface.

Protecting Server Access Using Authentication

The Finance department in Company XYZ is concerned about users in other departments accessing their Finance Web server. To alleviate this concern, IT has decided to limit access to the Finance server using the PIX firewall. A new server has been provided, which will serve as the AAA server that runs Cisco Secure ACS. Figure 4.8 illustrates this scenario.

To begin, execute the following:

```
pixfirewall(config)#write terminal
interface ethernet0 inside auto
interface ethernet1 outside auto
```

Figure 4.8 Protecting a server using AAA.

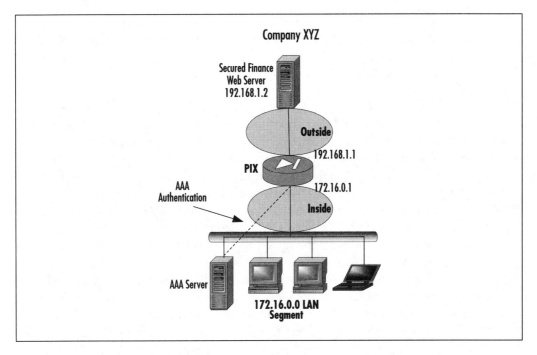

This sets each Ethernet interface to 10/100 auto negotiation.

```
ip address outside 192.168.1.1 255.255.255.0
ip address inside 172.16.0.1 255.255.255.0
```

This assigns unique IP addresses to each of the interfaces.

```
nat (inside) 1 0 0
```

This allows any address on the inside interface to be NAT'd.

```
global (outside) 1 192.168.10-192.168.20 netmask >255.255.255.0
```

This sets up a global pool using address 192.168.10-192.168.20 for NAT.

```
global (outside) 1 192.168.10.21 netmask >255.255.255.255
```

This sets up a global pool using 192.168.10.21 for NAPT. This is used when addresses from the NAT pool have been exhausted.

```
aaa-server AuthOutbound protocol tacacs+
```

This specifies TACACS+ for AAA protocol.

```
aaa-server AuthOutbound (inside) host 172.16.0.10 >cisco timeout 20
```

This specifies host 172.16.0.10 as AAA server.

```
aaa authentication include any outbound host >192.168.1.2 0 0
```

This authorizes any traffic with a destination address of 192.168.1.2.

Protecting Public Servers Connected to the Internet

Company XYZ management has discussed the possibility of hosting their public servers internally. Currently the Web servers are hosted elsewhere by another company in which connectivity, security, and maintenance is provided for them. The security policy dictates that the risks of having public servers on the internal network are unacceptable. A new perimeter (DMZ) will need to be defined to secure the public servers. Three web servers, one e-mail server, and one DNS server will be placed in the DMZ.

A class C subnet has been assigned to the company by their ISP. To allow the company to utilize as many of the class C public addresses as possible, Network Address Port Translation will be used instead of NAT.

Management would like to restrict the amount of traffic that traverses the PIX from their local LAN to the Internet. Administrators have decided that the only traffic permitted from the LAN will be HTTP, FTP, Telnet, and DNS requests to their DNS server. Figure 4.9 illustrates how the LAN will be set up.

To begin, execute the following:

```
pixfirewall(config)#write terminal
nameif ethernet2 dmz security 50
```

This names and assigns security value to ethernet2 interface.

```
interface ethernet0 inside auto
interface ethernet1 outside auto
interface ethernet2 dmz1 auto
```

This sets each Ethernet interface to 10/100 auto negotiation.

```
ip address inside 172.16.0.1 255.255.0.0
ip address outside 207.139.221.2 255.255.255.128
ip address dmz 207.139.221.129 255.255.255.128
```

This assigns unique IP addresses to each interface.

```
route (outside) 0.0.0.0 0.0.0.0 207.139.221.1
```

Figure 4.9 Three interfaces without NAT.

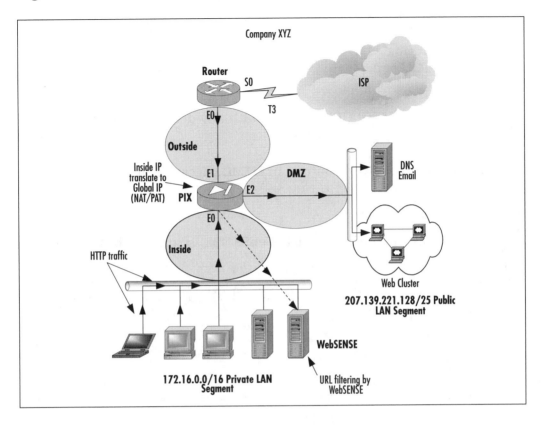

This sets static route for outside interface.

```
nat (inside) 1 0.0.0.0 0.0.0.0
```

This enables NAT for all traffic originating from the inside interface.

```
Nat (dmz) 0 0.0.0.0 0.0.0.0
```

This disables NAT feature on DMZ interface. Since hosts on DMZ interface will be using global IP addresses; NAT translations are not necessary.

```
global (inside) 1 207.139.221.3
```

This sets up a global pool using global IP address 207.139.221.3 for NAPT.

```
static (dmz,outside) 207.139.221.129 207.139.221.129 >netmask
 255.255.255.128
```

This creates a static translation for:

```
static (dmz,outside) 207.139.221.130 207.139.221.130 >netmask
  255.255.255.128
static (dmz,outside) 207.139.221.131 207.139.221.131 >netmask
  255.255.255.128
filter url http 0 0 0 0
```

This filters any HTTP URL requests with any destination address.

```
filter activex 0 0 0 0
```

This filters any ActiveX controls in HTML pages to any destination address.

```
url-server (inside) host 172.16.0.10 timeout 5
```

This specifies the server in which WebSENSE is running for URL filtering.

```
access-list acl_out permit tcp any any eq http
access-list acl_out permit tcp any any eq ftp
access-list acl_out permit tcp any any eq ftp-data
access-list acl_out permit tcp any any eq smtp
access-list acl_out permit tcp any any eq telnet
access-list acl_out permit tcp any any eq domain
access-list acl_out permit udp any any eq domain
access-list acl_out deny tcp any any
access-list acl_out deny udp any any
```

This specifies types of traffic that will be permitted through the PIX (inside, outside) with an explicit deny all statement to block any other traffic.

```
access-list dmz_in permit tcp any 207.139.221.128
    >255.255.255.128 eq http
access-list dmz_in permit tcp any 207.139.221.128
    >255.255.255.128 eq domain
access-list dmz_in permit udp any 207.139.221.128
    >255.255.255.128 eq domain
access-list dmz_in permit tcp any 207.139.221.128
    >255.255.255.128 eq smtp
access-list dmz_in permit tcp any 207.139.221.128
    >255.255.255.128 eq pop3
```

This specifies types of traffic that will be permitted through the PIX (outside, dmz). All traffic not explicitly permitted will be denied.

```
access-group acl_out in interface inside
```

This applies access-list acl_out to the inside interface.

```
access-group dmz_in in interface outside
```

This applies access-list acl_in to the DMZ interface.

```
telnet 172.16.0.0 255.255.0.0 inside
```

This permits Telnet access on inside interface from any host on 172.16.0.0/16 network.

Figure 4.10 illustrates an example of a DMZ that uses private IP addresses, therefore requiring NAT.

Figure 4.10 Three interfaces with NAT.

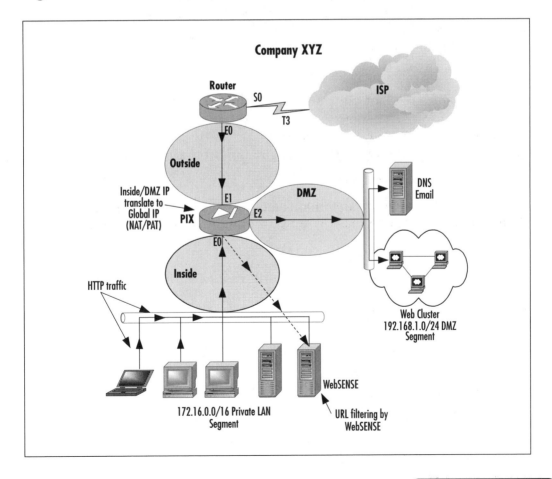

To continue with the configuration:

```
pixfirewall(config)#write terminal
nameif ethernet2 dmz security 50
```

This names and assigns security value to ethernet2 interface.

```
interface ethernet0 inside auto
interface ethernet1 outside auto
interface ethernet2 dmz1 auto
```

This sets each Ethernet interface to 10/100 auto negotiation.

```
ip address inside 172.16.0.1 255.255.0.0
ip address outside 207.139.221.2 255.255.255.0
ip address dmz 192.168.1.1 255.255.255.0
```

This assigns unique IP addresses to each interface.

```
route 0.0.0.0 0.0.0.0 207.139.221.1
```

This sets static route for outside interface.

```
nat (inside) 1 172.16.0.0 255.255.0.0
```

This enables NAT for all traffic originating from the inside interface.

```
nat (dmz) 1 0.0.0.0 0.0.0.0
```

This enables NAT for all traffic originating from the DMZ interface.

```
global (inside) 1 207.139.221.3
```

This sets up a global pool using global IP address 207.139.221.3 for NAPT.

```
global (dmz) 1 192.168.1.10-192.168.1.30
```

This sets up a global pool using IP addresses 192.168.1.10-192.168.1.30 for DMZ.

```
static (dmz,outside) 207.139.221.129 192.168.1.2 >netmask 255.255.255.0
```

This creates a static translation for DMZ host 192.168.1.2 to Global unique IP 207.139.221.129.

```
static (dmz,outside) 207.139.221.130 192.168.1.3 >netmask 255.255.255.0
```

This creates a static translation for DMZ host 192.168.1.3 to Global unique IP 207.139.221.130.

```
static (dmz,outside) 207.139.221.131 192.168.1.4 >netmask 255.255.255.0
```

This creates a static translation for DMZ host 192.168.1.4 to Global unique IP 207.139.221.131.

```
filter url http 0 0 0 0
```

This filters any HTTP URL requests with any destination address.

```
filter activex 0 0 0 0
```

This filters any ActiveX controls in HTML pages to any destination address.

```
url-server (inside) host 172.16.0.10 timeout 5
```

This specifies the server in which WebSENSE is running for URL filtering.

```
access-list acl_out permit tcp any any eq http
access-list acl_out permit tcp any any eq ftp
access-list acl_out permit tcp any any eq ftp-data
access-list acl_out permit tcp any any eq smtp
access-list acl_out permit tcp any any eq telnet
access-list acl_out permit tcp any any eq domain
access-list acl_out permit udp any any eq domain
access-list acl_out deny tcp any any
access-list acl_out deny udp any any
```

This specifies types of traffic that will be permitted through the PIX (inside, outside) with an explicit deny all statement to block any other traffic.

```
access-list dmz_in permit tcp any 207.139.221.129
    >255.255.255.255 eq http
access-list dmz_in permit tcp any 207.139.221.130
    >255.255.255.255 eq domain
access-list dmz_in permit udp any 207.139.221.130
    >255.255.255.128 eq domain
access-list dmz_in permit tcp any 207.139.221.131
    >255.255.255.131 eq smtp
```

This specifies types of traffic that will be permitted through the PIX (outside, dmz). All traffic not explicitly permitted will be denied.

```
access-group acl_out in interface inside
```

This applies access-list acl_out to the inside interface.

```
access-group dmz_in in interface outside
```

This applies access-list acl_dmz to the outside interface.

```
telnet 172.16.0.0 255.255.0.0 inside
```

Securing and Maintaining the PIX

Part of creating a security policy is not only to protect network resources but also to protect the PIX itself. PIX provides several mechanisms in assisting an administrator in limiting access to the PIX and reporting various items such as security violations.

System Journaling

As with most Cisco products, the system message logging feature can save messages in a buffer or redirect the messages to other devices such as a system logging server to be analyzed or archived. This feature allows administrators to reference these logs in case of security violations.

System journaling is often an overlooked security mechanism. Logging is essential to the security of the network. It can be used to detect security violations, and to help determine the type of attack. If logging is done in real time, it can be used to detect an ongoing intrusion. You can find more information on this in Chapter 7, "Intrusion Detection."

PIX also has the added feature that if for any reason the syslog server is no longer available, the PIX will stop all traffic.

UNIX servers by default provide a syslog server; on Windows NT/2000 servers, a syslog server must be downloaded. Cisco provides a syslog server on their Web site (www.cisco.com).

By default, system log messages are sent to the console and Telnet sessions. To redirect logging messages to a syslog server use the **logging** command. Some of the variables used with the **logging** command are as follows:

- **On** starts sending syslog messages to all output locations. Stop all logging with the **no logging on** command.

- **Buffered** sends syslog messages to an internal buffer that can be viewed with the **show logging** command. To clear the buffer, use the **clear logging** command.

- **Console** specifies that syslog messages appear on the console. You can limit which type of messages appear by using the *level* option.

- **Host** specifies a syslog server that will receive the messages sent from the PIX. You may use multiple **logging host** commands to specify multiple syslog servers.

- *In_if_name* is the interface in which the syslog server resides.

- *Ip_address* is the IP address of syslog server.

- *Protocol* is the protocol in which the syslog message is sent, either **tcp** or **udp**. PIX sends only **TCP** messages to the PIX syslog server unless otherwise specified. You cannot send both protocols to the same syslog server. Use multiple syslog servers in order to log both UDP and TCP traffic.

- *Level* specifies the syslog message level as a number or string. See Table 4.2 for the different syslog levels.

- *Port* is the port in which the PIX sends either UDP or TCP syslog messages. Default for UDP is port 514 and port 1470 for TCP.

- **Timestamp** specifies that the syslog messages sent to the syslog server should have a time stamp value on each message.

Table 4.2 lists the different SNMP trap levels.

Table 4.2 SNMP Trap Levels

Level	Type	Description
0	Emergencies	System unusable messages
1	Alerts	Take immediate action
2	Critical	Critical condition
3	Errors	Error messages
4	Warnings	Warning message
5	Notifications	Normal but significant condition
6	Informational	Information message
7	Debugging	Debug messages and log FTP commands and WWW URLs

An example of sending warnings to a syslog server is as follows:

```
pixfirewall>enable
pixfirewall#configure terminal
pixfirewall(config)#logging trap 4
pixfurewall(config)#logging host inside 172.16.0.38 tcp
```

NOTE

Syslog is *not* a secure protocol. The syslog server should be secured and network access to the syslog server should be restricted.

Securing the PIX

Since the PIX is a security device, limiting access to the PIX to only those who need it is extremely important. What would happen if individuals where able to Telnet freely to the PIX from the inside network? Limiting access to the PIX can be achieved by using the **telnet** command. Telnet is an insecure protocol. Everything that is typed on a Telnet session, including passwords, is sent in clear text. Individuals using a network monitoring tool can then capture the packets and discover the password to login and enable a password if issued. If remote management of the PIX is necessary, the network communication should be secured.

It is also a good idea to limit the idle-time of a Telnet session and log any connections to the PIX through Telnet. When possible, use a RADIUS, Kerberos, or TACACS+ server to authenticate connections on the console or vty (Telnet) ports:

```
telnet ip_address netmask interface_name
```

In this case:

- *Ip_address* is an IP address of a host or network that can access the PIX Telnet console. If an interface name is not specified, the address is assumed to be on the internal interface. PIX automatically verifies the IP address against the IP addresses specified by the **ip address** commands to ensure that the address you specify is on an internal interface.

- *Netmask* is the bit mask of *ip_address*. To limit access to a single IP address, use 255.255.255.255 for the subnet mask.

- *Interface_name* is the name of the interface in which to apply the security.

- **Timeout** is the number of minutes that a Telnet session can be idle before being disconnected by the PIX. Default is 5 minutes.

TIP

When permitting Telnet access to an interface, be as specific as possible. If an administrative terminal uses a static IP address, permit only that IP address for Telnet access.

The following is an example of limiting Telnet access to the PIX to one host on the inside network.

```
pixfirewall>enable
pixfirewall#configure terminal
pixfirewall(config)#telnet 172.16.0.50 255.255.255.255 inside
pixfurewall(config)#telnet timeout 5
```

If features are not used on the PIX they should then be disabled. If SNMP is not used, deactivate it. If it is used, changed the default communities and limit access to the management station only.

Finally, a security measure that is often forgotten is to keep the PIX a secure area. By locking it away in a server room or wiring closet, only limited individuals will be able to physically reach the PIX. How would your security policy be enforced if an individual was able to walk up to the PIX and pull out the power cable?

Take the extra time to secure the PIX according to the security policy. The PIX is typically the device that enforces the majority of a company's security policy. If the PIX itself is not secured, and an unauthorized individual gains access to it, the security of the network will be compromised.

Summary

The Cisco PIX Firewall is a very versatile security device. From the PIX 506 SOHO model to the Enterprise class PIX 520 model, the PIX can fulfill the security needs of any size network.

In this chapter we covered numerous topics including the design of a security policy and then implementing that security policy on the PIX. It is extremely important to design a policy thoroughly before implementing it.

Identifying the resources to protect, the services you wish to allow (HTTP, FTP etc), and requiring users to authenticate in order to access a resource ahead of time will permit an organization to implement the security policy in a quick and efficient manner. By creating a security policy on the fly, your resources can be compromised and data can be corrupted. Instead of being reactive to attacks and other security holes, creating a detailed security policy is a proactive measure in protecting your network.

Remember the key security features of the PIX: URL, ActiveX, and Java filtering; access control lists; DMZs; AAA authentication and authorization; DNSGuard, IP FragGuard, MailGuard, Flood Defender, and Flood Guard; IPSec; Stateful filtering; securing access to the PIX; and syslog. These features will aid you in creating and implementing your security policy. NAT and NAPT should not be relied on as a security measure. Using a syslog server will allow you to archive all of the traffic that passes through your firewall. By using syslog, you will always have a record of anyone attempting to attack your firewall from the inside or outside.

FAQs

Q: I have two inside networks. I would like only one of them to be able to access the Internet (outside network). How would I accomplish this?

A: Instead of using the NAT (inside) 1 0 0 statement, which specifies all inside traffic, use the NAT (inside) 1 *xxx.xxx.xxx.xx yyy.yyy.yyy.yyy* statement where *x* is the source network you wish to translate, and *y* is the source network subnet mask.

Q: I am setting up my outbound access control lists to specify which traffic I will permit users to use. How do I know which TCP or UDP port a particular application uses?

A: Usually the application vendor will have the TCP or UDP port(s) listed in the documentation, or available on their Web site. For a comprehensive list of Well Known Ports, Registered Ports, and Dynamic/Private ports, visit: http://www.isi.edu/in-notes/iana/assignments/port-numbers

Q: A user has informed me that he believes that his application is not running due to firewall restrictions. After researching the application, I am unable to figure out which TCP or UDP port the application uses. How can I find this information?

A: If you are using a syslog server or third-party application to analyze the syslog on the PIX, you can query the syslog for instances of the IP address being denied. From that output, you should be able to determine the port in question. Below is one line of output from the syslog:

```
106019: IP packet from 172.16.0.39 to 212.214.136.27, protocol 17
received from interface "inside" deny by access-group "acl_out"
```

From this output you can clearly see that host 172.16.0.39 is trying to access a foreign IP address on port 17. After checking to which service port 17 corresponds, you find that the user is trying use an application that gives "Quote of the day" messages.

Q: My organization uses Microsoft Exchange server for our mail. How would I allow our Exchange server to receive external mail if the server is located on the inside network and a PIX firewall is in place?

A: Since the server is physically located on the inside network, a static translation will need to be created to assign the Exchange server a global IP address. Once the translation has been created, use ACLs to limit to the type of traffic able to reach the server; in other words, SMTP. For example, the Exchange server's internal IP address is 172.16.0.16, and the globally assigned IP address will be 207.139.221.40:

```
pixfirewall(config)#static (inside,outside) 207.139.221.40 172.16.0.16
 >netmask 255.255.255.255
pixfirewall(config)#access-list acl_mailin permit tcp any host
 207.139.221.40 eq smtp
pixfirewall(config)#access-group acl_mailin in interface outside
```

Chapter 5

Virtual Private Networks

Solutions in this chapter:

- **Overview of the Different VPN Technologies**
- **L2TP, Layer 2 Transport Protocol**
- **Internet Protocol Security (IPSec)**

Introduction

The new economy is reshaping the world in which we live. Our organizations are changing the way they do business, the place in which they do business, and even the hours that their business is being conducted. Everything is changing!

New demands and challenges are placed on our networks on a daily basis. Not only do our networks need to keep pace with these changes, but often they are the vehicles for initiating them. Our networks need to be flexible, reliable, secure, and most of all, cost-effective. Traditional private line or Frame Relay-based WAN networks often don't allow enough flexibility or are not cost-effective. Remote Access Service (RAS) also suffers from these problems, since these services typically are built on the same infrastructure. Virtual Private Networks (VPNs) provide solutions for many of these issues.

Until recently, concerns about security (insufficient or proprietary) have severely hampered the deployment of VPNs. IPSec has changed all of this.

What Is a VPN?

Chances are, no two networking cognoscenti will give you the same definition for a VPN. Vendors and the press have not been able to agree on a definition; what makes things worse is that a VPN can be implemented in so many different ways and at so many different layers of the OSI reference model that virtually any vendor can claim that its product is a VPN solution.

Simply put, a VPN is a network deployed on a shared infrastructure, employing the same security, management, and throughput policies applied in a private network.

Figure 5.1 depicts a typical VPN. The VPN provider network carries traffic from both VPN1 and VPN2.

Overview of the Different VPN Technologies

As discussed in the introduction, VPNs can take many different forms and can be implemented in many different ways. Not only can a VPN be classified by the layer of the OSI reference model at which it is implemented, but also by which VPN model it employs.

Figure 5.1 A typical VPN.

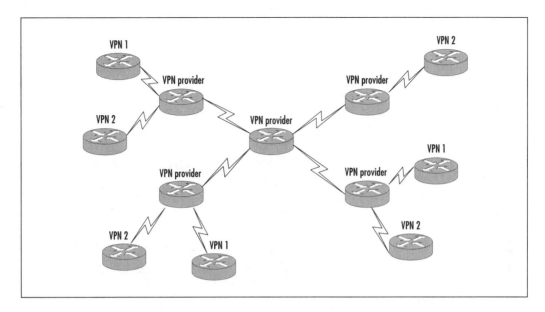

The Peer Model

A *peer* VPN model is one in which the path determination at the network layer is done on a hop-by-hop basis. The edge nodes (customer sites) form a network layer peering relationship with the VPN service provider network and use the best route through the network, rather than connecting to other edge nodes (customer sites) via a predetermined path though the network.

One of the major drawbacks of this model is that all network layer addressing must be unique within the VPN service provider network and the individual VPNs. A traditional routed network is an example of a peer model.

In Figure 5.2 a packet from network 1, destined for network 2, is first sent to router A. Router A determines that the best path for this packet to follow is via router B. Router B determines that the best path for this packet to follow is via router C. Router C determines that the best path for this packet to follow is via router D, who in turn delivers the packet to network 2.

Figure 5.2 Typical peer model.

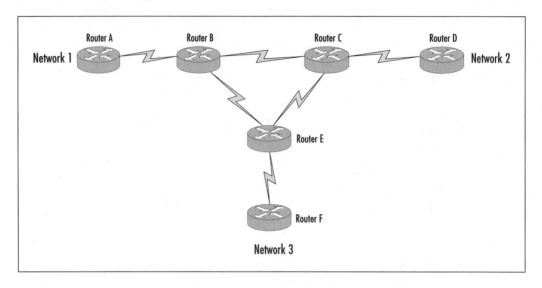

The Overlay Model

An *overlay* VPN model is one in which path determination at the network layer is done on a "cut-through" basis to another edge node (customer site). The network layer has no knowledge of the underlying infrastructure. All edge nodes (customer sites) are effectively one hop away from each other, no matter how many physical hops are between them.

An advantage of this type of VPN is that network addressing between the different VPNs and the VPN service provider networks does not have to be unique, except for within a single VPN.

It is generally accepted that the overlay model results in sub-optimal routing in larger networks and that full mesh overlay topologies have scalability problems, since they create large numbers of router adjacencies. Examples include ATM, Frame Relay, and tunneling implementations. In Figure 5.3, Network 1 is one hop away from Network 2, no matter how many physical hops are between them.

Link Layer VPNs

Link Layer VPNs are implemented at the link layer (Layer 2) of the OSI reference model. The link layer provides the networking platform, whereas discrete networks are built at the network layer. The different VPNs share the same infrastructure, but have no visibility of one another. The difference between this model and that of dedicated circuits is that there is no synchronized data clock shared by the sender and receiver and that there is no dedicated transmission path that is provided by the underlying network.

Figure 5.3 Typical overlay model.

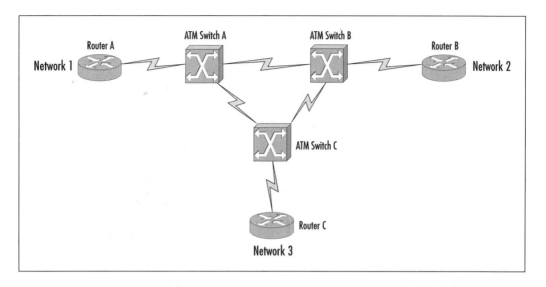

Frame Relay and ATM networks are examples of link layer VPNs.

Network Layer VPNs

These VPNs are implemented at the network layer (Layer 3) of the OSI reference model.

Tunneling VPNs are becoming increasingly popular, and most of the VPN growth is expected in this area.

Tunnels can be created either between a source and destination router, router-to-router, or host-to host. Tunneling can be point-to-point or point-to-multipoint, but point-to-point tunneling is much more scaleable than point-to-multipoint. This is because point-to-point tunneling requires substantially less management overhead, both from an establishment as well as a maintenance point of view.

One of the major advantages of tunneling is that the VPN backbone and the VPN connected subnets do not require unique network addresses. This is particularly important when you consider that the majority of organizations today use private address space.

A VPN using tunneling could be constructed with or without the knowledge of the network provider and could span multiple network providers. Obviously, performance might be a problem if the service provider is not aware of the tunneling and does not provide adequate Quality of Service (QoS).

Cisco's Generic Routing Encapsulation (GRE) is used for tunneling between source and destination router, router-to-router. GRE tunnels provide a specific pathway across a shared WAN and encapsulate traffic with new packet headers to ensure delivery to a specific destination. A GRE tunnel is configured between the source (*ingress*) router and the destination (*egress*) router. Packets designated to be forwarded across the tunnel are encapsulated with a GRE header, transported across the tunnel to the tunnel end-point address, and stripped of their GRE header.

The IETF's Layer 2 Tunneling Protocol (L2TP) and Microsoft's Point-to-Point Tunneling Protocol (PPTP) are used for host-to-host tunneling. PPTP should not be used without additional security features, such as those provided by IPSec, as it is known to have several security vulnerabilities. Some of these vulnerabilities have been addressed by the strengthening of PPTP's authentication mechanism, MS-CHAP, in the revised MS-CHAP version 2. Even with these changes, PPTP's security mechanisms provide only weak security and are vulnerable to attack.

Host-to-host tunneling is considerably more secure than router-to-router tunneling due to the fact that with host-to-host tunneling, the entire "conversation" can be encrypted. This is not the case in router-to-router tunneling, where only the tunnel can be encrypted and the host-to-router and router-to-host parts on both sides of the conversation are in cleartext. Tunneling is considered an overlay VPN model.

Virtual Private Dial Networks (VPDN) that utilize the Internet as carrier for RAS traffic are becoming very popular. Not only do they offer substantial cost savings over traditional RAS solutions, they also provide substantial flexibility. Any ISP point-of-presence (POP) could be used to provide secure RAS access services at a fraction of the traditional costs.

Layer 2 Tunneling Protocol (L2TP) and Microsoft's Point-to-Point Tunneling Protocol (PPTP) are fundamental to VPDN design and provide the tunneling features through which the RAS traffic reaches the desired services. VPDNs could be considered an overlay VPN model.

Controlled route leaking uses route filtering to control route propagation to only the members of a particular VPN. Multiple VPNs sharing the same network layer infrastructure are separated from one another only by the fact that routes to the other VPNs are blocked from each other. This is a rather simple and unsophisticated method of implementing a VPN but might be very effective in extranet or smaller network applications.

Controlled route leaking is considered a peer VPN model.

Transport and Application Layer VPNs

These VPNs are implemented at the transport and application layer (layers 4 and 5) of the OSI reference model. These implementations require the application to be VPN-aware and hence need to be written with this in mind. Although certainly possible, this form of VPN is not common.

With the IETF developing their Transport Layer Security (TLS) protocol, this form of VPN might become more important in the future. TLS 1.0 is at the proposed standard stage as RFC 2246.

Layer 2 Transport Protocol (L2TP)

Layer 2 Transport Protocol (L2TP) is an Internet Engineering Task Force (IETF) standard that combines the best features of two existing tunnelling protocols: Cisco's Layer 2 Forwarding (L2F) protocol and Microsoft's Point-to-Point Tunnelling Protocol (PPTP). L2TP has replaced Cisco's own proprietary Forwarding (L2F) protocol.

L2TP is a key building block for VPNs in the dial access space. Using L2TP tunnelling, an Internet Service Provider (ISP) or other access provider can create a virtual tunnel to link customers' remote sites or remote users with corporate networks. L2TP allows organizations to provide connectivity to remote users by leveraging a service provider's existing infrastructure. This often can be achieved at a lower cost and without the delays caused by establishing your own infrastructure.

The L2TP access controller (LAC), located at the ISP's point of presence (POP), exchanges messages with remote users and communicates by way of L2TP requests and responses with the customer's L2TP network server (LNS) to set up tunnels (see Figure 5.4). L2TP passes packets through the virtual tunnel between endpoints of a point-to-point connection. Frames from remote users are accepted by the ISP's POP, stripped of any linked framing or transparency bytes, encapsulated in L2TP, and forwarded over the appropriate tunnel. The customer's home gateway accepts these L2TP frames, strips the L2TP encapsulation, and processes the incoming frames for the appropriate interface. L2TP is an extension of PPP and is vendor interoperable.

Figure 5.4 L2TP architecture.

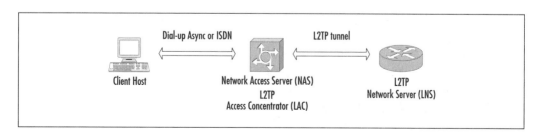

> **NOTE**
>
> L2TP is *not* a security protocol. This protocol is, however, very crucial to the operation of VPNs, in particular to dial VPNs. Security for L2TP is provided through IPSec.

L2TP uses a compulsory tunnelling model, which means that the tunnel is created without any action from the user and without allowing the user any choice in the matter.

In this scenario, a user dials into a Network Access Server (NAS), authenticates either against a locally configured profile or against a policy server, and, after successful authentication, an L2TP tunnel is dynamically established to a predetermined endpoint where the user's PPP session is terminated.

L2TP is supported in IOS from version 11.3(5)AA on limited platforms such as the Cisco AS5200, AS5300, AS5800, and the 7200 series. Platform support was extended to the 1600, 2500, 2600, 3600, 4000, 4500, 7500, and UAC 6400 in version 12.0(1)T.

Configuring Cisco L2TP

The following example illustrates how L2TP can be used to provide enterprise connectivity to remote users using a shared network such as a service provider. In this example, the user's domain name is very important because the LAC uses it to determine through which L2TP tunnel it needs to send the packet.

It is also important to understand that the client host gets an IP address from the remote network. The connection between the LAC and the LNS typically can be a series of IP networks, such as the Internet. Figure 5.5 shows a typical L2TP scenario, showing the L2TP access controller (LAC) as well as the L2TP network server (LNS).

Figure 5.5 L2TP configuration.

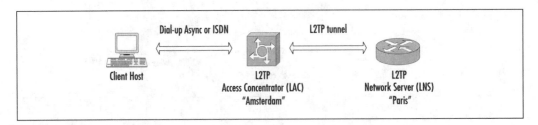

TIP

Throughout this chapter, the asterisks within the code listings represent a password being entered. Be sure you do not use simple passwords, as this is the most common security mistake made by network and security administrators. A simple way to improve your security is either to pick a good random password or to mask the password.

LAC Configuration Example

The following is a basic L2TP access controller (LAC) configuration for the scenario shown in Figure 5.5.

```
aaa new-model
aaa authentication ppp default local
username Amsterdam password 7 **********
vpdn enable
vpdn-group 1
   request dialin l2tp ip 172.25.1.19 domain test.com
```

To explain the previous code in more detail:

- Line 1 enables AAA.
- Line 2 enables AAA authentication for PPP.
- Line 3 defines the username as "Amsterdam."
- Line 4 enables VPDN.
- Line 5 defines VPDN group number 1.
- Line 6 allows the LAC to respond to dial-in requests using L2TP from IP address 172.25.1.19 domain test.com.

LNS Configuration Example

The following is a basic L2TP network server (LNS) configuration for the scenario shown in Figure 5.5. Note that the numbers in parentheses are for reference purposes only.

```
aaa new-model (1)
aaa authentication ppp default local (2)
username Paris password 7 ********** (3)
interface Virtual-Template1 (4)
```

```
   ip unnumbered Ethernet0 (5)
   no ip mroute-cache (6)
ppp authentication chap (7)
vpdn enable (8)
vpdn-group 1 (9)
   accept dialin l2tp virtual-template 1 remote Amsterdam (10)
```

To explain the previous code in more detail:

- Line 1 enables AAA.
- Line 2 enables AAA authentication for PPP.
- Line 3 defines the username as "Paris."
- Line 4 creates virtual-template 1 and assigns all values for virtual access interfaces.
- Line 5 uses the IP address from interface Ethernet 0.
- Line 6 disables multicast fast switching.
- Line 7 uses CHAP to authenticate PPP.
- Line 8 enables VPDN.
- Line 9 creates vpdn-group number 1.
- Line 10 accepts all dial-in L2TP tunnels from virtual-template from remote peer Amsterdam.

IPSec

Internet Protocol Security (IPSec) was developed by the Internet Engineering Task Force (IETF) to address the issue of network layer security. It is not a single protocol or specification but rather a framework of open standards for ensuring secure private communications over public IP networks. IPSec is documented in a series of RFCs. The overall IPSec implementation is guided by RFC 2401, "Security Architecture for the Internet Protocol."

The IETF maintains an official depository for its work on IPSec. This information can be found at www.ietf.org/html.charters/ipsec-charter.html.

Though IP dwarfs all other network protocols in sheer deployment numbers, and has been more successful than even its inventors could ever have imagined, it was not designed to be secure. IP has long been vulnerable to many forms of attack, including spoofing, sniffing, session hijacking, and man-in-the-middle attacks.

> **NOTE**
>
> IPSec's strength lies in the fact that it allows organizations to implement strong security without the need to change any of their applications. Only network layer infrastructure changes, such as routers, firewalls, and in some cases software client, are required. As with IP, IPSec is completely transparent from the end-user's perspective.

Initial security standards focused on application-level protocols and software, such as Secure Sockets Layer (SSL), which is used mainly for securing Web traffic; Secure Shell (SSH), which is used for securing Telnet sessions and file transfers; and Pretty Good Privacy (PGP), which is used for securing e-mail. These forms of security can be limiting, as the application itself needs to support these. However, in some cases, application-layer security provides additional features that are not supported by network-layer security. OpenPGP's digital signature is an example of such a feature.

Another place to implement security is at the network layer, as the applications are secured, even if they are not themselves aware of the security mechanisms. IPSec is based on this model.

Cisco has made IPSec support available since IOS release 11.3(3)T. It also supports IPSec in its PIX Firewall product range as well as its Cisco Secure VPN Client software available for the Microsoft Windows operating systems. It uses the approach that no matter what application is used, all packet level information has to travel through the network layer. By securing the network layer, the applications can automatically benefit from the security offered by that layer.

Due to its flexibility and strong security as well as its vendor interoperability feature, IPSec has found favor with all of the major networking and operating systems vendors. Most of these vendors have replaced, or at least supplemented, their own proprietary network layer security mechanism with IPSec.

Before the development of IPSec, the acceptance and large-scale deployment of VPNs was often hampered by security concerns. Existing solutions either were proprietary or used weak security algorithms.

The strength of proprietary solutions is often difficult to assess, as little information about them is generally made available, and their deployment is limited to a specific vendor. Multi-vendor interoperability was also a problem. This requirement was spurred on by the new economy where mergers and acquisitions and unlikely partnerships have become commonplace. IPSec addresses these concerns.

For Managers

Export Restrictions on Strong Encryption

IPSec uses encryption to offer *confidentiality* to VPN traffic. The RFCs provide for different encryption algorithms to be used in conjunction with IPSec.

The U.S. government places substantial restrictions on the export of *strong encryption*. Cisco is bound by these restrictions. This means that the only encryption algorithms that are exportable are the 56-bit DES encryption used by IPSec and the 40- and 56-bit encryptions used by CET.

Certain encryption algorithms, such as TripleDES, are available only under export licensing controls; these force Cisco to track each customer's deployment closely, and require lengthy legal documentation. Others are not available for export at all.

Cisco's Encryption Control Guidance site, www.cisco.com/wwl/export/crypto/index.html, provides comprehensive information on export-restricted encryption available from Cisco.

The U.S. government seems to be liberalizing its policy on encryption. Not long ago, only 40-bit encryption was exportable. On July 17, 2000, a further liberalization was introduced that allows more encryption technology to be exported to the European Union as well as to key trading partners.

The U.S. government encryption policy is strictly enforced through the Information Technology Controls Division, Office of Strategic Trade and Foreign Policy Controls, Department of Commerce. They maintain a Web site detailing commercial encryption export controls that can be found at www.bxa.doc.gov/Encryption. A breach of these export restrictions is considered a very serious offense. These export restrictions have a serious impact on security for many organizations outside the U.S.

In light of the many successful attacks on DES, this cipher and many others that use small key lengths are no longer considered secure. This is further aggravated by the fact that the IETF strongly discourages the use of ciphers with a key length smaller than 128 bits.

For a 128-bit key size, there are approximately 340,000,000,000,000,000,000,000,000,000,000,000,000 possible keys. The National Institute of Standards and Technology (NIST) is busy

Continued

developing a new open-standards-based encryption algorithm called Advanced Encryption Standard (AES). AES will replace the aging Data Encryption Standard (DES) that it adopted in 1977 as the Federal Information Processing Standard used by federal agencies to protect sensitive, unclassified information.

NIST is calling AES the "Crypto Algorithm for the Twenty-first Century..." and announced on October 2, 2000 that it has selected the *Rijndael* algorithm for their proposed AES.

IPSec Architecture

In simplified terms, IPSec provides three main functions:

- Authentication only, provided through the Authentication Header (AH) protocol

- Authentication and confidentiality (encryption), provided through the Encapsulating Security Payload (ESP) protocol

- Key exchange, provided either manually or through the Internet Key Exchange (IKE) protocol

IPSec provides secure communication between two endpoints, called IPSec peers. These types of communications are essentially sets of security associations (SAs) and define which protocols should be applied to sensitive packets, as well as the keying between the two peers. Multiple IPSec communications can exist between two peers, securing different data streams, with each communication having a separate set of Security Associations.

In Figure 5.6, IPSec is used in tunnel mode to protect the traffic between the two private networks that are connected via the public network.

In this scenario, the end hosts (John and Paul) do not need to support IPSec. Only the routers that connect the private networks to the public network need to support IPSec. Traffic on the private network is not encrypted (cleartext) and gets encrypted only when it has to pass over the public network.

IPSec over L2TP is also shown to provide secure remote access support for Peter, via PSTN dial-up, to access the corporate network. In this case, the end host (Peter) must also support IPSec.

Figure 5.6 IPSec deployed across a public network.

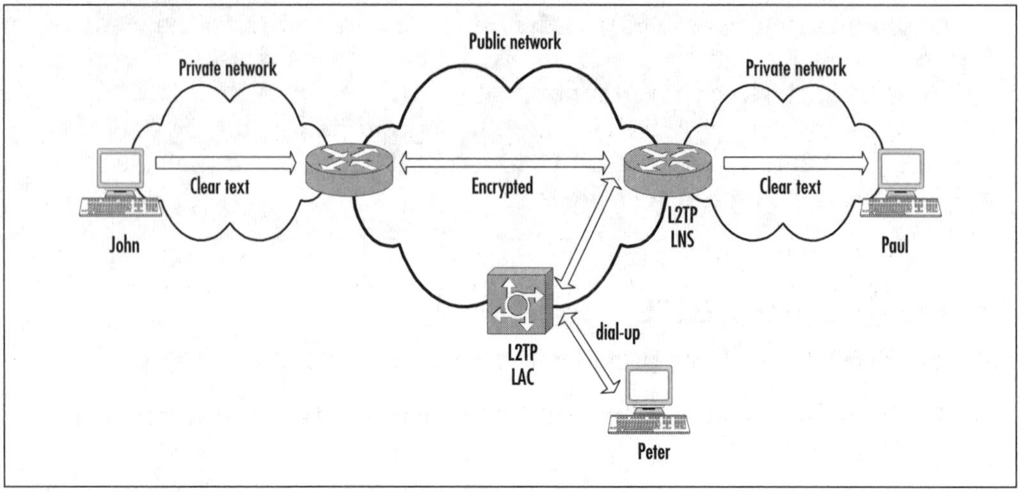

Security Association

IPSec Security Associations (SAs) define how two or more IPSec parties will use security services in the context of a particular security protocol (AH or ESP) to communicate securely on behalf of a particular flow. Among other information, SAs contain the shared secret keys that are to be used to protect data in a particular flow, as well their lifetimes.

SAs are uni-directional connections and are unique per security protocols (AH or ESP). This means that if both AH and ESP services are required, two or more SAs have to be created.

SAs can be created manually or automatically by using Internet Key Exchange (IKE). If created manually, the SAs are established as soon as they are created and do not expire. When created through IKE, SAs are established when needed and expire after a certain amount of time or after a certain volume of traffic, whichever is reached first. The default Cisco IOS lifetimes are 3,600 seconds (one hour) and 4,608,000 kilobytes. This provides an additional level of security because it forces a periodic security association renegotiation and thus periodically renews the encryption key material.

An SA is identified by three parameters:

- **Security Parameter Index (SPI)** A pseudo-arbitrary 32-bit value that is assigned to an SA when it is first created. Together with an IP address and security protocol (either AH or ESP) it uniquely identifies a particular SA. Both AH and ESP always contain a reference to an SPI. When SAs are manually created (i.e., IKE is not used) the SPI has to be specified manually for each SA.

- **IP destination address** The destination endpoint of the SA. This could be a host or network device such as a router or firewall.
- **Security protocol identifier** This could be either AH or ESP.

SAs specify whether IPSec is used in *transport* or *tunnel* mode:

- A *transport* mode SA is a security association between two hosts. The security provided by IPsec is end-to-end
- A *tunnel* mode SA is used when the IPsec peer is not the final destination of the IP traffic. This mode is typically used when either end of an IPsec security association is a security gateway or when both ends are security gateways. Thus, tunnel mode is used between two gateways or between a gateway and a host.

Use the following syntax to view the lifetimes:

```
show crypto ipsec security-association-lifetime
Security association lifetime: 4608000 kilobytes/3600 seconds
```

Anti-Replay Feature

Anti-replay is an important IPSec feature that uses sequence numbers together with data authentication to reject old or duplicate packets that could be used as an attack.

Replay attacks occur when an attacker intercepts an authenticated packet and later transmits it in order to disrupt service.

Cisco IOS always uses anti-replay protection when it provides data authentication services, except when Security Associations are manually established without the use of IKE.

Security Policy Database

Security Associations are used by IPSec to enforce a security policy. A higher level Security Policy Database (SPD) specifies what and how security services are to be applied to IP packets.

An SPD discriminates among traffic that is to be IPSec-protected and traffic that is allowed to bypass IPSec. If the traffic is to be IPSec-protected, it also determines which specific SA the traffic needs to use.

Each SPD entry is defined by a set of IP and upper layer protocol field values called selectors. In effect, these selectors are used to filter outgoing traffic in order to map it into a particular SA.

Authentication Header

The Authentication Header (AH) is an important IPSec security protocol that provides packet authentication and anti-replay services. AH is defined in RFC 2402 and uses IP Protocol 51. AH can be deployed in either transport or tunnel mode.

Transport mode is used to provide an end-to-end IPsec communication between two peers. Only the payload is encrypted, and the original IP header is left intact. It provides protection for upper layer protocols, in addition to selected IP header fields. In transport mode, the AH is inserted after the IP header and before an upper layer protocol (such as TCP, UDP, and ICMP), or before any other previously inserted IPSec headers.

In Figure 5.7 and Figure 5.8, the mutable fields referred to are fields like time-to-live, which cannot be included in authentication calculations because they change as the packet travels.

In tunnel mode, the entire original IP datagram is encrypted, and it becomes the payload in a new IP packet.

Figure 5.7 AH in transport mode.

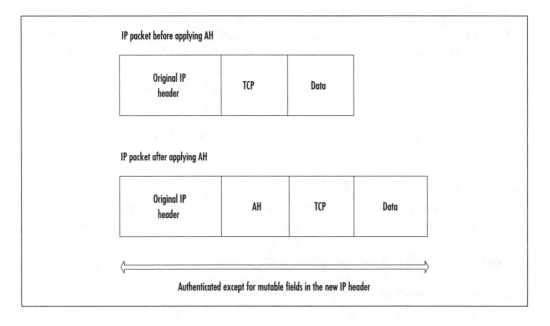

Figure 5.8 AH in tunnel mode.

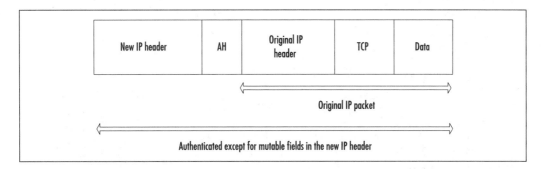

Encapsulating Security Payload

Encapsulating Security Payload (ESP) is an important IPSec security protocol that provides data encryption, data authentication, and anti-replay services. ESP can be used on its own or with AH packet authentication. ESP encapsulates the data that is to be protected and can be deployed in either transport or tunnel mode. ESP is defined in RFC 2406 and uses IP Protocol 50.

Transport mode provides protection for upper layer protocols but not for the IP header. This means that the ESP is inserted after the IP header and before an upper-layer protocol or any other IPSec headers. With IPv4, this means the ESP is placed after the IP header (and any options that it contains) and before the upper layer protocol. Since the IP header is available to any intermediate routers, ESP and AH are compatible with non-IPSec compliant routers.

Tunnel mode ESP may be employed in either hosts or security gateways. In tunnel mode, the inner IP header carries the ultimate source and destination addresses, and an outer IP header may contain distinct IP addresses (of security gateways, for example). In tunnel mode, ESP protects the entire inner IP packet, including the entire inner IP header. The position of ESP in tunnel mode relative to the outer IP header is the same as for ESP in transport mode.

Manual IPSec

In manual IPSec, all the Security Association parameters must be pre-defined by the network manager. Those parameters include the security protocol (AH, ESP), peer IP address, SPI, and keying material (session keys). This makes manual IPSec configuration-intensive and prone to incorrect configuration. Note that the Security Associations in manual IPsec never expire. This means that the keying material (session keys) will not expire and thus be more vulnerable to attacks. Also, the anti-replay security feature is not available in this type of configuration. Manual IPsec is generally used for initial test and debugging purposes.

For larger, more complex environments, the use of IKE is strongly advised since the Security Association management is automated.

Internet Key Exchange

Internet Key Exchange (IKE) is a key management protocol used in IPSec to create an authenticated, secure communication channel between two entities and then to negotiate the Security Associations for IPSec. This process requires that the two entities authenticate themselves to each other and exchange the required key material.

IPSec assumes that a Security Association is in place but does not itself have a mechanism for creating this association. IPSec uses IKE to create and maintain these Security Associations automatically.

IKE is defined in RFC 2409 and is a hybrid protocol that implements Oakley and SKEME key exchanges inside the Internet Security Association Key Management Protocol (ISAKMP) framework, which is in turn defined by RFC 2408.

IKE offers several advantages over manually defined keys (manual keying); IKE does the following:

- Eliminates manual configuration of keys.
- Allows you to specify a lifetime for IPSec Security Association.
- Allows encryption keys to change during IPSec sessions.
- Supports the use of public-key-based authentication and Certification Authorities, making IPSec scaleable.
- Allows dynamic authentication of peers.

IKE negotiation has two phases:

- **Phase one** The two peers mutually authenticate and negotiate how to set up a bidirectional ISAKMP SA. This ISAKMP SA provides a secure communication channel that will be used for phase two negotiation. One ISAKMP SA between a pair of peers can handle negotiations for multiple IPsec SAs.
- **Phase two** Using the ISAKMP SA, the peers negotiate IPSec (ESP and AH) as required. IPSec SAs are uni-directional (a different key is used in each direction) and are always negotiated in pairs to handle two-way traffic. More than one pair may be defined between two peers.

Both of these phases use the UDP protocol and port 500 for their negotiations. The actual IPSec SAs use the ESP or AH protocols.

In selecting a suitable key management protocol for IPSec, the IETF considered several different protocols and eventually chose IKE. Sun's Simple Key management for Internet Protocols (SKIP) seemed to be a favorite but eventually was not chosen. In an effort to be standards-compliant, SUN is now also offering IKE support. Another protocol, Photorus, described in RFC 2522 and RFC 2523, was considered too experimental.

TIP

Don't confuse IPSec SAs with IKE SAs. IKE SAs are used to negotiate the parameters for the IPSec SAs. There is only one IKE SA between two devices, but there can be multiple IPSec SAs for the same IKE SA.

Authentication Methods

IPSec peers must be authenticated to each other. The peers must agree on a common authentication protocol through a negotiation process.

The following authentication methods are supported:

- **Preshared keys** The same key is preconfigured in each device. The peers authenticate each other by computing and sending a keyed hash of data that includes the preshared key. If the receiving side can independently recreate the same hash using its preshared key, it knows that both parties must share the same key.

- **Public key encryption** Each party generates a pseudorandom number (nonce) and encrypts it in the other party's public key. The parties authenticate each other by computing a keyed hash containing the other peer's nonce, decrypted with the local private key as well as other publicly and privately available information.

- **Digital signatures** Each device digitally signs a set of data and sends it to the other party. This method is similar to the public key cryptography one, except that it provides non-repudiation (the ability for a third party to prove that a communication between the two parties took place).

IKE and Certificate Authorities

Even with IKE, the keys for enabling the strong security offered by IPSec become difficult to manage in larger secure networks. Digital certificates together with trusted third-party Certificate Authorities (CAs) offer a mechanism to scale IPSec to the Internet.

IKE interoperates with the X.509 certificate standard. X.509 certificates are the equivalent of digital ID cards and are the building block with which Certificate Authorities like VeriSign and Entrust authenticate IPSec connections.

Cisco and VeriSign, Inc. co-developed a certificate management protocol called Certificate Enrollment Protocol (CEP). CEP is an early implementation of Certificate Request Syntax (CRS), an emerging standard proposed by the IETF. CEP specifies how a device communicates with a Certificate Authority, including how to retrieve the CA's public key, how to enroll a device with the CA, and how to retrieve a Certificate Revocation List (CRL). CEP uses RSA's Public Key Cryptography Standard (PKCS) 7 and 10 as key technologies. The IETF's Public Key Infrastructure Working Group is working to standardize a protocol for these functions.

Figure 5.9 shows a typical scenario of multiple routers in a mesh topology where key management is not performed via a Certificate Authority. Every time a new router is added, keys need to be created between each of the participating IPSec routers.

Figure 5.9 Key management without Certificate Authority.

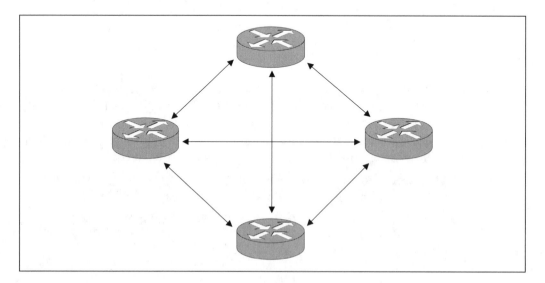

As an example, if you wanted to add an additional router to Figure 5.9, four additional 2-part keys would be required to add just a single encryption router. The key's numbers grow exponentially as you add more routers, and the configuration and management of these keys becomes problematic. Certificate Authorities offer an ideal solution to such an environment.

Figure 5.10 shows a typical scenario where key management is performed through a Certificate Authority.

Figure 5.10 Key management with Certificate Authority.

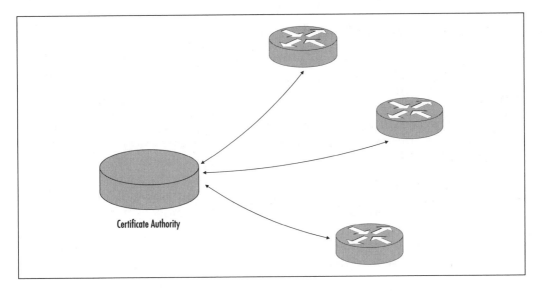

IPSec Limitations

One of the few limitations of IPSec is that it supports only unicast IP datagrams. No support for multicasts or broadcasts is currently provided.

Network Performance

IPSec can have a significant impact on your network performance, and the degree to which it does so is dependant on the specific implementation. Ensuring that the routers and firewalls have sufficient memory and processor capacity helps minimize performance degradation.

For larger implementations, hardware-based IPSec acceleration provided by the Integrated Services Adapter (ISA) adapter is strongly advised. The ISA can encrypt traffic at 90Mbps with up to 2,000 concurrent sites or users.

Network Troubleshooting

One of the drawbacks of network layer encryption is that it complicates network troubleshooting and debugging.

Intrusion detection, such as that offered by the Cisco Secure Intrusion Detection System (IDS) is also affected by IPSec. To determine if suspicious activity is occurring, the Cisco Secure IDS sensor analyses both the packet header information and packet data information. If these are encrypted by IPSec, then the sensor cannot analyze the packet to determine if the packet contains any suspicious information.

Interoperability with Firewalls and Network Address Translation Devices

For IPSec to work in conjunction with filtering devices such as firewalls and routers with access lists, it is important to remember that IKE uses UDP port 500, and IPSec ESP and AH use protocol numbers 50 and 51. This port and these protocols may not be blocked or filtered by these devices; otherwise, IPSec will not work.

Not all implementations of Network Address Translation (NAT) and Port Address Translation (PAT) will work in an IPSec environment. Authentication Header (AH), for example, will not work together with NAT. This is because AH uses an integrity check that is partially based on the source and destination addresses. Because NAT changes these addresses, IPSec rejects these packets as modified.

In general, NAT translation should occur before the router performs IPSec encapsulation; in other words, IPSec should be working with global addresses.

For a detailed discussion on what NAT and PAT configurations will and will not work, refer to "Deploying IPSec Reference Guide" on the Cisco Web site at the following link:

www.cisco.com/warp/public/cc/techno/protocol/ipsecur/ipsec/prodlit/dplip_in.htm

IPSec and Cisco Encryption Technology (CET)

Prior to IPSec's development and standardization, Cisco developed a proprietary network layer encryption technology called Cisco Encryption Technology (CET). CET was first introduced in IOS release 11.2 and was based on the 40- and 56-bit Data Encryption Standard (DES) encryption algorithm.

CET has now largely been replaced by the standards-based IPSec, although Cisco still maintains support for it. Although specific CET images will no longer be available in release 12.1, CET will continue to be included as part of the IPSec images (CET End-of-Life announced in Cisco Product Bulletin, No. 1118).

In many aspects, CET is very similar to IPSec. IPSec does, however, have some major advantages over CET, namely:

Multivendor interoperability Since IPSec is standardized, it interoperates not only with other vendors' equipment, but also on a variety of platforms such as routers, firewalls, and hosts (servers and clients).

Scalability IPSec deploys the Internet Key Exchange (IKE) key management technique and includes support for Certificate Authorities that allow virtually unlimited scalability.

Data authentication CET provides only for data confidentiality.

Anti-replay CET does not support this important feature and is vulnerable to this form of attack.

Stronger encryption CET supports only 40- and 56-bit DES, which is now considered unsecure.

Host implementations CET supports only router-to-router implementations.

CET does, however, have an advantage over IPSec:

Speed It's faster than IPSec, but this is mainly because it isn't as thorough. For instance, CET does not offer per-packet data authentication or packet expansion.

Like L2F and many other technologies developed by Cisco, CET is another prime example of where Cisco has developed a technology, worked with the Internet community to standardize it, and then replaced its own proprietary solution with the standardized version. Yet more proof that Cisco is a standards company!

Configuring Cisco IPSec

The following examples show how IPSec can be used to encrypt and protect network traffic between two networks. The first example demonstrates IPSec manual keying and the second, IPSec over a GRE Tunnel.

TIP

When using access lists or any form of filtering, remember that IKE uses UDP port 500, and IPSec ESP and AH use protocol numbers 50 and 51. These ports and protocols must not be blocked or IPSec will not function.

In very simplified terms, IPSec is configured by:

- Creating a Security Association (either manually or by using IKE).

- Defining the SPD (access lists that specify which traffic is to be secured).

- Defining the cryptographic algorithms and IPsec mode (transform-set).

- Applying the SPD and transform-set access lists to an interface by way of crypto map sets.

Here are some of the fundamental IPSec configuration commands and how they work.

transform-set This is how you match a security protocol (AH or ESP) to its authentication or encryption algorithm. For example, a possible transform-set is ESP with the DES encryption algorithm, as in the IPSec Manual Keying example to follow in the next section. A typical configuration might have multiple transform-sets with the peers agreeing on a particular transform-set for a particular data flow during IPSec security association negotiation.

access-list This is how you specify what traffic is to be secured. A typical access-list might look like this.

```
access-list 100 permit ip 10.1.1.0 0.0.0.255 10.1.3.0 0.0.0.255
```

crypto map This is how you pull together the various parts used to set up IPSec, including the crypto access-list, the transform-set, as well as the remote IPSec peer.

IPSec Manual Keying Configuration

The following example illustrates the use of IPSec Manual Keying to encrypt TCP/IP traffic between the 10.1.1.0/24 and 10.1.3.0/24 networks (see Figure 5.11).

If a host on network 10.1.1.x wants to send a packet to a host on network 10.1.3.x, the packet from host 10.1.1.x is sent in cleartext to the capetown router. The capetown router uses the IPSec tunnel between the capetown and london router to encrypt the packet and sends it to the london router, which decrypts the packet and sends it to the host on network 10.1.3.x in cleartext. Cisco 3640s with IOS release 11.3(8)T1 (IP Plus IPSec 56 feature set) were used for this example.

In this example, DES was used as the encryption cipher. This was done mainly to accommodate an international audience, where export restrictions might limit the availability of strong encryption. Please note that DES is no longer considered secure, and wherever possible a stronger cipher such as 3DES should be used.

NOTE

In IOS release 12.0, the crypto map statement **set security-association inbound...** has changed to **set session-key inbound**....

Figure 5.11 Network diagram for IPSec manual keying.

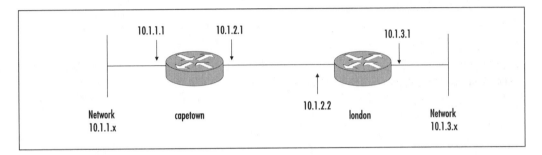

The configuration of the *capetown* router follows:

```
version 11.3

service timestamps debug uptime

service timestamps log uptime

!

hostname capetown

!

enable password 7 ********

!

ip subnet-zero

!

!

no crypto isakmp enable

!

!

crypto ipsec transform-set encrypt-des esp-des

!
```

```
!
crypto map test 8 ipsec-manual
set peer 10.1.2.2
set security-association inbound esp 1000 cipher ***************
    authenticator 01
set security-association outbound esp 1001 cipher ***************
    authenticator 01
set transform-set encrypt-des
match address 100
!
!
!
interface Serial0/0
 ip address 10.1.2.1 255.255.255.0
 no ip route-cache
 no ip mroute-cache
 crypto map test

!
interface Ethernet1/0
 ip address 10.1.1.1 255.255.255.0
!
ip classless
ip route 0.0.0.0 0.0.0.0 10.1.2.2
!
access-list 100 permit ip 10.1.1.0 0.0.0.255 10.1.3.0 0.0.0.255
!
!
line con 0
line aux 0
line vty 0 4
 login
!
end
```

The configuration of the *london* router is as follows:

```
version 11.3
service timestamps debug uptime
service timestamps log uptime
!
hostname london
!
enable password 7 ********
!
ip subnet-zero
!
!
no crypto isakmp enable
!
!
crypto ipsec transform-set encrypt-des esp-des
!
 !
 crypto map test 8 ipsec-manual
 set peer 10.1.2.1
 set security-association inbound esp 1001 cipher ***************
    authenticator 01
 set security-association outbound esp 1000 cipher ***************
    authenticator 01
 set transform-set encrypt-des
 match address 100
!
!
interface Ethernet0/0
 ip address 10.1.3.1 255.255.255.0
!
interface Serial0/0
 ip address 10.1.2.2 255.255.255.0
 no ip route-cache
```

```
 no ip mroute-cache
 no fair-queue
 crypto map test
!
interface Serial0/1
 no ip address
 shutdown
!
ip classless
ip route 0.0.0.0 0.0.0.0 10.1.2.1
!
access-list 100 permit ip 10.1.3.0 0.0.0.255 10.1.1.0 0.0.0.255
!
!
line con 0
line aux 0
line vty 0 4
 login
!
end
```

To verify and debug the preceding example, use the **show crypto engine connections active** and **show crypto ipsec sa** commands.

The command **show crypto engine connections active** shows all active encryption connections for all crypto engines. Of particular interest are the encrypt counters that show that the encryption is working.

```
capetown#show crypto engine connections active
```

ID	Interface	IP-Address	State	Algorithm	Encrypt	Decrypt
1	Serial0/0	10.1.2.1	set	DES_56_CBC	235	0
2	Serial0/0	10.1.2.1	set	DES_56_CBC	0	236

```
capetown#
```

The **show crypto ipsec sa** command shows the settings used by current security associations. Of particular interest are local and remote crypto endpoints, the transform set used (encryption algorithm), as well as statistics of the packets encrypted and decrypted. In the example to follow, the transform-set used is ESP-DES.

```
capetown#show crypto ipsec sa

interface: Serial0/0
    Crypto map tag: test, local addr. 10.1.2.1

   local  ident (addr/mask/prot/port): (10.1.1.0/255.255.255.0/0/0)
   remote ident (addr/mask/prot/port): (10.1.3.0/255.255.255.0/0/0)
   current_peer: 10.1.2.2
     PERMIT, flags={origin_is_acl,}
    #pkts encaps: 235, #pkts encrypt: 235, #pkts digest 0
    #pkts decaps: 236, #pkts decrypt: 236, #pkts verify 0
    #send errors 0, #recv errors 0

     local crypto endpt.: 10.1.2.1, remote crypto endpt.: 10.1.2.2
     path mtu 1500, media mtu 1500
     current outbound spi: 3E9

     inbound esp sas:
      spi: 0x3E8(1000)
        transform: esp-des ,
        in use settings ={Tunnel, }
        slot: 0, conn id: 2, crypto map: test
        no sa timing
        IV size: 8 bytes
        replay detection support: N


     inbound ah sas:


     outbound esp sas:
      spi: 0x3E9(1001)
        transform: esp-des ,
        in use settings ={Tunnel, }
```

```
      slot: 0, conn id: 1, crypto map: test

      no sa timing

      IV size: 8 bytes

      replay detection support: N




   outbound ah sas:




capetown#
```

IPSec over GRE Tunnel Configuration

The following example illustrates the use of IPSec over a GRE Tunnel to encrypt non-IP based traffic (see Figure 5.12). In this example Novell's Internetwork Packet Exchange (IPX) was used, but the same example holds true for other non-IP based protocols such as AppleTalk.

Cisco 3640s with IOS release 11.3(8)T1 (IP Plus IPSec 56 feature set) were used for this example. DES was used as the encryption cipher. This was done mainly to accommodate an international audience, where export restrictions might limit the availability of strong encryption. Please note that DES is no longer considered secure and wherever possible, a stronger cipher such as 3DES should be used.

Figure 5.12 Network diagram for IPSec over a GRE tunnel.

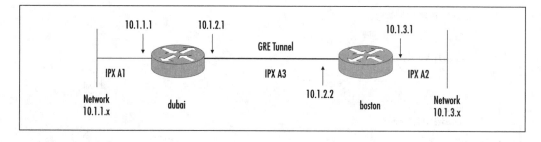

The configuration of the *dubai* router is as follows:

```
version 11.3

service timestamps debug uptime

service timestamps log uptime

!
```

```
hostname dubai
!
!
ip subnet-zero
ipx routing 0001.425f.9391
!
!
!
crypto isakmp policy 10
 authentication pre-share
 group 2
 lifetime 3600
crypto isakmp key ****** address 10.1.5.1
!
!
crypto ipsec transform-set tunnelset esp-des esp-md5-hmac
!
  !
  crypto map toBoston local-address Loopback0
  crypto map toBoston 10 ipsec-isakmp
  set peer 10.1.5.1
  set transform-set tunnelset
  match address 101
!
interface Loopback0
 ip address 10.1.4.1 255.255.255.0
!
interface Tunnel0
 no ip address
 no ip route-cache
 no ip mroute-cache
 ipx network A3
 tunnel source Serial0/0
 tunnel destination 10.1.2.2
```

```
crypto map toBoston
!
interface Serial0/0
 ip address 10.1.2.1 255.255.255.0
 no ip route-cache
 no ip mroute-cache
 no fair-queue
 crypto map toBoston
!
interface Ethernet1/0
 ip address 10.1.1.1 255.255.255.0
 ipx network A1
!
ip classless
ip route 0.0.0.0 0.0.0.0 10.1.2.2
!
access-list 101 permit gre host 10.1.2.1 host 10.1.2.2
!
line con 0
line aux 0
line vty 0 4
 login
!
end
```

Here is the configuration of the *boston* router:

```
version 11.3
service timestamps debug uptime
service timestamps log uptime
!
hostname boston
!
!
ip subnet-zero
ipx routing 0001.42a5.79a1
```

```
!
crypto isakmp policy 10
 authentication pre-share
 group 2
 lifetime 3600
crypto isakmp key ****** address 10.1.4.1
!
!
crypto ipsec transform-set tunnelset esp-des esp-md5-hmac
!
 !
 crypto map toDubai local-address Loopback0
 crypto map toDubai 10 ipsec-isakmp
 set peer 10.1.4.1
 set transform-set tunnelset
 match address 101
!
interface Loopback0
 ip address 10.1.5.1 255.255.255.0
!
interface Tunnel0
 no ip address
 no ip route-cache
 no ip mroute-cache
 ipx network A3
 tunnel source Serial0/0
 tunnel destination 10.1.2.1
 crypto map toDubai
!
interface Ethernet0/0
 ip address 10.1.3.1 255.255.255.0
 ipx network A2
!
interface Serial0/0
```

```
     ip address 10.1.2.2 255.255.255.0
     no ip route-cache
     no ip mroute-cache
     no fair-queue
     crypto map toDubai
    !
    interface Serial0/1
     no ip address
     shutdown
    !
    ip classless
    ip route 0.0.0.0 0.0.0.0 10.1.2.1
    !
    access-list 101 permit gre host 10.1.2.2 host 10.1.2.1
    !
    line con 0
    line aux 0
    line vty 0 4
     login
    !
    end
```

To verify and debug the preceding example, use the **show crypto engine connections active**, **show ipx route ping ipx ...**, and **show crypto ipsec sa** commands.

The command **show crypto engine connections active** shows all active encryption connections for all crypto engines. Of particular interest are the encrypt counters that show that the encryption is working.

```
dubai#show crypto engine connections active
```

ID	Interface	IP-Address	State	Algorithm	Encrypt	Decrypt
17	no idb	no address	set	DES_56_CBC	0	0
22	Tunnel0	unassigned	set	HMAC_MD5+DES_56_CB	0	20
23	Tunnel0	unassigned	set	HMAC_MD5+DES_56_CB	20	0

```
dubai#
```

The **show ipx route** command shows the ipx routing table and shows that network A2 is known via RIP through Tunnel 0. IPX traffic between network A1 and A2 is being encapsulated in TCP/IP and tunnelled through the network.

```
dubai#show ipx route
Codes: C - Connected primary network,    c - Connected secondary network
      S - Static, F - Floating static, L - Local (internal), W - IPXWAN
      R - RIP, E - EIGRP, N - NLSP, X - External, A - Aggregate
      s - seconds, u - uses, U - Per-user static


3 Total IPX routes. Up to 1 parallel paths and 16 hops allowed.


No default route known.


C         A1 (NOVELL-ETHER),   Et1/0
C         A3 (TUNNEL),         Tu0
R         A2 [151/01] via      A3.0001.42a5.79a1,    27s, Tu0
dubai#
```

The **ping ipx** … command proves that the remote IPX device is accessible through the encrypted IPSec Tunnel interface. The output of **show crypto engine connections active** and **show crypto ipsec sa** will confirm that five packets have been encrypted—the five IPX ping packets.

```
dubai#ping ipx a2.0001.42a5.79a1
Type escape sequence to abort.
Sending 5, 100-byte IPX cisco Echoes to A2.0001.42a5.79a1, timeout is 2
seconds:
!!!!!
Success rate is 100 percent (5/5), round-trip min/avg/max = 8/8/8 ms
dubai#
```

Here, the **show crypto ipsec sa** shows the settings used by current security associations. Of particular interest are local and remote crypto endpoints, the transform set used (encryption algorithm) as well as statistics of the packets encrypted and decrypted.

In the example to follow, the transform-sets used are ESP-DES and ESP-MD5-HMAC.

```
dubai#show crypto ipsec sa

interface: Tunnel0
    Crypto map tag: toBoston, local addr. 10.1.4.1

   local  ident (addr/mask/prot/port): (10.1.2.1/255.255.255.255/47/0)
   remote ident (addr/mask/prot/port): (10.1.2.2/255.255.255.255/47/0)
   current_peer: 10.1.5.1
     PERMIT, flags={origin_is_acl,}
    #pkts encaps: 57, #pkts encrypt: 57, #pkts digest 57
    #pkts decaps: 57, #pkts decrypt: 57, #pkts verify 57
    #send errors 1, #recv errors 0

     local crypto endpt.: 10.1.4.1, remote crypto endpt.: 10.1.5.1
     path mtu 1514, media mtu 1514
     current outbound spi: 71313FA

     inbound esp sas:
      spi: 0x111214EE(286397678)
         transform: esp-des esp-md5-hmac ,
         in use settings ={Tunnel, }
         slot: 0, conn id: 22, crypto map: toBoston
         sa timing: remaining key lifetime (k/sec): (4607992/2989)
         IV size: 8 bytes
         replay detection support: Y


     inbound ah sas:


     outbound esp sas:
      spi: 0x71313FA(118690810)
         transform: esp-des esp-md5-hmac ,
         in use settings ={Tunnel, }
```

```
      slot: 0, conn id: 23, crypto map: toBoston

      sa timing: remaining key lifetime (k/sec): (4607992/2989)

      IV size: 8 bytes

      replay detection support: Y



   outbound ah sas:



interface: Serial0/0

   Crypto map tag: toBoston, local addr. 10.1.4.1


  local   ident (addr/mask/prot/port): (10.1.2.1/255.255.255.255/47/0)

  remote ident (addr/mask/prot/port): (10.1.2.2/255.255.255.255/47/0)

  current_peer: 10.1.5.1

    PERMIT, flags={origin_is_acl,}

   #pkts encaps: 57, #pkts encrypt: 57, #pkts digest 57

   #pkts decaps: 57, #pkts decrypt: 57, #pkts verify 57

   #send errors 1, #recv errors 0


    local crypto endpt.: 10.1.4.1, remote crypto endpt.: 10.1.5.1

    path mtu 1514, media mtu 1514

    current outbound spi: 71313FA


    inbound esp sas:

     spi: 0x111214EE(286397678)

        transform: esp-des esp-md5-hmac ,

        in use settings ={Tunnel, }

        slot: 0, conn id: 22, crypto map: toBoston

        sa timing: remaining key lifetime (k/sec): (4607992/2989)

        IV size: 8 bytes

        replay detection support: Y
```

```
   inbound ah sas:



   outbound esp sas:
     spi: 0x71313FA(118690810)
       transform: esp-des esp-md5-hmac ,
       in use settings ={Tunnel, }
       slot: 0, conn id: 23, crypto map: toBoston
       sa timing: remaining key lifetime (k/sec): (4607992/2989)
       IV size: 8 bytes
       replay detection support: Y



   outbound ah sas:


dubai#
```

Connecting IPSec Clients to Cisco IPSec

A common design is to use IPSec between an IPSec-aware host client (such as a remote PC) and an IPSec router or firewall. This can be achieved either through the host client's operating system being IPSec-aware or through a third-party IPSec software client.

There seems to be a trend to include IPSec client technology into the operating system, reducing the requirement for a third-party IPSec client. Microsoft Windows 2000 as well as Linux (via FreeS/WAN) and the BSD variants (via Kame) now all offer built-in IPSec client capabilities.

Cisco Secure VPN Client

Cisco Secure VPN client is a software program that provides IPSec support to Windows 95, Windows 98, and Windows NT operating systems that do not have native IPSec support. It does this by integrating into the existing IP stack.

The latest release is Cisco Secure VPN Client 1.1, which is a component of the Cisco Secure VPN Software. With the recent acquisition of Altiga Networks, Cisco will be releasing a Unified VPN Client called Cisco Client that ultimately will replace the Cisco Secure VPN client.

For PIX Firewall, version 5.0 and router IOS release 12.0(5)T, 12.0(5.5)T and 12.0(5)XE version 1.0a of the Cisco Secure VPN client must be used.

For PIX Firewall version 5.1 and router IOS versions 12.1(1)T, 12.1(2)E, and 12.1(2), Cisco Secure VPN client version 1.1 is used.

The Security Policy Editor application is shown in Figure 5.13. This is the utility through which the Cisco Secure VPN client is configured.

Figure 5.13 Cisco Secure VPN client configuration.

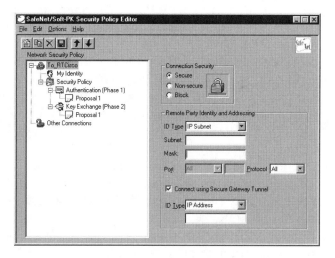

During installation of the client, a Cisco Secure VPN Client icon is added to the Windows Taskbar that shows if TCP/IP is secured or not. If it is secured, a key is displayed.

In Figure 5.14, the View Log utility is shown. This is a powerful tool to log and troubleshoot Cisco Secure client problems. In this example, Phase 1 client authentication was not been successful. The View Log can be accessed by right clicking the Cisco Secure VPN Client icon located on the Windows Taskbar.

Figure 5.14 Cisco Secure VPN client View Log.

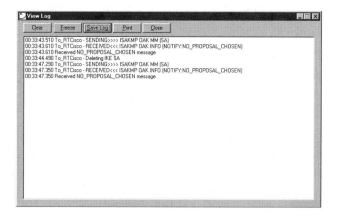

Windows 2000

The Microsoft Windows 2000 operating system (Server, Professional, Advanced Server, and Datacenter Server versions) now has native support for IPSec without the use of any third-party software. Full support of industry IETF standards is provided.

Configuration is via the IP Security Policy Management snap-in. A quick way to load this is to click Start, click Run, and then type **secpol.msc** and then click OK.

Microsoft makes a tool called IP Security Monitor available that administrators can use to confirm whether IPSec communications are successfully secured. The tool shows how many packets have been sent over the Authenticated Header (AH) or Encapsulating Security Payload (ESP) security protocols and how many security associations and keys have been generated since the computer was last started.

IP Security Monitor also indicates whether or not IPSec is enabled in a given computer. This information is located in the lower-right corner of the window. To start IP Security Monitor, click Start, click Run, type **ipsecmon**, and then click OK.

For remote Windows 2000 clients to use IPSec across a public IP network on a dial-up basis, the use of L2TP or Microsoft's PPTP protocol is required to establish a tunnel through the public IP network. Once the tunnel is established, IPSec can be used in transport mode to secure the communications through the tunnel.

There are some good Microsoft Knowledge Base documents that will help you in implementing the Windows 2000 client with Cisco's IPSec. These documents can be found at the following URL: http://www.microsoft.com/technet

Q249278 – Windows VPN Compatibility with Cisco VPN

Q249067 – How to Configure Cisco IOS for L2TP/IPSec in Windows 2000

Q249125 – Using Certificates for Windows 2000 and Cisco IOS VPN Interoperation

Q252735 – How to Configure IPSec Tunneling in Windows 2000

Q257225 – Basic IPSec Troubleshooting in Windows 2000

Q231585 – Overview of Secure IP Communication with IPSec in Windows 2000

Figure 5.15 and Figure 5.16 show the IP Security Policy Management snap-in that is used to configure IPSec in a Windows 2000 client.

Figure 5.15 Windows 2000 IP Security Policy Management snap-in.

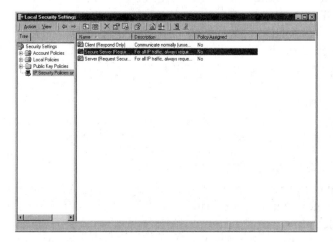

Figure 5.16 Secure Server option screen.

Linux FreeS/WAN

The Secure Wide Area Network project (FreeS/WAN) aims to make IPSec freely available on Linux platforms. It does so by providing free source code for IPSec. The project's official Web site can be found at www.freeswan.org.

It all started with John Gilmore, the founder and main driving force behind FreeS/WAN, who wanted to make the Internet more secure and protect traffic against wiretapping.

To avoid export limitations of cryptographic products imposed by the U.S. government, FreeS/WAN has been completely developed and maintained outside of the U.S. As a result, the strong encryption supported by FreeS/WAN is exportable.

Those interested in large-scale FreeS/WAN implementations should read the paper called "Moat: a Virtual Private Network Appliance and Services Platform," which discusses a large VPN deployment using FreeS/WAN. It was written by John S. Denker, Steven M. Bellovin, Hugh Daniel, Nancy L. Mintz, Tom Killian, and Mark A. Plotnick, and is available for download from www.research.att.com/~smb/papers/index.html.

BSD Kame Project

The Kame Project is a joint effort by seven leading Japanese companies to develop free reference implementations of advanced networking features on the BSD UNIX platform. Implementations for several BSD variants are being developed, including FreeBSD, NetBSD, OpenBSD, and BSDI. The project's official Web site can be found at www.kame.ne.

The project has three main focus areas:

- IPv6
- IPSec (IPv4 and IPv6)
- Advanced networking such as advanced packet queuing, ATM, and mobility

The Kame Project was started in April 1998 as a two-year project and has since been extended for a further two years.

In alphabetical order, the members of the project are:

- Fujitsu Limited
- Hitachi Limited
- IIJ Research Laboratory
- NEC Corporation
- Toshiba Corporation
- YDC Corporation
- Yokogawa Electric Corporation

Kame's aim is to provide standardized IPSec and IPv6 stacks providing advanced networking features across the BSD variants. Most of these features are in an advanced stage, with Kame-based code already merged into the current releases of FreeBSD, NetBSD, and OpenBSD.

For those more adventurous, both supply early releases, intended for hackers and researchers (termed SNAP).

Summary

IPSec addresses the security concerns that have held back large-scale VPN deployment for years. Not only is it a technically sound framework, but it has also passed the other important hurdle, that of vendor and market acceptance.

Cisco has recognized the fact that all of the features that will make VPNs even more successful in the future have only recently come together. They are constantly striving to provide their customers the competitive edge by offering innovative and cost-effective networking solutions.

The Cisco 7100 Series VPN router is just such an innovation. This product, together with the Integrated Services Adapter (ISA), a hardware-based IPSec acceleration adapter, can terminate thousands of IPSec protected tunnels.

Solutions like these will allow us to change network deployment times to days while reducing both capital and operating costs.

FAQs

Q: In which IOS release was IPSec first made available?

A: IPSec was first introduced in IOS version 11.3(3)T.

Q: Is IPSec supported in the standard IP-only IOS version?

A: No. IPSec images are identified as IPSec in the image description or are recognized by either 56i or k in the image filename.

Q: From which IOS version are specific CET images no longer available?

A: CET images have been discontinued from version 12.1 onwards. CET will, however, continue to be included in the IPSec images.

Q: If I deploy IPSec, will any of my applications need to change?

A: No. Because IPSec operates at the network layer of the OSI reference model, it is completely transparent to the applications. The applications will benefit by network layer security and encryption, but will not have to be modified.

Q: XYZ Networks, Inc. is offering a proprietary network layer encryption technology that it claims is far superior to IPSec. Should I buy this solution?

A: Probably not. Firstly, you won't have any vendor interoperability. Secondly, how do you go about assessing the strength of their encryption technology? Do you simply believe them because the brochure or presentation looks good? Ask yourself why XYZ Networks isn't working with the Internet community to standardize their solution.

Q: Does IPSec support hardware encryption acceleration?

A: Yes, IPSec uses the Integrated Services Adapter (ISA) available on the Cisco 7100 and 7200 router platforms to perform this function. The Encryption Service Adapter (ESA) that CET uses is not supported by IPSec, however.

Chapter 6

Cisco Authentication, Authorization, and Accounting Mechanisms

Solutions in this chapter:

- **Basic Authentication**

- **Cisco AAA Mechanisms**

- **Authentication Proxy**

Introduction

Authentication, authorization, and accounting (AAA) provide the required framework to configure access control. This chapter will give an overview of the AAA mechanisms provided on the Cisco router and RAS.

Authentication is the process of verifying the identity of an entity. This process is usually done by exchanging information to prove one's identity. This information can take many forms: password, token, and a one-time password, among others.

Authorization is the process of giving permission to an entity to access a system resource. For example, network access can be restricted based on the identity of a client.

Accounting enables the network manager to keep track of the services and resources that are used by the users. The accounting process collects information such as the connection time, identity, and billing information.

Cisco AAA mechanisms support security protocols such as the Remote Access Dial-In User Service (RADIUS), the Terminal Access Controller Access Control System Plus (TACACS+), and Kerberos. This chapter will provide configuration examples of how AAA is applied in such situations as remote dial-in users and a Cisco Secure PIX Firewall.

AAA Overview

In its most basic form, authentication typically consists of a username and password for an individual to gain access to services or resources. Although used quite frequently in network security, it is the weakest type of authentication. With this type of security, you are prompted for your username when accessing a resource or service; upon entering your username, you are prompted for a password. What if the resource to which you are gaining access is a payroll database that contains the salaries of everyone in your company? This resource is protected only by the username and corresponding password. What if the Human Resources individual was Justin Smith, whose username is jsmith, and he just happened to use a password that was easy to remember such as his last name, Smith? In a company consisting of thousands of employees, how many people could have a last name of Smith? Furthermore, what are the chances of several people with Smith as their last name having the same first initial as Justin?

As you can see, John Smith, Jim Smith, Joan Smith, Jack Smith, Jennifer Smith, Jacob Smith, Janet Smith, Judy Smith, Julianne Smith, Jason Smith, Jeff Smith, Jeremy Smith, Jessica Smith, Jillian Smith, Joanne Smith, Joel Smith, Joey Smith, Jordan Smith, Joyce Smith, and Julie Smith already have the half of the information needed to access that database without even attempting to hack into it. Now, let's assume that most of these individuals are not aware of good security practices that recommend against using your name as your password, and they decide to use only their last name for their passwords. How secure is that payroll database now?

Since usernames and passwords are commonly used to identify individuals and permit access to resources, additional security features can be added to help lower the risk of that payroll database being opened accidentally (or intentionally). Informing users to use passwords that would be hard for other individuals to guess and forcing them to change their passwords on a regular basis will lower the security risk. In a situation where the username and password is being sent over a network or the Internet, encryption will also assist in lowering the security risk. For example, any information sent through a Telnet session is not encrypted. That means that anyone who captures the packets destined to a network device originating from a user can easily look at the data portion of the packet and find out the username and password needed to access that device. If this information had been encrypted, anyone using a network monitor to capture the packets would have an extremely difficult (if not impossible) time decrypting the information.

Another example of where encryption can assist in security is in a configuration file on a Cisco router. Without encrypting the enable password, an administrator can use the **show running-config** command to display the current configuration. In that configuration, the enable password will be readily available to anyone looking over the administrator's shoulder at the screen. Furthermore, if the **show running-config** command is executed remotely through a Telnet session to the router, and someone happens to be capturing the packets, the **show running-config** output will be sent back through the Telnet session. This would make it readily available to the individual who is capturing those packets. To prevent this sort of security risk, use the following command while in configuration mode:

```
service password-encryption
```

This command directs the IOS software to encrypt the passwords, CHAP secrets, and similar data that is saved in the configuration file. Now when the **show running-config** command is executed, the enable password will resemble nothing more than random ASCII text with no obvious meaning.

Token cards can be used as another form of authentication. Typically, a token card is a credit-card-sized device that generates passwords at various time intervals. During the duration of each of the generated passwords life cycles, it may be used to access remote networks. Since the passwords change so often, it is very difficult for unauthorized persons to guess or obtain a valid password since a password's life cycle changes.

Another form of credential is a one-time password. In a situation where a user needs to access a resource only once, one-time passwords maybe used for authentication credentials. Once the user has successfully validated, that password is no longer valid.

AAA is a concept that consists of three mechanisms that provide authentication, authorization, and accounting services on Cisco devices. AAA is a concept used to describe a suite of mechanisms that provide the ability to validate the identity and grant rights, and to track the use of these rights and validations. This chapter will focus on implementing authentication, authorization, and accounting mechanisms through RADIUS, TACACS+, and Kerberos on various Cisco devices.

By definition, authentication is used to validate the proposed identity of a user, device, or other entity in a computer system. This commonly uses a challenge-and-response approach to validation. A challenge is issued to the request for access (such as a user logging into a workstation), and the workstation will consult an authentication database (either internal on the workstation or an external device such as an authentication server). If the proposed identity of the user matches the required criteria in the authentication database, access will be granted. If the identity cannot be matched, then access will be denied.

Authorization can be described as the act of permitting predefined rights or privileges to a user, group of users, system, or process.

Accounting is a method that records (or accounts) who, what, when, and where an action has taken place.

Examples of AAA happen in everyday life outside of computers and Cisco devices. For instance, when you go to an ATM machine to withdraw money, you must first insert your bank card and enter your personal identification number (PIN). At this point you are now authenticating yourself as someone who has the authority to withdraw money. If your card is valid, and your PIN is valid, you have successfully authenticated and can now continue the task of withdrawing money. If you have entered an incorrect PIN number, or your card has been damaged (or stolen) and the criteria cannot be validated, you will not be able to continue.

Once authenticated you will be permitted to perform certain actions, such as withdraw, deposit, check balances, and so on. Based on your identity (your bank card and your PIN), you have been pre-authorized to perform certain functions, which include withdrawing your hard-earned money. Finally, once you have completed the tasks in which you are authorized to perform, you are then provided with a statement describing your transactions as well as the remaining balance in your account. The bank will also record your transactions for accounting purposes.

In some cases, it may not be necessary to implement all AAA mechanisms. For example, if a company simply wishes to authenticate users when they access a certain resource, authentication would be the only element needed. If a company wishes to create an audit trail to reference which users logged in to the network at what times, authentication and accounting will be needed. Typically, AAA is used in remote access scenarios such as end users dialing into an ISP to access the Internet, or end users dialing into their company LAN to access resources. Figure 6.1 illustrates a common implementation of AAA.

Figure 6.1 Example AAA ISP implementation.

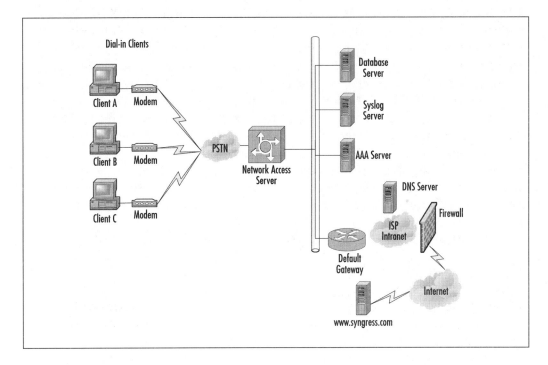

In Figure 6.1, Client A is attempting to access the Web site www.syngress.com. In order to accomplish this, Client A must first connect to their local Internet Service Provider (ISP) to gain access to the Internet. When Client A connects to the ISP, they are prompted for a set of logon credentials (authentication) by the Network Access Server (NAS) before they can fully access the Internet.

A NAS is a device that usually has interfaces connected to both the backbone and to the Telco (analog or ISDN modems) and receives calls from remote clients who wish to access the backbone via dial-up services. A security server is typically a device such as a Windows NT, UNIX, or Solaris server that is running a TACACS, RADIUS daemon, or other daemon that contributes to AAA policy. In Figure 6.1, the AAA Server and the SYSLOG server are examples of security servers. Once they have entered their credentials and the AAA server has validated them, if the security policy permits them to use the Internet (authorization), they can now connect to the desired Web site www.syngress.com. As a policy, the ISP has decided to log all of their customer connections on a SYSLOG server (Accounting). This example illustrates two of the elements of AAA, Authentication and Accounting.

AAA Benefits

AAA provides a security mechanism to protect a company's investments by permitting only certain entities (such as individuals or system process) to access those investments, by governing what those entities can do once they have authenticated, and by logging or auditing the actions that were performed for future reference and troubleshooting purposes.

AAA provides several benefits when implemented correctly. Picture a very large network consisting of over 100 Cisco devices (routers, PIX firewalls) located around the world. By default, each Cisco device requires a password to access EXEC mode (if configured on the console or VTY lines) as well as a password to enter privileged EXEC mode. If good security practices are implemented, then those passwords should be different on each device and should be changed at regular intervals. This is an administrative nightmare.

Instead of configuring passwords on each device, imagine if there were a centralized database in which user accounts were defined, policies defined what those users were permitted to do on each device, and an audit trail logged the changes that were made. Instead of maintaining various passwords to allow users to Telnet to each device (as well as the passwords to permit them into privileged EXEC mode on various devices) user accounts and privileges could be defined in one central location.

AAA is a template that allows dynamic configuration of the type of authentication, authorization, and accounting that can be done on a per-entity (user, group, system, or system process) basis. You have the ability to define the type of authentication and authorization you want by creating lists that define the method in which authentication will be performed, then applying those lists to specific services or interfaces.

Cisco documentation refers to these lists as *method lists*. For the purpose of clarity, these lists will be referred to as method lists throughout this chapter to avoid confusion.

AAA provides many benefits, such as increased flexibility and control, the ability to scale as networks grow larger, the ability to use standard protocols such as RADIUS, TACACS+, and Kerberos for authentication, and the ability to have a backup system in case an authentication server fails future authentication requests, which will automatically be redirected to another server in sequence.

Cisco AAA Mechanisms

AAA is composed of three mechanisms which are as follows:

- **Authentication** is a method of identifying users or processes. Typically, users or processes use a set of credentials such as a username or password to validate themselves.

- **Authorization** provides a method of controlling access to resources.

- **Accounting** provides a method for gathering and sending security information, which can then be used for billing, auditing, and reporting.

Each of these mechanisms can work in conjunction with, or independent of, one another to provide their respective functionality.

Supported AAA Security Protocols

As today's networks grow larger and larger, the need for remote dial-in access increases. In a company such as an ISP, managing Network Access Servers with modem pools for a large number of users can be an administrative headache. Since a pool of modems are typically how remote users will gain access to the Internet, great care and attention must be taken to secure them. In a company such as an ISP, their business revolves around granting access to the Internet for remote users. If the method in which remote users access the Internet is compromised, the ISP could lose a lot of money due to their customers' inability to use the services for which they have paid. Typically, user accounts will be stored in a single database, which is then queried for authentication requests by a NAS or router.

RADIUS

The RADIUS protocol was developed by Livingston Enterprises, Inc. as an access server authentication and accounting protocol. The RADIUS specification (RFC 2138 was made obsolete by RFC 2865 and updated in RFC 2868) is a proposed standard security protocol and RADIUS accounting standard (RFC 2139 was made obsolete by RFC 2866 and updated in RFC 2867) is informational for accounting purposes.

From large enterprise networks such as ISPs to small networks consisting of a few users requiring remote access, RADIUS can be used as a security protocol on any size network. RADIUS uses less CPU overhead and consumes less memory than TACACS+.

RADIUS is a client/server protocol. The RADIUS client is typically a NAS, router, or switch, which requests a service such as authentication or authorization from the RADIUS server. A RADIUS server is usually a daemon running on a UNIX machine or service running on a Windows NT/2000 server machine. The daemon is the software such as Cisco Secure ACS or another RADIUS or TACACS+ server program that fulfills requests from RADIUS clients.

When the client needs authorization information, it queries the RADIUS server and passes the user credentials to the designated RADIUS server. The server then acts on the configuration information necessary for the client to deliver services to the user. A RADIUS server can also act as a proxy client to other RADIUS servers or other kinds of authentication servers. Figure 6.2 illustrates what happens when a user attempts to log in and authenticate to a NAS or router using RADIUS.

Figure 6.2 Authenticating with RADIUS.

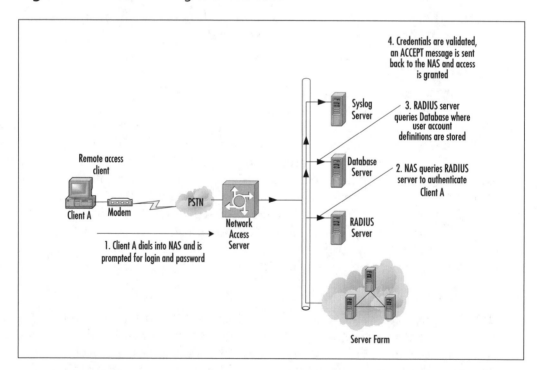

1. The remote user dials into a NAS and is prompted for credentials such as a username and password by the NAS.

2. The username and encrypted password are sent from the RADIUS client (NAS) to the RADIUS server via the network.

3. The RADIUS server queries the database where user account definitions are stored.

4. The RADIUS server evaluates the credentials and replies with one of the following responses:

   ■ **REJECT** The user is not authenticated. They are prompted to re-enter the username and password; otherwise, access is denied.

   ■ **ACCEPT** The user is authenticated.

   ■ **CHALLENGE** A challenge is issued by the RADIUS. The challenge may request additional information from the user.

   ■ **CHANGE PASSWORD** A request from the RADIUS server specifying that the user must change their current password.

Configuring RADIUS on Cisco

To configure RADIUS to use AAA security commands, you must specify the host running the RADIUS server daemon and a secret text string that it shares with the RADIUS client. Table 6.1 outlines the commands needed to define a RADIUS server and key.

Table 6.1 RADIUS Configuration

Command	Task
radius-server host [*hostname* | *ip-address*] [**auth-port** *port-number*] [**acct-port** *port-number*]	Specify the IP address or host name of the remote RADIUS server host and assign authentication and accounting destination port numbers.
	hostname Enter the hostname of the server in which RADIUS requests will be directed,
	or,
	ip-address Enter the IP address of the server in which RADIUS requests will be directed.
	auth-port *port-number* Specifies the UDP port for authentication requests.
	acct-port port-number Specifies the UDP port for accounting requests

Continued

Table 6.1 Continued

Command	Task
radius-server key *string*	Specify the shared secret text string used between the router and the RADIUS server.
	The specified key must be the same on both the RADIUS client and RADIUS server.
radius-server retransmit *retries*	Specify the number of times the router transmits each RADIUS request to the server before giving up (default is three).
radius-server timeout *seconds*	Specify the number of seconds a router waits for a reply to a RADIUS request before retransmitting the request.
radius-server deadtime *minutes*	Specify the number of minutes a RADIUS server, which is not responding to authentication requests, is passed over by requests for RADIUS authentication.

The following example creates a method list named *dialins*. A RADIUS server will be queried for authentication requests; if the RADIUS server is unavailable, the local user database on the device will be used instead.

```
aaa new-model
radius-server host 192.168.1.10
radius-server key RadiusPassword
```

This specifies the RADIUS server host and shared secret text string between the NAS and RADIUS server host.

```
aaa authentication ppp dialins radius local
```

This defines the authentication method list **dialins**, which specifies the RADIUS authentication. Then (if the RADIUS server does not respond), local authentication will be used.

```
aaa authentication login admins local
line async 1 4
 encapsulation ppp
 ppp authentication chap pap dialins
```

This applies the **dialins** method list to the lines specified. If both devices support Challenge Handshake Authentication Protocol (CHAP) it will be used; otherwise, Password Authentication Protocol (PAP) will be used.

TACACS+

Another available security protocol is the TACACS. TACACS provides a method to validate users attempting to gain access to a service through a router or NAS. The original Cisco TACACS was modeled after the original Defense Data Network (DDN) application. Similar to RADIUS, a centralized server running TACACS software responds to client requests in order to perform AAA requests.

TACACS+ allows an administrator to separate the authentication, authorization, and accounting AAA mechanisms and therefore provide the ability to implement each service independently. Each of the AAA mechanisms can be tied into separate databases.

Currently, the Cisco IOS software supports three versions of the TACACS security protocol:

- **TACACS** The original specification has the ability to perform authentication requests only.

- **XTACACS** In addition to authentication, extended TACACS has the ability to perform the accounting element of AAA.

- **TACACS+** The latest version of TACACS enhances the previous versions by providing all elements of AAA. Packets rely on TCP as the transport protocol thereby making the connection reliable. TACACS+ can also encrypt the body of traffic travelling between the TACACS+ server and client. Only the TACACS+ header is left unencrypted.

TACACS and XTACACS are now deprecated and are not compatible with the AAA security features in Cisco. This section will focus on the operation and configuration of TACACS+.

TACACS+ separates each of the functions of AAA by allowing configuration of each element independently of one another.

Figure 6.3 illustrates the process that occurs when a user attempts to log in by authenticating to a NAS using TACACS+.

1. When the connection is established, the network access server will contact the TACACS+ server to obtain an authentication prompt, which is then displayed to the user. The user enters their username and the NAS then contacts the TACACS+ server to obtain a password prompt. The NAS displays the password prompt to the user, and the user enters their password.

2. These credentials are then sent to the TACACS+ daemon running on a server.

3. The TACACS+ server will query a user database and compare Client A's credentials with those stored in the database server.

Figure 6.3 Logging on using TACACS+.

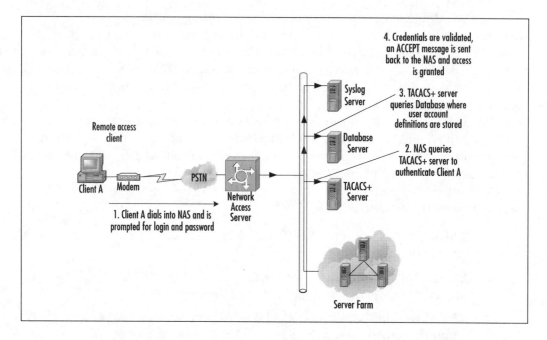

4. The NAS will eventually receive one of the following responses from the TACACS+ daemon:

   - **ACCEPT** The user is authenticated and the service may begin.

   - **REJECT** The user failed to authentication. The user may be denied further access, or will be prompted to retry the login sequence depending on the TACACS+ daemon.

   - **ERROR** An error occurred at some time during authentication. This can be either at the daemon or in the network connection between the daemon and the network access server. If an ERROR response is received, the network access server will typically try to use an alternative method for authenticating the user.

   - **CONTINUE** The user is prompted for additional authentication information.

If the user is using PPP to authenticate to a NAS—a PAP login, which is similar to an ASCII login except that the username and password arrive at the NAS in PAP protocol packet instead of being typed in by the user—the user is not prompted for their credentials. PPP CHAP logins are also similar to PAP; each of them send the credentials through the PPP link instead of prompting the user after a connection has been established. PAP and

CHAP are the authentication methods for point-to-point protocol (PPP) links. For example, when a user connects to an ISP with their modem, PPP is used to encapsulate the traffic to and from the remote user and the NAS. PPP can send authentication information in the form of PAP and CHAP to the NAS for authentication and authorization purposes. PAP sends passwords in cleartext, which can easily be viewed using a packet sniffer. CHAP uses a three-way handshake process to validate each side of the point-to-point link, and also encrypts the username and password that are exchanged during that handshake. CHAP is a much more secure protocol than PAP and should be used whenever possible.

Configuring TACACS+ on Cisco

To configure TACACS+ as your security protocol of choice, you must specify the host running the TACACS+ server software, and a secret text string that is shared with the TACACS+ client. Table 6.2 outlines the commands needed to define a TACACS+ server and key.

Table 6.2 TACACS+ Configuration

Command	Task
tacacs-server host *name* **[single-connection] [port** *integer*] **[timeout** *integer*] **[key** *string*]	Specify the IP address or host name of the remote TACACS+ server host and assigned authentication and accounting destination port numbers.
	name Enter the host name or IP address of the server in which TACACS+ requests will directed.
	single-connection Specify that the client maintain a single open connection when exchanging information with the TACACS+ server.
	port *integer* Specify the TCP port in which the TACACS+ client will send TACACS+ requests. This value should match the configuration of the TACACS+ server. The default is 49.
	timeout *integer* Specify the time (in seconds) that the TACACS+ client will wait for the TACACS+ server to respond.
	key *string* Specify the shared secret text string used between the TACACS+ client and server. The specified key must be the same on both devices. The key specified here will override the key specified in the **tacacs-server key** command.
tacacs-server key *key*	Specify the shared secret text string used between the TACACS+ client and server.

NOTE

Specifying the **key** string with the **tacacs-server host** command overrides the default key set by the global configuration **tacacs-server key** command.

The following example shows how to configure TACACS+:

```
aaa new-model
```

This enables the AAA security services.

```
aaa authentication ppp test tacacs+ local
```

This defines a method list **test** to be used on serial interfaces running PPP. The keyword **tacacs+** means that authentication will be done through TACACS+. If TACACS+ returns an error of some sort during authentication, the keyword **local** indicates that authentication will be attempted using the local database on the NAS.

```
tacacs-server host 192.168.1.10

tacacs-server key securekeypassword
```

This identifies the TACACS+ daemon as having IP address of 192.168.1.10 and defines the shared encryption key to be **securekeypassword**. This same key has to be configured on the TACACS+ server.

```
interface serial 0

 ppp authentication chap pap test
```

This selects the line and applies the **test** method list to this line. If CHAP is supported on both devices, it will be used; otherwise, PAP will be used.

Kerberos

A major security concern for today's networks is the usage of network monitoring tools to capture packets traversing a network. Sensitive information such as a user's login ID and password is contained in these packets. Protocols such as Telnet, FTP, POP3, and many others send the information in cleartext. This means that anyone who looks at the contents of the packet (data portion) will be able to see everything in plaintext.

Firewalls have been put in place to protect a network from intrusions originating from the outside. This assumption does not protect a network from attacks that originate from the inside. An often-overlooked security measure is having users on the inside network prove their identity to the services they are accessing.

The name Kerberos originates from Greek mythology—it is the three-headed dog that guards the entrance to Hades. Kerberos was developed by MIT as a solution to the fore-mentioned security problems. Kerberos uses a strong cryptography protocol which means that a client must prove their identity to a server or service, and a server or service must prove its identity to the client across an insecure network (such as the Internet). After a client has used Kerberos to prove his or her identity, data exchanged between the client and server will be encrypted. This renders networking monitoring tools useless when capturing packets that contain sensitive data.

How does Kerberos work? Well, Kerberos works in a way similar to the way your driver's license works as identification. For example, in a situation where you need to prove your identity, your driver's license contains enough unique information on it, so it is typically the only piece of ID you need to prove yourself. The unique information consists of a photo, your name and address, and your birth date. These pieces of identification, when used together, uniquely identify you from everyone else. In addition to the unique information, your driver's license is issued by a single authority; in other words, you can't get a (real) driver's license from anyone else but that government authority. Your driver's license also must be renewed regularly; once your license has expired, it is no longer valid.

In the Kerberos world, the governing agency would be the Kerberos *authentication server* (AS), and your driver's license would be called a *ticket*. The following steps outline the process in which Kerberos authenticates a client to use a service. Before the process actually occurs, both the user and service are required to register keys with the AS. The user's key is derived from a password that he or she chooses; the service key is a randomly chosen key since no user is required to type in a password for the service.

1. The user sends a message to the AS requesting "user would like to talk to server."

2. When the AS receives this message, it makes two copies of a brand new key called the *session* key. It will be used in the exchange between the user and service.

3. It then places one of the session keys in a packet (for clarity, the packet will be called *packet1*), along with the name of the service— for example, *sessionkey@email*. It then encrypts this packet with the user's key (recall that the user's key is derived from the password that he or she chose).

4. It places the other session key in another packet (for clarity, the packet will be called *packet2*), along with the name of the user—for example, *sessionkey@rlusignan*. It then encrypts this packet with the services key.

5. Both packet1 and packet2 are then returned to the user.

6. The user decrypts packet1 with the key, extracting the session key and the name of the service in it—for example, *email*.

7. The user will be unable to decrypt packet2 (since it is encrypted with the service's key). Instead, they place a note with the current time in another packet (for clarity, the packet will be called *packet3*), and encrypt this packet with the session key and then pass both packet2 and packet3 to the service.

8. The service decrypts packet2 with its own key, extracting the session key and note with the user on it. It then decrypts packet3 with the session key to extract the note with the current time on it. This process identifies the user.

The timestamp on packet3 is to prevent another individual from copying packet2 and using it to impersonate the user at a later time. What happens if the clocks on both machines are slightly off? A little leeway is allowed between the two computers (five minutes is a common time interval).

In Kerberos language, packet2 is called the *ticket* and packet3 is called the *authenticator*. The authenticator usually contains more information than what is listed in the example. Some of this information comes from other fields in the packet such as the checksum.

In the previous example, there is a small problem. This process must occur every time a user attempts to use a service. The user must enter a password each time this occurs (to decrypt packet1). The most obvious way around this problem is to cache the key that was derived from the user's password. This poses another security problem—caching keys and having them around is very dangerous. An attacker can use a copy of this cached key to impersonate the user at any time (or until the password is changed by the user).

Kerberos resolves this by introducing a new agent, called the *ticket granting server* (TGS). The TGS is logically separated from the AS; in other words, both of these agents may be running on the same machine but are two totally separate entities. These two entities are commonly referred to as the *key distribution center* (KDC). The KDC's purpose is as follows: before accessing any service, the user requests a ticket to contact the AS. This ticket is called the *ticket granting ticket* (TGT). After receiving the TGT, any time that the user wishes to contact a service, he or she requests a ticket not from the AS, but from the TGS. In addition, the reply is encrypted not with the user's key, but with the session key that the AS provided for use with the TGS. Inside that packet is a new session key for use with the regular service. The rest of the process continues as explained earlier.

If this extra process confuses you (how could it not?), think about it in this manner. When a visitor arrives at a company to take a tour, that visitor typically exchanges their regular ID (such as a driver's license) for a guest ID. During the tour, in order to get into the various areas of the company, the visitor will show their guest ID each time it is needed. If this guest ID was dropped or stolen, it is valid only for a limited time (until the visitor realizes that they have lost their guest ID, and in order to get their driver's license back, they report the guest ID as being lost or stolen) and a new guest ID would be issued.

Kerberos v5 is used in Windows 2000 as the default authentication protocol for domains that only have Windows 2000 domain controllers. This allows for the single logon concept that permits a user to enter a username and password only once. From that point on (assuming authorization has been granted), they will be able to access services that are available in foreign realms.

In the AAA model, Kerberos fulfills only the authentication mechanism. It does not provide any authorization or accounting functionality. If Kerberos is used for authentication, TACACS+ may be used in conjunction with Kerberos to provide authorization or accounting mechanisms.

Configuring Kerberos

To configure a Cisco router or NAS to authenticate users using the Kerberos v5 protocol, the following steps must first be taken:

1. Define a Kerberos Realm in which the router or NAS reside.
2. Copy the SRVTAB file from the KDC to the router or NAS.

NOTE

SRVTAB (also known as KEYTAB) is a password that a network service shares with the KDC.

3. Specify Kerberos authentication on the router or NAS.
4. Enable Credentials forwarding on the router or NAS.

Note that the previous steps assume that a Kerberos server is configured and running. Configuration of a Kerberos server is outside the scope of this chapter, but for more information on configuration of a Kerberos server, refer to the vendor's documentation. To configure the router to authenticate to a specified Kerberos realm, perform the tasks shown in Table 6.3 in global configuration mode.

Table 6.3 Configuring the Router to a Kerberos Realm

Command	Task
kerberos local-realm *kerberos-realm*	Define the default realm for the router.
kerberos server *kerberos-realm* [*hostname* | *ipaddress*] [*port-number*]	Specify the KDC the router or NAS will use in a given realm. *hostname* Host name of the KDC, or, *ipaddress* IP address of the KDC. *port-number* As an option, specify the port number Kerberos will use. The default port is 88.
kerberos realm [*dns-domain* | *host*] *kerberos-realm*	As an option, map a host name or DNS domain to a Kerberos realm. *dns-domain* Name of the DNS domain, or, *host* Name of the DNS host. *kerberos-realm* Name of the Kerberos realm to which the specified domain belongs.

In order for users to authenticate to the router or NAS using Kerberos, the device must share a secret key with the KDC. To accomplish this, the device needs a copy of the SRVTAB file that is located on the KDC. To copy the SRVTAB file, you must transfer it over the network via the Trivial File Transfer Protocol (TFTP).

NOTE

A TFTP server must be running on a network host in order for the router to successfully download the SRVTAB. A copy of a Cisco's version of a TFTP server is available at www.cisco.com.

To copy the SRVTAB files from the KDC to the router or NAS, use the **kerberos srvtab remote** command in global configuration mode, as shown in Table 6.4.

Table 6.4 The kerberos srvtab remote Command

Command	Task
kerberos srvtab remote [*hostname* | *ip-address*] [*file name*]	Retrieve a SRVTAB file from the KDC.
	hostname Specify the host name of the KDC from where the SRVTAB files will be downloaded,
	or,
	ip-address Specify the IP address of the KDC from where the SRVTAB files will be downloaded.
	file name Specify the name of the SRVTAB file to download from the KDC.

WARNING

The SRVTAB is the core of Kerberos security. Using TFTP to transfer this key is an *important* security risk! Be very careful about the networks in which this file crosses when transferred from the server to the router. To minimize the security risk, use a cross-over cable that is connected directly from a PC to the router's Ethernet interface. Configure both interfaces with IP addresses in the same subnet. By doing this, it is physically impossible for anyone to capture the packets as they are transferred from the Kerberos server to the router.

Once the SRVTAB file has been copied, Kerberos must now be specified as the authentication protocol using the **aaa authentication** command. For example:

```
aaa authentication login default krb5
```

You have the option to configure the router or NAS to forward users' TGTs with them as they authenticate from the router to another host that uses Kerberos for authentication. For example, if users Telnet to the router and Kerberos is used for authentication, their credentials can be forwarded to a host they are attempting to access (from the router). This host must also use Kerberos as its authentication protocol. To have all clients forward users' credentials as they connect to other hosts in the Kerberos realm, use the command as shown in Table 6.5.

Table 6.5 Forwarding Credentials

Command	Task
kerberos credential forward	Forward user credentials upon successful Kerberos authentication.

To use Kerberos to authenticate users when they connect to a router or NAS using Telnet, use the command shown in Table 6.6 in global configuration mode.

Table 6.6 Authenticating Users

Command	Task
aaa authentication login [**default** | *list-name*] **krb5_telnet**	Set login authentication to use Kerberos v5 Telnet authentication protocol when using Telnet to connect to the router.
	default Keyword to modify the *default* method list, which will be applied automatically to all interfaces.
	list-name Name of the method list to be referenced when applying the method list to an interface.
	krb_telnet Keyword to specify Kerberos as the authentication protocol when users establish Telnet sessions to the router or NAS. This is different than using **krb5** keyword, which specifies that Kerberos will be used for any login authentication, not just Telnet authentication.

Users have the ability to open Telnet sessions to other hosts from the router or NAS on which they are currently logged in. Kerberos can be used to encrypt the Telnet session using 56-bit Data Encryption Standard (DES) with 64-bit Cipher Feedback (CFB). To enable this when a user opens a Telnet session to another host, use the command shown in Table 6.7.

Table 6.7 Enabling 56-Bit DES with 64-Bit CFB

Command	Task
connect *host* [*port*] **/encrypt kerberos** or **telnet** *host* [*port*] **/encrypt kerberos**	Establish an encrypted Telnet session. *host* Specify the host name or IP address of the host to establish a Telnet session. *port* Optionally specify the port in which the Telnet session will be established. **/encrypt kerberos** Specify that data transferred during the Telnet session will be encrypted.

The following configuration example shows how to enable user authentication on a router via the Kerberos database. Remember that in order to enable Kerberos on a router, the necessary steps for configuring a Kerberos server must done before configuring the router.

```
aaa new-model
```

This enables the AAA security services.

```
kerberos local-realm syngress.com
```

This sets the Kerberos local realm to **syngress.com**.

```
kerberos server syngress.com krbsrv
Translating "krbsrv"...domain server (192.168.1.10) [OK]
```

This specifies the KDC for the **syngress.com** realm.

```
kerberos credentials forward
```

This enables the forwarding of credentials when initiating sessions from the router or NAS to another device using Kerberos authentication when the **/encrypt kerberos** command is specified.

```
kerberos srvtab remote krbsrv srvtab
[output ommitted]
```

This specifies the server from which the file **srvtab** will be downloaded via TFTP.

```
aaa authentication login default krb5
```

This specifies that the **default** method list will use Kerberos as the authentication protocol.

RADIUS, TACACS+, or Kerberos

The two most widely used security protocols are RADIUS and TACACS+. Which one should be implemented in your enterprise?

Several factors will influence your decision. Vendor interoperability and how the protocols are structured are typically the factors considered in choosing one over the other.

Transport Protocol Considerations

RADIUS uses User Datagram Protocol (UDP) as the Transport layer protocol, whereas TACACS+ uses Transmission Control Protocol (TCP) as its Transport layer protocol. What this means is that TACACS+ traffic is more reliable than RADIUS traffic. If any disruption occurs (such as corrupted or dropped packets), TACACS+ will retransmit those unacknowledged packets, whereas RADIUS will not.

Packet Encryption

RADIUS encrypts only the password portion of the access-request packet from the client to the server. The rest of the packet is sent in cleartext, which can be captured and viewed by a network monitoring tool.

TACACS+ encrypts the entire body of the packet but does not encrypt the TACACS+ header. The header contains a field that indicates whether the body of the packet is encrypted or not.

Authentication and Authorization

RADIUS combines both the AAA elements authentication and authorization. The **access-accept** packet exchanged by the RADIUS client and server contain authorization information. This makes it difficult to separate the two elements.

TACACS+ uses the AAA architecture. This architecture separates authentication, authorization, and accounting allowing for advantages such as multiprotocol use. For example, TACACS+ could provide the authorization and accounting elements, and Kerberos may be used for the authorization element.

Protocol Support

RADIUS does not support the following protocols, but TACACS+ does.

- AppleTalk Remote Access (ARA) protocol
- NetBIOS Frame Protocol Control protocol
- Novell Asynchronous Services Interface (NASI)
- X.25 PAD connection

For IT Professionals

Security Protocol Considerations

Selecting a security protocol is a daunting task for administrators. Many factors have to be taken into consideration. For example, will this security protocol facilitate only Cisco routers? Should I dedicate only one server or use two servers in case of failure? On which services should I configure any of the AAA mechanisms? Is one protocol easier to configure than the others?

Remember the key differences between RADIUS and TACACS+. At the transport layer of the OSI model, TACACS+ uses TCP whereas RADIUS uses UDP. TCP is a connection-oriented protocol; therefore, RADIUS does not have the ability to resend lost or corrupted packets. RADIUS packets are sent on a best-effort basis.

TACACS+ follows the AAA architecture by separating each of the AAA elements. We can take advantage of this in an environment where Kerberos is already used as an authentication protocol. TACACS+ can be used as an authorization or accounting protocol.

Authentication

Authentication on Cisco devices comes in many forms. There are many features that Cisco devices (especially PIX and routers) perform that would benefit from authentication—for example, accessing a router either through the console or VTY (Telnet) lines in order to perform configuration, diagnostics, or troubleshooting tasks. In an Internet Service Provider environment, users dialing in to a Network Access Server (NAS) must be authenticated (through PPP) before access will be granted to the Internet. Depending on how the device has been configured, authentication may be provided by security protocols such as RADIUS, TACACS+, Kerberos, or a user database that is stored locally on the device.

A basic form of authentication is already provided by default on Cisco devices. During the initial configuration of a router, you will be asked to enter an enable password. This password will allow access to privileged EXEC mode where modifications and diagnostics (which were not available in EXEC mode) may be done. The default authentication on these devices requires only one set of credentials (password) in order to continue. Worse yet, the Telnet protocol sends data in cleartext over the network. If a user Telnets into a device, the login and enable passwords will be readily available to anyone who captures the packets.

To configure authentication on Cisco devices, you must first define a method list of authentication methods and then apply that list to the various interfaces. A method list defines the various types of authentication such as network, login, or privileged EXEC mode authentication, to be performed as well as the order in which they will be performed.

Once the list has been defined, it must be applied to a specified interface such as VTY lines (Telnet), a console line, a group of asynchronous interfaces (modems), or a service such as the ability to use HTTP through a router or PIX before it will become active. There is also a default method list that may be altered; this default list is applied automatically to interfaces or services that require a login unless another method list is applied to that interface or service, thereby overriding the default method list. For example, a method list named **admin** is created and then applied to the VTY lines. The default method list will no longer apply to that interface because the **admin** method list was specified explicitly.

The purpose of a method list is to describe the authentication method, and the order in which this will occur to authenticate a user. This is where the security protocols (RADIUS, TACACS+, and Kerberos) may be specified. For example, if a method has been configured to do so, a RADIUS server may be queried first to validate a username and password. If the RADIUS server has failed and is not functional, a TACACS+ server may then be queried to validate that same username and password. If the TACACS+ server has failed, the local user database on the device maybe queried to validate the same username and password as a last resort. This process occurs only in the event that a security server has failed and is unable to perform validation. If the RADIUS server denies the credentials of the user (incorrect password or invalid username), the TACACS+ server would not be queried in this case.

There are several steps that need to be completed before authentication can be configured. The following steps are necessary to enable login authentication:

1. Enable AAA on the device by issuing the **aaa new-model** command while in global configuration mode.

   ```
   router(config)#aaa new-model
   ```

2. Once AAA has been enabled, security protocol parameters such as the IP address of the security server and the key to exchange with the authentication server need to be defined.

   ```
   radius-server host <ip-address | hostname>
   radius-server key <radius-key>
   ```

3. To specify a TACACS+ server by IP address or host name, and the key to exchange from the TACACS+ client to the TACACS+ server, use:

```
tacacs-server host <ip-address | hostname>
tacacs-server key <tacacs-key>
```

NOTE

The key used by the RADIUS or TACACS+ client *must* be the same as the key specified on the RADIUS or TACACS+ security server.

4. Define the method list and order in which authentication requests will be queried by defining a method list. Use the **aaa authentication** command to define a method list.

```
aaa authentication login auth_example radius tacacs+ local
```

5. Finally, apply the method lists to a particular interface, line, or service if required.

```
line vty 0 4
login authentication auth_example
```

Table 6.8 lists the commands needed to configure login authentication.

Table 6.8 Login Authentication Commands

Command	Task
aaa new-model	Enable AAA globally on the device.
aaa authentication login [**default** | *list-name*] *method1* [*method2*]	Create a local authentication list.
	default Keyword to modify the *default* method list, which will be applied automatically to all interfaces.
	list-name Name of the method to be referenced when applying the method list to an interface.
	method Keyword to specify security protocol such as RADIUS, TACACS+, and Kerberos.

Continued

www.syngress.com

Table 6.8 Continued

Command	Task
line [**aux** | **console** | **tty** | **vty**] *line-number* [*end-line-number*]	Enter interface configuration mode for the interface to which you want to apply the authentication list.
	aux Enter configuration mode for the **aux** port.
	console Enter configuration mode for the **console** port.
	tty Enter configuration mode for the **tty** line.
	vty Enter configuration mode for the **vty** (Telnet) line.
	line-number Starting line number.
	End-line-number Ending line number.
login authentication [**default** | *list-name*]	Apply the authentication list to a line or set of lines.
	default Specify to use the default method list for authentication.
	list-name Specify the method list to use for authentication.

Login Authentication Using AAA

A method list can define a variety of authentication methods. For example, TACACS+ may be selected as the authentication method for users attempting to log in via Telnet on a NAS, where as a RADIUS server may be selected by the NAS as the authentication method for authenticating users through the console. The following login authentication methods may be used:

- **enable** Use the enable password for authentication.
- **line** Use the line password for authentication.
- **none** Use no authentication.
- **local** Query the local user database stored on the device for authentication requests.
- **krb5** Use Kerberos v5 for authentication.
- **krb5-telnet** Use Kerberos v5 for authentication when accessing the device via Telnet. This must be the first method listed in the method list.

- **group radius** Query a RADIUS server for authentication requests.

- **group tacacs+** Query a TACACS+ server for authentication requests.

- **group** *group-name* Query a subset of RADIUS or TACACS+ servers that have been defined with the **aaa group server radius** or **aaa group server tacacs+** commands.

TIP

When specifying RADIUS and TACACS+ in a method list, remember that you must specify the server IP address, as well as the key to exchange from the client (Cisco device) to the server (server running RADIUS/TACACS+ software).

When specifying RADIUS or TACACS+ as the authentication protocol, security servers must be defined before RADIUS or TACACS+ can be used in a method list. To define RADIUS or TACACS+ servers, use the **aaa group server** command. For example:

```
aaa gropu server radius loginrad
server 172.16.1.10
```

This specifies that a RADIUS server at IP address 172.16.1.10 will be a member of the **loginrad** server group.

The following are examples for configuring each of the authentication methods.

```
aaa authentication login enable
```

This specifies the enable password as the login authentication method.

```
aaa authentication login line
```

This specifies the line password as the login authentication method.

```
aaa authentication login none
```

This specifies that no password is needed in order to authenticate.

```
aaa authentication login local
```

WARNING

Be careful when stating that no password is necessary for login authentication. This option defeats the purpose of a security policy entirely.

This specifies that the local database on the device will be queried to perform authenticated requests.

```
aaa authentication login krb5
```

This specifies that a Kerberos v5 server will be queried to perform authentication requests.

```
aaa server group radius radiuslogin

server 192.168.1.1

server 192.168.1.2

server 192.168.1.3

aaa authentication login group radiuslogin none
```

This specifies that servers at IP addresses 192.168.1.1, 192.168.1.2, and 192.168.1.3 are members of the **radiuslogin** group. Login authentication will use this group of servers to perform authentication requests. If the RADIUS server at IP address 192.168.1.1 is unavailable to perform the authentication request, the next server (192.168.1.2) will be queried. If the server at IP address 192.168.1.2 is unavailable, the next server (192.168.1.3) will be queried to perform the authentication request. If all of the RADIUS servers are unavailable, then no authentication will be required.

```
aaa server group tacacs+ logintacacs

server 172.16.1.1

server 172.16.1.2

server 172.16.1.3

aaa authentication login group logintacacs local
```

This specifies that servers at IP addresses 172.16.1.1, 172.16.1.2, and 172.16.1.3 are members of the **logintacacs** group. Login authentication will use this group of servers to perform authentication requests. If the TACACS+ server at IP address 172.16.1.1 is unavailable to perform the authentication request, the next server (172.16.1.2) will be queried. If the server at IP address 172.16.1.2 is unavailable, the next server (172.16.1.3) will be queried to perform the authentication request. If all of the TACACS+

servers are unavailable, the local user database will be used to perform authentication requests.

PPP Authentication Using AAA

In an environment such as an ISP, users often access network resources through dial-up via async (analog modem) or ISDN. When this occurs, a network protocol (such as PPP) takes charge of the network connection set-up and authentication. PPP authentication is very similar to login authentication, when a user configures a workstation to dial-up to their ISP, they must enter their login ID and password (as well as the phone number of the ISP). When the user connects to the NAS, the login ID and password are transmitted over the phone line. If they are successfully authenticated, they will then be able to access the Internet (or other services in which they are authorized to access). Table 6.9 illustrates how to configure authentication using PPP.

Table 6.9 PPP Authentication Commands

Command	Task
aaa new-model	Enable AAA globally on the device.
aaa authentication ppp [**default** | *list-name*] *method1* [*method2*]	Create a local authentication list.
	default Keyword to modify the *default* method list, which will be applied automatically to all interfaces.
	list-name Name of the method list to be referenced when applying the method list to an interface.
	method Keyword to specify security protocol such as group RADIUS, group TACACS, Kerberos, and so on.
ppp authentication [**chap** | **pap** | **chap pap**] [**if-needed**] [**default** | *list-name*] [**callin**] [**one-time**]	Apply the authentication list to a line or set of lines selected on the previous command.
	chap Select challenge handshake authentication protocol when exchanging login credentials.
	pap Select password authentication protocol when exchanging login credentials
	chap pap Select CHAP first; if the client does not support CHAP, then use PAP when exchanging login credentials.

Continued

Table 6.9 Continued

Command	Task
ppp authentication [chap | pap | chap pap] [if-needed] [default | *list-name***] [callin] [one-time]**	**if-needed** If specified, users will not need to authenticate if the user has already provided authentication (used on async interfaces). This is useful if a user has already authenticated via normal login procedure. This will avoid the user entering the username and password twice.
	default Keyword to modify *default* method list, which will be applied automatically to all interfaces.
	list-name Name of the method to be referenced when applying the method list to an interface.
	callin Specifies that authentication will be performed on incoming calls only.
	one-time Use one-time passwords such as token card passwords. Note that one-time passwords are not supported by CHAP.

The following example creates a method list named **remote-access**. This specifies that authentication requests will query a RADIUS server that is defined in the **loginradius** server group first. If the RADIUS server is unavailable, a TACACS+ server that is defined in the **logintacacs** server group will be queried. If the TACACS+ server is unavailable, the local database will be queried. PPP encapsulation has been selected on the async 4 interface, CHAP is enabled, and method list **remote-access** will be used for authentication.

```
aaa group server radius loginradius
server 192.168.1.1
aaa group server tacacs+ logintacacs
server 192.168.1.2
aaa authentication ppp remote-access loginradius logintacacs local
interface async 4
    encapsulation ppp
    ppp authentication chap remote-access
```

Enable Password Protection for Privileged EXEC Mode

When a user successfully authenticates on a device via the console (if configured) or via Telnet, they are in EXEC mode. To enter privileged EXEC mode, the user must use the **enable** command. Typically the **enable** password is stored locally on the device. By using the **aaa authentication enable default** command, a method list can be specified to authenticate anyone attempting to enter privileged EXEC mode. Table 6.10 illustrates how to use authentication with the **enable** command.

Table 6.10 Enable Authentication Commands

Command	Task
aaa authentication enable default *method1 [method2]*	Enable user id and password checking for users attempting to enter privileged EXEC mode
	method Keyword to specify security protocol such as RADIUS, TACACS, and Kerberos.

The following example creates a method list named **admin-enable**. When users attempt to enter privileged EXEC mode, a TACACS+ server will be queried to authenticate the user. If the TACACS+ server is unavailable, the previously configured enable password must be used for authentication.

```
aaa authentication enable admin-enable tacacs+ enable
```

Authorization

The second mechanism in AAA is authorization. Authorization can be defined as the act of granting permission to a user, group of users, system, or system process. For example, if a user logs into a server, their user account will be preauthorized to use certain services such as file access or printing. On a router or NAS, authorization may include the ability to access the network when logging in via PPP or the ability to use a certain protocol such as FTP.

A Cisco device can be used to restrict user access to the network so that users can only perform certain functions after they have successfully authenticated. Like authentication, a remote or local database can be used to define the ability of a user once they have authenticated.

An example of authorization that is enabled by default on Cisco devices is the ability to enter privileged EXEC mode. Once a user types **enable** at the EXEC prompt, he or she is prompted for a password (if the router or

NAS is configured with an enable password). If the correct enable password is entered, the user is now authorized to use privileged EXEC mode. Instead of the enable password, a database of users may be used that previously defines whether a user may or may not access privileged EXEC mode. If a RADIUS or TACACS+ server is configured for use with authentication, then the ability to enter privileged EXEC mode will be defined on the security server and will not rely on the configured enable password or rely on it in a fail-safe configuration on the Cisco device.

The following list defines the authorization types that may be used on a router or NAS:

- **EXEC** applies to the attributes associated with a user EXEC terminal session.

- **Command** applies to EXEC mode commands that a user issues. Command authorization attempts to authorize for all EXEC mode commands, including global configuration commands associated with a specific privilege level.

- **Network** applies to network connection. This can include a PPP, SLIP, or ARAP connection.

- **Auth-proxy** applies a specific security policy on a per-user basis. For more information on Authentication proxy, please refer to the section, "Authentication Proxy."

- **Reverse Access** applies authorization to reverse-Telnet sessions.

The following list defines the methods in which a user may be authorized:

- **TACACS+** As with authentication, a TACACS+ server is queried to authorize a user to perform a certain action. TACACS+ authorization defines specific rights for users by associating the appropriate user with the authorized services.

- **if-authenticated** The user is allowed to access the requested function provided the user has been authenticated successfully.

- **local** Similar to authentication, the router or NAS consults its local database, as defined by the **username** command, to authorize specific rights for users. Only a limited set of functions can be controlled via the local database.

- **RADIUS** As with authentication, a RADIUS server is queried to authorize a user to perform a certain action. RADIUS authorization defines specific rights for users by associating the appropriate user with the authorized services.

- **krb5-instance** The router or NAS uses the instance defined by the **kerberos instance map** command for authorization.
- **none** No authorization will occur.

Configure Authorization

The **aaa authorization** command allows you to set parameters that restrict a user's network access. To enable AAA authorization, perform the task shown in Table 6.11 in global configuration mode.

Table 6.11 Enabling AAA Authorization

Command	Task
aaa authorization {network | exec | command *level*} {*group-tacacs+* | if-authenticated | none | local | *group-radius* | krb5-instance}	Set parameters that restrict a user's network access.
	network Keyword to specify that authorization will run for all network-related service requests.
	or,
	exec Keyword to specify that authorization will run to determine if the user is permitted to run an EXEC shell,
	or,
	command Keyword to specify that authorization will run for all commands at the specified privilege level.
	level Specifies the command level that should be authorized. Valid level entries are 0–15.
	group-tacacs+ Keyword to specify that a TACACS+ server(s) will be queried to retrieve authorization information for the user,
	or,
	if-authenticated Keyword to specify that the user is allowed to access the requested function or service provided the user has already been authenticated successfully,
	or,
	none Keyword to specify that no authorization request will occur,

Continued

Table 6.11 Continued

Command	Task
aaa authorization {network | exec | command *level*} {*group-tacacs+* | **if-authenticated | none | local |** *group-radius* | **krb5-instance}**	or, **local** Keyword to specify that the local user database will be queried to retrieve authorization information for the user, or, *group-radius* Keyword to specify that a RADIUS server(s) will be queried to retrieve authorization information for the user, or, **krb5_instance** Keyword to specify will use the instance defined by the **kerberos instance map** command for authorization.

TACACS+ Configuration Example

The following example uses a TACACS+ server to authorize login and the use of network services, including PPP. In this example, two method lists named **admins** and **remote** have been created. The **admins** method list will be used to authenticate users logging into the console and vty lines (Telnet). The **remote** method list will be used to authenticate users logging into the async interfaces. Users will be authorized by the default method list for access to privileged EXEC mode, as well as network access from the async interfaces.

```
aaa new-model
```

This defines a new AAA model.

```
aaa server group tacacs+
server 192.168.1.10
aaa tacacs-server key ExchangKeyforServer
```

This specifies the IP address of the TACACS+ server and the secret text key to exchange with the TACACS+ server.

```
aaa authentication login admins group tacacs+ local
aaa authentication ppp remote group tacacs+ local
```

This specifies new authentication lists called **admins** and **remote** that will query the TACACS+ server defined in the TACACS+ server group for authentication. If the TACACS+ server is unavailable, it will default to the local user database.

```
aaa authorization exec default group tacacs+ local
```

This specifies that a TACACS+ server will be queried to authorize a user when entering EXEC mode. If the TACACS+ server is unavailable, the local database will be used instead.

```
aaa authorization network default group tacacs+
```

This specifies that a TACACS+ server will be queried to authorize the use of network services.

```
interface group-async1
 ppp authentication chap remote
```

This specifies that the **remote** method list will be used for PPP authentication.

```
 group-range 1 16
line console 0
 login authentication admins
```

This specifies that the **admins** method list will be used for authentication on the console.

```
line vty 0 4
login authentication admins
```

This specifies that the **admins** method list will be used for authentication on the VTY (Telnet) lines 0 to 4.

WARNING

Be extremely careful when specifying authentication to the console. It is very easy to lock yourself out of the device. The **admins** method list specifies that a TACACS+ server will be queried for authentication. If that TACACS+ is not available, the local user database on the device will be used. If **local** is not specified and the TACACS+ server is unavailable, you will then be locked out of the device until the TACACS+ is again available.

Accounting

Finally, the last mechanism of AAA is accounting. Accounting provides the method for collecting and sending information used for billing, auditing, and reporting, such as user identities, start and stop times, commands executed, number of packets sent and received, and the number of bytes sent and received.

Accounting enables you to track the services users are accessing as well as the amount of network resources they are consuming. When accounting is activated, the router or NAS reports user activity to the TACACS+ or RADIUS security server (depending on which security method you have implemented) in the form of accounting records. Each accounting record consists of accounting attribute value (AV) pairs meaning that a value will have a specific attribute—for example "address=192.168.2.1" where address is the attribute and 192.168.2.1 is the value of that attribute. These AV pairs are stored on the access control server that may be analyzed for network management, client billing, and auditing purposes.

All accounting methods must be defined through AAA. When accounting is activated, it is globally applied to all interfaces on the router or NAS. Therefore, you do not have to specify whether accounting is enabled on an interface-by-interface or line-by-line basis. The following types of accounting are available on the Cisco IOS:

Network Accounting provides information for all network sessions (PPP, SLIP, or ARAP) such as packet and byte counts.

Connection Accounting provides information about all outbound connections originating from the router or NAS, such as Telnet.

EXEC Accounting provides information about user EXEC terminal sessions (user shells) on the NAS or router, including username, date, start and stop times, the NAS or router IP address, and (for dial-in users) the telephone number from which the call originated if Caller ID is enabled.

System Accounting provides information about all system-level events such as system reboots.

Command Accounting provides information about EXEC shell commands being used for a specific privilege level on a NAS or router. Each accounting record includes a list of the commands that are executed for that privilege level as well as the date and time that the command is executed and the user who executes it.

Configuring Accounting

To enable accounting on a router or NAS, you must first issue the **aaa accounting** command, described in Table 6.12.

Table 6.12 Enabling Accounting

Command	Task
aaa accounting {system | network | connection | exec | command *level*} {default | *list-name*} {start-stop | wait-start | stop-only} {*method*}	Enable accounting.
	system Keyword to perform accounting for all system-level events
	network Keyword to perform accounting for all network-related service requests such as PPP, SLIP, and ARAP,
	or,
	EXEC Keyword to perform accounting for EXEC sessions (user shells),
	or,
	connection Keyword to provide information about all outbound connections from the router or NAS,
	or,
	commands Keyword to perform accounting for all commands at the specified privilege level.
	level Specify the command level to track for accounting. Valid entries are 0–15, where 15 is privileged EXEC mode commands and 0 is EXEC mode commands.
	default Keyword to specify that the listed accounting methods that follow will be used as the default list of methods for accounting services,
	or,
	list-name Specify the method list of accounting methods. For example, **group radius** or **group tacacs+,** or a named method list that define the way accounting will be performed.

Continued

Table 6.12 Continued

Command	Task
aaa accounting {system | network | connection | exec | command *level*} **{default |** *list-name*} **{start-stop | wait-start | stop-only}** {*method*}	**start-stop** Specify that accounting will start at the beginning of a process, and stop at the end of the process. The process will start regardless of whether the security server receives the **start** command or not. For example, if a command is executed on a router, a process runs in the background. This will trigger accounting to begin. Once the process is finished, accounting will halt. The process will execute whether accounting is functioning or not; for example, if the TACACS+ server is unavailable for accounting, the process will still execute.
	wait-start Specify that accounting will start at the beginning of the process and stop at the end of the process. The process will not begin until the **start** command has been acknowledged by the security server. Unlike the **start-stop** keyword, if all accounting servers defined in the method list are not responding, the process will not execute.
	stop-only Specify that a **stop** accounting notice will be sent at the end of the process.

TIP

To configure minimal accounting on a router or NAS, use the **stop-only** keyword. This will send a **stop-record** accounting notice at the end of the requested user process.

AAA accounting supports the following accounting methods:

- **group radius** Specifies that a list of RADIUS servers defined by the **aaa server group radius** command will be used for accounting.

- **group tacacs+** Specifies that a list of TACACS+ servers defined by the **aaa server group tacacs+** will be used for accounting.

- **group** *group-name* Specifies that a subset of RADIUS or TACACS+ servers will be used for accounting.

Suppress Generation of Accounting Records for Null Username Sessions

There may be a situation in which authentication is set to **none**. This means that users who connect to lines (VTY, tty, or con) are not required to authenticate. If accounting is activated, an accounting record will be created with NULL as the username. To avoid seeing these records, you can disable accounting of records with a username of NULL. To do this, use the command:

```
aaa accounting suppress null-username
```

This will prevent accounting records from being generated for users whose username string is NULL

RADIUS Configuration Example

The following example shows RADIUS-style accounting to track all usage of EXEC commands and network services, such as slip, PPP, and ARAP:

```
aaa server group radius accountradius

server 192.168.1.1

aaa accounting exec start-stop accountradius

aaa accounting network start-stop accountradius
```

Typical RAS Configuration Using AAA

In the following example, an ISP is using a Cisco AS5200 access server to enable remote analog customers to dial into the AS5200 (NAS) and access the Internet. The ISP has decided that authentication and accounting will be enabled, and the security protocol of choice will be RADIUS. Login authentication will occur on each of the asynchronous interfaces (modems), VTY lines on the NAS (Telnet), and the console. The AAA configuration examples are outlined in **bold**. Figure 6.4 illustrates this configuration.

Figure 6.4 AAA ISP example.

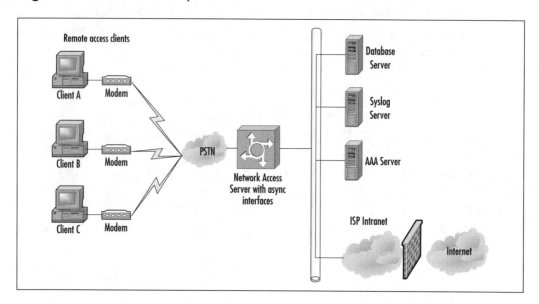

```
!
version 11.3
service timestamps debug datetime msec
service timestamps log datetime msec
service password-encryption
no service udp-small-servers
no service tcp-small-servers
!
hostname NAS
!
aaa new-model
```

This enables AAA globally.

```
aaa server group radius loginradius
server 172.16.1.200
server 172.16.1.210
```

This defines a group of RADIUS servers that will be used for authentication and accounting. If the server is at IP address 172.16.1.200, RADIUS will query the server at 172.16.1.210 as a backup.

```
aaa authentication login console enable
```

This enables login authentication for users accessing the AS5200 by the console port. The authentication uses the enable password.

```
aaa authentication login vty group loginradius
```

This enables RADIUS authentication when accessing the AS5200 by Telnet.

```
aaa authentication login dialin group loginradius
```

This creates a method list named **dialin** that will query a RADIUS server for authentication.

```
aaa authentication ppp default loginradius
```

This sets RADIUS authentication for the **default** method list for PPP sessions.

```
aaa authentication ppp dialin if-needed loginradius
```

This creates a method list named **dialin** that will query a RADIUS server for authentication unless the user has already been authenticated (**if-needed**).

```
aaa accounting login isp-accounting start-stop group loginradius
```

This creates a method list named **isp-accounting** that will execute accounting during login attempts. The accounting servers will be defined in the **loginradius** server group.

```
enable secret secretpass
!
async-bootp dns-server 172.16.1.5 172.16.1.6
isdn switch-type primary-5ess
!
controller T1 0
 framing esf
 clock source line primary
 linecode b8zs
 pri-group timeslots 1-24
!
controller T1 1
 framing esf
 clock source line secondary
```

```
  linecode b8zs
  pri-group timeslots 1-24
!
interface Loopback0
 ip address 172.16.1.254 255.255.255.0
!
interface Ethernet0
 ip address 172.16.1.2 255.255.255.0
!
interface Serial0
 no ip address
 shutdown
!
interface Serial1
 no ip address
 shutdown
!
interface Serial0:23
 no ip address
 encapsulation ppp
 isdn incoming-voice modem
!
interface Serial1:23
 no ip address
 isdn incoming-voice modem
!
interface Group-Async1
 ip unnumbered Loopback0
 encapsulation ppp
 async mode interactive
 peer default ip address pool dialin_pool
 no cdp enable
 ppp authentication chap pap dialin
```

This sets the authentication method for **Group-Async1** to be CHAP, then PAP (if the connecting party does not support CHAP) using the **dialin** method-list for authentication.

```
ppp accounting isp-accounting
```

This enables the accounting method that is defined in the **isp-accounting** method list on all **async** interfaces defined by **group-async1**.

```
 group-range 1 48
!
router eigrp 10
 network 172.16.1.0
 passive-interface Dialer0
 no auto-summary
!
ip local pool dialin_pool 172.16.1.10 172.16.1.250
ip default-gateway 172.16.1.1
ip classless
!
dialer-list 1 protocol ip permit
!
line con 0
 login authentication console
line 1 48
 autoselect ppp
 autoselect during-login
 login authentication dialin
```

This sets the authentication method for lines 1 to 48 to that specified in the **dialin** method list.

```
 modem DialIn
line aux 0
 login authentication console
```

This sets the authentication method for the console to that specified in the **console** method list.

```
line vty 0 4
```

```
login authentication vty
```

This sets the authentication method for Telnet to that specified in the **vty** method list.

```
transport input telnet rlogin
!
end
```

Typical Firewall Configuration Using AAA

The following sample configuration displays how authentication and authorization can be used on a Cisco Secure PIX Firewall. In this example, the following services will be permitted when authentication and authorization is enabled:

- **Telnet** When the user connects to a host on the outside network via Telnet, he or she will see a username and password prompt before the connection to the host is established. This is the PIX performing authorization (for the use of Telnet). If the authentication succeeds, a connection will be established to the target host and another prompt will appear (from the host) beyond the PIX.

- **FTP** When the user initiates an FTP session to a remote host, he or she will see a username prompt come up. The user needs to enter local_username@remote_username for username and local_password@remote_password for password. The PIX sends the local_username and local_password to the security server, and if the authentication (and authorization) succeeds at the PIX, the remote_username and remote_password are passed to the destination FTP server beyond.

- **HTTP** A window is displayed in the browser requesting username and password. If authentication (and authorization) succeeds, the user arrives at the destination Web site beyond the PIX. Keep in mind that browsers cache usernames and passwords.

Figure 6.5 illustrates AAA on a Cisco PIX Secure Firewall. For more information on the Cisco Secure PIX Firewall, please refer to Chapter 4, "Cisco PIX Firewall."

If it appears that the PIX should be timing out an HTTP connection but is not doing so, it is likely that re-authentication is taking place with the browser sending the cached username and password to the PIX, which then forwards this to the authentication server. If this problem occurs, clear the cache in the Web browser settings.

Figure 6.5 AAA PIX example.

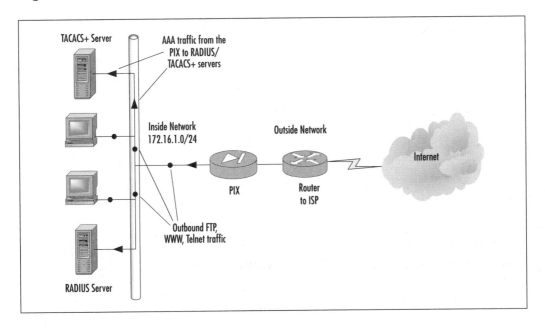

```
PIX Version 5.2

nameif ethernet0 outside security0

nameif ethernet1 inside security100

nameif ethernet2 dmz security10

enable password 8Ry2YjIyt7RRXU24 encrypted

passwd 2KFQnbNIdI.2KYOU encrypted

hostname firewall

fixup protocol ftp 21

fixup protocol http 80

fixup protocol smtp 25

fixup protocol h323 1720

fixup protocol rsh 514

fixup protocol sqlnet 1521

names

pager lines 24

no logging timestamp

no logging standby

logging console debugging
```

```
no logging monitor

no logging buffered

no logging trap

no logging history

logging facility 20

logging queue 512

interface ethernet0 auto

interface ethernet1 auto

interface ethernet2 auto

mtu outside 1500

mtu inside 1500

mtu dmz 1500

ip address outside 207.139.221.2 255.255.255.0

ip address inside 172.16.1.1 255.255.255.0

ip address dmz 127.0.0.1 255.255.255.255

no failover

failover timeout 0:00:00

failover ip address outside 0.0.0.0

failover ip address inside 0.0.0.0

failover ip address dmz 0.0.0.0

arp timeout 14400

global (outside) 1 207.139.221.10-207.139.221.50 netmask 255.255.255.0

nat (inside) 1 172.16.1.0 255.255.255.0 0 0

static (inside,outside) 207.139.221.5 172.16.0.22 netmask
255.255.255.255 >0 0

conduit permit icmp any any

conduit permit tcp any any

conduit permit udp any any

route outside 0.0.0.0 0.0.0.0 207.139.221.1

timeout xlate 3:00:00 conn 1:00:00 half-closed 0:10:00 udp 0:02:00

timeout rpc 0:10:00 h323 0:05:00

timeout uauth 0:05:00 absolute

access-list 100 permit tcp any any eq telnet

access-list 100 permit tcp any any eq ftp

access-list 100 permit tcp any any eq www
```

Create an access list that defines the traffic that will trigger authentication. This access list will be referenced by the **aaa authentication match** command.

```
aaa-server TACACS+ protocol tacacs+
aaa-server RADIUS protocol radius
aaa-server AuthInbound protocol tacacs+
```

This specifies that TACACS+ will be used to authenticate inbound traffic.

```
aaa-server AuthInbound (inside) host 171.68.118.101 cisco timeout 5
```

This specifies the TACACS+ server IP address to query for authentication requests.

```
aaa-server AuthOutbound protocol radius
```

This specifies that RADIUS will be used to authenticate outbound traffic.

```
aaa-server AuthOutbound (inside) host 171.68.118.101 cisco timeout 5
```

This specifies the RADIUS server IP address to query for authentication requests.

```
aaa authentication match 100 outside AuthInbound
```

This performs an inbound authentication on any traffic defined in access list 100.

```
aaa authentication match 100 inside AuthOutbound
```

This performs outbound authentication on any traffic defined in access list 100.

```
no snmp-server location
no snmp-server contact
snmp-server community public
no snmp-server enable traps
floodguard enable
telnet timeout 5
terminal width 80
Cryptochecksum:b26b560b20e625c9e23743082484caca
: end
[OK]
```

Authentication Proxy

Authentication proxy allows administrators to apply security policies on a per-user basis. Typically, authorization is associated with a user's IP address, or a subnet. For example, if an administrator wanted to restrict access to the FTP protocol, they create an access list denying (or permitting) use for a single IP address or specific range of IP addresses. This is difficult to implement especially if a DHCP server is dynamically assigning IP addresses to workstations. Careful IP management is needed to make sure that a group of workstations is assigned an IP from the correct pool; otherwise, the ability to FTP may not be permitted (or denied) because of their IP address.

Instead of implementing access control lists based on the IP address only, the authentication proxy allows the application of a security policy on a per-user basis. Users can be identified by their username (instead of IP address) and, based on their username, access profiles are retrieved automatically and applied from a CiscoSecure ACS server or some other RADIUS or TACACS+ authentication server. These profiles are in use only while there is traffic being passed to and from the specific user. For example, if a user initiates an HTTP connection to a Web site, the profile will be in use. After a certain amount of time, when no HTTP traffic unique to that profile passes through the PIX, the profile will no longer apply to that user.

The Authentication proxy feature is available on Cisco Secure PIX Firewall IOS and on Cisco routers running the IOS Firewall feature set 12.0 and later.

How the Authentication Proxy Works

The authentication proxy works like this:

1. A user initiates an HTTP session via a Web browser through the Cisco Secure PIX firewall and triggers the authentication proxy.

2. The authentication proxy will check if the user has already been authenticated. If the user has authenticated and the information is valid, the connection is completed. If the user information is not valid or does not exist, the authentication proxy will prompt the user for a username and password.

3. After the user has entered a username and password, the authentication profile is downloaded from the AAA (RADIUS or TACACS+) server. This information is used to create a dynamic access control entry (ACE), which is then added to the inbound ACL of an input interface and added to an outbound ACL of an output interface

(if an output ACLS exists). For example, after successfully authenticating by entering my username and password, my profile is downloaded to the PIX. ACLs will be altered dynamically (as opposed to being entered statically and having to change them manually) and then applied to the inbound or outbound interfaces. If my profile permits me to use FTP, then an outbound ACL will be added dynamically to the outbound interface (typically the outside interface) allowing this. If the authentication fails, then the service will be denied.

4. The inbound and outbound ACL is altered by replacing the source IP address with the IP address of the host (in this case, my workstation's IP address).

5. As soon as the user has successfully authenticated, a timer begins for each user profile. As long as traffic is being passed through the firewall, the user will not have to reauthenticate. If the authentication timer expires, the user must reauthenticate before traffic is permitted through the firewall again.

Comparison with the Lock-and Key Feature

Another feature that utilizes authentication and dynamic access control lists is the *Lock-and-Key Access List*, described in Chapter 2, "Traffic Filtering on the Cisco IOS." Table 6.13 compares the authentication proxy to the features of Lock-and-Key.

Table 6.13 Lock-and Key Comparison

Authentication Proxy	Lock and Key
Triggers on HTTP connection requests.	Triggers on Telnet connection requests.
TACACS+ or RADIUS authentication and authorization.	TACACS+, RADIUS, or local authentication.
Access lists are retrieved from AAA server only.	Access lists are configured on the router only.
Access privileges are granted on a per user and host IP address basis.	Access privileges are granted based on the user's host IP address.
Access lists can have multiple entries as defined by the user profiles on the AAA server.	Access lists are limited to one entry for each host IP address.
Allows DHCP-based host IP addresses, meaning that the users can log in from any host location and obtain authentication and authorization.	Associates a fixed IP address with a specific user. Users must log in from the host with that IP address.

Benefits of Authentication Proxy

Every policy or networking concept has its advantages and disadvantages. The following are some of the benefits provided by the authentication proxy:

- It provides dynamic, per-user authentication and authorization, authenticating users by querying a server through TACACS+ or RADIUS security protocols.

- It allows ACLs to be altered dynamically by changing the source IP address to the IP address assigned to the workstation. This makes it easier for administrators who use DHCP-assigned IP addresses.

- Since authentication and authorization are being used, it aids in the overall security policy of a company.

- User profiles can be tailored on a user-by-user basis. I may be able to access FTP, Telnet, and HTTP services, whereas another individual may be permitted to use HTTP only.

- Probably one of the greatest benefits of the authentication proxy is that no special client software is needed. Only an HTTP browser (which is typically installed on clients anyway) is needed. This makes it completely transparent to the client (apart from entering their username and password).

Restrictions of Authentication Proxy

As we stated earlier, there are always some minor restrictions when implementing a protocol or policy. The restrictions of the authentication proxy are as follows:

- Only HTTP connections will trigger the authentication proxy.

- HTTP services must be running on the default (well-known) port 80.

- Accounting is not currently supported in IOS 5.2.

- JavaScript must be enabled in the client browsers.

- The authentication proxy access lists apply to traffic passing through the PIX. Traffic destined to the router is authenticated by the existing authentication methods on the IOS software.

- The authentication proxy does not support concurrent usage. For example, if two separate users attempt to log in from the same workstation, authentication and authorization will apply only to the first user who successfully authenticated. The second user will be unable to authenticate and unable to pass traffic through the PIX until they authenticate.

- Load balancing through multiple AAA servers is currently not supported.

Configuring Authentication Proxy

The first step in configuring the authentication proxy is to specify the AAA server in which authentication will occur. This section will focus on the configuration of the authentication proxy on the PIX.

Use the **auth-proxy** keyword, for example:

```
aaa new-model
```

This command enables AAA functionality on the router.

```
aaa-server radiusserver protocol radius
```

This defines a list of authentication methods at login.

```
aaa authorization auth-proxy default
```

This uses the **auth-proxy** keyword to enable authentication proxy for AAA methods.

```
aaa-server radius (inside)host 192.168.1.10 radiuskey
aaa-server tacacs+ (inside) host 192.168.1.20 tacacskey
```

This specifies a TACACS+ and RADIUS AAA server. Specify TACACS+ and RADIUS encryption key for communications between the router and the AAA server.

```
access-list 110 permit tcp host 192.168.1.10 eq tacacs host 192.168.1.1
```

This creates an ACL entry to allow the AAA server to return traffic to the firewall. The source address is the IP address of the AAA server, and the destination is the IP address of the router interface where the AAA server resides.

The authentication proxy also requires a per-user access profile configuration on the AAA server. Refer to the vendor's documentation on how to configure authentication proxy on the AAA server.

Configuring the HTTP Server

To use the authentication proxy, the HTTP server must be enabled on the firewall or router, and the authentication method should be set to use AAA. To do this, perform these commands:

```
ip http server
```

This enables the HTTP server. The authentication proxy uses the HTTP server to communicate with the client for user authentication.

```
ip http authentication aaa
```

This sets the HTTP server authentication method to AAA.

```
ip http access-class 110
```

This specifies the access list for the HTTP server. Use the access list number that was configured previously.

Configure Authentication Proxy

Finally, to configure the authentication proxy, use the commands shown in Table 6.14 in global configuration mode.

Table 6.14 Configuring Authentication Proxy

Command	Description
ip auth-proxy auth-cache-time *min*	Set the global authentication proxy idle timeout value in minutes. If the timeout expires, user authentication entries are removed, along with any associated dynamic access lists. The default value is 60 minutes.
ip auth-proxy auth-proxy-banner	(Optional) Display the name of the firewall router in the authentication proxy login page. The banner is disabled by default.
Ip auth-proxy name *auth-proxy-name* **http [auth-cache-time** *min*] **[list** *std-access-list*]	Create authentication proxy rules. The rules define how you apply authentication proxy. This command associates connection initiating HTTP protocol traffic with an authentication proxy name. You can associate the named rule with an access control list, providing control over which hosts use the authentication proxy feature. If no standard access list is defined, the named authentication proxy rule intercepts HTTP traffic from all hosts whose connection initiating packets are received at the configured interface.

auth-proxy-name Name of the authentication proxy. |

Continued

Table 6.14 Continued

Command	Description
Ip auth-proxy name *auth-proxy-name* **http [auth-cache-time** *min*] **[list** *std-access-list*]	**auth-cache-time** Optional keyword to override the global authentication proxy cache timer. This provides more control over timeout values. If no value is specified, the proxy assumes the value set with the **ip auth proxy auth-cache=time** command.
	list Optional keyword to specify the standard access list to apply to a named authentication proxy rule. HTTP connections initiated from hosts defined in the access list are intercepted by the authentication proxy.
	std-access-list Specify the standard access list for use with the **list** keyword.
interface *type*	Enter interface configuration mode by specifying the interface type on which to apply the proxy. For example, **interface** *Ethernet0*.
ip auth-proxy *auth-proxy-name*	In interface configuration mode, apply the named authentication proxy rule at the interface. This command enables the authentication proxy with that name.

Authentication Proxy Configuration Example

The following example shows how to configure the authentication proxy on a firewall:

```
aaa new-model
aaa authentication login default tacacs+ radius
aaa authorization auth-proxy default tacacs+ radius
```

This sets up the aaa new model to use authentication proxy.

```
aaa-server radius (inside) 192.168.1.10 radiuskey
aaa-server tacacs+ (inside) 102.168.1.20 tacacskey
```

This defines the AAA servers and keys.

```
ip http server
```

This enables the HTTP server on the router.

```
ip http authentication aaa
```

This sets the HTTP server authentication method of AAA.

```
access-list 20 deny any
ip http access-class 20
```

This uses ACL 20 to deny connection from any host to the HTTP server.

```
ip auth-proxy auth-cache-time 60
```

This sets the global authentication proxy timeout value.

```
ip auth-proxy name Corp_users http
```

This applies a name to the authentication proxy configuration rule.

```
interface ethernet0
    ip address 192.168.1.1
    ip auth-proxy Corp_users
```

This enters interface configuration mode and apply the authentication proxy rule to the interface.

Summary

In this chapter we discussed the mechanisms (authentication, authorization, and accounting) that make up AAA, and we discussed how to configure them on Cisco devices.

As we stated earlier, authentication is the process of verifying the identity of an entity. Authorization is the process of giving permission to an entity to access a system resource. Accounting enables the network manager to keep track of the services and resources that are used by the users.

It is important to remember that a simple login and password may not be enough security to protect data or access to various services. AAA can be used to provide a complete solution in which authentication, authorization, and accounting will give a company complete control over their assets and who has the ability to access them, as well as an audit trail that can be logged for future reference.

FAQs

Q: Should I use RADIUS or TACACS+ as my security protocol?

A: Various factors come into play on this question. If encryption and a connection-oriented authorization request is important, then TACACS+ would be the best choice. Recall that TACACS+ uses TCP as its transport protocol and it encrypts the entire body of the packet when sending information back and forth; RADIUS uses UDP for its transport protocol, and it encrypts the password in the access-request packet only when sending information back and forth.

Q: Where can I find a RADIUS or TACACS+ server/daemon?

A: There are several programs available to be used as a RADIUS or TACACS+ server, for example:

- Cisco Secure ACS at www.cisco.com
- Lucent RADIUS at www.livingston.com
- RADIUS-VMS Server at www.radiusvms.com

Q: I want to use TACACS+ or RADIUS for authentication with the enable password, but what happens if my security server is unavailable?

A: There are two common ways in which you can us authentication for the enable password on a Cisco router. You can simply use the local router enable password, or if you are going to configure authentication with a security protocol, use the enable keyword when defining the methods in which the enable password will be authenticated. For example:

```
aaa authentication login admin-enable tacacs+ enable
```

In this case, if the TACACS+ server is unavailable, the locally config-ured **enable** password can be used for authentication.

Chapter 7

Intrusion Detection

Solutions in this chapter:

- **Network Attacks and Intrusions**

- **Network and Host-Based Intrusion detection**

- **Cisco Secure Scanner (NetSonar)**

- **Cisco Secure Integrated Software and IOS IDS (Firewall Feature Set)**

- **Cisco Secure Intrusion Detection System (NetRanger)**

Introduction

A properly configured firewall can do a good job at protecting servers, but if your server needs to be visible from a public network then total protection is impossible. From an attacker's view of your network, any visible services are likely to be chosen as the first ones to be probed and attacked. Also if the security policies applied on your firewall allow Web access to your public server, then that same service can be used to attack the server for known vulnerabilities.

A popular attack against public servers is called a Denial of Service (DoS) attack. This renders the service or server unavailable. Several other types of attacks and intrusions must be investigated in order to understand the role the intrusion detection system can play in your network.

Firewalls, workstation security, and well-written software all contribute to a secure network. Because we can never be completely sure that best practices have been followed, a detection system is a logical next step. The IDS is your best ally against intrusions.

An intrusion detection system gives the network or security manager a tool to detect and react rapidly to an attack on the network. This chapter will investigate the various types of attacks and intrusions as well as describe the tools available from Cisco to implement an intrusion detection system.

What Is Intrusion Detection?

Intrusion detection is the ongoing process of searching for security violations on your network; this includes proactive and reactive detection of vulnerabilities, analysis, and corresponding responses.

Network Attacks and Intrusions

Let's start with a simple analogy. Imagine you have spent time, money, and effort working hard on your house to make it just the way that you want it. Now you remove your curtains, leave the front door open, leave the keys outside the front door, and learn that the other doors are easily broken into. None of these issues make you feel comfortable, and you quickly realize that even though everything inside is perfect; anyone can get in easily and mess it up. Who knows? You might even meet someone at the door impersonating the telephone repairman.

As a measure to protect your home, you would probably install a burglar alarm and a good set of locks. As an analogy to systems that take action against intruders, you might even decide to install a trap door to aggressively identify and trap them! Part of the overall solution you would use to make your home secure is analogous to the intrusion detection system available from Cisco Systems.

The first step is for us to identify what an attack or intrusion is. Any action that violates the security policy of your organization should be considered a threat, but broadly speaking, attacks and intrusions can be summarized as an exploitation of:

- Poor network perimeter/device security
- Poor physical security
- Application and operating software weaknesses
- Human failure
- Weaknesses in the IP suite of protocols

Before we look at these threats in more detail, let me suggest that you assume a shrewd mindset; it helps when it comes to learning about intrusion detection.

Poor Network Perimeter/Device Security

This can be described as the ease of access to devices across the network. Without access control using a firewall or a packet filtering router, the network is vulnerable.

Network Sniffers

A few years ago I worked in the IT department for a large investment house. I remember helping to tune an application that some developers were working on. The application contained sensitive information regarding the company's financial strategies. My role was to analyze the traffic to compare performance from one version of code to the next. In the network trace I came across some frames containing usernames and cleartext passwords. I informed the application developers, and they quickly fixed the problem. If it wasn't for my upbringing, I could have easily signed on to the application and then used that information to tamper with the records.

This method of intrusion is called *eavesdropping*, or packet snooping, and the type of network technology implemented directly influences its susceptibility. For instance, shared networks are easier to eavesdrop on than switched networks.

Scanner Programs

Certain types of software such as Solarwinds are able to scan entire networks, produce detailed reports on what ports are in use, perform password cracking, and view account details on servers. Although this is a very useful tool if used for the purpose of legitimate network auditing, in the wrong hands, it could be devastating. Scanning software commonly uses one or more of the following methods:

- Ping sweep
- SNMP sweep
- TCP/UDP port scans
- Scanning logon accounts

Approaching the millennium, I performed a global scan for a company using an SNMP sweep program. The objective was to ensure that all network devices were running at a compliant release of software. This was surprisingly easy, and I even ended up accidentally scanning some devices outside the perimeter of our network inside the carrier's network. Incidentally, one device in their network was not Y2K compliant and was upgraded at our request!

Network Topology

Shared networks are easier to eavesdrop on as all traffic is visible from everywhere on that shared media. Switched networks on the other hand are more secure since by default, there is no single viewpoint for traffic. Cisco Catalyst switches have a feature that is used for troubleshooting where you can mirror traffic from VLANs or switch ports to a single designated switch port called the span port. Once you plug your sniffer into the span port, you easily can view traffic in different VLANs by making configuration changes.

Thankfully, most organizations are moving away from shared media for multiple benefits, including improved security and performance.

Unattended Modems

Installing a modem on a PC for remote access allows a quick and easy way to access the network from home. Unfortunately, this also means that the modem and PC may be prone to attack when you are not there. It is not generally possible to detect modems attached to PCs using most types of network auditing systems, so tighter software control and education of the user community is the best solution. If access is essential, you should explain the benefits of using the (secure) corporate remote access solution instead.

Poor Physical Security

There are simple security measures that can be taken in the physical world to ensure better security for your systems. Locking your doors is obviously a good common-sense start, but there are often a number of simple procedures and safeguards that companies could perform and implement that, for one reason or another, they do not.

I recently read an article in Packet that described a theft in California of a file server that contained over 300,000 credit card numbers. The thief just unplugged the server and walked out with it. A simple tagging system would have done the trick, as alarms would have sounded when the machine was removed; even a paper authorization system would have worked. After all, it's pretty simple to bypass security on routers and switches if you can get to the console port, or in the case of servers you can remove the hard disks and reinstall them elsewhere.

Application and Operating Software Weaknesses

In this context, software is a term that describes the operating system as well as the packages that run under its control. Most software is or has been deficient at some point in its life, and it is not always attributed to poor programming either. For example, sometimes commercial pressures can force a company to release software early, before it is debugged completely.

Software Bugs

Most bugs are based on buffer overflows, unexpected input combinations, and the exploitation of multithread scheduling. An example of this is where the cracker tries to race the legitimate code in making modifications to files in the hope of updating a password file and *not* causing a software failure; this is called a *race* condition.

Web Server/Browser-based Attacks

The Internet is one of the fastest moving areas at present and, as such, Web applications are often hastily written. General software bugs and browser configuration errors all provide vulnerabilities for the wily attacker to break in.

Getting Passwords—Easy Ways in Cracking Programs

Most people have created a simple password based on objects that are easy to remember, such as a name or favorite color at some point or other. In the ten to fifteen companies I've worked for, I don't recall seeing good pass-word practices being enforced very often. It's quite simple to get someone else's password; many times, all you have to do is ask.

Some other ways that passwords might be obtained are:

- Observation, over the shoulder.
- Gaining access to password files.
- Using a sniffer to look for clear text passwords.
- Replaying logon traffic recorded on a sniffer that contains the encrypted password.
- Dictionary-based attacks, where a software program runs through every word in a dictionary database.
- Brute force attacks, where the attacker runs a program that tries variations of letters, numbers, and common words in the hope of getting the right combination. Typical programs can try around 100,000 combinations per minute.

Trojan Horse Attacks

Legend says that the Greeks won the Trojan War by hiding in a big wooden horse and offering it as a gift just so they could get past the gates of Troy. At night the Greeks leaped out and seized control to win the war—brilliant! Today, some malicious computer programmers write software Trojan horses. These are disguised as something quite innocent such as an e-mail or a game, but once initialized start other hidden programs that proceed to wreak havoc.

A recent example of this would be the Love Bug virus, which caused huge disruption worldwide. An e-mail was sent out, which once opened, infected files on the hard disk, read your address book, and then propa-gated the same e-mail to everyone telling them that you loved them.

A primary effect of this Trojan horse was an overload of mail servers as they struggled to keep up with the exponential rise in e-mail traffic. The attack had a sizeable impact on the global business community.

Virus or Worm Attacks

Viruses are programs that target files on your computer, and worms have the ability to propagate themselves. These types of attacks are often con-tained within Trojan horses.

Human Failure

"If there is any one secret of success, it lies in the ability to get the other person's point of view and see things from that person's angle as well as from your own."

—Henry Ford

Everyone is an individual; we all have our own thoughts, feelings, and moods. Of course, the human failure factor spans far and wide across the security spectrum and is usually a common contributing cause for security breaches. These can be a result of malicious motives or simply innocent mistakes.

Poorly Configured Systems

The very first time I configured a Cisco router on a network, I used the default password of "cisco." If anyone had decided to choose that router to attack they could have logged on, looked at the routing tables, reloaded the router (causing user disruption), or changed the password.

Many new systems when taken out of the box use default accounts or passwords that are easy to obtain. Most allow you to decide whether or not to use security features without any objections. In brief, systems are poorly configured because of:

- A lack of thought during configuration
- Insufficient time to configure the product properly
- Poor knowledge of the product

Information Leaks

Rather than a sinister individual "leaking" information to the outside, this is usually a little more straightforward. You may have seen security PINs (personal identification numbers) or passwords in diaries or written on post-it notes. The list is long and an absolute feast for a nocturnal attacker wandering around the office late at night. Not shredding sensitive documents and drawings can also be a risky practice. If someone gets hold of the network diagram, they can start targeting devices and choosing points for maximum impact.

One time I was sitting in an open-space office one day where the LAN administrator was asked by a colleague from far across the room what the supervisor account password was. He shouted it back to him. Need I say more?

Malicious Users

For various motives, there are people who will perform or facilitate intrusions and attacks into your network. For example, an FTP download of all customers' account information onto a laptop, which could be removed from the building, could do serious damage to a business.

TIP

An attacker is also known as a *cracker*. Crackers are responsible for all kinds of negative and destructive attacks on systems. However, the term *hacker* used in the correct way refers to someone who uses his or her knowledge for beneficial or constructive purposes. Most hackers find the incorrect usage of this terminology misleading, but the general trend is toward mixing the terms.

Weaknesses in the IP Suite of Protocols

When most of the TCP/IP family of protocols was originally developed the world was a nicer place; perhaps there was not the need for the security we have today. Nowadays, it is possible for you to stroll into a bookshop and pick up a book on how to crack a network, and the success of the Internet also means that this type of information is readily available.

The TCP/IP stack is code written by programmers/developers; as such, it is probable that some implementations will contain errors. If the implementation of TCP/IP is poor then the system can be compromised in spite of the upper layer applications being used.

Taking advantage of these weaknesses requires an in-depth awareness of TCP/IP protocols. Flaws exploited by attackers are being countered by software developers and then recountered by attackers.

One example of improvement is IPSec, which is an addition to the IP protocol suite. IPSec provides privacy and authentication methods creating traffic security on a network. For more information on this interesting protocol, refer to Chapter 5, "Virtual Private Networks," where it is covered in more detail.

Any member of the TCP/IP suite, shown in Figure 7.1, can be the target of an attack. Some have flaws that are easier to exploit by the cracker than others.

Figure 7.1 TCP/IP protocol suite.

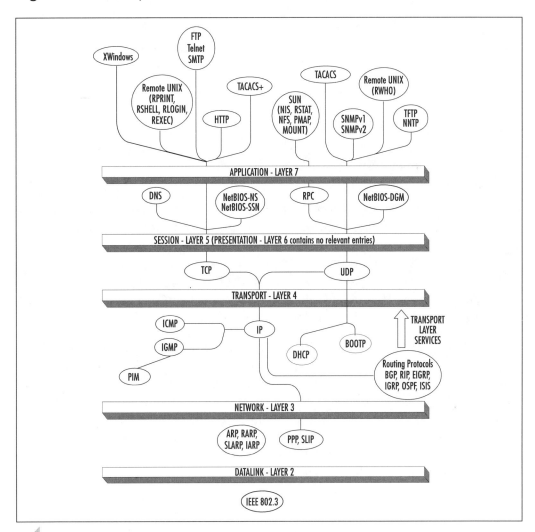

NOTE

Although we have discussed TCP/IP weaknesses in this section, application programs also can be poorly written or badly designed in the way that they interface with the lower layer protocols. Bad application software can provide the attacker with a foothold to penetrate a system.

Conversely, a server running well-written applications with solid code but using a bad TCP/IP implementation can still be compromised because the application relies on the TCP/IP stack for network services.

The next sections highlight some examples of the more common attacks to date; for the purpose of our discussion I've assumed that an Attacker (station C) can see traffic returning from its victims (stations A and B). In practice, this may not be the case, but the attack can still succeed; it just takes more skill on the part of the attacker. For each type of attack, I've tried to list the URL of the related CERT document for you to read. CERT is a central coordination center for Internet security problems worldwide.

Layer 7 Attacks

Here are a few examples of some of the more common attacks that can occur at the application layer of the OSI model.

SMTP Attacks

Simple Mail Transport Protocol (SMTP) has been used to send mail by a wide variety of mail programs for many years. A common method of attack is the buffer overrun where the attacker enters a larger number of characters in an e-mail field than expected by the e-mail server. The extra characters contain executable code that is run by the e-mail server following an error in the application. The code could then facilitate further cracking. Installing the latest security patches for the e-mail system may avoid this kind of attack.

It is good practice to use digital signatures and cryptography techniques in cases where sensitive information is to be sent across shared networks. These methods can offer you good protection against spoofing attacks. Digital signatures will ensure that each message is signed and verified, and encryption techniques will ensure that the mail content is viewable only by the intended receiving e-mail address. Details of these types of attack can be found at the following URLs:

www.cert.org/tech_tips/email_spoofing.html

www.cert.org/advisories/CA-97.05.sendmail.html

SMTP SPAM

This is when an e-mail is sent to a very large number of people, but not personally directed at any of them. Internet service providers can restrict spamming by the implementation of rules that govern the number of destination addresses allowed for a single message. For further information, go to www.cert.org/tech_tips/email_bombing_spamming.html.

FTP

Anonymous connections to servers running the FTP process allow the attacking station C to download a virus, overwrite a file, or abuse trusts that the FTP server has in the same domain.

FTP attacks are best avoided by preventing anonymous logins, stopping unused services on the server, as well as creating router access lists and firewall rules. If you require the use of anonymous logons, then the best course of action is to update the FTP software to the latest revision and to keep an eye on related advisories. It's probably a good idea to adopt a general policy of regular checks of advisories for all software you are responsible for to ensure the best protection. For further information go to the following URL:

www.cert.org/advisories/CA-93.10.anonymous.FTP.activity.html.

SNMP

It is possible to gain detailed information about a device by using SNMP get queries. Armed with this information, the cracker can facilitate further types of attacks. By using an SNMP set program, it is also possible to change the values of Managed Information Base (MIB) instances.

WARNING

A few years ago I had to modify the ISDN number called outbound by a non-Cisco router in South Korea. Based in London, I had no access to the configuration utility or any onsite engineers.

However, by viewing the entries in the MIB tree and performing multiple SNMP sets, I was able to change the phone number to the correct string. This allowed calls to be made successfully to the London router.

If public and private default strings are used for SNMP configuration without SNMP access lists, it's like leaving the door wide open for attack.

All applications and services can leak information that an attacker can use. In this section we have reviewed a few common ones but in reality there are hundreds that have been reported, with many more that remain unreported or undiscovered. Security personnel must keep up to date with advisories on all software (and operating systems) so that they are best prepared against attacks: in other words, a policy of security through prevention.

Layer 5 Attacks

Here are some examples of common attacks that occur at the session layer of the OSI model.

DNS Attacks

The DNS service in most companies is vital. Without it, nothing works as it should. For example, e-mail, Web services, and most communications applications use DNS names. One method of attack is to infiltrate the server in order to modify DNS entries directly. Another is where station C would pretend to be another DNS server responding to a request from a real DNS server. In this way, the DNS cache on all DNS servers could be poisoned, which would affect the whole network.

Modern DNS software has the capability of using authentication between servers. For further information, visit www.cert.org/advisories/CA-2000-03.html.

NetBIOS Win Nuke

Station C would send OOB (Out Of Band) data to station B with an URG flag on port 139 (NetBIOS Session/SMB). This could cause station B to fail. There are vendor software patches available to overcome these types of issues. For further information, go to www.cert.org/vul_notes/VN-2000-03.html.

Layer 3 and 4 Attacks

These occur at the Network and Transport layers of the OSI model; here are some examples of the more common attacks to date.

TCP SYN Flooding

This is best described in stages:

1. Station C sends lots of SYN packets to station B in rapid succession from nonexistent host addresses.

2. B sends back SYN/ACKs and maintains the half-opened connections in a queue as it waits for ACKs from the nonexistent hosts at the source addresses.

3. B runs out of resources waiting for ACKs back from non-existent hosts.

4. At this point B drops legitimate connections and is likely to hang and crash.

There is no widely accepted solution for this problem. On Cisco routers however, it is possible to configure TCP Intercept which protects against SYN floods.

TCP Intercept Configuration

This section covers the TCP Intercept feature available on Cisco routers that have Cisco Secure IS (Firewall Feature Set) installed. You configure it in the following way:

1. Ensure that you have the necessary IOS Firewall Feature Set installed.

2. Create an extended access list where the source is "any" and designate internal networks to protect against SYN flooding attack.

3. In global configuration mode enter the command:

```
ip tcp intercept list <access-list number>
```

4. Choose the mode in which you want to operate; if you don't specify any, it will be in *Intercept* mode. In *Watch* mode, the router "watches" TCP connection requests; if they do not become established within 30 seconds the router sends a TCP RST to the receiving station, thus allowing it to free its resources. When operating in *Intercept* mode the router acts as a middleman in the TCP handshake. It will keep the original SYN request; respond back to the originator with a SYN/ACK pending the final ACK. Once this happens, the router sends the original SYN and performs a three-way handshake with the destination; it then drops out of the way allowing direct communications between source and destination. To choose the mode enter the command:

```
ip tcp intercept mode intercept|watch
```

TCP intercept will monitor for the number of incomplete connections. When this figure goes over 1,100 or if a surge of over 1,100 connections is received within 60 seconds, then the router deletes the oldest connection request (like a conveyor belt) and then reduces TCP retransmission time by 50 percent. This aggressive behavior can be adjusted to fit security policy. For further information on TCP SYN flooding go to www.cert.org/advisories/CA-96.21.tcp_syn_flooding.html.

SMURF IP Spoofing Attack

This is based on IP spoofing where multiple broadcast pings are sent out by station C with victim A's IP address as the source. A system could be overwhelmed with ICMP response packets. Recommended solutions are as follows:

- To disable IP directed broadcasts at the router by entering the global command in the router configuration.

```
no ip directed-broadcast
```

- If possible, to configure the operating system not to respond to broadcast pings. For more information go to www.cert.org/advisories/CA-98.01.smurf.html.

- To use the global command on the router as follows:

```
ip verify unicast reverse-path
```

This will match the routing entries in the CEF (Cisco Express Forwarding) table against the source IP addresses of incoming packets. If there is no route back out of the interface then the router drops the packet. This will work only if CEF is enabled on the router.

- To use CAR (Committed Access Rate) on the Cisco routers to limit the inbound levels of ICMP traffic. Note that CAR configurations can also reduce the amount of SYN traffic to help against SYN flooding and DDoS attacks (discussed later in this section).

TCP/IP Sequence Number Spoofing/Session Hijacking

Let's imagine C wants to spoof B into thinking it is A.

1. Station C initiates a Denial of Service (DoS) attack on A and then impersonates A by spoofing its IP address. The purpose of this is to prevent the real A from interfering with the attack.

2. C initiates a connection to B and tries to guess the sequence number from frames it has sniffed.

3. If B is fooled into believing C is actually A then data will flow freely between the two.

Older TCP/IP implementations increment SEQ numbers in a predictable manner that makes the exchange easier to intercept and spoof.

> **TIP**
>
> Modern TCP/IP implementations are able to take advantage of a SYN cookie. If this were in place station B would create a cookie to store the sequence number and forget about it. This would free up B's resources and avoid it crashing. The same cookie could be referenced when traffic arrives back at station B. This method prevents a hijacking station from using a "guessed" sequence number as the cookie controls (the validity of) all TCP/IP exchanges. Some Linux implementations use SYN cookies enabled by default; Linux is an operating system upon which the Apache Web Server runs. Also Sun Systems offer a SYN cookie feature for use in the UNIX environment.

Hijack attacks from outside the network can be prevented by applying an access list to the WAN interfaces of the company router. This would prevent traffic with internal source addresses from being accepted from the outside. This type of filtering is known as input filtering and does not protect against attempts to hijack connections between hosts inside the network.

Another access list to prevent unknown source addresses from leaving the internal network should also be applied. This is to prevent attacks to outside networks from within the company. For more information on spoofing and session hijacking go to www.cert.org/advisories/CA-95.01.IP. spoofing.attacks.and.hijacked.terminal.connections.html.

Denial of Service Type Attacks

This is when the victim is left paralyzed and unable to provide services, or is overwhelmed by attack traffic.

Ping of Death

This type of attack takes advantage of an inability of poor IP implementations to cope with abnormally large IP packets. In this example, ICMP packets transmitted by the attacking station would exceed 65535 bytes (the maximum IP packet size). The packet would then be fragmented and the receiving station could fail the reassembly process and then crash or hang.

Several vendors have released software patches to overcome this problem. For more information, go to www.cert.org/advisories/ CA-1996-26.html.

Teardrop Attack

This attack targets a specific weakness in some TCP/IP implementations where the reassembly fails to work correctly when incorrect offset values are injected into IP traffic. The attack is based on the same principle as the Ping of Death attack.

Land Attack

Land is an IP spoofing-type attack—here's how it works:

1. C sends a SYN packet to B using B's IP address and identical source and destination port numbers.

2. B will never be able to complete this connection and may go into an infinite loop.

3. If B is susceptible to this type of attack it will hang or crash.

The recommended solution is to install vendor patches. For Land it is also advisable to install ingress filters to combat IP spoofing. For more information, go to www.cert.org/advisories/CA-97.28.Teardrop_Land.html.

Distributed Denial of Service Attacks (DDoS)

Recently this type of attack has become more common. Typical tools used by crackers are Trinoo, TFN, TFN2K, and Stacheldraht. How does a DDoS attack work? Refer to Figure 7.2.

Figure 7.2 Simplified DDoS attack scenario.

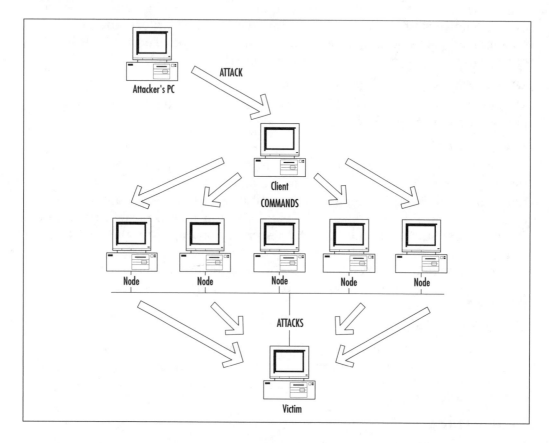

The attacker gains access to a client PC. From here, the cracker can use tools to send commands to the nodes. These nodes then flood or send malformed packets to the victim. Coordinated traceroutes from several sources can be used to probe the same target to construct a table of routes for the network. This information can be used as the basis for further attacks.

So what makes this so nasty? In practice there may be thousands of nodes. Billions of packets can be directed at the victim, taking up all available bandwidth or causing DoS.

At present there is no solution to the problem, nor is it easy to trace the attack origin.

A list of general suggestions is as follows:

- Prevent initial compromise of the client through good security practices.
- Keep software up-to-date with patches and upgrades.
- Keep all anti-virus software up to date.
- Run desktop firewall software where available.
- Install and activate the Cisco IDS.

Cisco also suggests the following recommendations:

- Use the global command:

```
ip verify unicast reverse-path
```

- Use ACLs to block private address range traffic coming inbound.
- Use ingress filtering (discussed earlier).
- Use CAR to limit ICMP and SYN packets inbound.

For more information, visit www.cert.org/advisories/CA-99-17-denial-of-service-tools.html and www.cert.org/reports/dsit_workshop.pdf.

For more details on Cisco's recommendations, go to www.cisco.com/warp/public/707/newsflash.html#prevention.

Network and Host-based Intrusion Detection

There has been a large amount of market hype around what IDSs are capable of. Cisco and other reputable IDS vendors maintain that the IDS is a key component to be used in conjunction with other tools to provide an end-to-end secure system.

The IT community is undecided on the best way to perform intrusion detection. Should it be network-based? Or host-based? The truth of the matter is that a combined approach is probably best. Let's describe both of these methods in order to understand their particular strengths and weaknesses.

Network IDS

The network-based IDS is usually composed of a sniffer or a sensor that examines frames on the wire and a reporting or analysis engine. The sensor and analysis engine can be packaged in a single host or as a distributed system. In the same way that you have a signature or thumbprint by which you are identified, an attack will display a unique signature or pattern, hopefully. The sensors in this type of system operate in promiscuous mode and will look at all traffic that passes by. The moment they spot something suspicious they will send notification messages to an analysis or management station.

The advantages are as follows:

- They can be configured to be non-obtrusive. You can pick up intrusion attempts, create log entries, and inform security staff of the event without the intruder's knowledge.

- You don't need application passwords, network operating system rights, or system logons in order for the software to run and return results.

- They are not dependent on OS or application types as they work at a packet level, identifying attack patterns or signatures.

- No infrastructure changes are usually required, the Network IDS can just slot into the existing network.

- There is no overhead nor changes on servers and workstations as the Network IDS does not require any software to be installed on these devices.

The disadvantages are as follows:

- Some vendors' systems are unable to collect data at higher speeds. Because collection and analysis is key, the Network IDS must not drop or miss packets. Some Network IDSs running at speeds of 100 Mbps or above may experience this problem.

- They are able to sniff only on the local segment. Ideally the Network IDS must be connected to a promiscuous hub or a span port on a switch. If visibility is limited then its capacity will be too.

- They are based on predefined attack signatures and as a result could be out of date or miss more complex types of attacks. Although every effort is made by authorities like Cisco Countermeasure Research Team (C-CRT) and the Computer Emergency Response Team (CERT) to keep the signature databases up to date, new attacks can only be protected against after the event has occurred.

- They perform impersonal analysis, and resulting actions can therefore be impersonal too. Due to the level at which the Network IDS works, it cannot "see" who the user is or what the business value of a service is, so this can result in a secure but sometimes severe action (for upper layer services) being taken.

- Depending upon the configuration, large amounts of data can be sent from collection devices back to the central management station. The more granular the collection, the more traffic there will be.

- A lot of events can be generated by the reporting engine. Trained personnel will need to spend time tuning the system by analyzing the reports and filtering out false positives.

- They have difficulty in dealing with attacks within encrypted sessions. The Network IDS relies on being able to identify attack signatures. If the traffic is encrypted then the signature will be hidden too, rendering the IDS ineffective.

For IT Professionals

False Positive, False Negative

A *positive* is where detection has been made. If this is a real attack then appropriate action must be taken. What if it isn't a real attack? This scenario is known as a *false positive*.

A perfectly legitimate transaction could trigger an IDS to believe that an attack was in progress. The solution is to investigate and review the IDS configuration to prevent the false positive from occurring again; this is possible if you use Cisco's Secure IDS (NetRanger).

The other end of the spectrum is where an attack takes place and the IDS doesn't detect it—this is called a *false negative*. You must avoid this situation—but how do you know that you've had a false negative? If this has happened it usually means that one tier of security in your defense has been compromised. Thankfully, responsible IDS vendors like Cisco are at the very forefront of technology and make every effort to keep their IDS detection database up to date.

Host IDS

These types of IDSs will use system, audit, and event logs from different operating systems and applications. They are able to generate reports based on user/system process activity and can highlight any suspicious behavior based on a set of rules.

The advantages are:

- They provide specific information about who did what, when, and to whom! This is great because there are no speculations or deductions to be made. Meaningful actions can be taken according to specific individuals or applications.

- Host IDSs are less likely to generate false positives as information is directly related to people and applications.

- They produce much less traffic than Network IDSs; there is little emphasis on multiple separate sensors and centralized management stations.

- They do not suffer from network visibility problems (like Network IDSs).

The disadvantages are a lack of portability between operating systems, which results in multiple software installations being required. Host IDSs are usually written for one operating system only.

> **NOTE**
>
> Cisco does not offer a host-based IDS solution; their IDS solution is made up of three network-based products. In this book, we are concerned with the Cisco security solution and will therefore concentrate on Network IDS.

What Can't IDSs Do?

Let's eliminate some of the common misunderstandings regarding IDSs:

- They are not "silver bullets" and cannot perform magic when it comes to stopping intruders.

- They cannot provide investigations without human assistance. Like a good tool, the IDS is most effective when in the right hands.

- They are not intuitive to company security policies, and they have to be configured to match.

- They are not self-correcting. If we don't take the time to configure the IDS properly, we will get poor results. The "garbage in, garbage out" principle still applies.

- They cannot necessarily sustain direct attacks (on the IDS itself). Just like any other system, the IDS itself can be compromised.

- They cannot track and defend against all types of attack.

- They cannot always analyze all traffic on a network. Sometimes the IDS is unable to keep up with all the traffic, or the location of the IDS is such that it has a limited view of the network.

- They cannot improve poor security strategy.

Deploying in a Network

The placement of a Network IDS requires careful planning. Cisco's Secure IDS product (NetRanger) is made up of a Sensor and a central management station called a Director (see Figure 7.3). Let's look at the best place to put the Sensor.

Figure 7.3 Distributed network IDS deployment example.

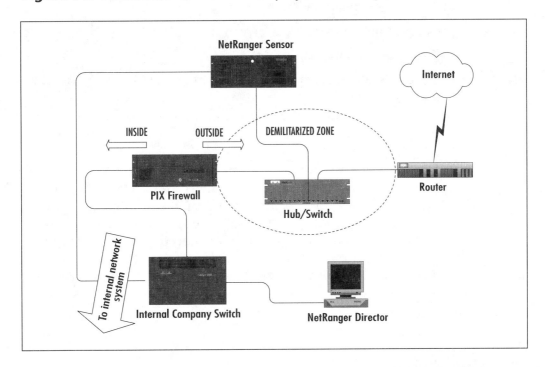

Sensor Placement

Most companies have a firewall that separates the internal network from the outside world; the network outside the firewall is known as the DMZ, or Demilitarized Zone.

Should we place the Sensor outside or inside? If the Sensor is outside, then it can monitor external traffic. This is useful against attacks from the outside but does not allow for detection of internal attacks. Also, the Sensor itself may become the target of an attack so it must be protected. If you place the Sensor inside, then it will be unaware of violations that have occurred that were prevented by the firewall. On the plus side it will detect internally initiated attacks and can highlight firewall rules that are not working properly or are incorrectly configured.

So which one do we choose? The answer is to install the Sensor so that one of its two interfaces is connected to the DMZ (monitoring port) and the other (control and communication port) is connected on the inside. The Sensor can then manage the outermost Cisco router in order to protect itself and the rest of the internal network while communicating back to the Director.

When you review your security policy you may decide that you need to install more Sensors at different points in the network according to security risks and requirements. Some example locations are the following:

- The Accounts department LAN

- Company strategic networks; for example, development LAN

- The Technical department's LAN

- LANs where staff turnover is rapid or hotdesk/temp locations exist

- A server LAN

NOTE

It is important that the firewall allows the Sensor to manage the router in the DMZ and the Director (behind the firewall) to communicate with the Sensor. Depending upon your Firewall setup, this may involve rules to allow communication on UDP port 514 for syslog traffic from the router to the Sensor, Telnet from the Sensor control interface to the router, and communication on UDP port 45000 between the Sensor and the Director.

Network Vulnerability Analysis Tools

Some time ago, I bought a 20-year-old car for a small sum. The only way that I achieved peace of mind was by taking it to a specialist, a mechanic, who performed a full safety check. After his inspection of the car, I had a long list of potential safety risks. Armed with this knowledge, I was able to repair, remove, and replace components in order to make my vehicle secure.

In the same sense, it is important to proactively scan for weaknesses in a network before they are exploited. Cisco Systems NetSonar can actively probe and perform passive investigation of devices around the network.

Cisco's Approach to Security

Cisco's view of security is that it is an ongoing process of monitoring, testing, improving, and securing the network. To achieve this a suite of products is available to us. In the following sections, we will investigate key features and review configurations of the three IDS products:

- Cisco Secure Scanner (NetSonar)
- Cisco Secure Intrusion Detection System (NetRanger)
- Cisco Secure Integrated Software/IOS Intrusion Detection System (Firewall Feature Set)

Cisco Secure Scanner (NetSonar)

Cisco's vulnerability scanner runs on a network-based machine, either Solaris or Windows NT-based. It takes a few minutes to install and has an easy-to-use, intuitive user interface that allows you to get results quickly. Why would this be useful for you? What does the product do? Let's begin by dividing the features into four sections:

1. Minimum system specifications for Secure Scanner v2.0
2. Searching the network for vulnerabilities
3. Viewing the results
4. Keeping the system up-to-date

Minimum System Specifications for Secure Scanner V2.0

Secure Scanner runs on NT 4.0 (Service Pack 3), Solaris 2.5.x, 2.6-2.8 with a Sun SPARC 5 station (or Solaris x86 if using an Intel CPU). All platforms require at least 64MB RAM, 2GB disk space, a network card with a TCP/IP stack, and a display capable of at least 800x600. A recent HTML browser is also essential.

NOTE

Each Secure Scanner license is not tied to a specific IP address range. This allows you to point the same scanner at multiple IP address ranges. With a single license you can scan up to 2,500 devices.

Searching the Network for Vulnerabilities

Once Secure Scanner has been installed you can create and initiate a Scanner session to search your network for vulnerabilities. The session can be designated as either a non-intrusive and passive scan or an intrusive and active probe (used to confirm any vulnerabilities found). Sessions can also be scheduled to start on recurring or specific dates and times, or at random.

Using your session configuration you can initiate an automatic discovery of host devices (all devices running a TCP/IP stack) and services on your network. TCP/UDP port interrogation and SNMP queries are used to gather information, which is compiled into a database. The latter can be used to develop and verify security policies as well as find unexpected machines and services on your network.

WARNING

It is possible to render a service or device unavailable by initiating a probe on the network. Active probing sessions should either run outside peak network usage hours or should omit sensitive devices to prevent loss of service/user disruption.

Although general clients may be unaware that a session is in progress, it is possible that a performance drop may occur. This is especially likely if a probe has been selected with a heavy vulnerability profile.

When you select the page icon from the main screen, the Session Configuration box opens (see Figure 7.4). This screen allows you to define multiple address ranges in a session. You can configure ranges to be aggressively scanned, to exclude certain ranges, to import data from previous session runs, as well as export data to files.

Choose the Vulnerability folder to see the screen in Figure 7.5. Here you can select the ports you want to scan, turning active probing on or off, and choose a predefined Active Probe profile that selects settings for 13 different categories of vulnerability.

Figure 7.4 Specifying network addresses.

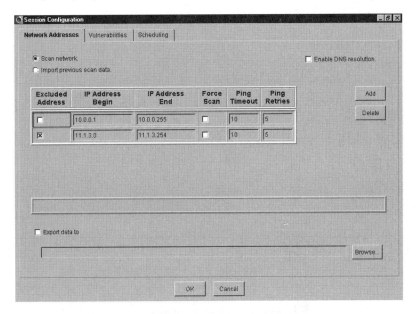

Figure 7.5 Specifying vulnerabilities.

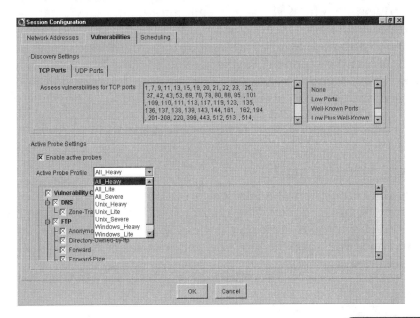

The following categories are available; each has further subcategories available for more specific selection:

- DNS
- NFS
- Telnet
- Finger
- NT security
- TFTP
- FTP
- Rlogin
- X Window
- HTTP
- SMTP
- RSH

The Network Security Database (NSDB) contains in-depth information about these items. We will discuss this in more detail later in the section.

NOTE

It is possible to configure user-defined and custom vulnerability rules. This could be useful if you are scanning for unique devices or non-standard port numbers. Once a custom rule has been defined then you should distribute that rule throughout the enterprise to ensure consistency across the scanners. Further details on how to create user-defined rules can be found at www.cisco.com/univercd/cc/td/doc/product/iaabu/csscan/csscan2/csscug/userrule.htm#13881.

Viewing the Results

Following the completion of a session, a result set folder is created in the main Secure Scanner screen. The result set contains folders for charts, grids, and reports. Right-click on the Results folder and then select View Grid Data; once you save the grid you can just select it by double-clicking from the main screen.

Grid Browser

The grid browser is used to view session results and is very flexible. You can change axes to refer to different data, drill down into cells to highlight specific factors, view host details, create totals or percentages for rows or columns, and create charts. It is also possible to save multiple grid browser views and charts for later use or incorporation into reports. To find out more about the icons you can just hold the mouse over each to display its function.

The grid is a 2-D matrix showing the information returned from the session. In Figure 7.6 the columns on the right represent the IP addresses of the hosts and the rows represent the vulnerabilities that were tested for; the six columns on the left detail the vulnerability details. Let's examine a row from left to right. Column one shows an overall classification for vulnerabilities. Column two shows a value that represents the severity level of the exploit (the higher the number the worse). Column three designates the type of exploit. Column four is the name of the exploit. Column five details whether the vulnerability is confirmed (Vc) or potential (Vp). Column six shows the corresponding ID in the NSDB database. The value of 1 indicates the number of intersections of a row and column value; in this context this value is always 1.

Figure 7.6 NetSonar grid browser.

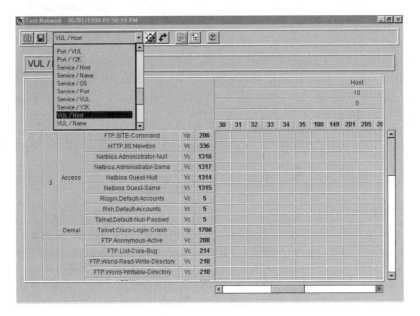

In Figure 7.6, you can see the pull-down menu; this changes the grid view. Let's say you want to change the grid to display the number of exploits and vulnerability types for hosts. Right-click on column 3 and then select Zoom Out, then right-click again and choose Show, Totals. As you can see from Figure 7.7, the cell values change to the number of vulnerabilities exhibited by each Host of each type. Along the bottom you can see the total number of vulnerabilities per host.

Figure 7.7 NetSonar grid browser—number of vulnerability types.

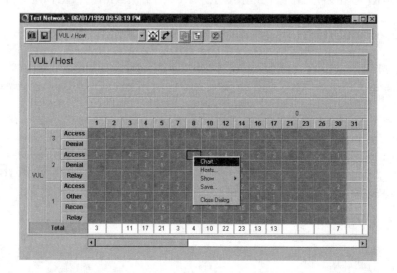

This allows you to represent the data found graphically. Using the wizard, you can create many different types of charts including 2-D and 3D, line, pie, and bar. You can also export the chart for use in a Microsoft PowerPoint slide show.

From our grid browser example in Figure 7.6, you would create a chart by selecting the cells required then choosing the "create chart" button from the tool bar. Once created selecting the right mouse button on the chart will allow you to customize the view completely.

The chart shown in Figure 7.8 is based on the grid view we just created in Figure 7.7. For this example, I've picked only a few stations for clarity, but you can easily select more and rerun the wizard. The chart is simple to use—right-click offers you most options, and by clicking around the chart you can tilt and pan the view. In our example, the height of the bars represents the number of vulnerability types exhibited by a host. Once you saved a graph, it can be incorporated into a NetSonar report or used externally as a .bmp or .gif file.

Figure 7.8 NetSonar Chart from grid selection.

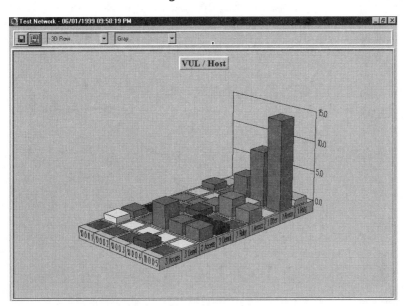

Reports and Wizards

Secure Scanner includes a flexible reporting and analysis tool. Three types of HTML reports can be generated from Secure Scanner: executive, brief technical, and full technical. As the names suggest, each type of report is aimed at different groups of people—the executive presents a high-level summary whereas the full technical provides an in-depth review of all security vulnerabilities found on the network.

Information layout is straightforward; it's easy to insert grids and charts into reports. Results can be ported to Microsoft Word for editing and printing, or to other platforms that support HTML format.

By selecting the options on the screen (see Figure 7.9) you can navigate the report easily.

Keeping the System Up-to-Date

Regular updates to the vulnerability scanner are easy to download and install directly from the Cisco Web site. Cisco employs a team called the Cisco Countermeasure Research Team (C-CRT) who work to ensure that Secure Scanner is up-to-date. C-CRT maintains the NSDB, which is a goldmine of information against intrusions and attacks.

The NSDB is accessible from within the application by selecting the icon from the main screen. It contains updates and fixes as well as links to other vendor's Web sites (see Figure 7.10).

Figure 7.9 NetSonar Report main menu.

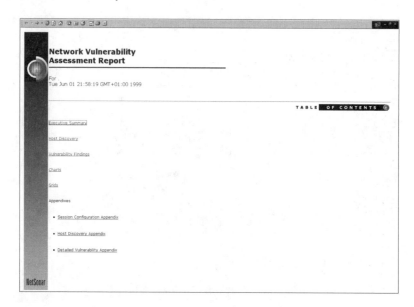

Figure 7.10 The NSDB Vulnerability Index.

You can select items on the index to view further details for a specific vulnerability. Let's select 208—Anonymous FTP (see Figure 7.11).

For a comprehensive guide on usage of NetSonar go to www.cisco.com/univercd/cc/td/doc/product/iaabu/csscan/csscan2/csscug/index.htm.

Figure 7.11 NSDB vulnerability details.

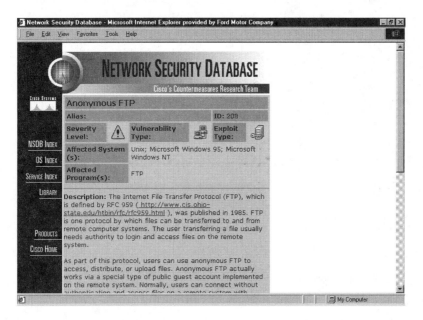

- As soon as new devices are added to the network, a scan should be run. This process should be integrated into the company change management system.

- Report any anomalies or new vulnerabilities you have found to Cisco Systems using the NSDB reporting mechanism. As a responsible user of the system you could help protect other companies from similar attacks.

Cisco Secure Intrusion Detection System (NetRanger)

NetRanger was originally developed by Wheelgroup Inc. but is now owned by Cisco Systems. We will tackle this product by dividing it into five sections:

1. What is NetRanger?

2. Before you install

3. Director and sensor setup

4. General operation

5. Data management package (DMP)

What Is NetRanger?

This is a solution that can be added to your network to perform dynamic intrusion detection. NetRanger will monitor for, and respond to, intrusions in real time. A simple NetRanger solution is made up of a distributed model with three main components: the Sensor, the Director, and the Post Office.

The Sensor

This is a specialized device that uses a rule-based inference engine to process large volumes of traffic in order to identify security issues in real time. The Sensor is either a ready-made appliance that is purchased from Cisco or a software-based one installed on an x86 or SPARC Solaris 2.5.1/2.6 station. The software to create your own Sensor can be found on the NetRanger CD. The Sensor either can capture traffic itself or can monitor syslog traffic from a Cisco router. Once an attack or security event is detected the Sensor can respond by generating alarms, logging the event, resetting TCP connections, or shunning the attack (by reconfiguration of managed router ACLs). Sensor events are forwarded to a central facility called the Director via a control/command interface.

Sensors have two interfaces, one for monitoring and one for control. The monitoring interface of the Sensor does not have an IP address and will not respond to detection attempts. There are several types of monitor interfaces available from Cisco, each selected for a particular network scenario. An example is the IDS 4230 Sensor which is capable of supporting LAN speeds of up to 100Mbps LAN or T3 WAN speeds. Another is the Catalyst 6000 IDS module which is designed for switched networks.

The Director

This is a GUI software solution used to "direct" or manage NetRanger from an HP Openview platform. It is installed on an HP UX or Solaris workstation. Directors are used to complete initial Sensor configuration, process and present information sent from Sensors (in HP Openview), and specify Sensor behavior. The Director contains drivers for the Oracle RDBMS and the Remedy trouble ticket system. It is possible to modify these drivers to interface with Sybase or Informix systems if required.

When the Director receives information from the Sensors it will initially log to a flat file and then push the data to a relational database. Once stored in the database, RDBMS tools such as SQL can be used to interrogate the data. Database details such as location of files and account information have to be configured using the nrConfigure utility (discussed later). Systems such as Oracle contain tools to generate reports containing graphical as well as numerical representation of data. To get you started, each Director ships with a sample set of SQL queries that can be easily modified and run from within your RDBMS system. It is possible to define custom actions based on events too (this is covered in more detail later in this section). The Director also provides you with access to the NSDB for reference material on exploits.

NOTE

Cisco recommends that no more than 25 Sensors should be configured to send information to a single Director. If more Sensors are required in your network, you should install multiple Directors and build a hierarchical structure of Sensors and Directors.

The Post Office

This is a messaging facility between Directors and Sensors that uses a proprietary UDP transport protocol for communication. Rather than being unacknowledged, the protocol guarantees transmissions, maintains connection status, and provides acknowledgment for packets received with lower overhead than TCP/IP. It uses an enhanced addressing structure that is ideal for building hierarchical fault tolerant structures upon. Up to 255 alternate routes between each Sensor and its Director can be supported. The structures are composed of multiple Directors and Sensors; in this way, you can support a theoretically unlimited number of Sensors. Sensors can forward updates onto one or more directors, which can then propagate the message to other Directors in the hierarchy.

Figure 7.12 shows these basic components in context.

Figure 7.12 NetRanger daemons and associated components.

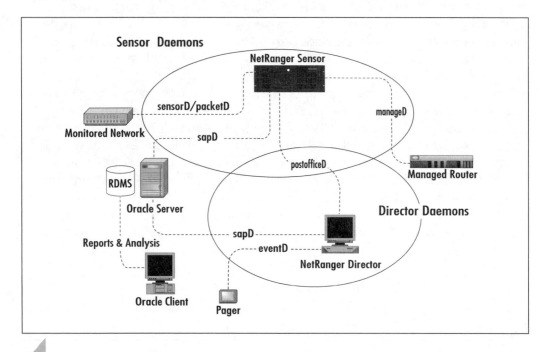

NOTE

If you need to perform any traffic filtering on routers between Directors and Sensors (control interface), then you must allow traffic using UDP port 45000 to pass between the two.

You can see the NetRanger components with the main daemons that are responsible for running the system. Each daemon performs a specific function:

sensord/packetd sensord is used to relay intrusion detection information that is sent from other devices capable of detecting attacks and sending data; packetd is used when the Sensor itself does the intrusion detection.

loggerd This is used to write to log files to record events such as alarms and command instructions.

sapd This provides file and data management functions including the transfer of data to database systems such as Oracle.

postofficed This manages and provides all communications between the Director and Sensors.

eventd This performs notification management on events to pager and e-mail systems.

managed This controls configuration of managed Cisco routers.

Here are some other daemons not displayed in Figure 7.12:

smid This is a Director daemon that converts raw information into data that ndirmap uses.

nrdirmap This displays icons for NetRanger components and events such as alarms and status conditions for other daemons.

configd This interprets and manages commands entered through ndirmap to interface with the other daemons.

Now that we understand the components, let's discuss some of the more general features. NetRanger is a network-based IDS system that captures packets and then performs signature analysis using an inferencing engine. The analysis involves examination of each packet's payload for content-based attacks and examination of the header for patterns of misuse. NetRanger classifies attacks into two types: atomic (single, directed at one victim) and composite (multiple, over a period of time involving many victims).

The Director uses an internal (upgradeable) security database (NSDB) for signature analysis, which provides information about exploits and matching countermeasures. There are two types of signatures, embedded and string matching. As the name suggests, embedded signatures are contained within the Sensor's system files; they cannot be modified and protect against misuse by matches against the packet header fields. String matching signatures, on the other hand, are user configurable and work by examining the payload of the packet. A description of how to do this is included later in this section.

Before You Install

It is imperative that you spend time thinking out your NetRanger design to avoid its being ineffective. You should consider all connections from your network to outside as well as the volumes and types of traffic in use. Also, if your network is large, perhaps a multi-national one, then you may want to consider internal boundaries too. You should consider how many sensors are required to monitor the network effectively.

Sensors have two interfaces, one for data collection and the other, called the control interface, for remote communication (always Ethernet-based). The placement of the Sensor is important in order to protect the control port and to "sense" correctly (this is covered earlier in the chapter in the section "Deploying in a Network").

Director placement is also important; it is a focal point and compromise could have serious consequences. The Director must be easily accessible for security staff yet physically secure, that is, protected on the network (perhaps through a firewall) yet able to communicate with its Sensors.

Director and Sensor Setup

Here are the minimum requirements for Director installation; the amount of RAM required will vary depending upon configuration.

HP UX 10.20 (with HP Openview 4.1) requires 125MB disk space for software directories, whereas Sun Solaris 2.5.1 or 2.6 requires 172MB. Both platforms require 1GB disk space for logging, 96MB RAM, a CD drive, a TCP/IP enabled network card, and a current HTML browser.

Next we will investigate how to install and configure the Director and Sensor. Let's start with the Director installation procedure for UNIX.

Director Installation (HP-UX or Solaris)

Once you have decided on where you want to place the Director, and you have a workstation that meets the minimum system requirements, you can power up and begin the installation.

1. Logon as **root** on the chosen Director station.
2. Make sure the date and time are correct.
3. Ensure /usr/sbin is in the PATH.
4. Enter /etc/set_parms initial and restart the machine.
5. Configure the IP address, subnet mask, default gateway, and host-name.
6. Install HP Openview.

7. Add these lines to the root profile (watch the space between . and /):

```
. /opt/OV/bin/ov.envvars.sh
PATH=$PATH:$OV_BIN
```

8. Modify semaphores to read:

```
semmns - 256, semmni - 128, semmnu - 90, semume - 20
```

9. Restart the machine.
10. Insert the NetRanger CD into the drive and exit Openview.
11. From the CD type **./install** and follow the on-screen instructions.
12. Restart the machine.

Director Configuration

Now that we have completed the basic installation of NetRanger, we must perform the following steps to configure it:

1. Logon as netrangr.
2. Stop all services by typing **nrstop** at the prompt.
3. Start configuration by typing **sysconfig-director**.
4. Enter all Director information, Host ID and Name, Organization ID and Name, and the IP address.
5. Exit sysconfig-director and then type **nrstart** at the prompt to restart services.

Sensor Installation

The Director base configuration is complete; you should already know where you want to place your Sensor. Sensor installation and configuration is done using a program called sysconfig-sensor. Here's how it works:

1. Connect all cables and attach the Sensor to the network where required.
2. Sign on as **root** and enter **sysconfig-sensor** at the prompt.
3. A menu will appear where you can enter values for the IP address, subnet mask, default gateway, and hostname. It should look like Figure 7.13.

Figure 7.13 The sysconfig-sensor menu.

```
#sysconfig-sensor

NetRanger Sensor Initial Configuration Utility

Choose a value to configure one of the following parameters:

1 - IP Address

2 - IP Netmask

3 - IP Hostname

4 - Default Route

5 - Network Access Control

6 - Netranger Communications Infrastructure

7 - System Date, Time and Timezone

8 - Passwords

x - Exit


Selection:
```

4. Connect a terminal server to the COM1 port for out-of-band access.

5. Using option 5, define IP addresses that are allowed to Telnet or perform file transfer to the Sensor.

6. Using option 6, set the Sensor Host and Organization details. The corresponding Director details must also be entered.

7. Exit sysconfig-sensor and restart the Sensor device.

8. Using UNIX system administration tools, modify the **netrangr** password. By default the password is attack.

Completing the Sensor Installation

We have almost finished; all that remains is to relate the Director and Sensor configurations together. Follow these steps:

1. On the Director station, select Security, Configure.

2. Select File, Add Host, and choose Next.

3. Enter the Sensor details in the next screen; select Next.

4. Choose Add new Sensor reporting to this Director.

5. Next, enter Shunning preferences—the amount of time to wait before shun and how long to log for.

6. Enter the Sensor interface performing the data collection, for example, **/dev/spwr0 for Ethernet**.

7. Select Add, and then choose the IP subnets the Sensor is protecting.

8. The next screen is optional; here you can enter details of a Cisco router managed by the Sensor.

9. Select Next and Finish.

General Operation

The Director runs under HP Openview; the top-level icon is NetRanger, which when double-clicked, shows submaps containing NetRanger nodes. As more Directors and Sensors are configured, these will also become visible. Each submap can represent different security regions across the company. Once you select the Director or Sensor icon the application daemons running on that machine are displayed. These can be selected in turn to show alarm icons generated by each. Each type of icon describes a different classification of attack based on the signatures found in the NSDB.

From HP Openview selecting the Security option displays further NetRanger options. Some of the more significant options are as follows:

Show (select icon first) This provides information on devices, configuration, alarms, the NSDB, and others.

Configure (select Sensor first) This starts nrConfigure, which is used to configure Sensors and Directors.

Network Device (select device first) This starts the network device configuration utility.

Shun (select alarm first) This allows you to shun devices and networks.

Advanced (select Sensor first) This allows various options; one of the most useful is the Statistics, Show option.

nrConfigure

When started, nrConfigure shows information regarding the device selected. You can configure communications, notification information, and setup device management; log policy violations; configure shunning; and perform intrusion detection. Here are some examples of how to use nrConfigure.

Configuring Logging from a Router to a Sensor

On the router in privileged exec mode, enter global configuration mode and type:

```
logging <ip address of Sensor control interface>
logging trap info
```

Modify your access list entries to include the log extension where required. This completes half of the configuration; the next step is to configure the Sensor.

In HP Openview, highlight the Sensor. From nrConfigure select Configure, then select Intrusion Detection, Data Sources, Add. Now enter the IP address of the sending router and select Profile, check the Manual box, Modify Sensor. Pull down and select Security Violations–choose the ACL, choose the level of severity, and then select Apply.

Syslog traffic between the router and the Sensor is sent in the clear; if any networks the traffic traverses is untrusted, it constitutes a security risk and should be avoided at all costs.

Configuring Intrusion Detection on Sensors

This can be done by using manual or profile-based methods. The manual method allows you to configure individual signatures with complete control over configuration, whereas the profile-based method allows selection of only predefined groups of signatures. You would probably use profiles if you were integrating new signatures following a software upgrade.

Highlight the Sensor you wish to configure then select one of the following methods for configuration:

Profile-based Select Configure, Intrusion Detection, Profile, then choose the Profile-based radio button, Response. You can then set the type of Response, disable Signatures if required, or choose the View Sensor button to view settings. Once complete, select OK in the Signatures box, and then OK.

Manual Select Configure, Intrusion Detection, Profile, then choose the Manual radio button. Now choose Modify Sensor; from the General Signatures box configure corresponding actions. Select OK and OK again to exit.

By selecting the Configure, Intrusion Detection, Protected Networks tab, you can set up networks upon which you wish to perform IP packet logging using the Sensor.

Customizing the NSDB

This is useful for protection against vulnerabilities that are not defined in the NSDB. You can create an NSDB record that the inferencing engine will use as part of its analysis. Custom signatures can also be used to track host and port usage for general information. For example, you might want to look for a particular string inside the content of the packet.

Here are the steps involved in adding your own signature to the NSDB to look for the string "do not ftp" in an FTP session and then to perform a session reset.

1. On the Director station, select the Sensor | Security | Configure.

2. Select Intrusion Detection | Profile.

3. Select Manual Configuration | Modify Sensor.

4. Choose Matched Strings from the scroll box, then Expand.

5. Select Add then enter **do not ftp** in the String column.

6. Enter a unique ID for the signature.

7. Enter port 20 for FTP data.

8. To specify the direction select To & From.

9. Enter the Occurrences as 1 to specify a condition to initiate an action.

10. Specify the Action as Reset and enter 5 in the destination.

11. Select OK, OK, and Apply.

The new rule will reset any FTP connections where the data contains one occurrence of the words "do not ftp" and will send out level 5 alarms to all configured logging destinations.

Upgrading the NSDB

To do this you must have a valid CCO logon. Download instructions for the NSDB file can be found at www.cisco.com by searching for "NetRanger Update" then following instructions in the update readme file.

Data Management Package (DMP)

The DMP is contained within NetRanger and performs two functions: the collection of data in flat file logs and the manipulation of data into relational database file format to facilitate Oracle SQL analysis (on the normalized data).

You can configure these options through nrConfigure and the Data Management option on the Director. It is possible to create triggers for execution on condition, setting log file size and other settings. The DMP contains a basic set of SQL reports that provide detail on attack signatures with dates and times. What other components do we need to make this work? Oracle server will have to be installed either remotely or locally. It must reference the NetRanger data. Using nrConfigure, tokens must be created to allow the Oracle server access. Further details of this can be found at www.cisco.com/univercd/cc/td/doc/product/iaabu/netrangr/nr220/nr220ug/rdbms.htm#27755.

Once the data is viewable from Oracle, you can either use native scripts or third-party tools to manage the data, create graphs, and draw correlations to highlight specific areas.

E-mail Notification Example

First you must configure event notification:

1. In HP Openview, select Configure | Security | Event Processing.
2. Select the Application tab.
3. Add a severity level to execute a script and reference to the script. Enter the path to /bin/eventd/event in the script name field.
4. Select the Timing option and set the thresholds of events which will trigger the script and the interleave between sampling the event data.
5. Select OK, then ensure that Daemons, nr.eventd has a status of Yes. Select OK.
6. Configure the Sensor to send notifications to eventd, select Destinations from nrConfigure, then Add.
7. Enter the Sensor ID, choose the application of eventd and a security level required to send the notification, and select the type of event to act upon.
8. Select Event Processing | E-mail.
9. Enter the Organization ID, the Type of event, and the Severity Level to trigger the mail.
10. Enter the e-mail addresses of the person(s) that you wish to notify and select OK.
11. The next time the event occurs, an e-mail notification will be sent.

TIP

Whenever a change is made to the system using nrConfigure it is advisable to use nrstop and nrstart to restart the services.

Cisco IOS Intrusion Detection System

This is one feature that puts the Cisco solution ahead of the competition because intrusion detection is integrated into the router IOS. Any traffic that passes through the router can be scrutinized for intrusions. The router acts as a sensor checking for intrusions in a similar fashion to a NetRanger Sensor device.

IOS IDS is useful to install at network perimeters such as intranet/extranet borders or branch office routers. You may decide to deploy this method of intrusion detection where a NetRanger Sensor is not financially viable or where a reduced set of signatures to be checked will suffice. Despite not having the same level of granularity during signature identification and checking against a much smaller signature base than NetRanger, it is still capable of detecting severe breaches of security, reconnaissance scans, and common network attacks. The signatures it uses constitute a broad cross-section selected from the NSDB. IOS IDS will protect against 59 different types of network intrusions.

It is possible to disable checking for individual signatures through modification of the router config in order to avoid false positives. The signatures can be categorized into two main types: Info and Attack. Info refers to reconnaissance scans for information gathering and Attack refers to DoS or other intrusions. Each type can also be further divided into atomic (directed at an individual station) or compound (directed at a group of stations perhaps over an extended period of time).

IOS IDS is fully compatible with NetRanger and can appear as an icon on the Director GUI. The router can send alarms back to a syslog server, a NetRanger Sensor, or can take action through dropping unwanted packets and terminating TCP/IP sessions. Dropping packets happens transparently without the router interacting with end stations, but session termination involves the router sending a TCP RST to source and destination devices. It is usually best to use both these actions together when configuring the router.

One important consideration is the impact of IOS IDS on the router. This will vary depending upon the specification of the router, the number of signatures configured, as well as how busy the router is. The most significant impact on the router is caused by audit rules that refer to access control lists. It is probably a good idea to keep an eye on the router memory by using the **sh proc mem** command from the privileged exec prompt after configuration.

Unlike NetRanger, IOS IDS (as the name suggests) contains the signatures within the image. For future updates to the IOS IDS signature base the image on the router flash has to be upgraded. It is not possible to modify or add new signatures to the existing set, which is a useful feature available on NetRanger.

We can divide IOS IDS into two main sections: configuring IOS IDS features and associated commands.

Configuring IOS IDS Features

Configuration begins by initializing the IOS IDS software and then creating audit rules to specify signatures and associated actions. Rules can be applied inbound or outbound on the router interfaces. The audit rule command ip audit has the following extensions available:

smtp spam This sets e-mail spamming restrictions.

po This is used for all Post Office configurations when using a NetRanger Director.

notify This sends event information to syslog servers or NetRanger Director.

info This specifies the action on a reconnaissance scan.

attack This specifies the action to take when an attack is detected.

name This specifies the name of the rule; also used to apply the rule to an interface.

signature This disables individual signatures and sources of false alarms.

po protected This selects which interfaces are to be protected by the router.

To investigate these commands further we can look the example in Figure 7.14.

Our objective is to protect the Ethernet network from attackers from the untrusted Internet. The example assumes that a NetRanger Director is present and that there is a trusted Token Ring network also attached to the router. The configuration displayed shows a subsection of commands from the router configuration.

Figure 7.14 Secure IS (IOS IDS) configuration scenario.

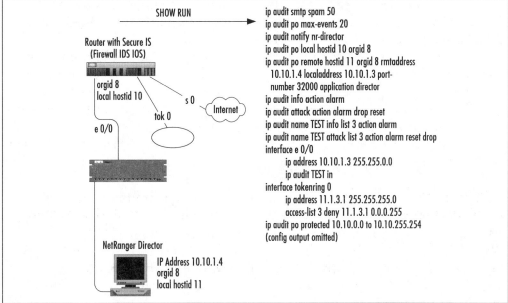

Let's describe the commands in turn:

```
ip audit smtp spam 50
```

This sets a threshold of 50 recipients in an e-mail to denote spam e-mail.

```
ip audit po max-events 20
```

This defines that 20 entries can be queued up for sending to the Director; above this value events will be dropped. You need to be careful when using this command as each queue entry uses 32KB of RAM. You can monitor levels of RAM using the show proc mem command.

```
ip audit notify nr-director
```

This configures the NetRanger Director as the destination for the alarms.

```
ip audit po local hostid 10 orgid 8
```

This defines the local router's post office details. The hostid is unique and the orgid is the same as the NetRanger Director group.

```
ip audit po remote hostid 11 orgid 8 rmtaddress 10.10.1.4 localaddress
10.10.1.3 port-number 32000 application director
```

This is the same as the previous command but defines the NetRanger Director hostid as 11, the Director orgid as 8, the IP address for the Director, the router's IP address, the UDP port the Director is listening on as 32000, and the type of application being used as director (logger in this field would be used if logging to a syslog server).

Note that the router has to be reloaded after all Post Office config changes.

```
ip audit info action alarm
```

The default response to take on information signature is to send an alarm.

```
ip audit attack action alarm drop reset
```

The default response to take on an attack signature is to send an alarm, drop the packet, and reset the audited session.

```
ip audit name TEST info list 3 action alarm
```

This defines an audit rule called TEST where traffic permitted by access list 3 will be processed and an alarm will be raised on an information signature match.

```
ip audit name TEST attack list 3 action alarm reset drop
```

This defines an audit rule called TEST where traffic permitted by access list 3 will be processed and an alarm raised, the connection reset, and the packet dropped on an attack signature match.

```
interface e 0/0
ip address 10.10.1.3 255.255.0.0
ip audit TEST in
```

This applies the audit rule to inbound traffic on the Ethernet interface.

```
interface tokenring 0
ip address 11.1.3.1 255.255.255.0
access-list 3 deny 11.1.3.1 0.0.0.255
```

This prevents Token Ring traffic from being audited. The Token Ring can be considered a trusted network.

```
ip audit po protected 10.10.0.0 to 10.10.255.254
```

This specifies the IP address range of the ethernet network to be protected. Note that you can omit addresses from being protected by defining multiple ranges.

By using another command, **no ip audit signature <signature-id>**, or **ip audit signature <signature-id> <disable / list ACL number>** it is possible to omit the auditing of a particular signature globally or for a range of addresses.

Associated Commands

These are IOS IDS commands you can enter at the Privileged EXEC prompt:

```
clear ip audit configuration
```

This disables IOS IDS and removes all IDS entries from the configuration.

```
show ip audit interface
```

This shows IOS IDS configuration from an interface perspective.

```
show ip audit configuration
```

This is used to display the active IOS IDS configuration on the router.

```
show ip audit debug
```

This shows the current IDS debug flag entries.

```
show ip audit statistics
```

This shows you signature-audited counts and TCP session statistics. You would use **clear ip audit statistics** to reset these figures.

Cisco Secure Integrated Software (Firewall Feature Set)

The Firewall feature set contains IOS features to allow you to configure the router as a firewall, as well as providing intrusion detection services. Apart from IDS the Firewall feature set also contains the following features:

Access Control Lists Standard, Extended, Dynamic (to provide temporary access), and Reflexive (to permit/deny traffic based on its direction).

TCP Intercept See the earlier section on protection against SYN flood attacks.

Authentication Proxy Service Implements user access security policies.

Port to Application Mapping (PAM) This allows TCP/UDP port customization.

Security Server Support For RADIUS, TACACS+, and Kerberos.

Network Address Translation (NAT) Translation of unregistered addresses.

IPSec Network Security Cryptography techniques across untrusted networks.

Neighbor Authentication Checking of routing updates for authenticity.

Event Logging This can be sent to the console, virtual terminals, and syslog servers.

User Authentication and Authorization This protects against unauthorized access.

Context-based Access Control This protects against attacks by inspecting traffic.

CBAC (Context-Based Access Control)

This part of the feature set is particularly relevant to this section as it provides protection against attacks by inspecting traffic and taking action. CBAC can inspect a variety of traffic types and is able to disconnect idle sessions, drop packets, or log inspection results to a server. Here is a summary of what CBAC can protect against:

- **Denial of Service Attacks** The dynamic monitoring, interception, and response to DoS-type network attacks. For example, the router can drop suspicious packets and notify the administrator. The router should also be configured with TCP Intercept to protect against SYN floods as discussed earlier in the chapter.

- **Java Applet Blocking** Allows blocking of unauthorized or malicious Java applets. Java has gained popularity with developers over the last few years due to its features. Java applets can be embedded within HTTP traffic. Websites can be permitted or denied to send traffic to your network using access lists on boundary routers.

- **Audit Trails** A comprehensive audit trail showing source, destination, timestamps, duration of connection, and bytes transmitted. This is configurable to highlight specific applications and features.

CBAC is discussed in more detail in Chapter 2, "Traffic Filtering on Cisco IOS."

Summary

The IDS has been in the spotlight lately, for good reason. The concept has been evolving for many years and is now more important due to the increasing growth of the Internet and abundant IT knowledge.

In this chapter we have reviewed network intrusions and defined the different types of attacks performed by intruders. We investigated the different approaches to IDS implementation, and covered the Cisco products in detail.

No one would like to think so, but threats to your system are more likely from inside rather than outside—and, of course, a combination of threats described in this chapter may be used. Our wily intruder has a large underground community that can be called upon to assist with an attack; it's a bit of a cyberwar. Fortunately there are also many ways that you can improve security, either to defend your network when it is threatened or to be prepared in advance.

We should now understand that a single product will not solve the problem, nor is it advisable to rely entirely on an IDS for protection. This balanced approach is the key and is discussed in Chapter 9, "Security Processes and the Cisco Security Fast Track" of this book.

We must aim to get to a comfortable point using excellent security practices, educating the user community and keeping a close eye on intrusion detection developments.

If you've been the victim of an attack, now is the time to get started with an IDS. If you haven't been attacked yet (or don't know it), you are doing the right thing by reading this book. Follow the principles within, apply them, and you can achieve greater peace of mind.

FAQs

Q: If I have a firewall why do I need an IDS? Isn't it just a waste of money?

A: Let's go back to the analogy of the house. Look upon the firewalls as being guards at the front and back garden gates. They will do their best to stop any obviously nasty individuals from coming to your door. The firewall is pretty rigid in its security. If you knew that the server had a rule that allowed Web cookies to pass then you could take advantage of it with an embedded file upload program. On the other hand, the IDS is a much more flexible and comprehensive solution. There are cameras, trap doors, a central control team, and a security patrol. The IDS is integrated into the very heart of the networking infrastructure (through Secure IS). It is complemented by a comprehensive vulnerability and attack scanning solution.

Cost-wise you could save money in the short term by leaving out the IDS, but you need to ask yourself whether it is worth leaving yourself exposed. Consider the IDS as an insurance policy that works for you and helps you live longer.

Q: I need to make my network secure. What do I do, where do I start?

A: Gain senior management approval first for your initiative. The next step is to implement a change "freeze" so that all network-related documentation can be brought up-to-date and compiled. Bad documentation is usually the road to ruin. Once this stage is complete you can start an investigation to classify the types of protocols, devices, and software applications/revisions in use. This does not need to be extensive, just enough to get a good feel for what you have. Assemble a security team and evaluate the real risks, hire expert consultancy if required. On the basis of your findings, make a proposal for an IDS and firewall security solution. Implement other sound security practices as suggested in this book. Once the solution is in place tie in other procedures, such as change control and new project designs into the security process.

Q: What should I do if my IDS detects a serious security breach?

A: Ideally you should be prepared for the worst well before the event. First, you must verify that it is not a false positive. If security is indeed compromised, then stay cool and work through these steps:

1. Establish a working party made up of key people from across the company. There should be representatives from senior management, technical departments, human resources, and, of course, your security experts. Present the security capabilities of your system and the impact of the attack to the team.

2. Gather and discuss information regarding the attack, investigate and correlate information. Involve outside authorities such as the Police, if necessary.

3. Based upon severity decide whether to monitor for recurring attacks (if they are nondestructive) or remove access entirely to protect the company. Gain authority to take draconian measures to protect the network if required.

4. Design a plan that all relevant teams will execute upon intrusion.

5. Document all incident-handling procedures, including actions according to severity. This should include responses to attacks from your IDS.

6. Record all suspicious activity. Take further advice from law enforcement on the next steps to take. Review the outcome in a meeting with the working party. Update any procedural documentation as required.

Q: Would a firewall or other security product interfere with the IDS?

A: In short, not if the system is configured correctly. Sensors should be made aware of NetSonar scans for example; this prevents unnecessary auditing. Likewise, a firewall should not be configured to restrict the IDS from performing its function properly. Because this is a detection system we would expect it to pick up all intrusions including other legitimate operations from security products.

Q: What is Signature Analysis?

A: Signatures are identifiable attack patterns, either strings within data or more complex events. The signature can be defined as an event or process with a resulting outcome. Systems that are compromised can be monitored to identify what types of attacks are in progress. The analysis portion involves pattern matching against a database. For further details, have a look at www.cisco.com/univercd/cc/td/doc/product/iaabu/netrangr/nr220/nr220ug/sigs.htm.

Chapter 8

Network Security Management

Solutions in this chapter:

- PIX Firewall Manager
- CiscoWorks 2000 ACL Manager
- Cisco Secure Policy Manager
- Cisco Secure ACS

Introduction

The goal of network security management is to control access to network resources according to your business requirements and policies. With the appropriate authorization and authentication, access to sensitive information can be controlled; only people with the appropriate access codes will have access.

With an ever-increasing number of devices on your network that are used to secure your network resources against intruders, you need an uncomplicated and straight-forward way to control and manage your network security policy. The Cisco applications covered in this chapter let you manage the security devices on your network effectively.

PIX Firewall Manager

When you need to administer a large network, you will have one or more firewalls on the border of your network, connecting either to the Internet or to a customer's company with whom you need to communicate. The firewalls installed on your network will play an important role in protecting against intruders from outside your network. It is critical that you manage them effectively and efficiently.

Cisco has developed PIX Firewall Manager for their PIX Firewall product range to do just this. The rules for accessing your network are defined at a central point and can be distributed to multiple firewalls on the border of your network.

PIX Firewall Manager Overview

When you have one or more PIX Firewalls installed on your network protecting the resources inside your network against potential intrusion from outside, you can use PIX Firewall Manager to administer and manage the PIX Firewall device security policy. PIX Firewall Manager can manage one or more PIX Firewalls from any host with a Graphical User Interface (GUI). The most basic use of PIX Firewall Manager is to add, remove, and change the security policy and rules for all communication between your network and the outside world.

PIX Firewall Manager, or PFM, can be installed on a Microsoft Windows NT Server or Workstation and includes two components:

- Management Server
- Management Client

After the installation of the PFM software on your server is complete, the new service added to the Windows NT server called PIX Firewall Manager Server is started automatically. This service is used for the Management Server component and runs in the background. It handles all requests from the Management Client and sends the requests to the selected PIX Firewall. All the responses for the requests are redirected back to the Management Client.

NOTE

There is no shortcut created on the desktop or task bar to control the PIX Firewall Manager Server. You can start and stop this service only within the Services application in the Control Panel.

The Management Client component is an extra Java applet that is installed with the PFM software. You use this applet from any host on the network that has an Internet browser installed and that is Java 1.02 compliant. This makes it very easy to manage your PIX Firewalls from any PC on the network; just make sure that you pick a good, nonguessable password to log on to the Management Server and that the client is well protected.

When using your Internet browser to connect to the Management Client on the PFM server, you are able to set custom alarms for specific events that happen on the specified PIX Firewall that will alert you if any potential problems occur. PIX Firewall Manager Server includes a SYSLOG server. The PIX Firewalls in your network can be configured to use PFM as the logging server. In PFM, the SYSLOG notification settings can be changed to inform you of the necessary or most useful method. You can also generate reports based on the usage and view the SYSLOG messages of the specified PIX Firewall.

You can change the common configuration, using the corresponding tab in PFM, on your PIX Firewall using the same GUI of the Management Client. This common configuration allows you to configure all the authentication and authorization settings on the PIX Firewall including Remote Authentication Dial-In User Service (RADIUS) and Terminal Access Controller Access Control System Plus (TACACS+) configuration. You can also change or manage all Telnet session connections to the PIX Firewall allowing specific access and closing unwanted active sessions.

If you have a new PIX Firewall to configure, you can use PIX Firewall Setup Wizard or a terminal connection using CLI to configure the PIX

Firewall for the first time. You need the console cable to connect to the Firewall console port and to the host COM port for the initial configuration of the PIX.

PIX Firewall Manager Benefits

All of Cisco's equipment can be managed via a Telnet connection to the device, using a normal Telnet client. This interface, or configurations mode, is called a Command Line Interface (CLI), and you can use commands specific to the device to add, remove, and change the configuration file. The CLI may sometimes be required to access commands not available on the PIX Firewall Manager software. Overall, PFM has the most commonly used configuration and settings used on the PIX Firewall.

When you use PFM to manage PIX Firewalls on your network, you will be able to connect to the Management Client from anywhere on your network. With this connection, you will use the Management Server to relay requests and responses to and from any PIX Firewall on your network. This means that you always have one central point to manage all PIX Firewall policies.

Conversely, if you use the CLI to manage and configure your PIX Firewalls, you will always connect to the specific IP address of the PIX Firewall to alter the configuration. This could become very time-consuming if your policy for the network security changes and you needed to implement this change on all the PIX Firewalls in your administrative domain and your network.

When you are using the alarms to notify you when a possible intrusion occurs, the PFM can be used as a central point for all notifications configured in all the PIX Firewalls on the network. If you need to implement this kind of policy, it would take you more than half the time to set specific alerts with PFM than it would with the CLI.

NOTE

The customized alarms configured in PFM will allow you to set specific SYSLOG message-received thresholds based on time. If a specific SYSLOG message is received in more than the set threshold in one minute, it will generate a notification as configured in the notification configuration tab of PFM.

In general, PFM is used for centralized administration of all your PIX Firewalls on the network, and, with the easy-to-use GUI of the

Management Client Java applet running on the Internet browser, you can change all the common configuration settings on the managed PIX Firewalls with ease—no commands to remember and no mistypes. The Management Client Java applet can be used from any host that is compliant with the Management Client requirements (discussed later in this chapter). This allows you to use any operating system that meets the requirements to manage your PIX Firewalls.

Supported PIX Firewall IOS Version Versus PIX Firewall Manager Version

Cisco has released quite a few versions of PIX Firewall IOS running on the PIX Firewall device and of PIX Firewall Manager running on the Windows NT server. The idea behind all these releases is to fix problems reported or detected by Cisco and to add new functionality. The PFM software will also be upgraded as new versions of the PIX Firewall IOS becomes available, including bug fixes for PFM itself.

The most recent versions of PFM will be compatible with most of the new PIX Firewall IOS versions available. Table 8.1 shows that the latest PFM software will not support some of the older PIX Firewall versions. Use Table 8.1 as a reference when installing your licensed copy on your Windows NT server; check to see if your PIX Firewall IOS version will be compatible with PFM.

Table 8.1 PIX Firewall IOS Version Supported by PIX Firewall Manager Version

PIX Firewall Manager Version	PIX Firewall IOS Version
4.1(7)	4.1(7)
4.2(5)	4.2(4)
4.3(2)	4.3(2) and later
4.3(2) b	4.3(2); 4.4(1) and later
4.3(2) c	4.3(2); 4.4; 5.0 and later
4.3(2) d	4.3(2); 4.4; 5.0 and later
4.3(2) e	4.3(2); 4.4; 5.0 and later
4.3(2) f	4.3(2); 4.4; 5.0; 5.1; 5.2 and later

TIP

You can check the PIX Firewall IOS version using the Show Version console command on the selected PIX Firewall and, if you connect to the PFM Management Client with your Internet browser, you will always have a header that includes the version number installed on your Windows NT server.

Installation Requirements for PIX Firewall Manager

For any installation of PIX Firewall Manager software, you have to check the requirements necessary for your successful installation. As mentioned in Table 8.1, you first have to ensure that your current version of PFM is compatible with the PIX Firewall IOS version used.

NOTE

All requirements and topics discussed in the chapter about PIX Firewall Manager software relate to the latest available version 4.3(2)f. This version has minor changes compared to the earlier versions released.

If you would like to manage the PIX Firewall from a host using the Management Client on an outside network, you need to configure a PIX Firewall on the outside network with a private link communicating to the local PIX Firewall and using the same private link. The PIX Firewall private link consists of an encryption card and software. These allow the PIX Firewall devices to encrypt the communication over an insecure link or public line like the Internet using the Data Encryption Standard (DES) or the IETF Authentication Header/Encapsulating Security Payload (AH/ESP) protocol. This permits you to build private, encrypted tunnels through any public network to create VPNs. To configure this private link on both PIX Firewalls, you need to have console access which is used by the PIX Firewall Setup Manager. Call the remote site administrator to help you with the initial configuration of the private link.

This is not the only requirement for a successful installation of PFM—you will also need to verify the server and host requirements that you will use to manage the PIX Firewalls.

PIX Firewall Management Server Requirements

The PIX Firewall Management Server requires the following for a successful installation on a Windows NT Server:

- Microsoft Windows NT Workstation or Windows NT Server version 4.0
- IBM-compatible Pentium computer
- At least 32MB of RAM
- All servers running the PIX Firewall Management Server component on the inside network
- For customized audio playback when a SYSLOG alarm is triggered, an .AU format sound file with mu-low as 8-bit, sample rate of 8,000Hz, and Channel mode as mono

TIP

To use the custom audio file, put the file in the installed path of PFM under the Jclient\Netscape directory of the target Management Server. This will allow you to select the custom audio file when you configure the SYSLOG notification settings.

Requirements for a Host Running the PIX Firewall Management Client

The PIX Firewall Management Client is installed on the Management Server, but it runs the Management Client Java applet on the host's Internet browser. The host running this applet in the browser needs to meet the following requirements to use the Management Client successfully:

- Microsoft Windows 95 or 98, Windows NT 4.0 Workstation, Windows NT 4.0 Server, Windows 2000, or Solaris
- For hosts running Windows 95 and Windows NT 4.0, 32MB of RAM is highly recommended.

- Browsers supported on the host are:
  - Microsoft Internet Explorer 4.0 with Service pack 1
  - Netscape Navigator version 3.0 or 3.01
  - Netscape Navigator Gold version 3.0 or 3.01
  - Netscape Communicator version 4.0, 4.01, 4.02, 4.04, 4.05
  - Netscape Navigator (standalone) version 4.0, 4.01, 4.02, 4.04, 4.05

- The host used to run the Management Client must be on the internal network of the PIX Firewall.

You have to disable any proxy settings that have been configured on the Internet browser used, or you can exclude the specific Management Client IP Address from the proxy settings.

WARNING

Later releases of Netscape Navigator and Communicator specified are not compatible with the Management Client. The following versions are not compatible:

- Netscape Navigator and Communicator 4.04 or 4.05 with the JDK 1.1 Patch installed

- Netscape Navigator and Communicator 4.06 and later

You can download the old browser versions of Netscape Navigator and Communicator from ftp://archive:oldies@archive.netscape.com/archive/index.html.

PIX Firewall Manager Features

The PIX Firewall Manager consists of many features that can help you manage all your PIX Firewalls on your network more efficiently. When connecting to the Management Client of the PFM with your Internet browser, you will use four tabs to configure the PIX Firewalls on your network, as shown in Figure 8.1. We will refer back to this figure later in the chapter when we discuss the usage of PFM.

As you can see in Figure 8.1, the first tab is the Administrator tab. This tab will allow you to add firewalls to the Main Tree on the left of the screen so you can manage it with the Management Client. The Main Tree will list all the PIX Firewalls available for management with their inside IP

Figure 8.1 The Administrator tab in the Management Client for PIX Firewall Manager.

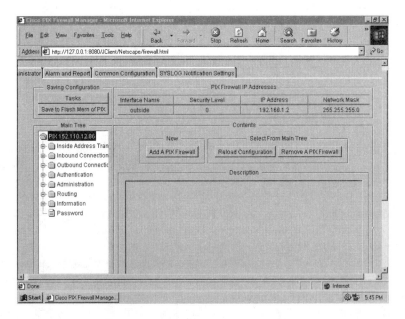

addresses. The inside IP address will be the IP address on the interface connected to your inside network. The Administrator tab will also allow you to perform tasks for granting outbound and inbound connections using the Tasks button. You can save the configuration to permanent flash memory on the PIX Firewall by using the Save to Flash MEM of PIX button just below the Tasks button.

With the Administrator tab, you can also reload the configuration with the Reload Configuration button. This will load the latest configuration values of the selected PIX Firewall to the screen. The last button on this tab will allow you to remove the currently selected PIX Firewall from the Management Client.

The Administrator tab also allows you to change most of the PIX Firewall IOS configurations with regard to the rules and security policy.

The Alarm and Report tab's features include generating alarms based on the PIX Firewall system messages and generating reports based on PIX Firewall usage. This view has a SYSLOG Message Folder that will list all the PIX Firewalls you are administrating as folders. You can double-click the specific folder for the PIX Firewall to view the SYSLOG messages. You can select one of the messages and use it to configure the Control Worksheet on the right panel of the screen. In the Control Worksheet, you can view a detail of the selected message and configure alarms if the selected message occurs more than the specified threshold per minute. For each alarm you configure, you can specify a custom notification message and specify the method to send the notification. If you click on the Report button, it will open the Report Wizard dialog box, which will help you generate reports that map system usage by host and FTP or HTTP activity by host. The Report button on this tab does not affect any alarm settings and vice versa.

For Managers

The Accounting Feature

You can use PIX Firewall Manager to analyze and account for activity on the PIX Firewall. The accounting feature enables you to track the services users are accessing as well as track the amount of network resources they are using.

Network accounting provides information for all remote dial-up sessions and includes packet and byte counts. The connection accounting information pertains to the outbound connections made from the network access server, such as Telnet, local-area transport (LAT), TN3270, packet assembly-disassembly (PAD), and rlogin. These types of accounting are used primarily for client activity on your network.

EXEC accounting provides information about user EXEC terminal session on the network device and includes username, date, start and stop times, the access server IP address, and the telephone number used by dial-up users. System accounting provides information about system-level events such as a system reload. Finally, command accounting provides information about the EXEC shell commands being executed on the network access server. These types of accounting are used primarily for logging activity on you network devices.

By using Cisco Secure, TACACS+, or RADIUS servers that provide the appropriate information (like the date and time of connections, total duration of connections, and total amount of data transferred per user or application), you can use these reports to plan for future growth or for billing purposes.

Refer to Chapter 6, "Cisco Authentication, Authorization and Accounting Mechanisms," for more information about configuring accounting on your network.

The Common Configuration tab allows you to configure authentication and administration settings common to all your managed PIX Firewalls. Under the authentication folder on the left, you can find a few options to configure your user authentication security policy. You can configure a TACACS+ or RADIUS server IP address that will be used by the PIX Firewall to authenticate user access to the network and to authorize the user's usage of service on the network. Under the administration folder, you can use the options to determine which host on your network can access the PIX Firewall console with Telnet, receive SYSLOG events, or process SNMP events.

The last tab in the Management Client is the SYSLOG Notification Settings tab. This tab is easy and straightforward to use. Here you can configure the method used to signal triggered alarms. You can change the method setting by e-mail address, pager address, audio filename, and SMTP server IP address to specify the action and where to send alarm notification.

Another important feature of PFM is the ease in administrating the users that have access to the Management Client. You can give users who have been created on the NT domain or the local host access to the Management Client to view, or to view and change, the configuration on the PIX Firewalls. During the PFM installation, two user accounts and two local groups are created. The two user accounts are pixadmin and pixuser, which are part of the local group PIX Admins and PIX Users, respectively. All the users that you add to the PIX Admins group will have access to view and change the configuration with the Management Client. All the users that are part of the PIX Users group will have access only to view the configuration with the Management Client. So, all you need to do is add the specific username to the relevant group to give the specific access to the user.

NOTE

Each PIX Firewall Manager supports up to 10 PIX Firewalls for full logging and configuration. This will allow you to manage the boundary security for your small- to medium-sized network. Later in the chapter we will discuss the Cisco Secure Policy Manager that will allow you to manage up to 100 PIX Firewalls on a large-scale network.

Using PIX Firewall Manager

This part of the chapter will give you more insight into the logical steps and procedures to get the PIX Firewall Manager working. You will also have some examples that you can look at and compare to your own environment. The following configuration steps let you get your PFM up and working, ready to connect to your PIX Firewalls. You can then start changing the rules for inbound and outbound connections to and from your network. We will also illustrate how to change some of the other configuration features discussed previously.

Configuration

First, you'll have to get the PIX Firewall ready to accept requests to view, change, or add the configuration from the Management Server that was actually relayed from your connection to the Management Client. Using a Telnet session to the PIX Firewall or using the PIX Firewall Setup Wizard to permit the Management Server access to the PIX Firewall does this. If the Management Server component has permission to access the PIX Firewall, it will respond to all the requests.

Make sure that the PIX Firewall is running the correct version of the IOS for the PFM install (refer to Table 8.1). The next step is to check the PIX Firewall requirements as mentioned earlier in this chapter.

You will need the **enable** password and the Telnet password that has been set on the PIX Firewall to configure the PIX Firewall successfully. You will also need the administrator password for the local host if it is a work-station or member server or the domain if you are installing PFM on a domain controller.

Installing the PIX Firewall Manager

If all your requirements are met, you can start with the installation of the PIX Firewall Manager software. This procedure can be trouble-free, but you can get into problems that will prevent you from continuing with the installation, causing the installation to terminate. These limitations were discussed in the previous section; please check them before you attempt to install the software.

If you are installing PFM on an existing server, please ensure that you have sufficient disk space, memory, and processing power for adding the PFM software as well as for the other software already running on the server. If you are using a new server, or a server that you formatted and reinstalled with Windows NT 4.0, please check the Management Server requirements before attempting to install the PFM software.

TIP

If you need the latest version of PIX Firewall Manager, you can find it on the Cisco Web site at www.cisco.com/cgi-bin/tablebuild.pl/pix.

The description of the file for PFM will be "Manager PC Executable" and will have the version of the released software in the next column.

Next, we will install the PFM software. All previous versions of PFM installed on the target installation server will be replaced with the newer version of PFM. Please make sure you have the necessary backups if needed.

1. Log in as the Administrator of the target server or workstation or with a user account that has the equivalent user rights on the local host or domain.

2. Verify that you have closed all Windows applications.

3. Locate the installation executable file and double-click the file to run the installation.

4. The InstallShield asks you to verify the start of installation; click Yes to start the PFM installation.

5. The welcome screen appears; click Next to continue.

6. At this point, if you have a previous version installed, you are asked to click Yes to uninstall the old version and continue with the new version installation. If you click Yes, it will run the uninstallation of the previous version before continuing.

7. In the next dialog box, you can change the installation directory if needed. Click Next to continue.

8. Specify the program group name in which the new icons should be created. You can leave it as default, then click Next.

9. The next screen asks you to specify the TCP port number to use for the Management Client connection. You can change this to any port number that is not in use on the server. I recommend using an available and unused port number above 1024.

10. After all the files are copied, click Finish to finish the installation and start the Management Server.

11. The last step is very important. You have to change the new user account names and passwords that were added during the installation. The two new user accounts are **pixadmin** and **pixuser**.

WARNING

If you are using an NT server with more than one Network Interface Card (NIC) installed, please verify that you are using the IP address that is used by the NIC that is connected to the segment of the PIX Firewall internal network.

Now that you have installed PFM on you server, you probably want to start using it. However, you find that there is no icon. This is where you need the host running the Internet browser to connect to the Management Client on the new PFM server. Check that you have the correct version of the Internet browser installed and that you meet the Management Client requirements before you attempt the connection.

To open the connection to the Management Client you have to open your Internet browser and use the host name or IP address where the PFM was installed together with the port number specified during the installation, that had a default value of 8080. In the address field, type **http://servername_ip:port**.

TIP

All the configuration information sent between PIX Firewalls and the PIX Firewall Manager is protected by a shared secret/secure hash algorithm (MD5) that allows for a very strong encryption for the packet crossing the physical network layer. This means that all communications and configurations are done using a secure protocol across the network.

Installation Errors in PIX Firewall Manager

When you install the PFM software, you might experience some difficulty. If you use it to manage your PIX Firewalls on your network, you might encounter some problems and limitations in conjunction with the PIX Firewall IOS. In the following sections, I have listed a few problems here and added the correct procedures to bypass the limitations of the software and related components.

When you install the PFM software on your Windows NT server, and the Windows NT server is a backup domain control, you have to make sure that the domain controller has a connection to the primary domain for the specific domain used. If you lose connection to the primary domain controller, you will receive an error message and will be unable to install PFM successfully. The error will read like this:

Could not find the domain controller for the domain.

This error message results from security requirements on the NT domain. The PFM installation needs to add the new PFM users and NT local groups to the Windows NT domain Security Accounts Database (SAM), so you need to communicate with the primary domain controller for the installation to continue. Generally, it is recommended that you do not add extra service to a domain controller, allowing the bulk of the processing load of the server for other domain functions.

Another limitation occurs when you install the PFM software on an NT server when you use an account that is not part of the Windows NT domain or local sever administration logins for the installation or uninstallation process. If you attempt to do so, you will receive the following error:

You are not authorized to run this installer.

Terminating...

You can add the username, used to log in to the server where you want to install PFM, to the domain administrator group or to the local server administrator group. When you are done with the installation, you can connect to the PIX Firewall and start using its features. If you installed the PIX Firewall prior to the PFM installation and used the CLI to configure and manage the PIX Firewall, you could have problems with some of the PIX Firewall commands currently used on the PIX Firewall. Use the PIX Firewall console port to change the current configurations, or use the interactive commands. Note that the following commands cannot be used from the PFM client:

`Hostname`

This changes the PIX Firewall host name.

`Name`

This permits users to map host names to an IP address.

`Ping`

This determines if a specific IP address is available for communication from the PIX Firewall.

`Clock set`

This hangs the clock in the PIX Firewall.

`Clear logging disabled`

This enables all previously disabled system messages.

`Config net`

This copies the running configuration from the TFTP server.

You also have configuration settings that PFM can read and can be viewed with the Management Client, but cannot be changed or added by PFM. These changes and additions have to be made on the PIX Firewall with a direct connection to the console cable. These features include:

- **MTU size** This is the Maximum Transmission Unit size for each interface (although you need to change this value only on the Token Ring interface).

- **Interface configuration** Use the interface commands to change the values only if needed.

- **Failover** Use this if you need to configure a failover using two PIX Firewalls to eliminate the single point of failure.

- **Private Link** As mentioned previously, use this when you need to manage the PIX Firewall from the outside network.

A Configuration Example

After the installation is successful and you are able to connect to the specific PIX Firewalls you would like to manage, you can start configuring the PIX Firewall for the specific security policy you have for the network traffic between your internal network and the outside network. As you can see in Figure 8.2, you can configure the most basic and accepted use for a firewall and have your network protected from the outside network or from the Internet.

The first item that you would need to implement on the firewall is the proper configuration for the hosts on your internal network that need to connect to the external network or Internet (also called the outbound access). You can use the following steps to configure the outbound access for your network.

1. Click on the Tasks button on the Administrator tab to open the wizard that will help you with the configuration of the out- or inbound rule on your PIX Firewall. The screenshot in Figure 8.3 illustrates where you select either inbound access or outbound access.

Figure 8.2 The most basic configuration of the PIX Firewall and the manager on the internal network.

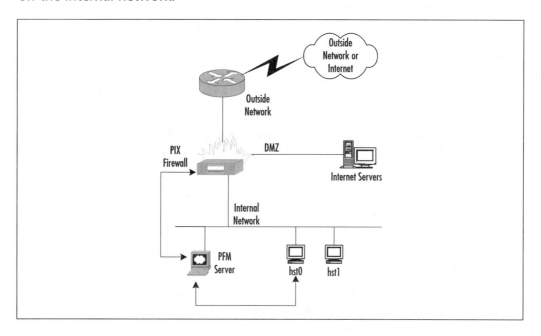

Figure 8.3 The first step for configuring outbound or inbound access.

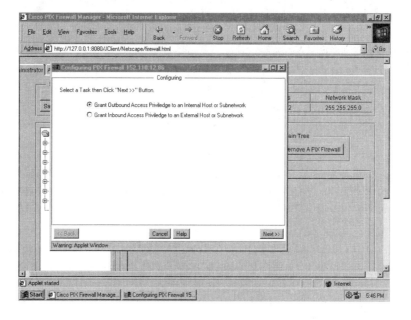

2. Specify the internal host or the range of internal IP addresses that is on your network for the outbound access rule you create. As you can see in Figure 8.4, you should enter the IP address and the relevant IP address mask to specify the network section.

Figure 8.4 Configure the internal IP host or IP range.

TIP

If you configure access only for a specific host, you can use the subnet mask of 255.255.255.255 to single out the host. If you would like to specify class C IP network range, use the subnet mask 255.255.255.0.

3. Specify if you need to configure and use NAT on the PIX Firewall. If you use a private IP address range on your internal network, you need to select Yes to configure NAT as shown in Figure 8.5.

4. On the next configuration screen, select the NAT type, either Dynamic Global Address Pool or Static Addresses depending on your preference and needs. If you don't need specific IP addresses on the internal network to define specific IP addresses on the external network, select the dynamic global addresses pool option. This simplifies your configuration, as shown in Figure 8.6.

Please refer to Chapter 3, "Network Address Translation" for more information on NAT.

Figure 8.5 Select the option for configuring NAT on the PIX Firewall.

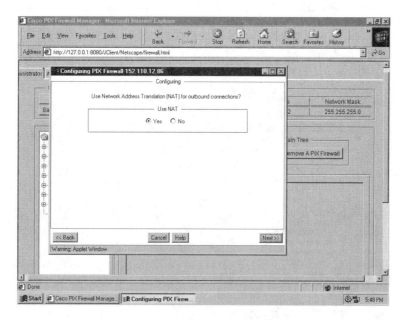

Figure 8.6 Selecting a Dynamic Global Addresses Pool or Static Addresses NAT type.

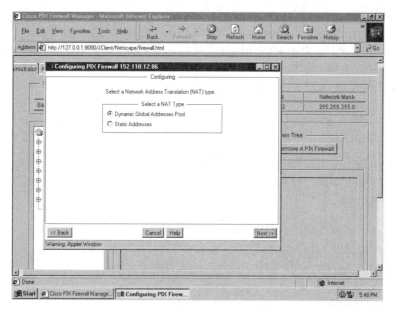

5. As displayed in Figure 8.7, if you selected the dynamic global
    addresses pool, you either need to select a global pool that you
    created in the Administrator tab, or you can specify a new global
    pool of legal IP address for the external network, specifying the
    start and end IP address with the associated subnet mask.

Figure 8.7 Specify the global pool of external NAT IP addresses.

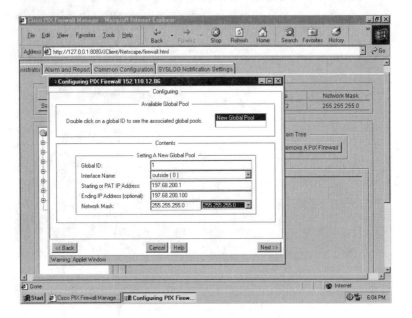

6. Figure 8.8 shows the last screen used to configure the PIX Firewall
    for a specific outbound access rule. You need to specify the set-
    tings for the associated NAT ID. You can configure the total
    amount of concurrent TCP connection allowed on the PIX Firewall
    for the access rule and the maximum embryonic connections. You
    can specify if the PIX Firewall should pick a random address from
    the dynamic global pool of addresses used with the Randomize
    Sequence selection option.

The procedure in this example can also be used to configure an
inbound access rule for specific access from the external network to your
internal network.

Figure 8.8 Changing default settings for NAT on the new outbound access rule.

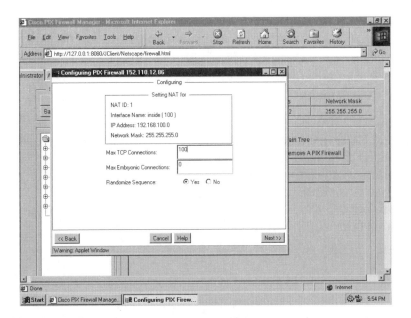

CiscoWorks 2000 ACL Manager

Now that you have configured and deployed your security policy to the PIX Firewalls on the outer boundary of your network with PIX Firewall Manager (protecting your network from the outside world) you need to ensure protection from people within your network from accessing confidential and restricted data or services. You have to manage your internal network security policy just as well as your external policy to ensure good security on your enterprise network.

This section will describe the use and features of the Access Control List Manager, which you can use to deploy and manage your internal network security policy.

ACL Manager Overview

CiscoWorks 2000 is a few applications bundled together to make up an entire suite for managing Cisco enterprise networks and devices. The products include solutions for managing local area networks (LAN) and for wide area networks (WAN) of your enterprise network. All the products fall into three categories (or solutions):

The LAN Management Solution This feature will support your local network and devices and includes Web-based applications for advanced management using an Internet browser.

The Routed WAN Management Solution This is used for your routed and multi-service wide area networks and provides traffic management, monitoring, and access control. (This is where ACL fits in.)

The Service Management Solution This is used to manage and monitor service-level agreements.

CiscoWorks 2000 gives you the option to integrate other third-party management software that is available on the market. This allows you to develop customized Web-based tools that you can use on your intranet. This feature is available with the Cisco Management Connection integration tool that is included in CiscoWorks 2000.

You can look on Cisco's Web site for more information on the products in the CiscoWorks 2000 family.

TIP

ACL Manager links to the new CiscoWorks 2000 Management Server multi-level security system. This allows for more secure access to the ACL Manager and the configuration of the access control list on network devices.

The Access Control List (ACL) Manager is one of the products included in the CiscoWorks family and fits into the Routed WAN Management solution bundle. It runs as an add-on to the Resource Manager Essentials. You use ACL Manager to view, add, or change all the access control lists on multiple Cisco devices that are part of your network and that are running IOS Release 10.3 and later. The Web interface provides the applications needed to manage the access control list from a central point of the network and can be accessed with an Internet browser from anywhere on your network. It can be used for IP and IPX traffic filters, also known as access control lists, and to manage access to specific devices. The ACL Manager is a lot easier to use than the CLI through a Telnet session to configure access control lists on Cisco devices. It will save you countless hours of configurations on new filters and managing existing traffic access lists in a large-scale network and will ensure consistent and accurate deployment of your security policy across the enterprise.

> **NOTE**
>
> You can configure access control lists (ACLs) only on routers running IOS version 10.3 or later. The ACLs on the routers consist of one or more access control entries (ACE) that would permit or deny traffic based on specified criteria like source or destination address. More information on access lists can be found in Chapter 2, "Traffic Filtering on the Cisco IOS."

The following tools are used to manage filters and access to specific devices on your network:

- **Template Manager** allows you to create and edit ACL templates. It can be used as a standard configuration for the ACL Manager when implementing your security policy. You would add common rules and ACLs that you need on your network to the templates.

- **Class Managers** let you create and edit specific networks and services for scalability and efficiency. The classes defined within Class Manager are a grouping of networks or services, like FTP and HTTP that you can use in your ACLs.

- **Hits Optimizer** lets you change the order of the ACEs inside the ACL based on the hit rate of the associated ACEs.

- **Optimizer** lets you check the ACL and streamline your access lists after changes, if possible.

- **Downloader** lets you schedule and download modified ACLs to specific devices or groups of devices.

- **Job Browser** allows you to list and view the status of all the download jobs.

- **Template Use Wizard** helps you select the type of template for a selected group of devices and the ACL or template to use on these devices.

- **Diff Viewer** allows you to display the configuration changes that you made since you created the scenario.

If you have a large internetwork that has multiple devices with access control lists configured, the Policy Template Manager can use the auto deployment feature to centralize the deployment of access control lists for a group of users, devices, or network services. The ACL Manager will also allow you to optimize the access lists configured for deployment. It will automatically remove redundant entries and merge access list entries to ensure that the device lookup time for a match in the access control list is reduced, resulting in increased packet forwarding.

ACL Manager Device and Software Support

The ACL Manager version 1.1 will support most Cisco devices running IOS. You can manage devices like routers, access servers, switches, and hubs. The IOS version on the managed devices must be at least release 10.3 to support the ACL Manager.

When it comes to the configuration of the access control list on the devices, you can view all the access lists on the device, but you can manage only the following types:

- Standard IP access lists and Extended IP access lists
- Standard IPX access lists and Extended IPX access lists
- SAP IPX access lists
- Summary IPX access lists
- Rate limit MAC access lists
- Rate limit Precedence access lists

Installation Requirements for ACL Manager

When you plan to install ACL Manager on your server, you have to verify that your server meets the software requirements. The most important requirement for installing ACL Manager is to install CiscoWorks 2000 (also known as CD One) first, followed by Cisco Resource Manager Essentials (RME) version 3.0, and then ACL Manager. ACL Manager is not a stand-alone application, and it depends on this software to work properly. CiscoWorks 2000 can be installed on a Windows NT Server or on a Solaris system. If you need to install ACL Manager on a Windows NT Server or Windows NT Workstation system, make sure that the server meets the specifications shown in Table 8.2.

Table 8.2 Minimum Windows NT Server Requirements for ACL Manager and Associated Software

Requirement Type	Required for ACL Manager
Processor	Pentium III 450MHz
Memory (RAM)	256MB
Window NT Virtual Memory (Page file)	512MB

Continued

Table 8.2 Continued

Requirement Type	Required for ACL Manager
Available Drive Space	4GB of free space
Additional Hardware	CD-ROM drive and 17-inch Monitor
System Software	Windows NT 4.0 Workstation or Server with Service Pack 5 (not Service Pack 6)
Internet Browser	If used as a client, same browser requirements as those in Table 8.4

If you are installing the ACL Manager software on a Solaris system, check that it fulfills the requirements in Table 8.3.

Table 8.3 Minimum Solaris Requirements for ACL Manager and Associated Software

Requirement Type	Required for ACL Manager
Processor	Sparc Ultra 10
Memory (RAM)	256MB
Swap Space	512MB
Available Drive Space	4GB free space
Additional Hardware	CR-ROM drive and 17-inch Monitor
System Software	Solaris 2.6 and Patches 105181-11, 105210-17, 105490-05, 105529-07, and 105568-13
Internet Browser	If used as a client, same browser requirements as those in Table 8.4

After you installed the ACL Manager and associated software on the server, you can use any operating system with an Internet browser installed to access and configure the ACL Manager. The system that you use has to comply with the minimum client requirements of the relevant operating system. Table 8.4 gives you the minimum requirements for running the ACL Manager client. The total amount of memory and the specifications for the Internet browser is the same for all operating systems and, therefore, put into a single column.

Table 8.4 Minimum Client Requirements for Accessing ACL Manager from the Network

Operating System	Hardware	Memory	Internet Browser
Windows NT 4.0, Windows 9x	IBM-Compatible with Pentium 300 MHz	128MB	Microsoft Internet Explorer 5.0 or 5.01 with Java Virtual Machine version 5.0.0.3186 or newer.
Solaris SPACstation, Sun Ultra 10	Solaris 2.6	128MB	
HP-UX Work-station	HP-UX 10.20 or 11.0	128MB	Netscape Navigator 4.61 or 4.7
IBM RS/6000 Workstation	AIX 4.3.3	128MB	

ACL Manager Features

The features added when you install ACL Manager are related to the access control lists (ACLs) that you manage on the Cisco devices for your enterprise network. After you install ACL Manager on your server you can access it through CiscoWorks 2000 from any host running an Internet browser and complying with the client requirements specified earlier. All the ACL Manager tools can be found under the RME section selected on the left panel of CiscoWorks 2000. Next, I'll describe some features that you can use, and the tool you can use to access these features.

Using a Structure Access Control Lists Security Policy

When you have multiple routers on your enterprise network and need to manage and configure ACLs to control the traffic that flows through your network, ACL Manager can help ensure consistency across your enterprise security policy.

You can use the Template Manager and the Class Manager to configure templates and classes that you can use for all your ACLs. This will allow you to use a standard selection of networks and hosts for all the templates you created with the Template Manager. This method can help to successfully manage a structured policy for all your ACLs on the entire network.

Increase Deployment Time for Access Control Lists

You can use the Template Manager to configure ACL templates for configuring general network security. It will help you to define a template that needs to be deployed on your network for optimal operation. When your network security policy for the ACL templates changes, you need to update only the template initially created. ACL Manager will indicate to you that the templates have changed and which devices will be affected. It automatically generates the appropriate configurations that need to be deployed on your enterprise network, thus decreasing deployment time for changes to ACLs.

You can also use the ACL Use Wizard to increase the deployment time for new ACLs that you would like to enforce on your network. It will take you through a step-by-step process to configure the ACL for a router or Telnet access to a router, or so-called line access, by adding a template to the device security policy. This allows you to concentrate on creating the ACLs on your network topology for your security policy; that way, you won't have to spend precious time learning the different syntax used on all your network devices

Ensure Consistency of Access Control Lists

When you define ACLs on your enterprise network, you have to ensure consistency throughout your network. This reduces the possibilities for errors getting into your security policy; it not only blocks unauthorized traffic from reaching their destinations but also allows authorized people to access restricted networks or hosts. This is why you have to implement standards for your security policy. Use the Template Manager together with the Class Manager to define network classes and services, as discussed previously. This will allow you to implement ACLs on your network a lot quicker and reduce the time to make changes on selected ACLs.

When you update the template defined with Template Manager, the ACL Manager will indicate to you the changes made and give you a list of devices affected by the change. In this way, you can confirm your newly configured ACL and redo any errors you pick up before making the change.

When you make changes on your network security policy, the changes on the ACLs can be viewed with the Diff Viewer. If you open the Diff Viewer from the Tools menu, the left side will show only the devices that are affected by the change and that will receive new or changed ACLs. In the middle of the Diff Viewer, you have the list of current configured ACLs for the selected device on the left. The right side of the Diff Viewer shows the new ACLs for the selected device. Using this to check and confirm your ACL configuration changes, you can reduce possible errors on your security policy.

Keep Track of Changes Made on the Network

ACL Manager should be installed on the same server where you installed CiscoWorks 2000 and Resource Manager Essentials version 3.0. Since ACL Manager is an add-on to RME, it uses the Change Audit service that is part of RME. The Change Audit is a central point where you can see network configuration changes. It will display information about types of changes made, who made the changes and when, and whether the changes were made from a Telnet connection, from the console port, or from a CiscoWorks 2000 application like ACL Manager.

TIP

With Resource Manager Essentials Change Audit service, you can filter the report using simple or complex criteria to find the specific changes you are looking for. You can even identify network changes made during critical network operation time.

Troubleshooting and Error Recovery

When you experience problems on your network where someone can't access the necessary segment on the network, first you have to confirm that your physical network and your routing and protocols are working properly. Only then should you start troubleshooting your ACLs on your network. The next step is to check when you started to experience the problem and check the latest changes made on your security policy using the Change Audit component. This will give you a good idea about recently made changes, and this could be your new problem on the network.

Once you identify the problem on the specific ACL, you can use the Template Manager to change the ACL template. You can generate the appropriate configurations that you need to deploy it on your network. The Template Manager greatly reduces the time spent to rectify the error on the network.

When you use the ACL Downloader to deploy the new ACLs on your network, you'll have a few options to select to prevent errors from occurring during the deployment. The first option in the Downloader is called Abort on error. This allows you to revert to the original router configuration, remove any changes, and abort the download if an error occurs during the ACL deployment. By default when you select this option the next option in ACL Downloader, Rollback, will be selected. This option will attempt to revert to the router's original configuration if an error occurs during the download. Any change prior to the download error will be removed.

Basic Operation of ACL Manager

Now that you know the features that ACL Manager provides for managing your ACLs on the enterprise network, We'll discuss some basic operations of ACL Manager components.

Using Templates and Defining Classes

As we discussed previously, you need to use templates to ensure consistency across your network and to reduce the time spent to deploy your ACLs. Before you start using the Template Manager, it is important first to configure networks, network classes, services, and service classes. Use the Class Manager to view, add, and change the classes.

The services in the Class Manager include standard service and port numbers for well-known applications like FTP, HTTP, and Telnet. You can add your own service to this list of services. First, you select the type of IP service, UDP or TCP, then you enter a name to identify the new service. Lastly, you can enter the associated port number.

Class Manager also allows you to configure service classes. This is used to create a custom service class, identified by a user-defined name, which includes multiple services. You can add a custom service class with the following steps. First, you have to specify a name that will identify this service class and select the associated IP protocol type, UDP or TCP. Next, you can specify one of the following to be part of your services class definition:

- One or more service port numbers
- A range of ports specified with a low and high port value
- One or more previously defined service classes

In addition, the Class Manager allows you to create, remove, and change networks and network classes. The networks created will be named and will include the IP address of the network with its corresponding subnet mask. You should use this to define the smallest logical network segment on the enterprise. This will allow you to be more specific when defining ACLs, and you can use the network classes to define more general group of networks.

The network classes you create with the Class Manager allow you to create a named class that will include one or all of the following:

- One or more specific host IP addresses

- One or more range of IP addresses specified using start and end IP addresses

- One or more networks created in the network folder

- One or more previously created network classes created in this folder

These specific services and networks can be removed and added to the new service classes and network classes as necessary. These are applied to an ACE within an ACL template configuration and create a standard for the security policy that you can easily reuse.

Using the Difference (Diff) Viewer

As you use the ACL Manager to change the ACLs on your network routers, all the changes will not take effect immediately. You can use the ACL Downloader to apply the changes to the specific routers now or at a scheduled time after hours. When you are finished with all the changes on the ACLs on your network, you can use the Diff Viewer to check all the current configurations on the routers and the changes you made on the ACLs.

In the right panel of the Diff Viewer, Modified Objects lists all the network devices to which you have made changes or which are affected by your changes. This panel will have subfolders under the specific devices that will include more information about the ACLs that changed and which interfaces have been affected. Using this, you can select a specific view for your changes based on ACL or interface.

The Original Config in the middle panel lets you view the current configurations of the ACLs affected by your change corresponding to the selected item on the right panel.

On the left, Modified Config lists all the changes that will be applied to the selected router. It's easy to identify the change by using the following colors:

- Red for all the change ACEs

- Green for all the newly added ACEs in the ACL

- Blue for all the removed ACEs from the ACL

There are two buttons that will give you more information about the new changes to ACLs on the devices. The first button, Config..., will display the entire new configuration for the selected device, including the changes. The other button, Delta..., will show the IOS commands that will be downloaded to the selected device to make the necessary changes for the new security policy.

Using the Optimizer and the Hits Optimizer

These two tools in the ACL Manager will help you optimize your ACL configuration to reduce processor cycles on the router where the ACLs are located and to increase throughput for packing forwarding.

When you use ACLs on one or more interfaces on a network device, you could impact the performance of the network traffic through the device for the following reasons:

- When a packet is received or sent out on an interface, it first has to be compared to all the ACEs in the ACL used on the interface. Once the packet finds a match for one of the ACEs in the ACL, it is denied or permitted according to ACE.

- The packets follow the ACEs in sequence until a match is found.

To prevent problems in lengthy ACLs configured on network devices, the ACL Optimizer minimizes the number of ACEs used in ACLs by merging ACEs, removing redundant ACEs, or removing duplicate ACEs. This will allow you to free up processing on the device and improve network performance. In Table 8.5, you can see the effect of using the Optimizer on some ACEs in an ACL that can be optimized.

Table 8.5 Using the ACL Optimizer to Optimize ACEs within an ACL

Original ACEs	Optimized ACEs
permit ip from host 192.168.50.8	permit ip from 192.168.50.8/0.0.0.7
permit ip from host 192.168.50.9	
permit ip from host 192.168.50.10	
permit ip from host 192.168.50.11	
permit ip from host 192.168.50.12	
permit ip from host 192.168.50.13	
permit ip from host 192.168.50.14	
permit ip from host 192.168.50.15	

As you can see, this process is similar to using route summarization on your network to improve network routing performance.

When you have no changes to apply to your ACLs for your network security policy, but want to improve performance related to ACL, you can use the Hits Optimizer to improve the network performance. The Hits Optimizer places the most frequently matched ACEs, for packet passing the interface, at the top of the ACL and moves the less frequently matched

ACEs to the bottom. This can be done based on the number of matches that the device IOS tracks, and it will reorder the sequence according to this tracked value.

> ## WARNING
>
> When you use the Hits Optimizer to reorder the sequence of ACEs in an ACL, it may not always change the order based on the number of matches for the ACEs. Reordering ACEs is performed only when the new order does not change the ACL statement. Careless reordering of access list entries can completely disable the security of an access control list.

Using ACL Manager

Before using the ACL Manager on your network devices, you need to successfully install the ACL Manager software and prepare the network devices you would like to manage. You will need a lot of preparation before you can even start using the ACL Manager to add and change ACLs on your network. The procedures to get everything successfully installed and working will be explained in the configuration section, and the example section will illustrate some of the steps necessary to create ACL configurations.

Configuration

When you are preparing your network for the ACL Manager, you need to take note of some information and configurations on all the Cisco devices that you would like to manage.

The first important step to add devices to Resource Manager Essentials (RME) using a DNS name is to define a DNS entry into your local DNS server for all your devices on the network with the relevant primary IP address for the devices. The DNS entry should be a fully qualified domain name. You can also use an IP address to add the devices to the Inventory of RME within CiscoWorks 2000. When you add devices to the RME, you need the following information from each device on your network:

- Read Community String for SNMP
- Read/Write Community String for SNMP
- TACACS username and password if used
- Local device username and password
- Telnet username and password

- Enable TACACS username and password if used
- Enable password (less secure, or non-encrypted, password)
- Enable secret password

This means that you have to configure SNMP on the managed devices with the relevant public and private community strings. All devices that you manage should be added using the Add Device tool under the Inventory folder in the RME section of CiscoWorks 2000 before you can make any changes to the ACLs of the device.

TIP

To configure the SNMP service on a router that you manage, use one of the following two commands in the global configuration mode:

```
Rt1(config)#snmp-server community Se9m4r7Yo ro
```

This command will configure read-only access for the specified community string Se9m4r7Yo.

```
Rt1(config)#snmp-server community 3eeTi5.w1w rw
```

This command will configure read-write access for the specific community string 3eeTi5.w1w.

Installing the ACL Manager and Associated Software

Before you begin the installation process, ensure that the recommended hardware requirements are met. Then, be sure that you have the following installation CD-ROMs, or files, available:

- CiscoWorks 2000 CD One
- Resource Manager Essentials version 3.0
- Access Control List Manager

You have to follow a predefined sequence of software installation to install the ACL Manager successfully on your server. You first need to install the CiscoWorks 2000 CD One on a server that is not a primary or backup domain controller on the NT domain. The installation can be installed only to an NTFS volume on your server, and not FAT. It's recommended that you use a dedicated server on which to install the software. This would mean more protection from intruders using other installed services or applications to access the Cisco software.

Secondly, you need to install the Resource Manager Essentials on the same server. Double-click on the install file to start the installation and follow the onscreen dialog wizard, which will guide you through the installation. The installation will take approximately 30 minutes—there are no trick questions that you need to answer for the installation; it's straight-forward.

NOTE

When using CiscoWorks 2000, be sure that Java, JavaScript, and Accept All Cookies are enabled in your Internet browser settings. If the settings are not correct, you will not be able to log on to CiscoWorks 2000.

When the RME installation is finished, you can finally start the installation of ACL Manager. Execute the ACL Manager installation file and follow the onscreen installation wizard. This installs the ACL Manager add-on to RME into CiscoWorks 2000 and is also a straight-forward installation with no configuration questions asked during the installation.

An ACL Manager Configuration Example

In the following example, we will walk through the procedure for creating an ACL on a router ready to be applied to the router-specific interface. These steps will include a simple illustration of adding a device to your CiscoWorks 2000 configuration, opening a new scenario to edit your ACLs on the selected devices, and adding an ACL and a specific ACE to the router. The Scenario is used to define a collection of devices that are affected by the policy and the applied ACLs.

You could also follow these steps in the ACL Template editor, and you can use the templates on the related router for your security policy.

1. To use your CiscoWorks 2000 GUI in your Internet browser, you have to open an HTTP connection to the specific host name or IP address on your internal network. Use the IP address you used during installation: either the default (port number 1741) or the port number of the CiscoWorks 2000 server to which you want to connect. Use the following format for your address in the browser: http://severname_ip:port.

   The first screen, as shown in Figure 8.9, will prompt you for a username and password to log in to the CiscoWorks 2000 GUI.

The default username is **admin** and the default password is **admin**. For security purposes, it's recommended to change the admin password when you log in for the first time using the Modify My Profile tool under CiscoWorks 2000 | Setup | Security folder.

Figure 8.9 The login screen for CiscoWorks 2000.

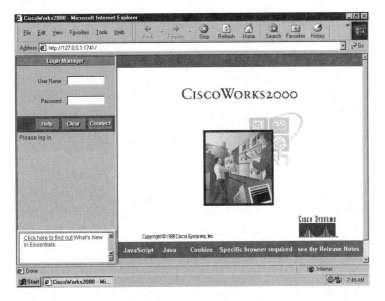

2. Once you are successfully logged into CiscoWorks 2000, click on the Resource Manager Essentials tab on the left of the screen. Click on the Administration tree selection followed by the Inventory sub-selection. Lastly, click on the Add Devices tool to add the devices you have on your network and would like to manage.

3. Figure 8.10 shows you the screen used to add a device to your configuration. Fill in the required information including passwords and SNMP community strings.

4. On the next screen, as shown in Figure 8.11, you need to configure a scenario that will be associated with the new ACL that you configure on the selected devices. Give a specific name for the new scenario and select the relevant information. Click Next to select the devices that would be used in this scenario.

5. In the next screen, select the devices based on a filter on custom view. Use the Add button to add the related device for the new scenario. If you click the Next button on the screen, it will open a new window called ACL Manager, running a Java applet, which you use

Figure 8.10 Adding a single network device to your network for administration.

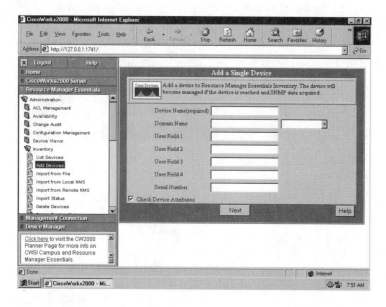

Figure 8.11 Creating or opening a scenario to edit the ACL.

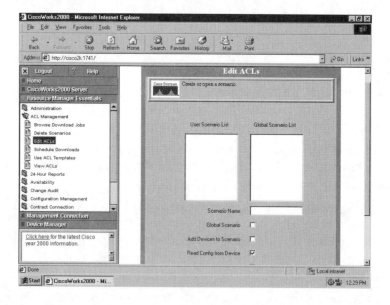

to configure the ACL and apply it to the selected device. Figure 8.12 shows the applet windows, ACL Manager, and some of the subselections you can use.

Figure 8.12 The ACL Manager used to Configure ACLs on selected devices.

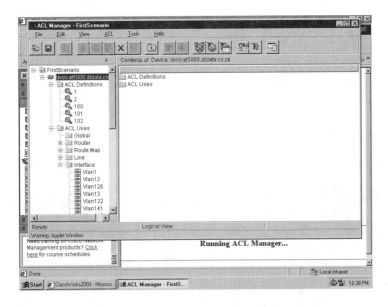

6. Right-click on the ACL Definitions folder and select New ACL to insert the new ACE for your new security policy. Figure 8.13 shows the screen you use to add an ACL to your selected router.

Figure 8.13 Adding an ACL to your selected router.

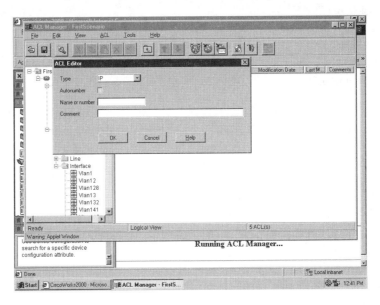

7. After you select the OK button, you will notice the new ACL in the ACL Definition section. Right-click on the new ACL to get a list of options related to your new ACL.

8. Add the relevant ACEs for the specific security policy. Figure 8.14 shows you the first ACE for the new ACL for a standard access control lists that will deny all traffic from 192.168.200.0. If you click on the Expand... button, you will get the list of IOS commands used to configure the selected router. If you would like to add another ACE to your ACL, click on the New button.

Figure 8.14 Add an ACE to your new ACL.

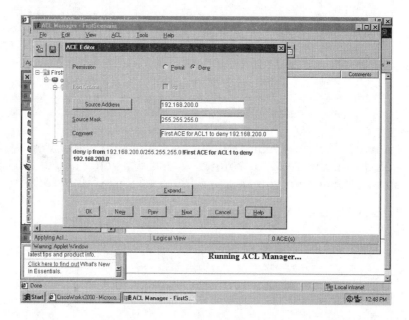

The ACE added to the ACLs will be applied to the selected devices in the scenario. You can change, add, and remove the ACE and ACL on the devices using the same procedures used in this example to build your security policy towards faultlessness. It is not recommended that you change the ACL on your devices configured by the ACL Manager because this will leave your ACL Manager information inconsistent.

Cisco Secure Policy Manager

Network security becomes more critical to any organization that incorporates intranets, extranets, and the Internet for e-commerce solutions. The associated security risk becomes very high with most organizations configuring and deploying firewalls to improve network boundary security and

Virtual Private Networks (VPNs) to protect the integrity of the network and also to establish secure business-to-business communications.

You would use Cisco Secure Policy Manager to minimize administrative costs and ensure consistent security policy on your network. This includes the ability to manage your secure network and associated services with a consolidated management system. It supports the different network requirements of your organization that are used to establish a secure connection for your intranets with multiple firewalls and VPN routers.

Cisco Secure Policy Manager Overview

With Cisco Secure Policy Manager (CSPM) you can define, distribute, enforce, and audit your entire network security policies from a central location. You can use CSPM to configure your PIX Firewalls on the boundary of your enterprise network, configure Network Address Translation (NAT), and IP Security (IPSec) based Virtual Private Networks. This allows for easy and simple deployment of your security policy to your PIX Firewalls and your VPN and builds the cornerstone of your security policy.

With CSPM's distributed architecture, using more than one policy enforcement point and its secure remote management allows you to deploy the policy in different environments. If you are administrating a large enterprise network, you can install the policy administrator (the Graphical Users Interface (GUI) used for policy administration) in different locations across your network for distributed management of your network security policy.

The CSPM software is really an immense product and could be the subject of an entire book, so this will be only a brief summary of the benefits, features, and example configurations included in this application.

The Benefits of Using Cisco Secure Policy Manager

Using CSPM on your network provides you with a great number of products to use to create, deploy, and change your enterprise network security policy. Some benefits of using CSPM and all the relative products include:

- Scalability, which enables you to meet large-scale security policy requirements and network growth. It provides the capability to manage up to several hundred PIX Firewall and VPN routers on your network.

- Built-in auditing and reporting, which provides up-to-date information on network and system events. It allows you to configure notifications according to your needs.

- The ability to define network-wide security policies based on your organization's business objectives. You can accurately define your security policies for different devices on your network and can reduce the time needed to deploy the security configurations.

- A centralized standalone policy management environment or a distributed architecture policy management environment to support your needs on the Internet, intranet, and extranet environments.

- The ability to configure and test your security policies without connecting to your live network. You can do your configurations offline and verify that your security policies are working correctly, as intended, and then deploy the policy to your live network.

- A Windows NT-based system, which provides you with an easy-to-use GUI to manage your security policy.

As discussed in this chapter, CSPM version 2.2 (formerly known as Cisco Security Manager) is the latest Cisco security policy management product available. In future releases of CSPM, Cisco will add support for Cisco intrusion detection services and user-based policy services and will incorporate the CSPM software into CiscoWorks 2000.

Installation Requirements for Cisco Secure Policy Manager

Before installing CSPM on your target server, you should ensure that all the devices on the network that you intend to manage is configured properly and active on your network. You should have IP communication between the device and the target CSPM server on your network for Telnet sessions.

Next, you should ensure that your target CSPM server meets the following hardware requirements:

- 200MHz Intel-based Pentium Processor

- 96MB of RAM

- 2GB of free hard disk space

- One or more properly configured NICs

- 1024x786 video card with 64KB colors or more

- SVGA color monitor

- CD-ROM with Autorun enabled

- Mouse

- Optional modem for pager notifications

- Optional sound card with speakers for tutorial videos

If you are installing the stand-alone or client-server system option on your target CSPM server, these minimum requirements would be sufficient, although not optimal for a distributed system. The Policy Server component is a multi-threaded application that can benefit from multiple processors and available memory when used in a large network managed environment.

You can install the GUI client for CSPM on a computer that runs Windows NT 4.0, Windows 95, or Windows 98. This allows you to manage the network security policy from any host on your network.

The following minimum software requirements should be met before attempting the CSPM installation:

- Windows NT 4.0 with Service Pack 6a

- Microsoft Internet Explorer 5.0

- HTML Help 1.3 Update

- NTFS file partition

- TCP/IP protocol stack installed and working properly

- Static IP address with DHCP disabled

- TAPI for pager notifications

- MAPI for e-mail notifications

Before installing CSPM on your target server, you have to check the Cisco Web site for the latest information about the compatible list software that has been tested for coexistence with CSPM on the same host. CSPM already supports the co-existence of Cisco Secure VPN Client 1.1, CiscoWorks 2000 with Resource Management Essentials version 3.0, and the QoS Policy Manager version 1.1 on the same computer.

TIP

One of the requirements for installing the CSPM software onto a target server is to create a user account that is used to install the new services for CSPM. This account will be used for starting the relevant services at system boot-up and should have Logon as a Services user rights on the local server.

Cisco Secure Policy Manager Features

Some of the features included in the CSPM product have the same intention as the PIX Firewall Manager and the ACL Manager. The difference with CSPM is that you have a more centralized management approach and more functionality for managing your enterprise network security policy.

Cisco Firewall Management

This feature allows you to easily define the boundary security policy on PIX Firewall and Cisco IOS routers running the firewall feature set. This allows for centralized configuration management of Cisco PIX Firewalls and Cisco routers using the firewall feature set on your enterprise network. It will simplify your network-wide firewall and NAT management, reduce the need for management skills to manage the security policy, and reduce costs.

> **NOTE**
>
> A Cisco router running the firewall feature set is called a Cisco Router/Firewall. A Cisco router running the IPSec VPN feature set is called a Cisco VPN Gateway. These feature sets are part of the Cisco Secure Integrated Software and Cisco Secure Integrated VPN Software solutions for Cisco routers.

Using this component within CSPM, you can specify the downstream, or outside, and the upstream, or inside, interface addresses of the specific PIX Firewall. When you configure either of the interfaces settings, you need to define the network to which the interface is connected and specify the IP address assigned to the interface on the specific network.

You use the Mapping panel of the PIX Firewall to define any Network Address Translation (NAT) handled by the PIX Firewall. You would not use the Firewall management component, defined in the Network Topology, to configure any of the rules that apply to the PIX Firewall on your network; use the security policies abstractors, used to configure any traffic filters on PIX Firewall and specific routers, to define the traffic filter rules that are part of your firewall security policy.

VPN and IPSec Security Management

The IPSec protocol suite is used to seamlessly integrate security features, such as authentication, integrity, and confidentiality into IP packets. You can configure an encrypted and authenticated communication path between two clients, routers, or firewalls.

When you configure IPSec, it can function in two modes. The first, transport mode, is used for end-to-end security between two nodes. The transport mode will protect all traffic between the source and the destination node with IPSec.

The second mode is the tunnel mode. This will use an IPSec-enabled security gateway or firewall that functions as an IPSec peer for communication between the two end nodes. It does not use end-to-end IPSec between the nodes. The IPSec tunnel is only used on the public, unsecure section of the network connection. The communication on the local protected network, behind the firewall or router, is not encrypted using the IPSec protocol.

Two types of IPSec protocols exist. The first is the Authentication Header (AH) protocol, which provides data integrity, data source authentication, and protection against replay attacks. The original IP packet is encapsulated into a packet that contains a new IP header followed by the AH header. The payload of this new packet is transmitted from clear across the tunnel, which means no data confidentiality is provided.

The second type of IPSec protocol is based on the Encapsulating Security Payload (ESP) protocol, which provides data confidentiality, data integrity, data source authentication, and protection against replay attacks. The data confidentiality is accomplished by basically encrypting the IP packet before encapsulating it into a new IP packet with the ESP header and trailer attached, half encrypted and half cleartext. The IPSec based on the ESP protocol can be used for Virtual Private Network (VPNs) communications across a public or insecure network.

The IPSec Security Association (SA) entails how to protect the data using either ESP or AH, what data to protect across this tunnel, and which two endpoints to use for the encrypted path. CSPM supports the configuration for IPSec SAs through the use of tunnel templates, tunnel groups, and policy. You use the tunnel template to define the algorithms and protocols that will be used for encryption of data across the connection for confidentiality or authentication purposes. The tunnel group is based on one associated tunnel template and defines the connection peers or endpoints. This ensures that your peers that are part of one tunnel group will reference the same protocols and algorithms. This will reduce your risks for introducing errors when manually configuring each peer or endpoint for the connections. You can use the security policies to determine between services that should be routed through the connections, and services routed using other methods.

For more information on IPSec, see Chapter 5, "Virtual Private Networks."

Security Policy Management

CSPM is a centralized, policy-based management solution for Cisco security devices on your network. You can use CSPM to deploy a company security policy throughout your network. It uses a simple management process for implementing network-wide policies by using policy, definition, enforcement, and auditing.

Security Policy Definition

Using CSPM, you can create high-level security policies based on the company security objectives. You can create security policy abstracts that define access and the associated level of security to specific network devices. By adjusting the parameters for the type of network service or application and the source and destination address of the abstracts, you can control network traffic across your enterprise network.

To simplify the creation of the policies on your network, the policy abstracts can be generated for a collection of services to reduce the number of policies created. When you first install the CSPM software on your server, there will be predefined abstract bundles ready for use in your security policies. CSPM also provides grouping constructs for supported devices and hosts that allow you to reference multiple networks or hosts in a single policy.

You can also use CSPM to easily define NAT policies on your PIX Firewall or router on the boundary of your network.

Security Policy Enforcement

After you have defined the security policy, you should deploy the policy to the specific Cisco security device on your network. You can easily create a network topology and identify where the policy should be enforced using a drag-and-drop method to apply the security policies to the target network segments. The CSPM translates the policy into the device commands to deploy it to the necessary PIX Firewalls and VPN routers on the specified network section. You don't need to use the time-consuming CLI to configure each router for the new security policy deployed.

Depending on your preferences and needs, you can deploy the policy to the network automatically or manually. The communication between the CSPM host and the managed devices is secure to use across the network. It provides a flexible, robust, and secure mechanism to distribute the configurations and enforce the policies.

It allows consistent and proper policy enforcement on your network that you can easily verify and modify as required. You can, at any time, use the consistency check feature to ensure network policy integrity and to enforce status, or you can configure a notification if an error occurs with the policy enforcement.

Security Policy Auditing

The final part of the policy management process is the policy auditing. CSPM provides for an auditing system that enables you to log, monitor, alert, and report on the security policy events on your network where you enforced a policy. This is critical for checking the status of the policies on your network.

Define filters and actions for the events that are related to SYSLOG messages generated on your network for the policies enforced. Any possible network attacks and security breaches on your network can be configured for a real-time automated response using e-mail or a visual display. You can categorize the alerts based on specific events and messages for your policies to trigger only important notifications when needed. All the SYSLOG messages can be redirected to other hosts or servers on your network that could be used by third-party applications for reporting and analysis.

CSPM's most useful tool for auditing and reporting is the Web-based reporting system that enables you to easily diagnose system security and integrity of your policies by using any host with an Internet browser.

Network Security Deployment Options

CSPM can be used for a wide range of networks ranging from small- or medium-sized businesses that need a secure intranet and secure connection to the Internet, to large enterprise networks distributed across multiple geographical locations using PIX Firewalls and VPN routers for intercommunication.

CSPM uses a distributed architecture and has remote management capabilities that enable you to deploy your security policy to a multitude of environments. However, CSPM is most useful in network environments where new devices like PIX Firewalls and VPN routers are being deployed. This allows you to distribute policy configurations for new installations and reduce the deployment time in implementing new security services.

When using CSPM on a large-scale enterprise network, you can deploy secure intranet connections, using the configured IPSec VPN connection, between multiple remote sites. Using CSPM as a centralized solution for your network, security management will benefit from the flexible and distributed architecture. On a large enterprise network, you could deploy CSPM in a distributed mode in which the GUI, or policy administrator, is installed on hosts on different locations on the network. The policy server includes the fundamental database, the policy translation, and configuration distribution for CSPM. A policy server can also be installed on multiple servers in different locations on the network.

If you administer a small- to medium-sized network, you would use the perimeter, or boundary, security deployment policy available from CSPM. This gives you a simple security model and requires minimal configuration and ongoing maintenance for your security policy. To protect themselves from the Internet, small companies usually enforce this deployment option. The small office environment is comprised of several internal networks with a single connection to the Internet. Shared resources such as Web and file servers are placed in a publicly accessible isolated services network, the demilitarized zone (DMZ), and are protected with a firewall. The internal network is also protected by the firewall.

Cisco Secure Policy Manager Device and Software Support

When you use CSPM to manage your security policies in your enterprise network, you need to ensure that the devices managed comply with the list of devices, software, or IOS version supported by CSPM before attempting to enforce any policies.

For all the Cisco PIX Firewalls, Cisco IOS routers, and VPN routers that are on your network, you need to verify that they support the platform or model, and software or IOS version as shown in Table 8.6.

Table 8.6 Devices and Related Software Supported by Cisco Secure Policy Manager

Device Platform or Model	Supported Version
	4.2(4), (5)
PIX Firewall 515	4.4(x)
PIX Firewall 520	5.1(x)
	5.2.1
Cisco 1702 router	
Cisco 2610 router	
Cisco 2620 router	IOS 12.0(5)T, XE
Cisco 3620 router	IOS 12.0(7)T
Cisco 3640 router	IOS 12.1(1)T, E1, XC
Cisco 7120 router	IOS 12.1(2), T, (2) T, E, XH, (3) T, X1
Cisco 7140 router	
Cisco 7204 router	
Cisco 7206 router	

To ensure the appropriate device types are managed, CSPM includes a software version-checking mechanism that would display a warning message indicating a difference in software version. Table 8.7 lists the supported IOS router images and memory requirements to be managed by CSPM.

Table 8.7 Cisco Secure Policy Manager Supported IOS Images and Memory Requirements

Platform	Features	Flash Memory	RAM Memory
c1700	IP/IPX/AT/IBM/FW Plus IPSec 56	8	24
c1700	IP/FW Plus IPSec 56	8	20
c2600	IP/FW/IDS IPSec 56	8	32
c2600	Enterprise/FW/IDS Plus IPSec 56	16	40
c3620	IP/FW/IDS IPSec 56	16	32
c3620	Enterprise/FW/IDS Plus IPSec 56	16	48
c3640	IP/FW/IDS IPSec 56	16	48
c3640	Enterprise/FW/IDS Plus IPSec 56	16	48
c7100	IP/FW/IDS IPSec 56	16	64
c7100	Enterprise/FW/IDS Plus IPSec 56	16	64
c7200	IP/FW/IDS IPSec 56	16	64
c7200	Enterprise/FW/IDS Plus IPSec 56	16	64

When it comes to access control lists, some will need to be deployed on the specific device on the network. To do this, use the Policy Abstract tool to define, store, and manage your security policy abstracts that will be changed to access control lists. Do this before you enforce the policy on devices. The policy abstracts that you create with this tool will support the following configuration settings:

- **Source** IP address range, specific host name, network object, policy domain, or interface defined in the network topology
- **Destination** IP address range, specific host name, network object, policy domain, or interface defined in the network topology
- **Service type** Single or a defined bundle of service types
- **Tunnel** Using specific IPSec tunnel groups
- **Java** Blocking Java

As you can see, you can define only standard IP ACLs and extended IP ACLs. All other access lists have to be configured using the CLI.

Using Cisco Secure Policy Manager

To successfully install the CSPM on your network servers, first identify the type of deployment option you will use, as discussed previously. This will affect the number of servers on which you need to run the CSPM installation, the physical location of the servers on your network, and which option you would choose during the installation based on the server's responsibility on your enterprise network.

Verify that your network devices meet the necessary requirements before you can enforce any of the policies on the selected network section and related devices. In addition, check the minimum hardware requirements needed for the target hosts on which you install the CSPM software.

Next, we will discuss the necessary steps to follow to get CSPM installed, some basic examples for configuring CSPM, and the necessary steps to get CSPM up and working. Given the large amount of configuration and optional tools available in CSPM, it is impossible to describe everything here. Consequently, only a few configurations and examples of the CSPM product will be discussed. Any additional information can be found on the Cisco Web site.

Configuration

When you insert the CSPM software installation CD-ROM into your computer's CD drive, it will autostart the Installation Wizard for CSPM. Select the Install Product option and click Next. This will start the installation; follow the onscreen instructions to complete the installation.

It will ask you for a location of the license file; use the one supplied with the CD-ROM allowing limited use of the software. Use the password **cisco** to continue. If you do have a license file that you purchased from Cisco, you can specify the location and enter the appropriate password.

WARNING

When you are currently running CSPM version 2.0 and would like to upgrade to CSPM version 2.2, you need to run the installation for CSPM version 2.1 first. After the upgrade is completed successfully, you can run the installation for CSPM version 2.2 and upgrade the older version.

The next option selection screen is determined by your deployment option type on your network. You can select Standalone CSPM | Client-Server CSPM, which has two subselections: Policy Server or Policy Client.

You can then select Distributed CSPM with a subselection of one of the following:

- Policy Server
- Policy Proxy-monitor
- Policy Proxy
- Policy Monitor
- Policy Admin

You can find a brief description for your selection in the Installation Option Box. On this window you also specify the installation path for CSPM. The next screen allows you to enter the password for the username that will be used to install and start the relevant services on your server.

Next, you can specify the IP address on your target installation server that will be used to access and configure your CSPM. This IP address is associated with a port number, or service port, used for the connection to the primary policy database. You can export the primary policy database key to a file into a selected path if required. If you export the primary database key, make sure to keep it safe and secure; otherwise, you might compromise the security of your network. This will start the installation of the files needed to run CSPM and configure your preferred settings.

Now that you are ready to start your CSPM, you need to get the access information for the routers and PIX Firewalls that you would like to manage. You will need the usernames and passwords to add the relevant devices to your CSPM application.

NOTE

Cisco Secure VPN Client version 1.1 enables you to secure the command communication channel between the Cisco Secure Policy Manager system and a managed IPSec-enabled Policy Enforcement Point.

CSPM Configuration Example

The examples in this section will give you a general view of the related configuration screens available in CSPM. You can see some of the settings for the topics discussed previously. All the configurations can be used without connecting to your network devices and you need to deploy your new security policy only if you are satisfied with the new configuration.

When you open the CSPM, enter the username and password that you configured during the installation. You have the option to connect either to the local database or to a remote database and the option to change your connection port number.

When you have successfully logged in, you will get the GUI to configure your network security policy. In Figure 8.15 you can see most of the options available in CSPM.

Figure 8.15 Available options and features for Cisco Secure Policy Manager.

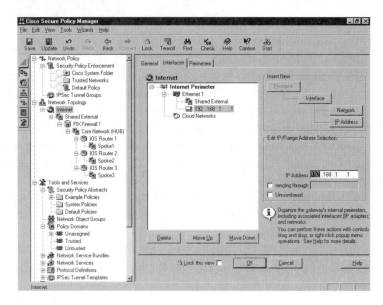

When you need to define a security policy that you would like to use on your network, you can use the Security Policy Abstracts tool. Figure 8.16 shows you a simple configuration to deny mail traffic from a specific desti-nation network.

Figure 8.17 shows the screen for the policy enforcement point used to deploy the policy to the network. The selected device has been installed as a stand-alone server and includes the Policy Database, Distribution, Monitor, and Reports installed options.

Figure 8.18 shows the general configuration settings for an IOS router. From this screen, you can change the router IP address, select the feature set installed on the router, and specify the effective version used. You also have other tabs like Interfaces, Routes, Mappings, and IPSec.

Figure 8.16 Configuration with the Security Policy Abstracts tool.

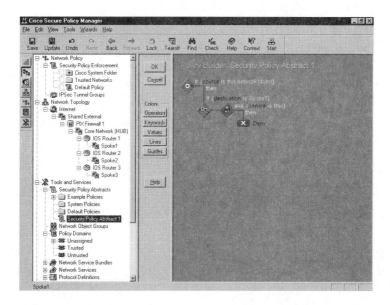

Figure 8.17 Configuration for the policy enforcement point on your network.

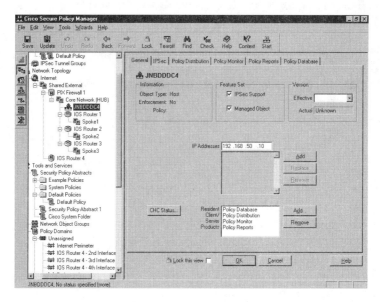

Figure 8.18 General configuration for an IOS router on your network.

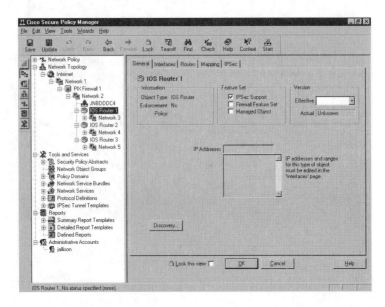

Figure 8.19 shows you the general configuration settings for a PIX Firewall on your network. The General tab has the same settings as the IOS router. The other tabs are Interface, Routes, Mappings, IPSec, Command, Control, and Settings 1.

Figure 8.19 General configuration for a PIX Firewall.

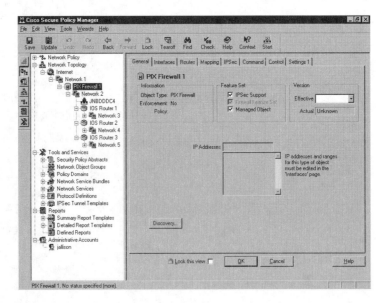

Cisco Secure ACS

To support your network's increasing amount of network devices that are used to control your network users connections to the Internet, your intranet, and specific devices, you can use Cisco Secure Access Control Server (ACS). It installs on Windows NT and runs as a service. Cisco Secure ACS is used for authentication, authorization, and accounting of users accessing your network.

With Cisco Secure ACS for Windows NT, you have a central point of access control and accounting for dial-up access servers and firewalls and the management of access control to switches and routers. You can quickly manage user accounts and groups of users on your entire network, changing their levels of security and network policies. It allows you to configure remote VPN access and dial-up services when you expand your network and services. You can leverage your existing network by using the Windows NT network and the Windows NT user account database.

Cisco Secure ACS Overview

With the installation of Cisco Secure ACS on your network, you can specify who can access the network and what services they are authorized to use. Each user on your network is associated with a profile created in Cisco Secure ACS that contains authentication and authorization information. Authentication information validates the user's identity, and authorization information determines what your users can access on your network. You can use an ACS server on the network at the same time with a dial-up access server, routers, and PIX Firewalls, and it can be configured to use the ACS server. You can use the ACS server for centralized access control for dial-in access and to secure your devices on the entire network from unauthorized access.

NOTE

All the information about Cisco Secure ACS in this chapter will be for version 2.4. Please refer to the Cisco Web site if you need more information about earlier versions and relevant changes made to the latest versions available.

Cisco Secure ACS Benefits

Cisco Secure benefits are defined in three categories: authentication, authorization, and accounting. For these, you can control all information and configurations from a central point connecting from any host on your network with an Internet browser, making the access control to your network easy to manage and always accessible.

Authentication

When a user needs access to your network, he or she needs to be authenticated to verify his or her identity and related information. The authentication method used could be a simple method like cleartext usernames and passwords (which is not very secure) or a more complex and secure method using One-Time-Password (OTP) like CHAP or a token card.

With Cisco Secure ACS, you can use several methods for authentication. We will discuss the most commonly used methods here.

The most popular and simplest method is a username and password that you or the client have to remember. This is the least expensive because no special equipment is required. This is not a very secure authentication mechanism because it could be guessed, captured, or can be told to someone else.

If you would like to reduce the risk of the password being captured on your network, you can use encryption on the password. This is made possible by the TACACS+ and RADIUS protocol used between the Network Access Server (NAS) and the ACS.

The next level of authentication uses OTP, which allows for increased security services. With Cisco Secure, you have support for several types of OTP solutions, like token cards for example.

WARNING

There is an important rule to remember when you configure the authentication and authorization for a user on your network: the people on your network with more authorization should require stronger authentication to access your network.

Authorization

Authorization on your network determines what a specific user is allowed to use. When a user tries to access a network service on a network device or access server, the Cisco Secure ACS will send the user's profile to the device to determine the level of service. This gives different users and groups different levels of services, access times, or security.

You can restrict any user based on the time of day, or restrict to any one or a combination of PPP, ARA, Serial Line Internet Protocol (SLIP), or EXEC service on a device. After the service is selected on the network, you can restrict access to layer 2 and layer 3 protocols. You can also apply access lists to a user or a group of users to deny or allow access to a specific network or service like FTP or HTTP.

Accounting

When you enable accounting on your network you will be able to get reports on what users are doing and for how long. Cisco Secure ACS will write accounting records to a Comma Delimited (CSV) log file daily. This file can be imported into popular spreadsheet and database applications to generate reports, billing, or security audits.

For more information, see Chapter 6, "Cisco Authentication, Authorization, and Accounting Mechanisms."

Installation Requirements for Cisco Secure ACS

Before you install the Cisco Secure software onto your server, you need to check the following requirements for your hardware and software as shown in Table 8.8.

Table 8.8 The Minimum Requirements for Installing Cisco Secure ACS

Hardware Requirements	Software Requirements
200MHz Pentium processor	Windows NT 4.0 or higher with Service Pack 4
64MB of RAM	Microsoft Internet Explorer 4 or Netscape Navigator 4.0x
150MB free disk space	Java and JavaScript enabled
CD-ROM drive	n/a
Color monitor with 256 colors and 800x600 resolution	n/a

Cisco Secure ACS Features

When it comes to the features provided by Cisco Secure ACS, you have an entire range available to use in your enterprise network security access control policy. This is a list of only the most important features that you can use:

- This first important feature provided by Cisco Secure ACS is the user interface, help, and relevant documentation. This easy-to-use interface can be accessed from anywhere on your network with an Internet browser, and includes all-around help and documentation for implementations and operations. This allows you to configure the user's level of authorization and authentication for your network effortlessly from a central point.

- With support for using the Windows NT user database, you can change the domain user account to allow the user access to the network. When you initially install Cisco Secure ACS on your network, you don't have to redo the user database on your ACS server. This also allows you to administer only one database instead of two. You can also use an external authentication server for strong authentication like one-time password (OTP) used by token cards.

- Performance Monitor can be used to gather real-time information proactively for performance viewing or capacity planning. Use the NT performance monitor to check the performance of the Cisco Secure ACS, like transactions per second, or total users logged in. Statistics are displayed for TACACS+ and RADIUS.

- The support for token cards increases the level of security on your network. The user has a token card and a password to enable the token. This process represents one of the most secure authentication methods.

- You can configure the Cisco Secure ACS server to restrict users based on the time of the day. This will increase your security and allow you to set authentication and authorization for a specific part of the network during a specific time of the day using ACLs. This feature supports TACACS+ and RADIUS.

- You should not forget access to the router on your network. You can use Cisco Secure ACS to control who has access to which router and services on your network. Use it to control access to the router from a central point and cut out the need to change authentication on all the routers on your network manually.

For more information on available features, refer to the Cisco Web site.

Placing Cisco Secure ACS in Your Network

When you configure a Cisco Secure ACS server on your network, you can use it to control access to many devices and services on your network. Figure 8.20 shows the placement of the Cisco Secure ACS server on your network.

Figure 8.20 Using Cisco Secure ACS in your network architecture.

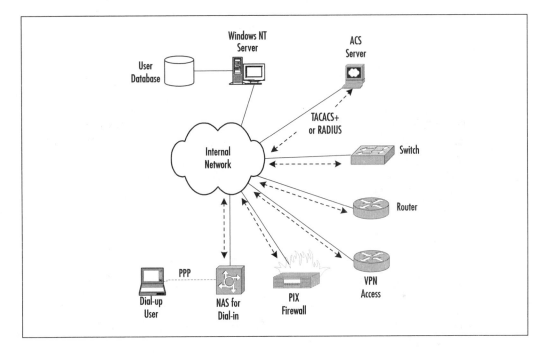

As you can see, you can use Cisco Secure ACS together with dial-up access servers for remote dial-up users, routers, PIX Firewalls, switches, and VPN Access gateways. You can use the Windows NT server to manage the username database for access to network devices and dial-up user access. Centralizing control of your network access simplifies access management and helps you establish a constant security policy.

Between the access client and the Cisco Secure ACS server, use the TACACS+ or the RADIUS protocol to do the authentication and the authorization for the network users. The ACS server will check the user database on the Windows NT server if you configured the users on the NT domain. If you like, you can configure local usernames and passwords on the local ACS server. The user that dials in to your network from remote locations will use a PPP protocol to the NAS, and the NAS will then use TACACS+ or RADIUS to the ACS server.

Cisco Secure ACS Device and Software Support

Cisco Secure ACS supports any device that can be configured with the TACACS+ or RADIUS protocol. All the Cisco devices on your network support these protocols and can use the ACS server for the authentication, authorization, and accounting (AAA) of network users. Some examples of supported devices are:

- Cisco 2509
- Cisco 2511
- Cisco 3620
- Cisco 3640
- AS5300
- AS5800
- PIX Firewall

When you use the TACACS+ and the RADIUS protocols with third-party devices that use the ACS server, please verify that they conform to the following specifications:

- TACACS+ as defined by Cisco Systems in draft 1.77. Check the Cisco Web site for more information on this draft.
- RADIUS as defined in RFC 2865, RFC 2868, RFC 2866, and RFC 2867.

The next list describes which user databases can be used with Cisco Secure ACS for authentication. If you don't have a user database, you can create usernames and passwords in the local Cisco Secure ACS database for authentication; otherwise, you can use an existing database of usernames, passwords, and relevant settings using one the following:

- Windows NT
- Token-card servers including AXENT, CRYPTOCard, and RSA Security
- Novell Directory Services (NDS)
- Directory Services (DS)
- Microsoft Commercial Internet System Lightweight Directory Access Protocol (MCIS LDAP)
- Microsoft Open Database Connectivity (ODBC)

When dial-up users dial into the NAS server on your network, the NAS directs the dial-in user access request to the Cisco Secure ACS for authentication and authorization of privileges using the TACACS+ or RADIUS protocol. If the Cisco Secure user database is not local, it sends the authentication request to the relevant username database for authentication. The success or failure response from the Cisco Secure ACS server is relayed back to the NAS that permits or denies user access to your network. After the user is authenticated on your network, Cisco Secure ACS sends a set of authorization attributes to the NAS and the accounting functions take effect.

Using Cisco Secure ACS

The necessary steps to get your Cisco Secure ACS server up and working will be discussed here. Like all the other products, you need to verify that the server, managed devices, and the necessary software versions meet the installation requirements. This will ensure a successful installation of Cisco Secure ACS on your enterprise network.

Configuration

When you start the installation for Cisco Secure ACS on your server, the first screen (after the acceptance of the agreement) displays a list of four requirements before you attempt to install the software on your server:

- Ensure that a dial-up client can successfully dial in to the NAS.

- The Windows NT server should have IP connectivity to the NAS.

- The NAS requires Cisco IOS release 11.1 or later.

- The Windows NT server should have Microsoft Internet Explorer v4.0 or later or Netscape Navigator v4.04 or later installed.

If you have verified this list, click Next. On the following screen, choose the database to use for your username and password authentication process. Select either the local Cisco Secure ACS database or the Windows NT User Database. If you use either one of the databases, use the option in the User Manager for Domain on the Windows NT server to allow or deny dial-up access to your network.

WARNING

If you are upgrading, be sure to back up your Cisco Secure ACS system files and database and your Windows Registry. If you do experience any problems with the upgrade, you will have a fallback plan and have all the files backed up.

On the next screen for the installation, you need to enter the information used to communicate with the first NAS server on your network. First, select the protocol to use for authenticating the user. Enter the NAS server name and its IP address. The IP address of the Windows NT server will be the local Windows NT server IP address. Next, enter the TACACS+ and the RADIUS key to use between the NAS and the ACS server for security and encryption.

During the installation, you can specify if you would like advanced options to be displayed in the Cisco Secure ACS user interface. These options are:

- **User-level network access restrictions** If selected, it will display the NAS and Dial-up filter sections in the User Setup when unused.

- **Group-level network access restrictions** If selected, it will display the NAS and Dial-up filter section in the Group Setup when unused.

- **Max sessions** If selected, it will display the Max Sessions sections in the User Setup and Group Setup screen if not used.

- **Default time-of-day/day-of-week specification** If selected, it will display the default Time-of-Day/Day-of-Week grid in the Group Setup screen if not in use.

- **Distributed system settings** If selected, it will display the AAA server table and the Distribution table in the Network Configuration screen.

- **Database replication** If selected, it will display the CiscoSecure database replication page in the System Configuration screen.

These selections can also be changed after the installation using the Cisco Secure ACS GUI. On the next options screen, you can enable login monitoring and configure notifications using your SMTP server and account information. It also gives you the option to help configure the NAS on your network.

The last screen will have three options:

- Start the new ACS service

- Start your Internet browser to connect to Cisco Secure ACS

- Open the readme.txt file for more information

After installing the software to your server, you will have a new icon on your desktop to access the Cisco Secure GUI using the Internet browser. If you want to connect to the Cisco Secure ACS server form a different host on your network, enter the server name or IP address in your Internet browser with the port number 2002. Use the following format for your address in the browser: http://servername_ip:2002.

Cisco Secure ACS Configuration Example

After connecting to the Cisco Secure ACS server on your network, you can start with the configurations needed for authentication, authorization, and accounting (AAA).

From the Network Configuration shown in Figure 8.21, you can add the devices on your enterprise that need to use the ACS server for AAA. The ACS server will handle all requests from a NAS1 server, PIX1 Firewall, and a Router1 configured for TACACS+ or RADIUS.

Figure 8.21 Configurations of your network and devices using Cisco Secure ACS.

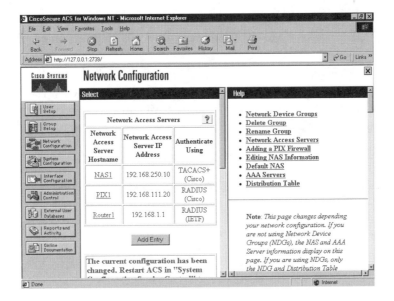

When you have to make changes for the specific device in your network configuration, click on the device name in Cisco Secure ACS. It will open the configuration settings for the selected device as shown in Figure 8.22. Use this screen to change the settings like the authentication protocol used by the device, the IP address, and the key used between the ACS server and the device. Please note that it is not recommended that you use a key that is easy to guess, like the one used in the example.

Figure 8.22 Changing the configuration of a network device in Cisco Secure ACS.

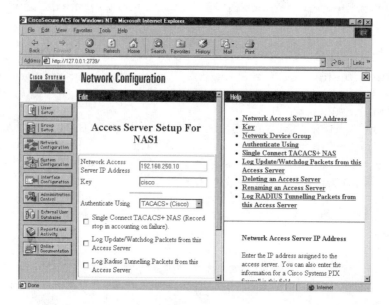

In Figure 8.23, you have the options to add, change, or delete user-names from your local user database in Cisco Secure ACS. You have plenty of additional settings that you can change for each user that needs access to your network resources and services.

Figure 8.23 Changing user information and settings.

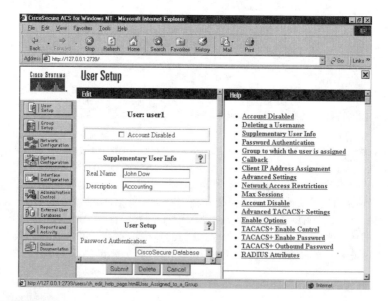

When you are using an alternative database for your username and password information, you can configure the specific database using the External User Database as shown in Figure 8.24. The list of available username databases that you can use is shown; click on the necessary one to change the configuration.

Figure 8.24 Selecting the necessary external user database used for your network access.

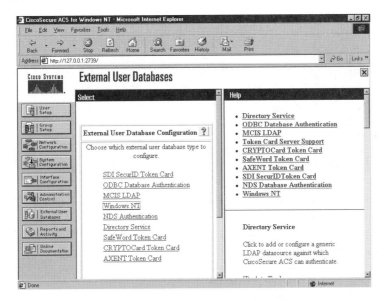

If you need to change the configuration for the protocol used between the access device and the Cisco Secure ACS server, you can use the Interface Configuration button on the left of the screen as displayed in Figure 8.25 to change the TACACS+ settings. As you can see, you can change the services used with TACACS+ on your network and you have more optional, related configurations that you can change.

The screen shown in Figure 8.26 can be used for all your reports and for getting information on the activity on your network. You can export all the reports to a file that can be used in other applications. You also have the option to back up and restore the database used for the reports on your ACS server.

In the example, you will notice that many configuration options are available in Cisco Secure ACS. You can use the excellent help and documentation displayed on the right hand of the GUI for more information about any available configuration options.

Figure 8.25 Changing configuration of TACACS+ on Cisco Secure ACS.

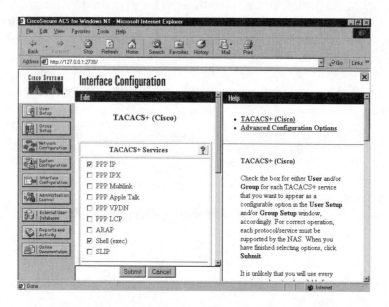

Figure 8.26 Generate reports and examine the activity in Cisco Secure ACS.

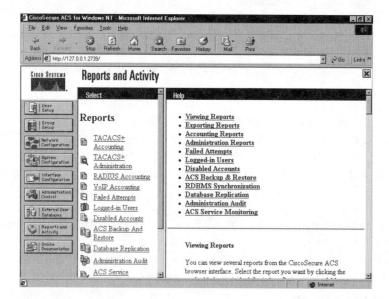

Summary

The products discussed in this chapter can and should be used to manage your network security policy successfully. Each one has advantages, but it's important to use the correct application for your environment.

The PIX Firewall Manager product is included if you purchase a Cisco PIX Firewall, and you should use it when you have a few PIX Firewalls to manage on your network. Make sure to check the requirements for the software installation on your target server and which PIX Firewall version is compatible with the PFM software. Always configure the inside and outside of your firewall with strong security and use the configured DMZ on a different port for access to your Internet services that need to be accessed from the outside network.

After you are confident that you have a strong protection policy for your network against the outside world, you have to ensure that your policy can protect your critical service and information from internal threats. Using the ACL Manager to configure specific access on your entire network will help to perform internal security. Because the Cisco ACL Manager is a plug-in for the Resource Management Essentials in CiscoWorks 2000, you will need to install both before you install the ACL Manager.

Finally, the Cisco Secure Policy Manager is used for larger networks using multiple Cisco products and is useful in defining the security policies for your enterprise network. It allows for the configuration of your PIX Firewalls and the ACLs on your network to control access to specific sections of the network. You have the option to deploy your security policy from one location, or distributed deployment from multiple locations on your network. In addition, you can configure all the VPN tunnels using IPSec and NAT on the boundary of your network to change your private IP address range to communicate with outside networks.

FAQs

Q: Why does the Windows NT system speaker beep constantly after the installation of the PIX Firewall Manager software?

A: If you have installed an application like CiscoWorks 2000 that uses the UDP port 514 for SYSLOG, or the TCP port 8080 used by the default installation of PFM, the Windows NT server will beep to inform you about this conflict. You can stop the relevant services in Windows NT Services to disable the application using the conflicting port.

Q: Why do you get an error message during the installation of PFM that you don't have permission to run the installer?

A: This error occurs when you don't have administrator permission on the local Windows NT computer or when you try to install PFM on a Windows NT domain controller. Check that you have the correct permission to create accounts in the local NT Security Accounts Manager (SAM) required for the installation.

Q: Can you use the ACL Manager to apply change ACLs on your network at a specific time?

A: Yes, you can define all changes required and apply them to the selected devices at a specified time.

Q: When does a device in CiscoWorks become unreachable?

A: This will happen when you have a connection problem between the CiscoWorks 2000 server and the manager device. It could also be the case when you have configured an ACL that denies the server access to the specific device.

Q: Does CSPM integrate with third-party network management applications?

A: No, CSPM has no support for integration with any third-party applications for network management.

Q: Can you use third-party devices with Cisco Secure ACS for access control and to authenticate the usernames and passwords on your network?

A: Yes, you can use any third-party device that supports the standard TACACS+ and RADIUS protocols used by the Cisco Secure ACS server for AAA.

Chapter 9

Security Processes and Managing Cisco Security Fast Track

Solutions in this chapter:

- **What Is a Managing Cisco Security Fast Track?**

- **A Rapid Review of the Important Concepts in Each Chapter**

- **General Security Configuration Recommendations on Cisco**

Introduction

In this chapter, we will present some of the salient issues, products, and processes that make up Cisco security solutions. After we lay the foundation, we can move onto such questions as "What is my organization's security like?" "Do we have a clear security policy?" "If not, what do I do?" These types of security issues must be addressed if we are going to have a proper context in which to evaluate any product in terms of its security features, strengths, and weaknesses.

In order to understand the good, bad, and indifferent issues surrounding Cisco security solutions, you must know what is important to you and your organization. If a certain component of the security model presented here is not supported, or supported well-enough as defined by the user's security plan, then the administrator, manager, or executive should go into the deployment process with this in mind. These are the critical factors that should be understood beforehand to choose the right Cisco security solutions for your business.

What Is a Managing Cisco Security Fast Track?

Do you need a quick and succinct rundown on all IP network security features covered in this book? Just check the subject headings in this chapter and jump to the topic you are interested in. Here we present a high-level view of the subject that will allow you to be familiar with the essential concepts.

The chapter also includes a general security recommendation section that lists useful security advice to help you improve the overall security of your network architecture. It can be used as a quick checklist to help you assess the security of your network.

Introduction to Cisco Network Security

Every network manager aims to achieve the best possible security. However, *perfect* security is still a myth in internetworking. An enterprise must decide on what level of security is required, what assets need to be protected, and what impact the security measures will have on the productivity of the personnel. It is a matter of weighing certain pros and cons and assessing risk management.

One needs to define what assets and information needs to be protected and what level of protection or risk the enterprise is willing to take on those assets. Defining the enterprise security policy should be one of the first steps in implementing good security.

Network Security

System and network security is made up of many pieces. Protecting information against unwanted disclosure, tampering, or loss requires the following security mechanisms:

Availability This ensure that information and services are accessible and functional when needed. The standard approach to achieve availability is by performing regular backups of important data and by introducing redundancy and fault tolerance in important network components.

Integrity Integrity is essential as it assures that the software or information is complete, accurate, and authentic. Data integrity is important for system configuration and for protecting against unauthorized system modification. Network traffic integrity is possible through cryptographic methods.

Confidentiality Confidentiality or secrecy allows the owner of some information to specify who should be allowed to view that information. Confidentiality can be applied to actual files or to network traffic. This process uses some encryption mechanisms.

Another important aspect of system and network security is authentication, authorization and accounting. These provide the framework to configure access control.

Authentication Authentication is the process of verifying the identity of an entity. This process is usually done by exchanging information to prove one's identity. This information can take many forms including password, token, and a one-time password among others.

Authorization Authorization is the process of granting permission to an entity to access a system resource. For example, network access can be restricted based on the identity of a client.

Accounting Accounting enables the network manager to keep track of the services and resources that are used by the users. The accounting process is able to collect such information as the connection time, identity, and billing information.

Network Communications in TCP/IP

In order to understand the different security mechanisms available in IP network security, a good understanding of TCP/IP is needed.

A TCP connection is uniquely identified by a connection "quadruplet" consisting of a source IP address, a source port number, a destination IP address, and a destination IP port. This quadruplet is also used to uniquely identify a UDP session between two nodes, though UDP is a connectionless protocol

Conversely, TCP is a connection-oriented protocol. By looking at the packets travelling on the wire, it is possible to determine who is initiating the connection, when the connection is established, and when the connection is being closed. These connection controls use special flags within the TCP header. For example, when a connection is established, the SYN flag bit is on in the first exchanges between the two hosts. When a TCP packet is part of an existing connection, the ACK flag bit is on. This type of information is used heavily in IP traffic filtering.

Because UDP is a connectionless protocol, it is not possible to determine if that packet is part of a connection or if it is the first packet sent to initiate a new session just by looking at one packet on the network.

Security in TCP/IP

Security can be applied to virtually any layer in the ISO model (data link, network link, transport link, application, and so on). To understand the different security protocols that are available today, it is essential to understand how applicable each is in a given situation and at which layer the security is applied.

For example, a commonly used security protocol is SSL in HTTP. SSL provides authentication, integrity, and confidentiality mechanisms for TCP based protocols.

Although SSL is widely available, it is not well-suited to provide secure communication between sites when a number of diverse protocols are used (FTP, SMTP, database synchronization and replication, and directory access).

IPSec offers strong security that can be applied on any (unicast) IP traffic without requiring any changes to the applications. IPSec is a security framework well-suited to use in building Virtual Private Networks (VPNs). Table 9.1 illustrates some security protocol examples that can be used on the various ISO layers.

These topics are covered in more detail in Chapter 1, "Introduction to IP Network Security."

Table 9.1 Security Protocols on ISO Layers

ISO Layer	Security Protocol Example	Features
application	OpenPGP, S/MIME	▪ Provides security for email. ▪ Application specific: must be integrated in the application. ▪ Security is applied to the data. The data stays protected up to the recipient.
transport (TCP)	SSL, TLS	▪ Provides security to TCP/IP application (HTTP, POP, SMTP, and so on). ▪ Security is applied on the traffic, during the transport. ▪ Both client and server software must support SSL or TLS.
network (IP)	IPSec	▪ It can provide security to any (unicast) IP traffic. ▪ Security is applied on the traffic during the transport. ▪ No change to applications is required.

Cisco products offers a wide range of security solutions in the Cisco Secure product line, as shown in Table 9.2.

Table 9.2 The Cisco Secure Product Line and Solutions

Product	What Function It Serves	Chapter Coverage
Cisco Secure PIX Firewall	Access control and policy enforcement	Chapters 3 and 4
Cisco Secure Integrated Software	Access control and policy enforcement	Chapter 2
Cisco Secure Integrated VPN Software	IPSec	Chapter 5
Cisco Secure VPN Client	IPSec	Chapter 5
Cisco Secure Scanner	Vulnerability scanner	Chapter 7
Cisco Secure Intrusion Detection System	Intrusion Detection	Chapter 7

Continued

Table 9.2 Continued

Product	What Function It Serves	Chapter Coverage
Cisco Secure Policy Manager	Security Management	Chapter 8
Cisco Secure Access Control Manager	Security server for authentication, authorization and accounting	Chapter 6

Traffic Filtering on the Cisco IOS

Access control is often one of the first security features deployed on an IP network. That control can be enforced in many places in a network; most often, this is applied at the network boundary such as on a router or firewall.

Traffic filtering is used to implement access control on traffic flowing in and out of a router or firewall. This requires a good understanding of TCP/IP and a good security policy.

Cisco routers offer different types of access lists, from the simplest standard access list, where only the source address is used to make a filtering decision, to the more extensive control based access control, where the transport layer and the application data is examined by the router. Depending on the security policy that needs to be implemented and the application protocols that will be used on the network, the network manager will be able to decide which type of access list is more appropriate.

Access Lists

An access list consists of a list of rules or statements that are sequentially tested against incoming or outgoing IP packets. Those rules can test for specific information inside an IP packet, such as the IP addresses or port numbers.

Once defined, an access list is applied to an interface (Ethernet, serial, ATM, and so on) where it will inspect packets going in or out of that interface.

Standard and Extended Access Lists

These are the simplest access lists that can be installed, and they are often sufficient for implementing many security policies.

Standard access lists can be used to filter packets based on the source IP address in the packet. For example, one could define a standard access list that would deny all incoming traffic on the router except if the traffic is from a specific IP address (source). The source address specified in the standard access list can be configured to represent a host or a network.

An extended access list allows better control when defining filtering rules: one can create a filtering rule based on the source address, destination address, type of protocol (for example, TCP or UDP), source and destination port numbers, and other various fields in the IP and TCP headers. A commonly used parameter is **established** which will match all TCP packets that have the ACK or RST flag bit set. The ACK flag indicates that the packet is part of an open TCP session.

The drawback of standard and extended access lists is that they do not understand the state of a connection in that every packet received is checked individually; it does not consider whether it is part of an existing connection between two hosts.

To allow TCP traffic, this means that one must configure the access list to allow return connections through the router.

To allow UDP traffic, an extended access list must simply allow UDP traffic through without any way to restrict from which direction the session initialization is permitted.

Although this filtering technique is suitable in many cases, it does not protect against forged TCP packets (commonly used to probe networks). It also does not offer any facility to effectively filter UDP sessions nor protocols that embed IP addresses within the protocol (RPC, SQL*Net, H.323, and so on) nor FTP in non-passive mode.

Reflexive Access Lists

Using extended access lists, one can install an access list that will permit allowed traffic through the router, but an access list is also required to allow the return traffic through as well. This can be a problem since it leaves permanent openings in the access lists.

This is where reflexive lists can be of help. Using reflexive access lists, one can install an access list that will permit allowed traffic through the router. Once traffic is initiated and allowed through by the access list, a reflexive list will automatically be installed in the router that will allow the return traffic through.

Reflexive access lists automatically create and delete temporary access list entries that will allow traffic associated with an IP session. This offers a stronger control over what traffic is allowed into a network.

Reflexive access lists are a feature added to an extended access list and can only be defined using extended named IP access lists.

One shortcoming of reflexive access lists, similar to extended access lists, is that it cannot be used with protocols that embed IP addresses within the protocol (RPC, SQL*Net, H.323, and so on) or FTP in non-passive mode.

Context-based Access Control

Compared to the other types of access lists, Context-based Access Control (CBAC) goes one step further and examines the application-layer protocol information in order to learn the state of the connection. This information is used to provide greater control over what traffic should be allowed or denied.

By examining the application-layer protocol, CBAC can effectively filter traffic from protocols like RPC, SQL*Net, H.323 and FTP. However, since every application protocol is different, CBAC must explicitly support that protocol. CBAC also offers protection against certain types of network attacks.

These topics are covered in more detail in Chapter 2, "Traffic Filtering on Cisco IOS."

Network Address Translation (NAT)

The Internet is comprised of an ever-growing number of hosts. Each of those hosts has a unique and globally routable IP address. This is the "ideal" Internet. However, in real-world application, IPv4 addresses have become a scarce resource. The majority of today's IPv4 network deployments require more addresses than are made available by ISPs. ISPs are being monitored by Regional Internet Registries which in turn are responsible for IP address allocation throughout the world.

With the ongoing IPv6 deployment on the Internet, this issue will eventually become a thing of the past.

Private Addresses

To get around the address shortage, a site can use addresses from a private space for its internal IP networks. Private addresses are part of a reserved network range defined in the document RFC1918 "Address Allocation for Private Internets" found at the following link:

www.normos.org/ietf/rfc/rfc1918.txt

A site using private addresses can allocate as many IP networks as required, and normal IP connectivity between those internal networks can be achieved without any special configuration. This site will have a private addressing realm, in that all nodes within that site will have full IP connectivity, but the connectivity is restricted to that site.

The Internet is part of the public addressing realm. In that respect, hosts within a site using private IP addresses cannot communicate directly with hosts on the Internet since addresses from the site are not part of the valid IP addresses on the Internet. Thus, they are non-routable.

Network Address Translation

Network Address Translation (NAT) is a mechanism that allow a site using a private addressing realm to achieve connectivity with another realm, like the Internet. (The Internet is part of the public addressing realm.) NAT is usually implemented in a router or a firewall at the boundary of the two networks or realms.

When a packet leaves the internal network, the NAT device will modify the source address of the packet such that the new source address is a valid address in the network it is forwarded on. A packet flowing in the other direction, towards the internal network, will be modified by the NAT device, this time by changing the destination address. Depending on the type of network address translation, the source and destination port numbers can be modified.

We can categorize NAT functions into static NAT and dynamic NAT. In static NAT, there is a pre-determined, one-to-one mapping between an internal IP address and an outside IP address. In dynamic NAT, the IP address mapping is done on demand (dynamically) and there can be a one-to-many mapping on the IP address.

Cisco IOS and PIX can be configured to offer these types of NAT functions.

Static NAT

In this type of configuration, an internal host can be reached externally from its external IP address.

Whenever an internal host initiates a communication with an external host, the NAT device allocates an external IP address for that host. The NAT is preconfigured with the address translation table such that an internal host will always be assigned the same external IP address. The NAT modifies the source address for the outgoing packets and the destination address for the incoming packets.

Since there is a fixed one-to-one mapping between internal addresses and external addresses, this type of NAT configuration requires one external IP address for each internal host that require static NAT.

Static NAT can be a useful tool when renumbering the IP address of servers. A static NAT can be configured so that during a transition, a server can be reached from its new and deprecated IP address.

Traditional or Outbound NAT

Whenever an internal host initiates a communication with an external host, the NAT device allocates an external IP address for that host. The NAT modifies the source address for the outgoing packets and the destination address for the incoming packets.

This type of NAT has a limit on the number of internal hosts that can simultaneously access the external networks. For example, if 10 external (public) address are available and configured in the NAT, there will be a limit of 10 internal hosts that will be able to simultaneously communicate with the external (public) network.

Network Address Port Translation (NAPT or PAT)

Network Address Port Translation (NAPT) is referred to as Port Address Translation (PAT) in Cisco documentation. In this configuration, a number of internal hosts can use the same external IP address. Whenever an internal host initiates a communication with an external host, the NAPT device modifies the source address and source port number for the outgoing packets. In doing so, the outgoing communications can be multiplexed through the same external source IP address.

By allocating multiple internal hosts to the same external IP address, this type of NAT makes an efficient use of external IP address.

Table 9.3 illustrates the various types of NAT and some of their features.

Table 9.3 Types of NAT and Features

NAT Types	Address mapping	Public to private address mapping	Number of address public required
Static NAT	Static	One-to-one	One public IP address per host
Traditional NAT	Dynamic	One-to-one	One public IP address per host simultaneously accessing the external network(s)
NAPT	Dynamic	One-to-many	One public IP address per 64,000 simultaneous session

Considerations

There are advantages and drawbacks to consider when implementing. NAT is a stateful device that maintains the state of every connection that requires address translation. This property can be a weakness since the NAT device becomes a single point of failure.

Some application protocols that embed IP addresses inside the application data will not work with NAT, unless that protocol is specifically supported by the NAT.

NAT often increases the complexity of network debugging tasks, such as logging records that may contain translated addresses.

Also, access control based on the source IP address breaks when a NAT is used. This is especially true when NAPT is used because many hosts will share the same IP source address assigned by the NAPT device. Note also that IPSec cannot be used through NAT.

These topics are covered in more detail in Chapter 3, "Network Address Translation (NAT)."

Cisco PIX Firewall

A firewall is a device that is used to create a security perimeter using programmed security rules. The security provided by the firewall will directly depend on having a good security policy, and keeping the system and the policy up-to-date.

A firewall allows the security manager to enforce a network security policy at a single point in the network. A properly configured firewall can do a good job at protecting servers and limiting your network exposure.

Many security features that the PIX offers are also available in a Cisco router through context based access control (CBAC). Indeed, it is difficult to differentiate the two. PIX is a dedicated hardware device built to provide security, so the PIX will usually support high network loads better.

Table 9.4 lists some of the main features of Cisco PIX.

Table 9.4 Cisco PIX features

Feature	Description
Packet filtering	Controls which systems can establish network connections.
Cut-through proxies	User-based authentication for inbound or outbound connections.
Stateful filtering	Keeps the state of every connection. Every inbound packet is checked connection state information and security rules to ensure they are valid and allowed.
Network Address Translation	Supports NAT and NAPT (PAT).
IPSec	Virtual Private Network.
Flood Defender	Protection against SYN flood attacks.

Continued

Table 9.4 Continued

Feature	Description
Flood Guard	Protection against denial of service attacks.
IP Frag Guard	Protection against IP fragmentation attacks.
DNS Guard	DNS proxy
FTP and URL logging	Log FTP and HTTP (URL) sessions of inbound and outbound connections.
Mail Guard	Protects internal mail server from attacks.
ActiveX Blocking	Stops ActiveX controls downloads.
Java Filtering	Stops Java applets downloads.
URL Filtering	Supports third party products to do URL filtering (HTTP).
AAA	Supports AAA services through RADIUS or TACACS+.

Security Policy Configuration

This is an important part of designing the security architecture. Defining the security perimeters (external networks, demilitarized zone (DMZ) for public servers, internal networks) and the assets to protect them will define where the firewall should be located and what security policies should be applied. Creating a new perimeter where the public servers are located allows for tighter control over the traffic that will be allowed into the internal network.

Securing and Maintaining the PIX

Securing the PIX is a task that should not be neglected. This task should include:

- Restricting remote access to the PIX to the management hosts only
- Activating idle session timeouts
- Deactivating all unused services and unused features
- Making sure the PIX is physically secured
- Activating system logging to an external syslog server

These topics are covered in more detail in Chapter 4, "Cisco PIX Firewall."

Virtual Private Networks (VPNs)

A VPN is a network deployed on a shared infrastructure that employs the same security, management, and throughput policies applied in a private network. They can take many different forms including peer, overlay, transport and application layer, and link layer VPNs. Each can be utilized and implemented in a network infrastructure in many different ways; Chapter 5 covers this in greater detail, but we will highlight some of the keys points here.

L2TP

Layer 2 Transport Protocol (L2TP) is an Internet Engineering Task Force (IETF) standard that combines the best features of two existing tunnelling protocols: Cisco's Layer 2 Forwarding (L2F) protocol and Microsoft's Point-to-Point Tunnelling Protocol (PPTP). L2TP has replaced Cisco's own proprietary forwarding (L2F) protocol.

L2TP is a key building block for VPN's in the dial access space. Using L2TP, an ISP can create a virtual tunnel between the remote user and the user's corporate network. From a remote user's point of view, the modem dials to the local ISP infrastructure, but the PPP connection is established to the corporate network.

L2TP doesn't provide for any security. In fact, L2TP uses IPSec for that function.

IPSec

IPsec is a framework of open security protocols developed at the IETF and has become the industry standard security protocol for IP networks. An IPSec-enabled node offers many security features such as:

- The authentication of the peer
- The confidentiality of the communication
- The integrity of the traffic with protection against replay attacks

IPSec can provide strong security to any IP traffic. When IPSec is integrated in the corporate router or firewall, the corporation can use IPSec to secure traffic between distant sites over a public network. When IPSec is integrated in hosts, such as in Windows 2000, IPSec can be used to allow the remote host to connect to the corporation using strong security to protect the IP traffic.

The benefits of IPSec are clear: the security features are transparent and are immediately available to all IP applications. If IPSec is available, there is no need to upgrade or recompile any application. IPSec is being implemented by many vendors and recent operating systems such as Windows 2000, Solaris 8, Unix *BSD (OpenBSD and FreeBSD), and others are bundled with IPSec. Futhermore, the IPv6 standard specification mandates that IPSec be built-in the new IP protocol

IPSec can be incrementally deployed in a network. It is not necessary to enable or install IPSec on every host and router in a network. IPSec traffic can flow through non-IPsec routers.

IPsec is supported on most Cisco routers running Cisco Secure Integrated VPN Software and on Cisco PIX. Also, Cisco Secure VPN is an IPSec client that is compatible with Windows 9x and Windows NT 4.0.

Table 9.5 outlines some useful IPSec terms.

Table 9.5 IPSec Terms and Definitions

Term	Definitions
IPsec tunnel mode	This encapsulates the entire IP packet within a new IP packet. The entire original packet is protected by IPsec, and is usually used with an IPSec gateway or router
IPsec transport mode	This provides an end-to-end IPSec communication between two peers. IPSec protects the upper-layer protocols in the packet.
Authentication Header (AH)	This is an IPSec security protocol that provides packet authentication.
Encapsulating Security Payload (ESP)	This is an IPSec security protocol that provides data encryption and data authentication.
Security Association (SA)	This is a one-way relationship between a sender and a receiver. This relationship defines the security services that will be applied to the traffic.
Security Policy Database (SPD)	This defines the traffic that will use IPsec security services. In Cisco, this is defined using access lists.
Internet Key Exchange (IKE)	This is the key management protocol used by IPSec to negotiate the security associations (SA).

Network Troubleshooting

One of the drawbacks of network layer encryption is that it does complicate network troubleshooting and debugging.

Intrusion detection, such as that offered by the Cisco Secure Intrusion Detection System (IDS) works by inspecting packet data information to detect known attack signatures. If IPSec is used to protect the IP traffic (through ESP), the packet becomes opaque to the sensor and detection can no longer function.

Interoperability with Firewalls and Network Address Translation Devices

IPSec cannot be used between two peers if a NAT device is in the path of the traffic. The NAT device essentially changes the source IP address and needs to recompute the checksum inside the packet. These changes in the packet will be detected by the integrity verification in IPSec, and the packet will be rejected.

If NAT is used, one must use IPSec in tunnel mode, and the NAT device has to be the IPSec peer. This implies that the NAT device must support IPSec.

If a firewall or packet filtering router is used in the network and if IPSec traffic is to be allowed on that network, one must configure the firewall or router to allow IPSec traffic through. The traffic characteristics of IPSec are shown in Table 9.6.

These topics are covered in more detail in Chapter 5, "Virtual Private Networks."

Table 9.6 IPSec Traffic Characteristics

Protocol Name	Protocol Type	Protocol Number
ESP	IP	50
AH	IP	51
IKE	UDP	500

Cisco Authentication, Authorization and Accounting Mechanisms

Cleartext passwords are bad—period. AAA security services on Cisco give you the means to centralize and strenghten the AAA mechanisms used throughout your site.

These security features can be used for login access on a Cisco device (router or firewall), PPP access, or even network access. Authentication, authorization, and accounting provide the required framework to configure access control.

AAA is the recommended access control mechanism on Cisco devices. An example of access control is the login authentication on a Cisco router where one configures a password for console access (serial port) or through telnet access on the router (VTY line). Without AAA, these configurations and passwords are stored locally on each and every router. This task quickly becomes unmanagable when the number of routers and other Cisco devices in use is significant. This is where AAA security services on Cisco can help.

When AAA is activated on a Cisco device, it can function as a client to a centralized security server. The security server protocols supported on Cisco are RADIUS, TACACS+ and Kerberos. Using a centralized security server for AAA brings many benefits, such as a centralized database that contains information for:

- User accounts for PPP, router access, firewall access, and so on.
- User authorization information
- User activities (accounting)

Having a centralized security server also allows the network manager to administer all the user accounts and accounting information from a single database. This makes user account management scalable. Table 9.7 outlines the various security server protocols and the AAA functions they perform.

Table 9.7 Security Server Protocol Comparison

Protocol	Authentication	Authorization	Accounting
RADIUS	yes	yes	yes
TACACS+	yes	yes	yes
Kerberos	yes	yes	no

Authentication

Authentication is the process of verifying the identity of an entity, most often, a user. This process is usually done by exchanging information to prove one's identity. This information can take many forms: a password, a one-time password or anther form of challenge/response.

When AAA security services are activated, a user's authentication information is stored on a security server. The router or NAS that need to authenticate the user will communicate with the security server to get that information, and the security server will tell the router or NAS if the user has successfully authenticated.

The authentication part of the AAA security services can be used to authenticate console and login access (routers, NAS, firewall), PPP access, and others.

The security servers RADIUS, TACACS+ or Kerberos can be used to provide authentication services.

Authorization

Authorization is the process of giving permission to an entity to access a system resource. For example, a PPP account network access can be restricted based on the authorization profile of that client, or authorization can define a user's privilege level to a router.

When AAA security services are activated, a user's authorization information is stored on a security server. Authentication must also be defined as authorization relies on it.

Cisco IOS supports the following types of authorization:

- **Exec** This type applies to the attributes associated with a user EXEC terminal session.

- **Command** This type applies to EXEC mode commands a user issues. Command authorization attempts to authorize for all EXEC mode commands, including global configuration commands associated with a specific privilege level.

- **Network** This type applies to network connection such as PPP, SLIP or ARAP.

The security servers RADIUS, TACACS+, or Kerberos can be used to provide authorization services.

Accounting

Accounting enables the network manager to keep track of the services and resources that are accessed and used by the users. The accounting process collects information such as the connection time, identity, billing information.

When AAA security services are activated, the accounting information can be sent by the router or NAS to a RADIUS or TACACS+ security server. The source of the accounting information can come from:

- PPP connections, terminal sessions on a router or NAS (**EXEC**).

- User sessions on a router or NAS where all commands are logged (**command**).

- Outgoing network sessions from the router or NAS (**connection**).

- Any system generated events (**system**).

These topics are covered in more detail in Chapter 6, "Cisco Authentication, Authorization, and Accounting Mechanisms."

Intrusion Detection

Intrusion Detection is an important component of the overall network security infrastructure. Intrusion detection can be done on a host level or at the network level by listening in on the network and looking for signature attacks in the IP packets traveling on the wire.

Cisco offers different tools to manager and implement intrusion detection:

- Cisco Secure Scanner (NetSonar), a network vulnerability scanner.

- Cisco Secure Intrusion Detection System (NetRanger), a complete network intrusion detection system.

- Cisco Secure Integrated Software, an network intrusion detection system integrated in Cisco IOS.

What Is Intrusion Detection?

Intrusion detection is the ongoing process of searching for security violations on your network; this includes proactive and reactive detection of vulnerabilities, analysis, and corresponding responses.

Intrusion detection can be host-based or network-based. For host-based intrusion detection systems, the intrusion detection takes place on individual hosts. This offers good protection for the host. For network-based intrusion detection systems, the intrusion detection is done on the network where a device monitors all the network traffic and checks for known attack signatures.

Both host-based and network-based intrusion detection come with advantages and disadvantages. Using both is best whenever possible, but when the network is composed of a large number of different types of hosts and devices, network-based intrusion detection may be the most practical solution.

Cisco Secure Scanner (NetSonar)

Cisco Secure Scanner is a network vulnerability scanner. It is important to proactively scan for weaknesses in the network before they are exploited. Cisco Secure Scanner can actively probe the devices used on your network. This type of tool is invaluable in maintaining a high level of security in a network.

Using your session configuration, you can initiate an automatic discovery of host devices (all devices running a TCP/IP stack) and services on your network. TCP/UDP port interrogation and SNMP queries are used to gather information which is compiled into a database. The latter can be used to develop and verify security policies as well as find unexpected machines and services on your network.

Cisco Secure Scanner contains a database of vulnerabilities that must be updated from time to time. Regular updates to the vulnerability scanner are easy to download and install directly from the Cisco Website. Cisco employs a team called the Cisco Countermeasure Research Team (C-CRT) who work to ensure that Secure Scanner is up-to-date.

Cisco Secure NetRanger

NetRanger is a network based intrusion detection system that can monitor your network and perform dynamic intrusion detection to respond to intrusions in real-time.

NetRanger uses sensors to capture traffic and can monitor syslog traffic from a Cisco router to detect network intrusions. If an attack or security event is detected, NetRanger can respond by generating alarms, logging the event, resetting TCP connections, or blocking the attack by instructing a router to deny the attack traffic through an access control list.

NetRanger uses a security database for signature analysis which provides information about exploits as well as countermeasures. Updates to the security database are made available through Cisco's Website. Custom attack signatures can also be defined by the security manager.

NetRanger is made up of three main components:

The Sensor This is a specialized device that uses a rule-based inference engine to process large volumes of traffic in order to identify security issues in real-time. The Sensor is either a ready-made appliance that is purchased from Cisco, or it can be a software based one installed on an x86 or SPARC Solaris 2.5.1/2.6 station.

The Director This is a GUI software solution used to "direct" or manage NetRanger from a HP Openview platform; it is installed on a HP UX or Solaris workstation.

The Post Office This is a messaging facility between Directors and Sensors that uses a proprietary UDP transport protocol for communication.

Cisco Secure Intrusion Detection Software

Cisco Secure Intrusion Detection Software is available on Cisco routers. It allows a router to act as a sensor checking for intrusions in a similar fashion to a NetRanger Sensor device. Any traffic that passes through the router can be scrutinized for intrusions. Cisco Secure IDS contains attack signatures to protect against 59 different types of network intrusions and attacks. It is possible to disable checking for individual signatures through modification of the router **config** in order to avoid false positives. Contrary to NetRanger, it is not possible to modify or add new signatures to the existing set.

The router configured with Cisco Secure IDS can signal a detected intrusion in a number of different ways:

- By sending an alarm to a syslog server
- By sending an alarm to a NetRanger Sensor
- By dropping the attack traffic
- By terminating the attack traffic by reseting the connection

Cisco Secure IDS cannot protect against attacks originating from within the protected network. It only detects and protects against attacks that travel through the router.

These topics are covered in more detail in Chapter 7, "Intrusion Detection."

Network Security Management

As a network grows, security management can quickly become a daunting task. In order to be able to perform a good job, the network security manager must be able to constantly get a clear view of the network security policies that are enforced on the network. Also, whenever there is a policy change that needs to be applied across the network, one must be certain that everything is applied consistently.

Without a centralized security management software, this is a difficult task when there number of security enforcement points (firewalls, routers, and NAS).

Table 9.8 outlines some of the security management software available from Cisco.

Table 9.8 Cisco Security Management Software

Cisco Security Management Software	What It Manages
Cisco PIX Firewall Manager	PIX firewall
CiscoWorks 2000 ACL Manager	Access control lists in routers
Cisco Secure Security Manager	PIX, VPN, access control lists
Cisco Secure Access Control Manager	AAA

Cisco PIX Firewall Manager

PIX Firewall Manager (PFM) can be used to centralize administration of the PIX firewalls on a network by providing a GUI to manage the security rules on the PIX. PFM also supports a syslog server that can be used to centralize the logging information generated by all PIX firewalls. Alarms can be configured in PFM based on the logs generated from the PIX firewall

PIX Firewall Manager can support up to 10 PIX firewalls.

CiscoWorks 2000 ACL Manager

CiscoWorks 2000 ACL Manager can be used to view, add, or change all the access control lists on multiple Cisco devices that are part of your network. A Web interface is used to manage the access control list from a central point.

The main benefits of ACL Manager are as follows:

- Structure Access Control Lists Security Policy through the use of templates
- Faster deployment time of access control lists
- Ensures consistency in ACL definition
- Keeps track of changes in ACL definitions
- Faster error recovery/troubleshooting structured filter policy

The ACL Manager supports most Cisco devices running IOS. You can manage devices like router, access servers, switches and hubs. The IOS version on the managed devices has to be release 10.3 or higher to support the ACL Manager.

ACL Manager version 1.1 can view all the types of access list on the device, but you can only manage standard and extended IP access control lists and other non-IP access lists

ACL Manager is supported on Windows NT and Solaris.

Cisco Secure Policy Manager

Cisco Secure Policy Manager (CSPM) can be used to define, distribute, enforce, and audit network security policies from a central location. CSPM can be used to configure PIX firewalls, Cisco routers, and other devices supporting IOS. CSPM also supports the configuration of NAT- and IPSec-based Virtual Private Networks (VPNs).

In a large enterprise network, CSPM's GUI is used for policy administration and can be used to distribute the network security policy to different locations across your network.

Some of the features included in the Cisco Secure Security Manager (CSPM) product have the same intent as the PIX Firewall Manager and the ACL Manager. The difference is that CSPM offers a centralized management platform for different devices including PIX firewall and routers, and CSPM includes more functionality for managing your enterprise network security policy.

Some benefits of using CSPM include:

- It enables you to meet large-scale security policy requirements and network growth. It provides the capability to manage up to several hundred PIX Firewall and VPN routers on your network.

- The built-in auditing and reporting provides up-to-date information on network and system events. It allows you to configure notifications according to your needs.

- It allows you to define network-wide security policies. You can accurately define your security policies for different devices on your network and can reduce the time needed to deploy the security configurations.

- You can either use a centralized standalone policy management environment, or you can use a distributed architecture policy management environment.

- You can configure and test your security policies without connecting to your live network. You can do your configurations offline and verify that your security policies are working correctly then deploy the policy to your live network.

Cisco Secure Policy Manager version 2.2 is supported on Windows NT.

Cisco Secure Access Control Manager

Cisco Secure ACS provides a central point of access control and accounting for dial-up access servers and firewalls, as well as a central point for managing access control to switches and routers. Using this, you can manage user accounts as well as groups of users. It also allows you to configure remote VPN access and dial-up services when you expand your network and services.

Cisco Secure ACS acts as a security server for authentication, authorization and accounting security services. The access protocol used between the Cisco Secure ACS and the client (PIX firewall, router or NAS) can be either TACACS+ or RADIUS.

Some of the functionalities of Cisco Secure ACS are as follows:

- The easy to use interface can be accessed from the network with an Internet browser and includes on-line help and documentation.

- It supports Windows NT user databases and external authentication databases to provide strong authentication schemes such as token cards.

- Performance Monitor can be used to proactively gather real-time information for performance viewing or capacity planning.

General Security Configuration Recommendations on Cisco

Throughout this book, many security products are introduced and configurations presented to secure your network. An important issue that needs to be addressed is the security of the infrastructure itself. For example, if your border router connected to the Internet protects your internal network using access lists but is also running an HTTP server open to the public, your security is compromised.

The default configuration of many operating systems, including the Cisco IOS, can leave the system exposed to many security risks.

We will cover some general security recommendations to limit the exposure of your security infrastructure.

Remote Login and Passwords

Operating systems and software packages are often configured with simple default passwords. These passwords are the first thing that should be changed.

Remember that using telnet to manage routers means that everything that is typed during a session is sent in cleartext. Don't do this over a public network! One should consider using SSH, a secure remote terminal that allows encrypted connections to the router. As of IOS version 12.x, SSH is available on high-end routers only (7200, 7500 and 12000). Kerberos can also be used to provide an encrypted telnet session for remote management. Another option is to use Telnet over IPSec. IPSec is supported on most platforms.

Activate **service password-encryption** in your router configuration. This will encrypt all passwords in the configuration file. Note, however, that this is a weak encryption and anyone can decrypt the passwords if they get ahold of your configuration. Keep you configuration backup in a secure place.

Use **enable secret** to protect the **enable** password, as this provides a much stronger encryption. Unfortunately, this encryption method is not available for other passwords.

Don't forget to add passwords to the console port (serial) and VTY ports (telnet). Activate the **autologout** timer on all access ports (console, VTY) and log all access to an external syslog server.

Table 9.9 lists some of the commands you should implement.

Table 9.9 Useful Security Commands

Command	Function
service password-encryption	Enable password encryption in configuration file
access-list 2 permit 192.168.31.0 0.0.0.255 log	Allow connection from 192.168.31.0 network
access-list 2 deny all log	Deny all other sources and log the failed attempt
line vty 0 4	Configure VTY 0 through 4
access-class 2 in	Apply the access list
exec-timeout 5 0	Disconnect after 5 minutes of inactivity
password 7 XXXXXXXXXXXXXX	Configure a password (encrypted)

If you are using an AAA security server, configure your routers to use that facility for login and console access.

Another important factor that is often overlooked is the default password configuration of software. A great deal of software (including operating systems), comes with a common, pre-configured default username and password. While this is convenient for the initial installation of the system, users and administrators often forget to change the default passwords before putting the system in production.

Needless to say, this has a serious security implications, and you should be careful to change all initial passwords, and preferably the usernames as well, whenever possible.

Disable Unused Network Services

The default configuration of many operating systems, including the Cisco IOS, leaves many network services activated. As a rule of thumb, a server, router, firewall, or any devices that is publicly visible should contain the minimum number of network services. The reason is simple: any software can potentially contains bug that can be exploited for attacks. If the software is not used or activated, chances are that the attack will not succeed.

If a service is enabled on a server, router, or firewall, it should always be protected against network attacks or misuse. This protection is accomplished by installing access lists to prevent traffic from unauthorized sources from ever reaching the service, as well as by configuring the service to require authentication.

A fairly recent example of this was the HTTP server vulnerability found in Cisco routers. An HTTP server was introduced in the Cisco IOS to allow router and switch management using a Web browser. If the HTTP service is running, anyone can remotely create a denial-of-service attack against the router or switch. You can find more information on this at the following link: www.cisco.com/warp/customer/707/ioshttpserver-pub.shtml

A careful network manager should install strict access control (access lists) in order to limit access to the HTTP server or even deactivate the HTTP server.

HTTP

The HTTP service can be used to manage the router through a Web browser. If you use this feature, be sure to install strict access control and authentication to that service. Use the same precautions as you would for the remote login access.

To deactivate the HTTP server, use the following global command:

```
no ip http server
```

SNMP

The Simple Network Management Protocol is commonly used by network management stations to monitor and control network devices. Unfortunately, the security provided in SNMP (version 1 which is the most common version used today) is weak. Authentication is done using community strings that are sent in cleartext over the network. For that reason, it is not recommended that you use SNMP over a public network.

The default configuration in many SNMP implementations is to use "public" as the community for read-only access and "private" as the read-write access. These community names should never be used. Also, access control should be enforced on the SNMP server by installing an access list.

Table 9.10 lists some of the commands you should consider using:

Table 9.10 Useful SNMP Security Commands

Command	Function
access-list 2 permit 192.168.9.33	Allow host 192.168.9.33
access-list 2 deny all log	Deny all other hosts and log the failed attempt
snmp-server community S0meGiDpa22 RO 10	Configure SNMP read-only community as "S0meGiDpa22" and apply access list 10

If SNMP is not required, it can be disabled using the following command:

```
no snmp-server
```

Finger

The finger protocol is used to find out who is currently connected to the router. This has no useful function on a router and should be deactivated:

```
no service finger
```

NTP

Network Time Protocol (NTP) is activated be default. If you have a good and trusted time source, NTP is a good way to synchronize the time base on all your routers and network devices. If not, deactivate this service using the following interface command:

```
no ntp enable
```

CDP

Cisco Discovery Protocol (CDP) is used for some network management functions. If this service is not required in your environment, deactivate it using the global command:

```
no cdp running
```

Other TCP and UDP Servers

You should also disable minor services. These services are activated by default on most TCP/IP implementations, so use the following global commands to deactivate those services:

```
no service udp-small-servers
no service tcp-small-servers
```

Logging and Backups

System logging is an often-overlooked security mechanism. Logging is essential to the security of the network. It can be used to detect security violations and help to gather information and evidence during an attack.

Logging should be centralized on a server where an analysis of activity can be done on a regular basis. This server will need to run a syslog service and accept network logs from different network devices. Syslog is a UDP based protocol and doesn't offer any security. It is important to protect the syslog server through strict access control, such as allowing network access to the syslog service from specific IP addresses only.

It is strongly recommended to log all suspicious traffic. For example, use the **log** keyword in the access list to deny suspicious traffic like IP spoofing and unauthorized access to a VTY port. Also, logs should be periodically rotated and analyzed.

A backup of the configuration files of routers and other network devices should be stored in a secure place. TFTP is used to upload and download configuration files and IOS images. You should be careful not to leave any configuration files in the TFTP server directory or in any publicly readable directory. The information contained in the configuration is very sensitive and can have serious consequences if in the wrong hands.

Traffic Filtering

Many network attacks can be avoided if some basic precautions are taken. In many cases, adding simple access lists on the border routers can block many attacks that use spoofed IP addresses or other types of forged IP packets. See Chapter 7, "Intrusion Detection" for a description of some of the common attacks.

Cisco's Website offers a lot in the way of security advice and advisories; you can consult the Cisco security web page at the following URL: www.cisco.com/warp/public/707/

IP Spoofing

To prevent IP spoofing, install access lists on your border router or firewall. For example, if a class C network 192.168.99.0 is connected to the Internet using an Ethernet interface on a router, the IP spoofing access list would look like the following (comments are preceded with the bang "!" symbol):

```
! Inbound access list denies packets that have a source address
! that is part of our network. Log such packets
```

```
access-list 199 deny ip 192.168.99.0 0.0.0.255 any log
access-list 199 permit ip any any
! Outbound access list denies packets that have a source address
! that is NOT part of our network. Log such packets
access-list 198 permit ip 192.168.99.0 0.0.0.255 any
access-list 198 deny ip any any log
interface Ethernet0
  ip access-group 199 in
  ip access-group 198 out
```

More information on IP spoofing can be found in "Network Ingress Filtering: Defeating Denial of Service Attacks which employ IP Source Address Spoofing" at www.normos.org/ietf/rfc/rfc2267.txt.

TCP SYN Flooding Attacks Protection

TCP SYN flooding attacks are a Denial-of-Service attack targeted to disable a server on the network. They are accomplished by sending a large amount of TCP connection establishment requests to a server running a TCP service, such as a Web server. The attack forges the TCP packet such that the connection request sent to the victim comes from a non-existent host.

Consequently, the TCP connection can never be completely established, and these incomplete connections will rapidly consume the server's resources. The end result is that the server can no longer accept new TCP connections.

Cisco offers features in PIX, Flood Defender, and in the IOS, **tcp intercept access list**, to protect against such attacks. For example, the following commands can be used to activate the **tcp intercept** feature for a server (192.168.99.2) behind a Cisco router:

```
ip tcp intercept list 198
access-list 198 permit tcp any 192.168.99.2 0.0.0.0
```

A description of **tcp intercept** is found in Chapter 7, "Intrusion Detection."

Directed Broadcast

Most Denial-of-Service attacks are difficult to prevent or block. It is important to prevent your site from becoming an unwilling participant in such an attack. This type of attack sends a forged packet inside your network with a broadcast IP destination address. It is possible to block such packets with the following global command:

```
no ip directed-broadcast
```

This is the default in Cisco IOS software version 12.0 and later.

ICMP Filtering

ICMP is a protocol that is part of all IP implementations and is used to communicate error messages to the IP layer or higher layer protocols, such as TCP or UDP. For example, if a client initiates an HTTP connection to a server where the HTTP service is not available, the server will return an ICMP error message back to the client. In this situation the client is immediately notified that the service is not available. Many network debugging tools use ICMP in order to find out if a machine is alive (ping) or to trace the path taken by packets to reach a specific destination (traceroute).

Unfortunately, ICMP can be used for attacks as well. In general, ICMP traffic can be used to probe and map your network or even do Denial-of-Service attacks against your hosts and servers. Some tools are used to insert a data payload inside an ICMP packet in order to bypass security rules in a firewall.

ICMP filtering is recommended. How much filtering should be done depends on which tools (ping or traceroute) you want to be able to use normally. The most prudent solution would be to deny everything and to log the denied ICMP packets.

One ICMP message which can cause network problem if blocked is the "Fragmentation needed but don't fragment bit set" message. This message is used by IP for path MTU computation and may cause communication problems with some hosts when sending large IP datagrams.

The denied packet log file will help diagnose network problems should they occur.

Other Filtering Recommendations

Border routers connected to the Internet should deny any packet that uses a private source IP address. These addresses should never be routed on the Internet.

Physical Access

No matter how good your network security is, if the physical access to your routers, firewall or servers is not secure, your network can be compromised. If the console is not protected, anyone can easily send a BREAK signal on the console port, modify the system configuration, and reboot the modified system.

Keeping Up-to-Date

Staying up to date on all the new technologies is a full-time job. A new software version comes out, a new bug is found, the exploit is published, and the software vendor sends out a patch. This cycle happens on a regular basis. As a network security manager, keeping in touch with the most current information is crucial in order to keep your systems up-to-date.

A lot of information on network security is available on the Internet. This section will list some of the good sources of information related to Cisco security and network security in general.

Cisco's Web site is the first resource you should look at for security information on Cisco products. A large number of good resources are available.

The Cisco Product Security Incident Response Web page reports useful information on security incidents related to Cisco products. You can visit the URL at: www.cisco.com/warp/public/707/sec_incident_response.shtml.

Electronic mail addresses and telephone numbers are listed to report incidents directly to the Cisco Product Security Incident Response Team (PSIRT).

That Web page also gives the information on how to subscribe to the security announcement mailing list. As a network security manager, this mailing list is *a must*.

Cisco also provides a great deal of security-related Web pages with tips on such topics as configuring access lists, AAA security servers, IPSec, and others, as shown in Table 9.11.

Table 9.11 Cisco Websites on Security

Website URL	Topics covered
www.cisco.com/warp/public/707/	Good starting point for information on security tips and advisories.
www.cisco.com/warp/public/707/index1.shtml	Security Technical Tips: Hardware
www.cisco.com/warp/public/707/index2.shtml	Security Technical Tips: Software
www.cisco.com/warp/public/707/21.html	Improving Security on Cisco Routers
www.cisco.com/tac	Cisco Technical Assistance Center

As was previously mentioned, a lot of information on network security is available on the Internet. Table 9.12 lists some of the Web sites that offer good information on host and network security.

Table 9.12 General Websites on Security

Website URL	Topics covered
www.sans.org	System Administration, Networking and Security Institute
www.cert.org	CERT/CC (security advisories)
http://cve.mitre.org	Common Vulnerabilities and Exposures. Database of all publicly known vulnerabilities and security exposures.
www.trusecure.com	Security assurance services
www.l0pht.com	Various security issues
www.securityportal.com	Various security issues
www.ntbugtraq.com	Various security issues
www.counterpane.com/crypto-gram.html	Monthly newsletter on security

Summary

In this chapter, we have taken a high-level view of some of the important topics discussed in this book. After reading this Fast Track chapter, you can now go to the chapter that covers the material of interest to get a more thorough account of the subject.

Each chapter explores each subject area in-depth and contains helpful figures, charts, tables, and screen shots that will aid you in understanding and implementing the IP network security technologies offered by Cisco.

FAQs

Q: What is Kerberos, and where does it come from?

A: Kerberos is an open specification for authentication. In the strictest sense, it is an algorithm. It originated at MIT and has been widely used in large information systems. It is well-tested, mature, and regarded as being very secure. In its complete implementation, it is also fairly complicated. For more information, visit: www.isi.edu/gost/info/kerberos.

Q: How secure is IPSec and can I trust my network if I use it?

A: IPSec is a framework for implementing security components at several stages of the data transmission process. If they are used diligently, IPSec-specified techniques are not only a good idea, but an absolute must if you plan to conduct business across the Internet. It might be a good idea to consider some of the ways IPSec architecture and techniques might be used inside your organization, behind your firewall as well. You need to understand what it is you are protecting, from whom, and why before any security architecture will be of any benefit.

Q: We don't have a security plan. How can I get or make one?

A: You might consider starting with the suggestions presented in this chapter and see where that takes you. There are more books on the subject of computer and information system security, now more than ever, and your local bookstore is a great place to start. If you have the budget, you might consider retaining a security consultant, even if it's just to look at your organization and make suggestions. Full-service consulting organizations are a good place to go for this type of assistance, even if you are simply looking for advice. If you find later that you are in over your head, you can always go back to the consulting firm should the need arise. You might also want to take a look at the many newsgroups that discuss security issues in general and Cisco security specifically.

The Global Knowledge Advantage

Global Knowledge has a global delivery system for its products and services. The company has 28 subsidiaries, and offers its programs through a total of 60+ locations. No other vendor can provide consistent services across a geographic area this large. Global Knowledge is the largest independent information technology education provider, offering programs on a variety of platforms. This enables our multi-platform and multi-national customers to obtain all of their programs from a single vendor. The company has developed the unique CompetusTM Framework software tool and methodology which can quickly reconfigure courseware to the proficiency level of a student on an interactive basis. Combined with self-paced and on-line programs, this technology can reduce the time required for training by prescribing content in only the deficient skills areas. The company has fully automated every aspect of the education process, from registration and follow-up, to "just-in-time" production of courseware. Global Knowledge through its Enterprise Services Consultancy, can customize programs and products to suit the needs of an individual customer.

Global Knowledge Classroom Education Programs

The backbone of our delivery options is classroom-based education. Our modern, well-equipped facilities staffed with the finest instructors offer programs in a wide variety of information technology topics, many of which lead to professional certifications.

Custom Learning Solutions

This delivery option has been created for companies and governments that value customized learning solutions. For them, our consultancy-based approach of developing targeted education solutions is most effective at helping them meet specific objectives.

Self-Paced and Multimedia Products

This delivery option offers self-paced program titles in interactive CD-ROM, videotape and audio tape programs. In addition, we offer custom development of interactive multimedia courseware to customers and partners. Call us at 1-888-427-4228.

Electronic Delivery of Training

Our network-based training service delivers efficient competency-based, interactive training via the World Wide Web and organizational intranets. This leading-edge delivery option provides a custom learning path and "just-in-time" training for maximum convenience to students.

Global Knowledge Courses Available

Microsoft
- Windows 2000 Deployment Strategies
- Introduction to Directory Services
- Windows 2000 Client Administration
- Windows 2000 Server
- Windows 2000 Update
- MCSE Bootcamp
- Microsoft Networking Essentials
- Windows NT 4.0 Workstation
- Windows NT 4.0 Server
- Windows NT Troubleshooting
- Windows NT 4.0 Security
- Windows 2000 Security
- Introduction to Microsoft Web Tools

Management Skills
- Project Management for IT Professionals
- Microsoft Project Workshop
- Management Skills for IT Professionals

Network Fundamentals
- Understanding Computer Networks
- Telecommunications Fundamentals I
- Telecommunications Fundamentals II
- Understanding Networking Fundamentals
- Upgrading and Repairing PCs
- DOS/Windows A+ Preparation
- Network Cabling Systems

WAN Networking and Telephony
- Building Broadband Networks
- Frame Relay Internetworking
- Converging Voice and Data Networks
- Introduction to Voice Over IP
- Understanding Digital Subscriber Line (xDSL)

Internetworking
- ATM Essentials
- ATM Internetworking
- ATM Troubleshooting
- Understanding Networking Protocols
- Internetworking Routers and Switches
- Network Troubleshooting
- Internetworking with TCP/IP
- Troubleshooting TCP/IP Networks
- Network Management
- Network Security Administration
- Virtual Private Networks
- Storage Area Networks
- Cisco OSPF Design and Configuration
- Cisco Border Gateway Protocol (BGP) Configuration

Web Site Management and Development
- Advanced Web Site Design
- Introduction to XML
- Building a Web Site
- Introduction to JavaScript
- Web Development Fundamentals
- Introduction to Web Databases

PERL, UNIX, and Linux
- PERL Scripting
- PERL with CGI for the Web
- UNIX Level I
- UNIX Level II
- Introduction to Linux for New Users
- Linux Installation, Configuration, and Maintenance

Authorized Vendor Training
Red Hat
- Introduction to Red Hat Linux
- Red Hat Linux Systems Administration
- Red Hat Linux Network and Security Administration
- RHCE Rapid Track Certification

Cisco Systems
- Interconnecting Cisco Network Devices
- Advanced Cisco Router Configuration
- Installation and Maintenance of Cisco Routers
- Cisco Internetwork Troubleshooting
- Designing Cisco Networks
- Cisco Internetwork Design
- Configuring Cisco Catalyst Switches
- Cisco Campus ATM Solutions
- Cisco Voice Over Frame Relay, ATM, and IP
- Configuring for Selsius IP Phones
- Building Cisco Remote Access Networks
- Managing Cisco Network Security
- Cisco Enterprise Management Solutions

Nortel Networks
- Nortel Networks Accelerated Router Configuration
- Nortel Networks Advanced IP Routing
- Nortel Networks WAN Protocols
- Nortel Networks Frame Switching
- Nortel Networks Accelar 1000
- Comprehensive Configuration
- Nortel Networks Centillion Switching
- Network Management with Optivity for Windows

Oracle Training
- Introduction to Oracle8 and PL/SQL
- Oracle8 Database Administration

Custom Corporate Network Training

Train on Cutting Edge Technology
We can bring the best in skill-based training to your facility to create a real-world hands-on training experience. Global Knowledge has invested millions of dollars in network hardware and software to train our students on the same equipment they will work with on the job. Our relationships with vendors allow us to incorporate the latest equipment and platforms into your on-site labs.

Maximize Your Training Budget
Global Knowledge provides experienced instructors, comprehensive course materials, and all the networking equipment needed to deliver high quality training. You provide the students; we provide the knowledge.

Avoid Travel Expenses
On-site courses allow you to schedule technical training at your convenience, saving time, expense, and the opportunity cost of travel away from the workplace.

Discuss Confidential Topics
Private on-site training permits the open discussion of sensitive issues such as security, access, and network design. We can work with your existing network's proprietary files while demonstrating the latest technologies.

Customize Course Content
Global Knowledge can tailor your courses to include the technologies and the topics which have the greatest impact on your business. We can complement your internal training efforts or provide a total solution to your training needs.

Corporate Pass
The Corporate Pass Discount Program rewards our best network training customers with preferred pricing on public courses, discounts on multimedia training packages, and an array of career planning services.

Global Knowledge Training Lifecycle
Supporting the Dynamic and Specialized Training Requirements of Information Technology Professionals

- Define Profile
- Assess Skills
- Design Training
- Deliver Training
- Test Knowledge
- Update Profile
- Use New Skills

Global Knowledge

Global Knowledge programs are developed and presented by industry professionals with "real-world" experience. Designed to help professionals meet today's interconnectivity and interoperability challenges, most of our programs feature hands-on labs that incorporate state-of-the-art communication components and equipment.

ON-SITE TEAM TRAINING

Bring Global Knowledge's powerful training programs to your company. At Global Knowledge, we will custom design courses to meet your specific network requirements. Call (919)-461-8686 for more information.

YOUR GUARANTEE

Global Knowledge believes its courses offer the best possible training in this field. If during the first day you are not satisfied and wish to withdraw from the course, simply notify the instructor, return all course materials and receive a 100% refund.

REGISTRATION INFORMATION

In the US:
call: (888) 762–4442
fax: (919) 469–7070
visit our website:
www.globalknowledge.com